Shojo Beat

S.A

Special A

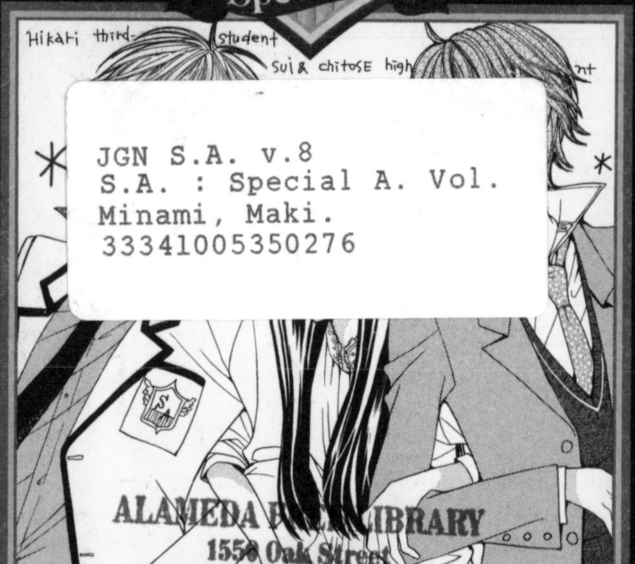
Hikari third-
student
sui & chitose high

Volume 8

Story & Art by

Maki Minami

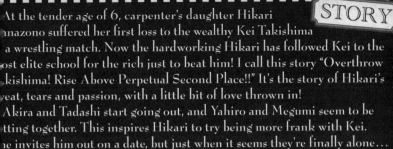

At the tender age of 6, carpenter's daughter Hikari anazono suffered her first loss to the wealthy Kei Takishima a wrestling match. Now the hardworking Hikari has followed Kei to the ost elite school for the rich just to beat him! I call this story "Overthrow kishima! Rise Above Perpetual Second Place!!" It's the story of Hikari's eat, tears and passion, with a little bit of love thrown in!

Akira and Tadashi start going out, and Yahiro and Megumi seem to be tting together. This inspires Hikari to try being more frank with Kei. e invites him out on a date, but just when it seems they're finally alone...

Kei Takishima

Ranked number one in SA, Kei is a seemingly flawless student who not only gets perfect test scores but also runs his family business, Takishima Group, from behind the scenes. He is in love with Hikari, but she doesn't realize it.

Ryu Tsuji

Ranked number seven in SA, Ryu is the son of the president of a sporting goods company...but wait, he loves animals, too! Megumi and Jun are completely infatuated with him.

Megumi Yamamoto

Megumi is the daughter of a music producer and a genius vocalist. Ranked number four in SA, she only talks to people by writing in her sketchbook.

Jun Yamamoto

Megumi's twin brother, Jun is ranked number three in SA. Like his sister, he doesn't talk much. They have both been strongly attached to Ryu since they were kids.

S·A CHARACTERS

Hikari goes to an elite school called Hakusenkan High School. This school divides each grade level into groups A through F, according to the students' test scores. Group A includes only the top seven students in each class. Then the top seven students from all grades' A-groups are put into a group called Special A, which is considered much higher than all others. Known as SA, they are "the elite among the elite."

What is "Special A"?

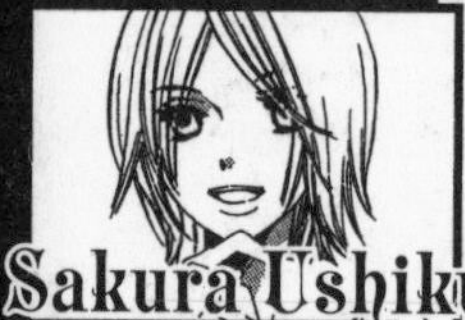

Sakura Ushikubo

Sakura's family set her up with Kei via a matchmaker. But if she married Kei, it would only be for her family's convenience. Right now she is head-over-heels for Jun.♥

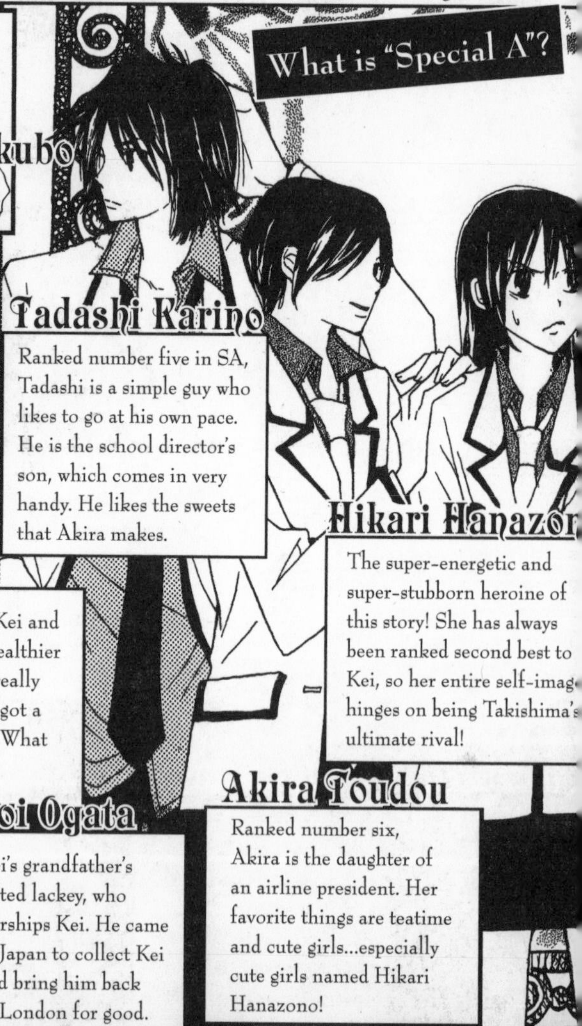

Tadashi Karino

Ranked number five in SA, Tadashi is a simple guy who likes to go at his own pace. He is the school director's son, which comes in very handy. He likes the sweets that Akira makes.

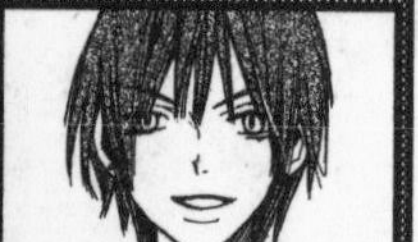

Yahiro Saiga

A childhood friend of Kei and Akira, Yahiro is even wealthier than Kei. He seems to really care for Akira, but he's got a mysterious side as well. What is his real objective?

Hikari Hanazon

The super-energetic and super-stubborn heroine of this story! She has always been ranked second best to Kei, so her entire self-imag hinges on being Takishima's ultimate rival!

Akira Toudou

Ranked number six, Akira is the daughter of an airline president. Her favorite things are teatime and cute girls...especially cute girls named Hikari Hanazono!

Aoi Ogata

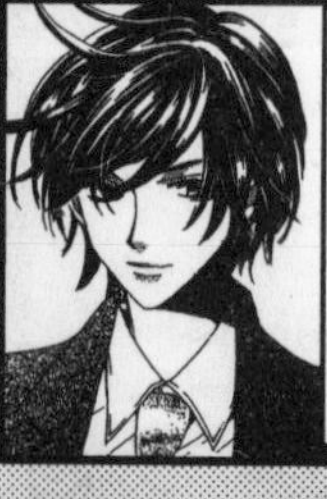

Kei's grandfather's gifted lackey, who worships Kei. He came to Japan to collect Kei and bring him back to London for good.

Contents

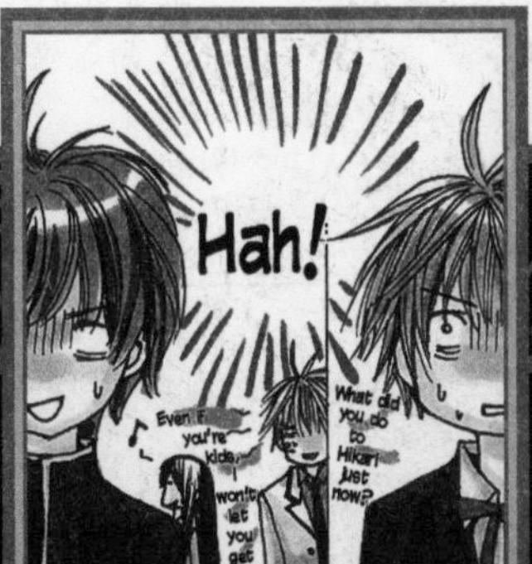

Hah!
What did you do to Hikari just now?
Even if you're kids, I won't let you get away with it.

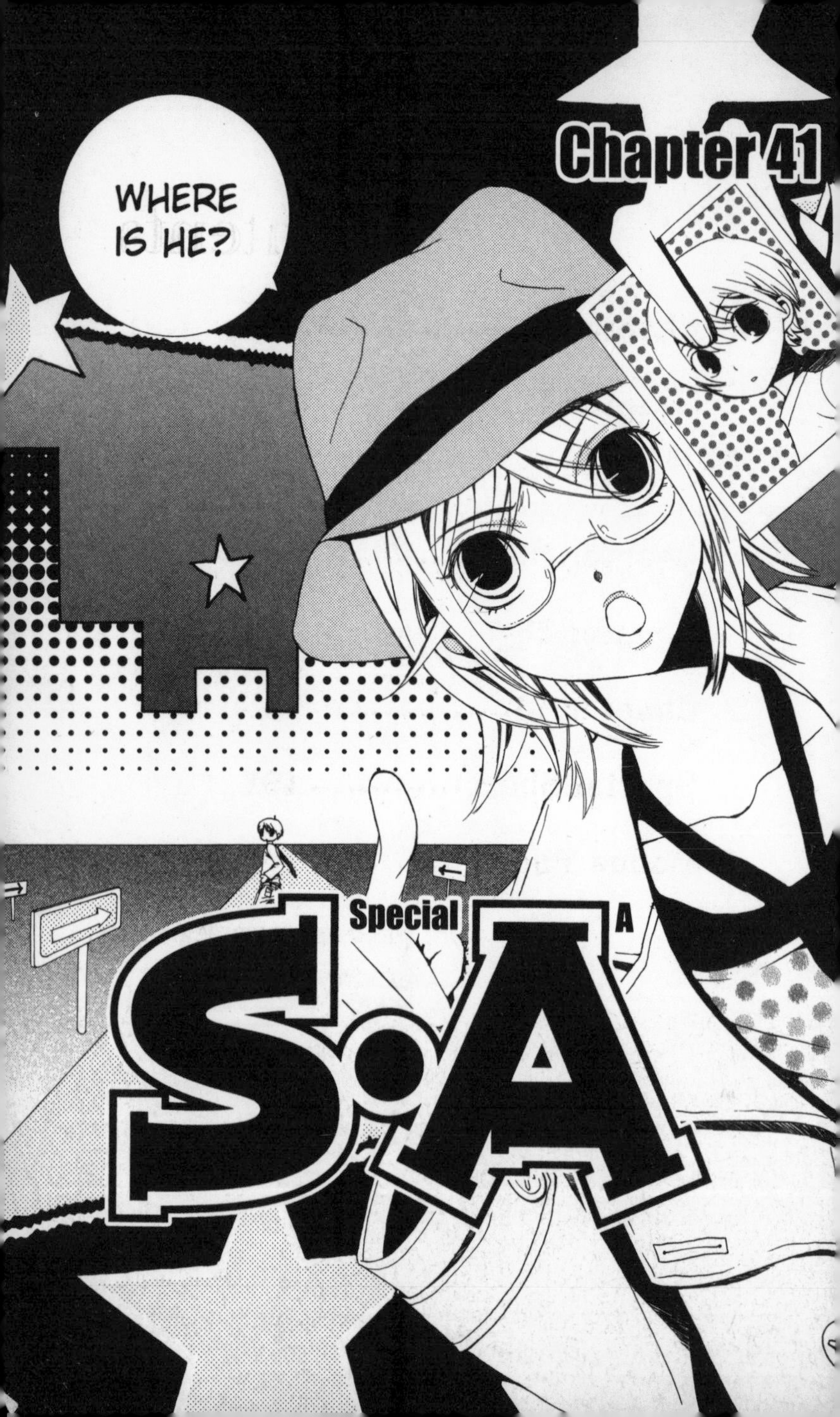
Chapter 41
WHERE IS HE?
Special A
S·A

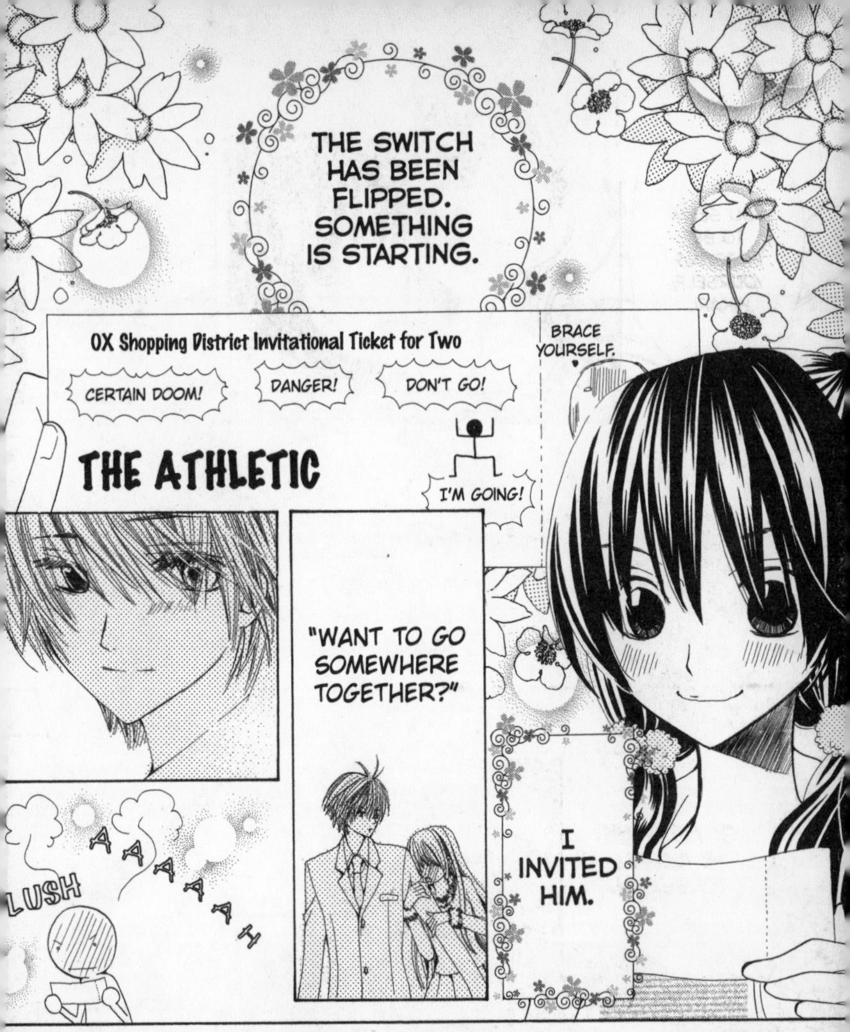
THE SWITCH HAS BEEN FLIPPED. SOMETHING IS STARTING.
BRACE YOURSELF.
OX Shopping District Invitational Ticket for Two
DON'T GO!
DANGER!
CERTAIN DOOM!
I'M GOING!
THE ATHLETIC
I INVITED HIM.
"WANT TO GO SOMEWHERE TOGETHER?"
AAAAAAH
LUSH

•COVER•

THE COVER FOR THIS ISSUE DEPICTS KEI'S YOUNGER BROTHER SUI AND YAHIRO'S YOUNGER BROTHER CHITOSE. THEY HAVEN'T APPEARED MUCH, BUT DRAWING THEM SEEMED LIKE FUN SO I DID IT. ALSO, THE TITLE PAGE DEPICTS OLDER VERSIONS OF SUI, CHITOSE AND HIKARI. APOLOGIES TO ANYONE WHO THOUGHT, "WHO ARE THEY?!" IT WAS A LOT OF FUN DRAWING THEM TOO. CHITOSE LOVES GIRLS AND SUI PROBABLY STILL HAS A MAJOR BROTHER COMPLEX. I'D LIKE THEM TO APPEAR IN SOME FUTURE STORY. MEANWHILE, WHO SHOULD I PUT ON THE COVER OF VOLUME 9? IT'S COMING OUT IN FEBRUARY, SO I'LL HAVE TO DECIDE SOON!!!

HUP!!

A

I HAVEN'T USED HIKARI OR KEI'S DADS YET, HAVE I?

MEH HEH HEH!

CREEPY.

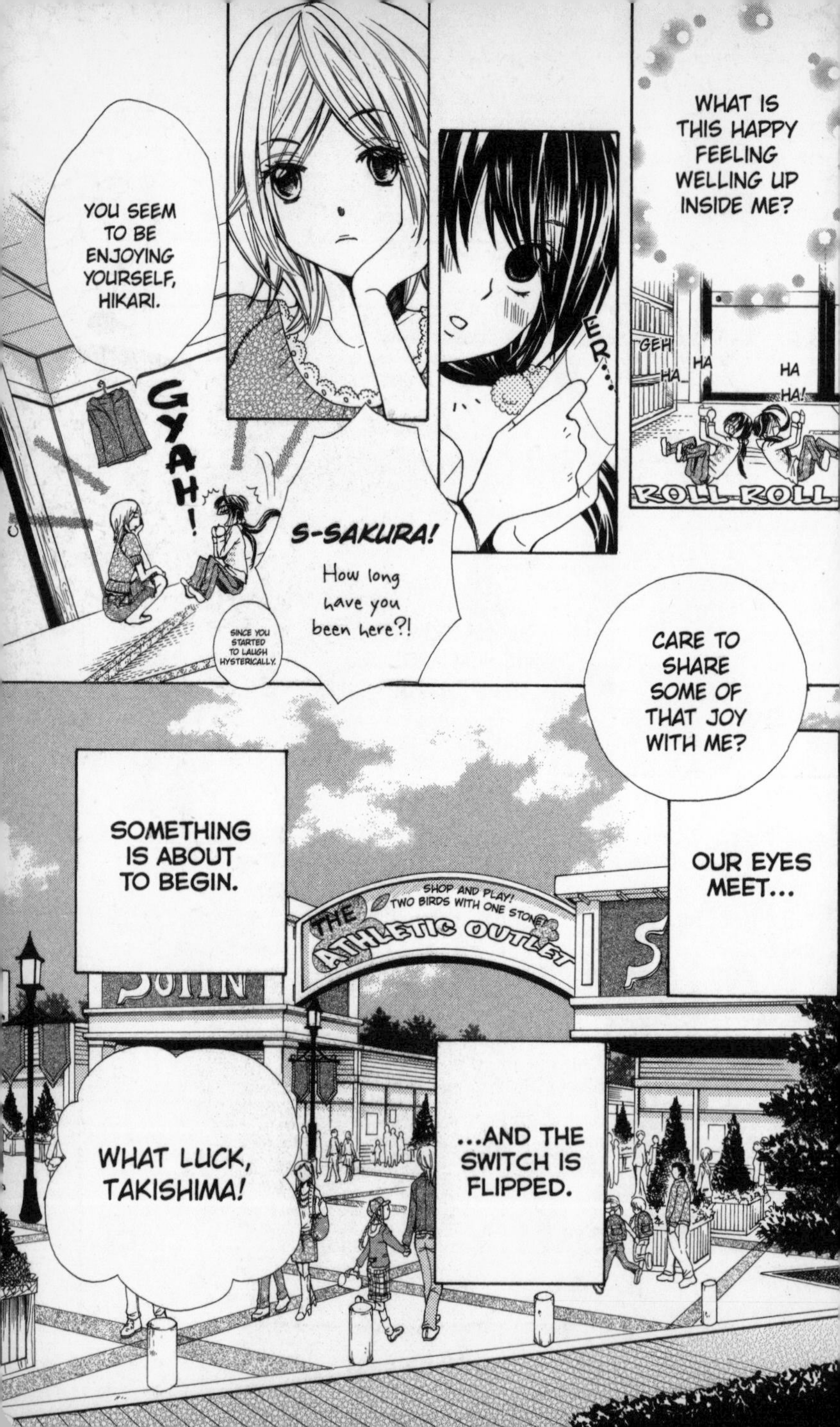
WHAT IS THIS HAPPY FEELING WELLING UP INSIDE ME?
GEH HA HA
HA HA!
ROLL ROLL
ER...
YOU SEEM TO BE ENJOYING YOURSELF, HIKARI.
GYAH!
S-SAKURA!
How long have you been here?!
SINCE YOU STARTED TO LAUGH HYSTERICALLY.
CARE TO SHARE SOME OF THAT JOY WITH ME?
OUR EYES MEET...
SOMETHING IS ABOUT TO BEGIN.
SHOP AND PLAY! TWO BIRDS WITH ONE STONE!
THE ATHLETIC OUTLET
...AND THE SWITCH IS FLIPPED.
WHAT LUCK, TAKISHIMA!

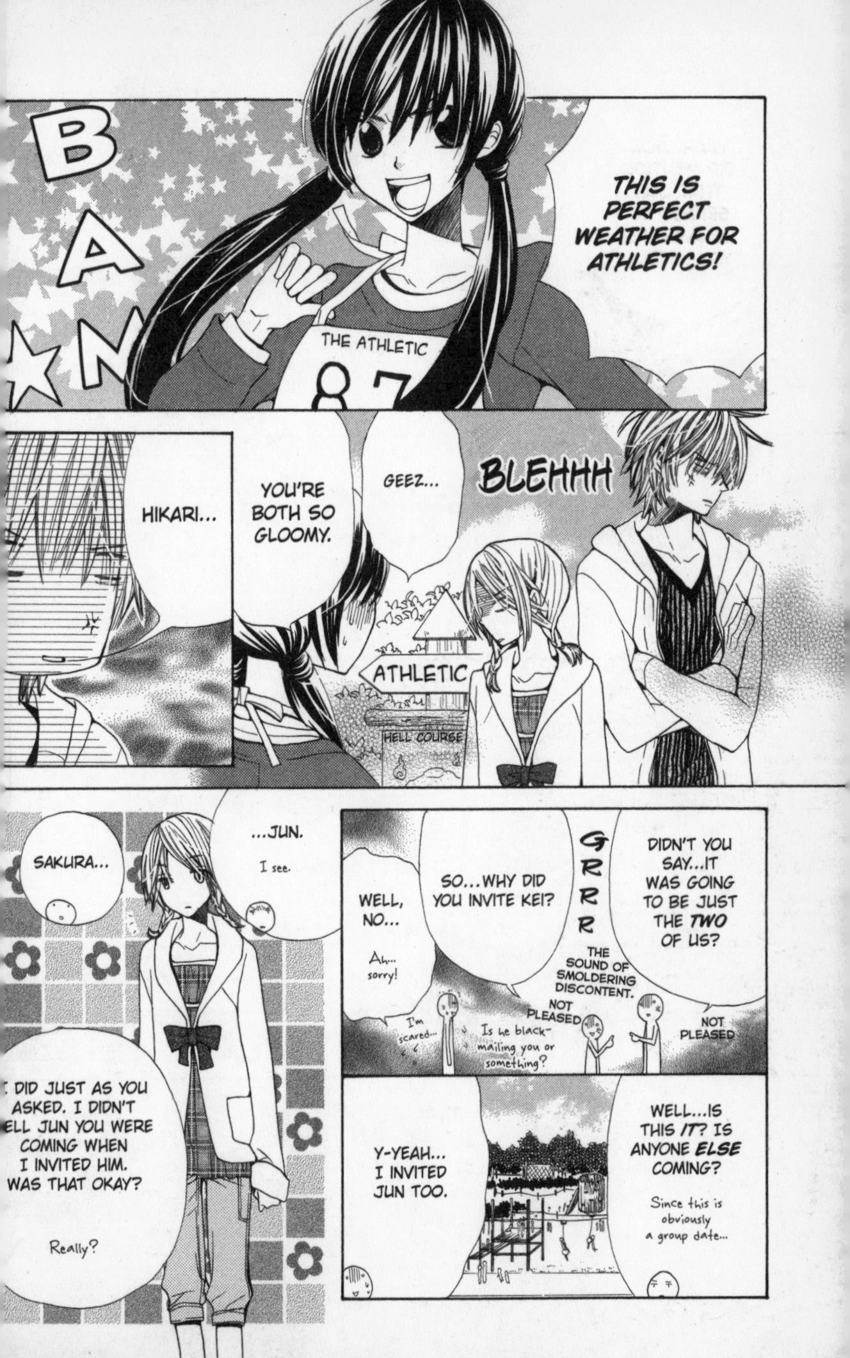
THIS IS PERFECT WEATHER FOR ATHLETICS!
BAM
THE ATHLETIC
87
BLEHHH
GEEZ...
YOU'RE BOTH SO GLOOMY.
ATHLETIC
HELL COURSE
HIKARI...
DIDN'T YOU SAY...IT WAS GOING TO BE JUST THE *TWO* OF US?
GRRR
THE SOUND OF SMOLDERING DISCONTENT.
NOT PLEASED
NOT PLEASED
SO...WHY DID YOU INVITE KEI?
Is he blackmailing you or something?
WELL, NO...
Ah... sorry!
I'm scared...
WELL...IS THIS *IT*? IS ANYONE *ELSE* COMING?
Since this is obviously a group date...
Y-YEAH... I INVITED JUN TOO.
...JUN.
I see.
SAKURA...
I DID JUST AS YOU ASKED. I DIDN'T TELL JUN YOU WERE COMING WHEN I INVITED HIM. WAS THAT OKAY?
Really?

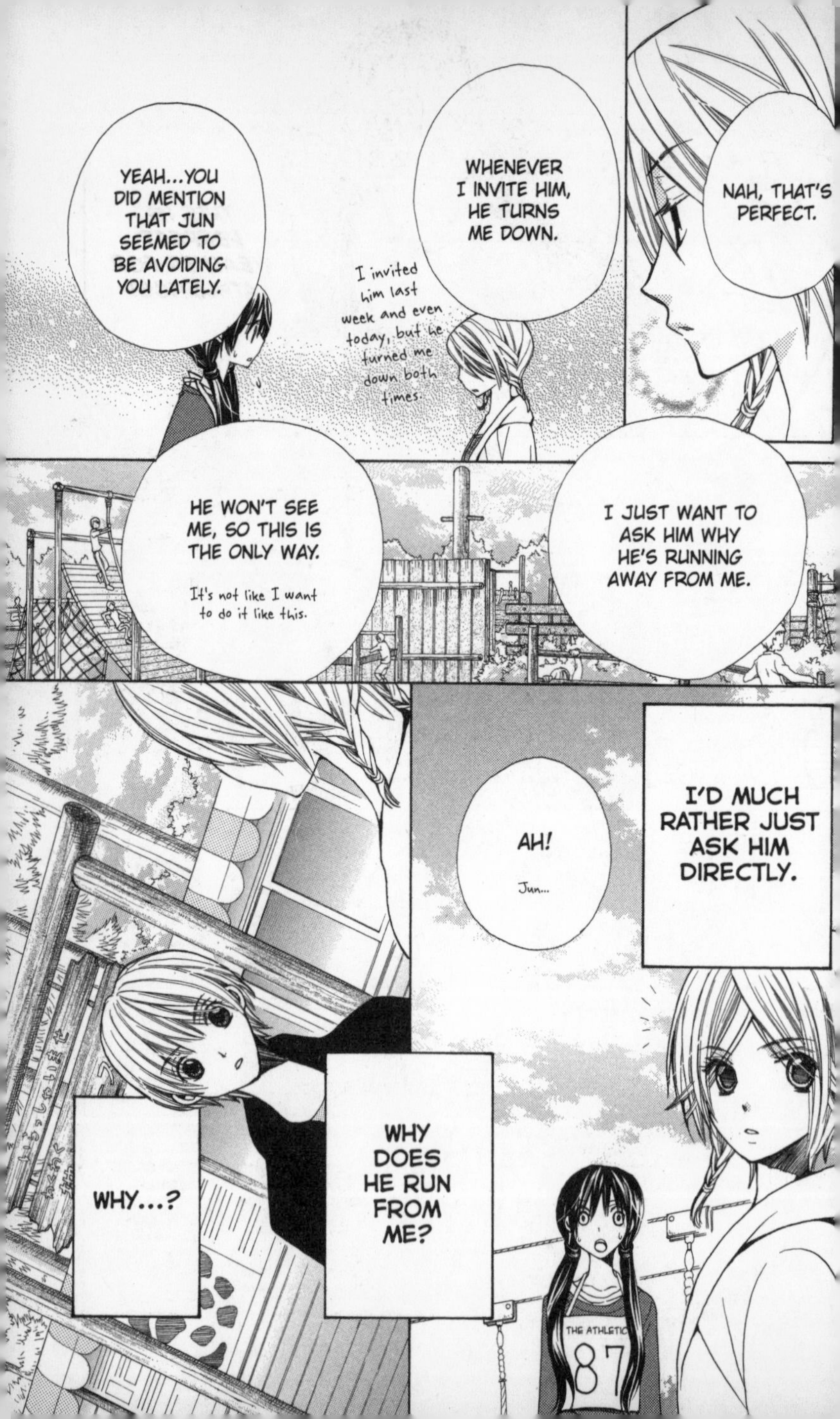
NAH, THAT'S PERFECT.
WHENEVER I INVITE HIM, HE TURNS ME DOWN.
I invited him last week and even today, but he turned me down both times.
YEAH...YOU DID MENTION THAT JUN SEEMED TO BE AVOIDING YOU LATELY.
I JUST WANT TO ASK HIM WHY HE'S RUNNING AWAY FROM ME.
HE WON'T SEE ME, SO THIS IS THE ONLY WAY.
It's not like I want to do it like this.
I'D MUCH RATHER JUST ASK HIM DIRECTLY.
AH!
Jun...
THE ATHLETIC
87
WHY DOES HE RUN FROM ME?
WHY...?

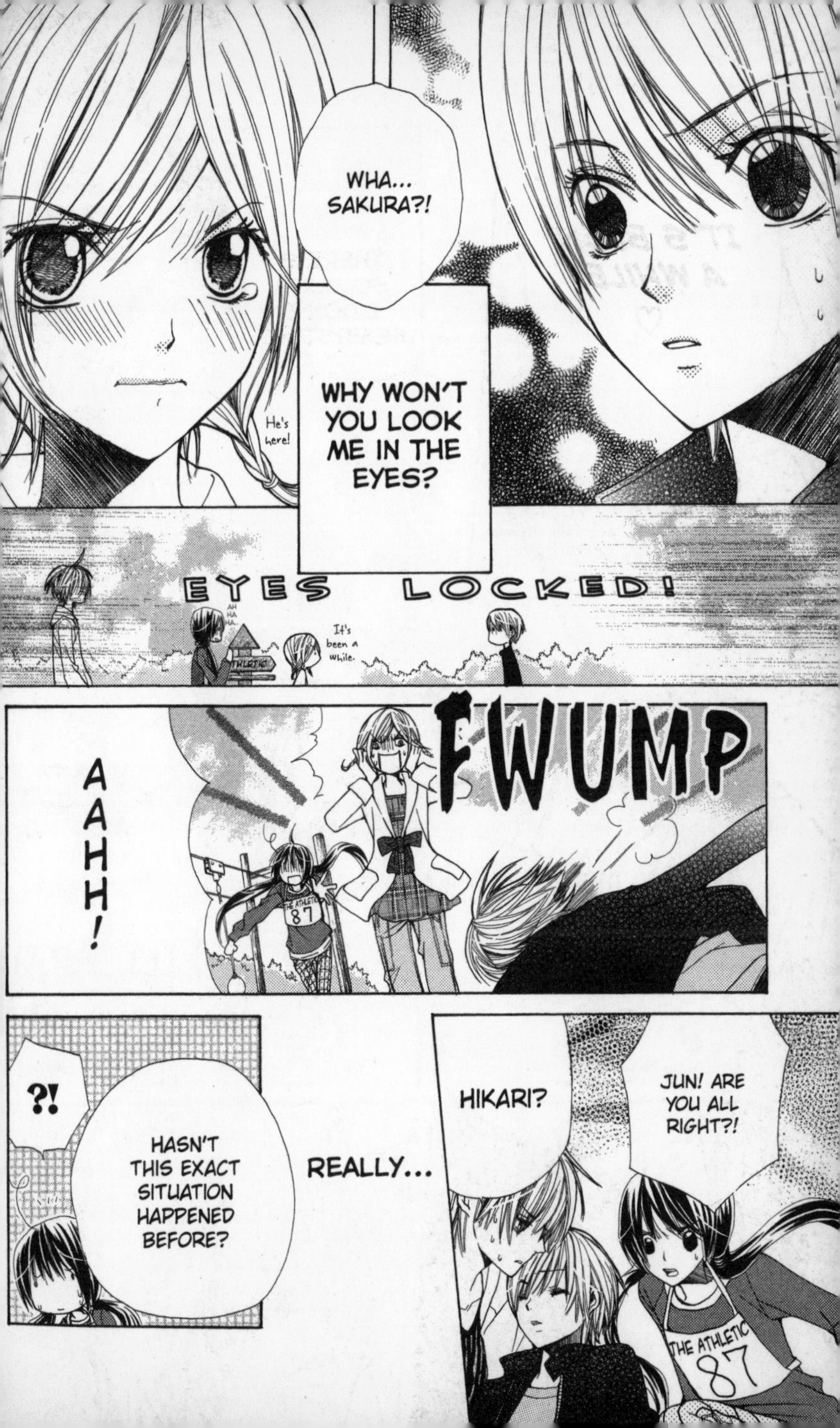
WHA... SAKURA?!
WHY WON'T YOU LOOK ME IN THE EYES?
He's here!
EYES LOCKED!
It's been a while.
AH HA HA...
FWUMP
AAHH!
JUN! ARE YOU ALL RIGHT?!
HIKARI?
REALLY...
HASN'T THIS EXACT SITUATION HAPPENED BEFORE?
?!

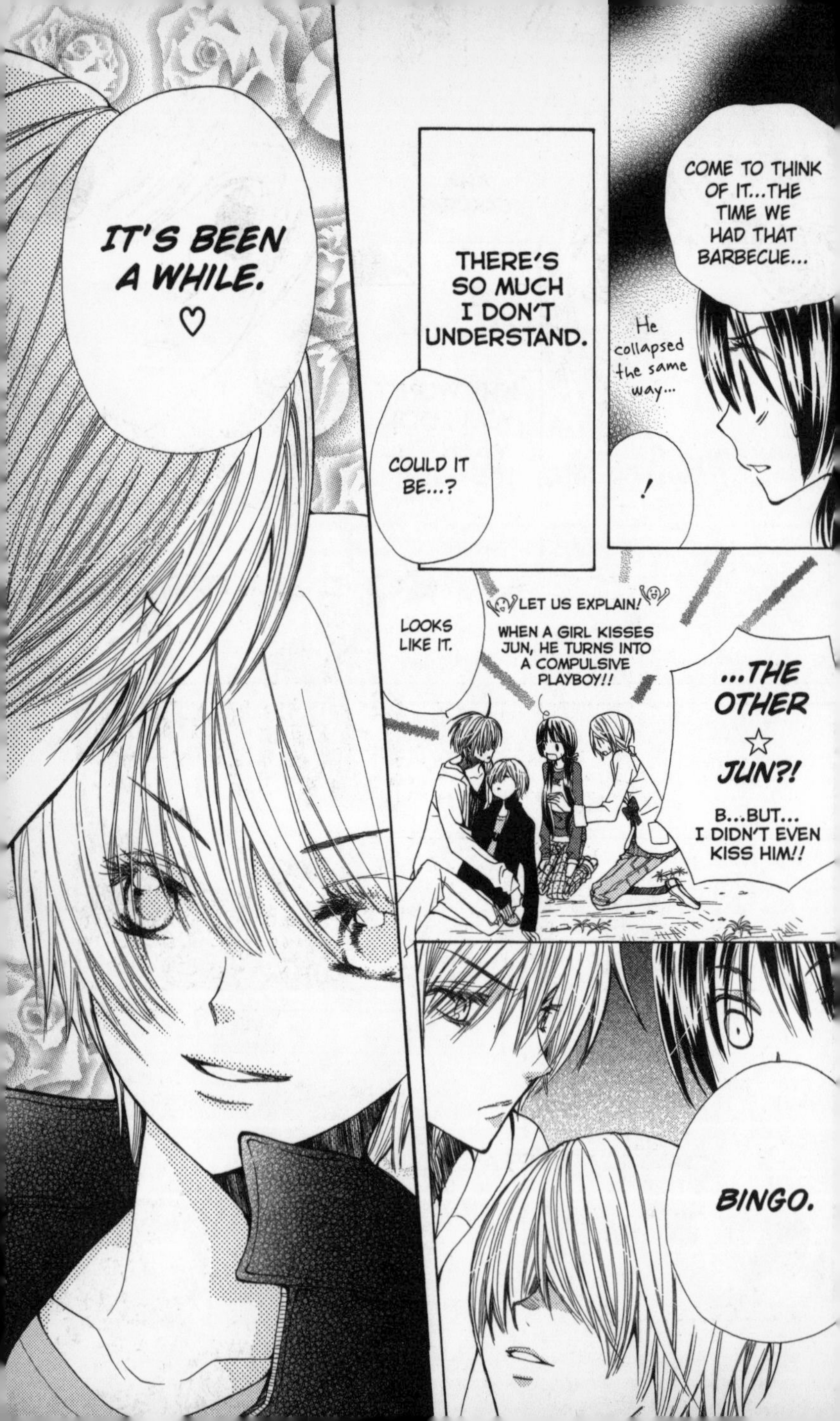
COME TO THINK OF IT...THE TIME WE HAD THAT BARBECUE...
He collapsed the same way...
!
THERE'S SO MUCH I DON'T UNDERSTAND.
COULD IT BE...?
...THE OTHER ☆ JUN?!
B...BUT... I DIDN'T EVEN KISS HIM!!
LET US EXPLAIN!
WHEN A GIRL KISSES JUN, HE TURNS INTO A COMPULSIVE PLAYBOY!!
LOOKS LIKE IT.
BINGO.
IT'S BEEN A WHILE. ♡

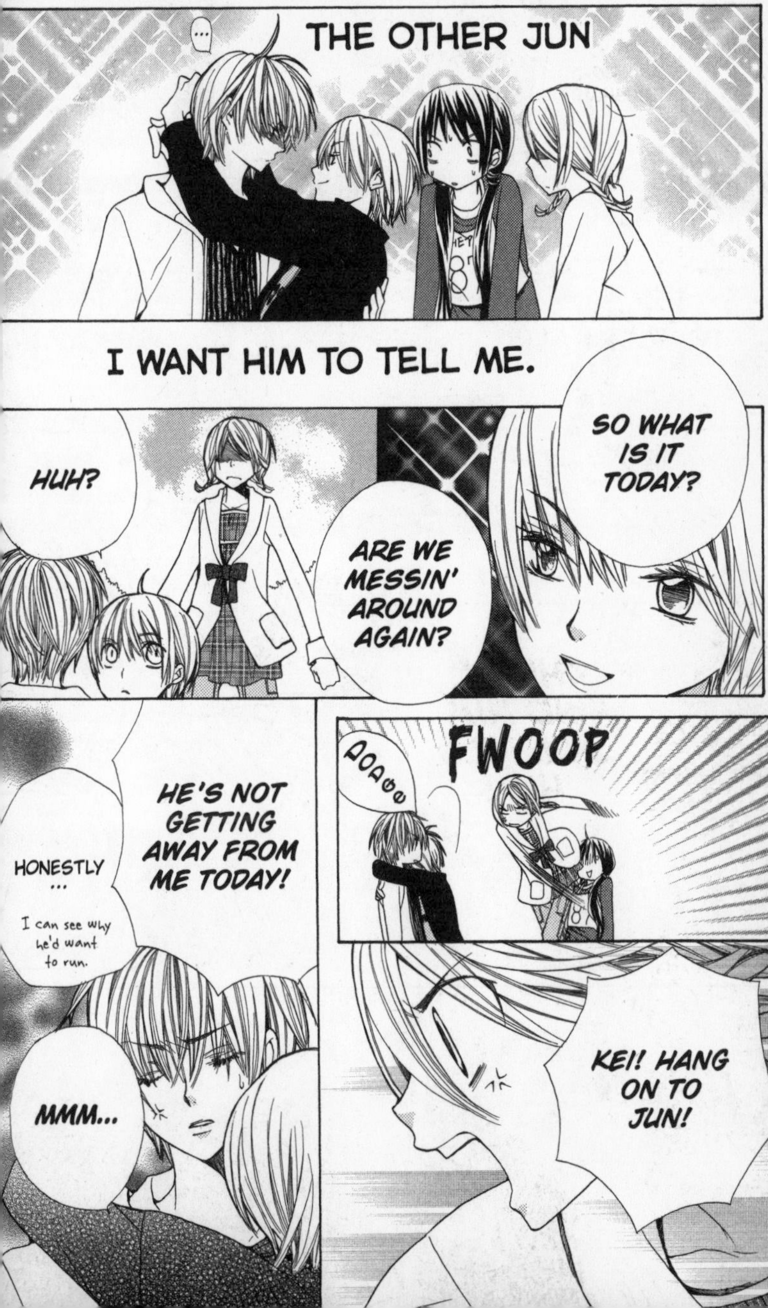
...
THE OTHER JUN
I WANT HIM TO TELL ME.
SO WHAT IS IT TODAY?
ARE WE MESSIN' AROUND AGAIN?
HUH?
FWOOP
KEI! HANG ON TO JUN!
HE'S NOT GETTING AWAY FROM ME TODAY!
HONESTLY ...
I can see why he'd want to run.
MMM...

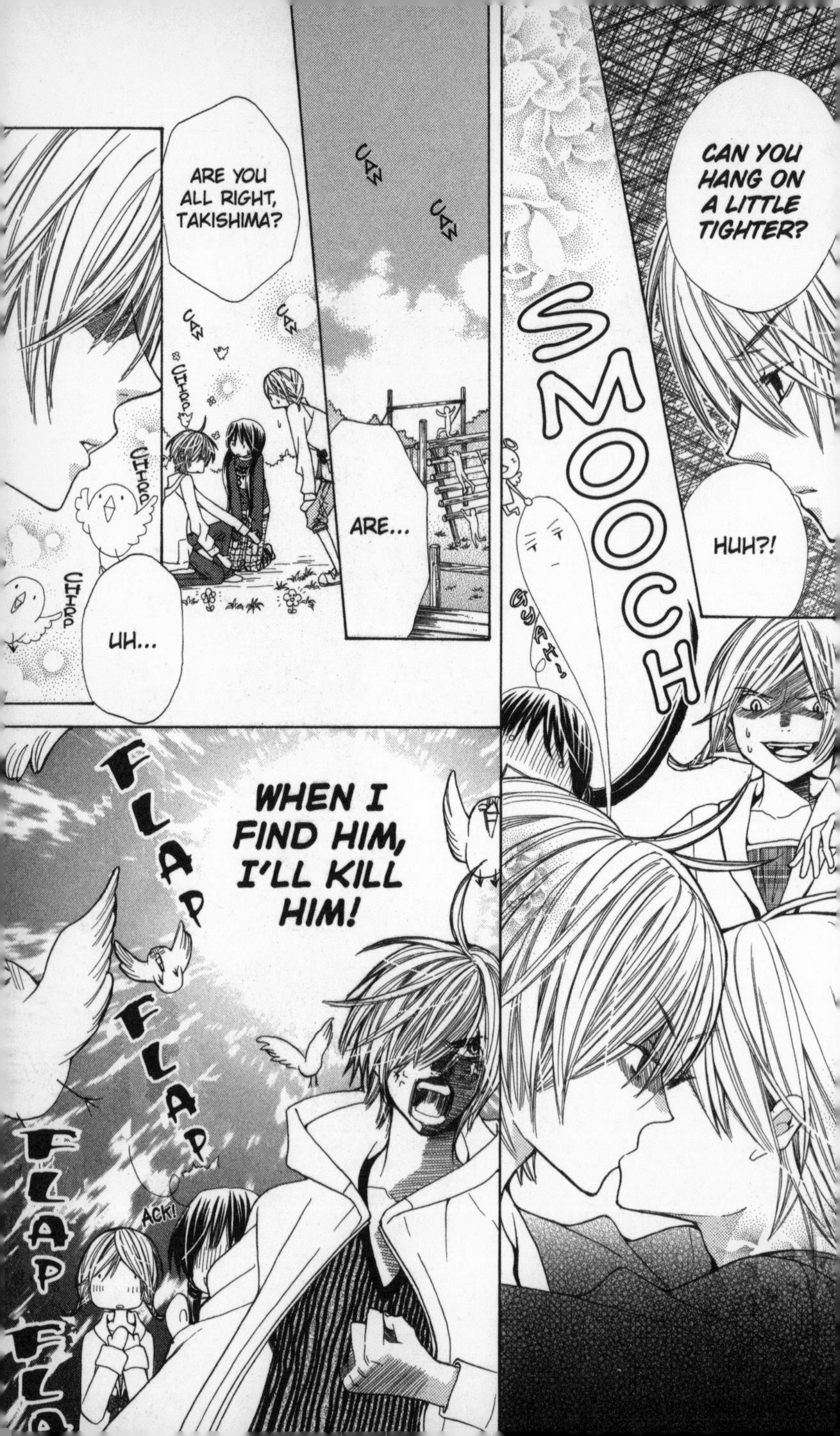
CAN YOU HANG ON A LITTLE TIGHTER?
HUH?!
SMOOCH
GYAAH!
ARE YOU ALL RIGHT, TAKISHIMA?
CHIRP
ARE...
CHIRP
CHIRP
UH...
WHEN I FIND HIM, I'LL KILL HIM!
FLAP
FLAP
FLAP
FLAP
ACK!

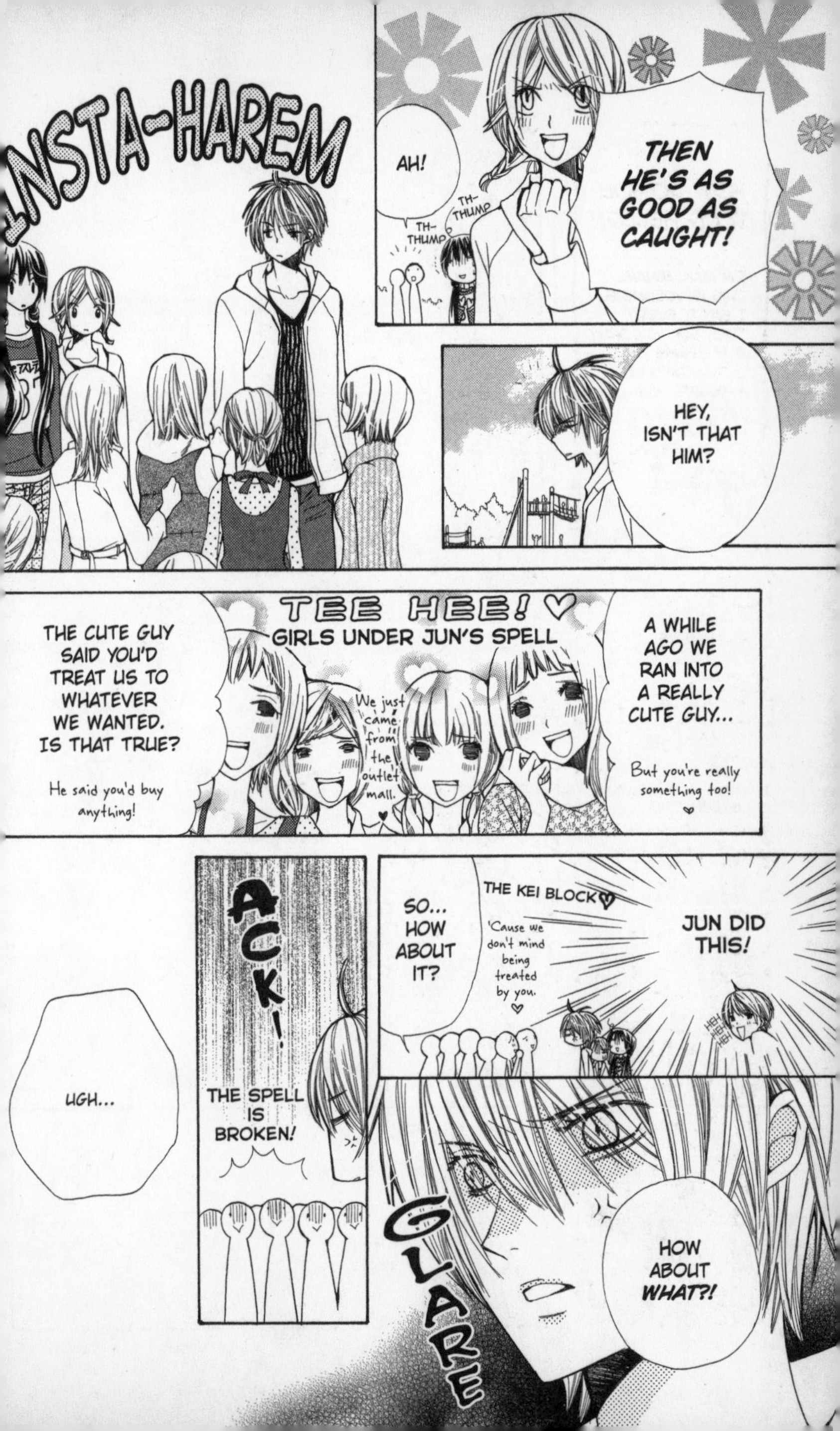
THEN HE'S AS GOOD AS CAUGHT!
AH!
TH-THUMP
TH-THUMP
HEY, ISN'T THAT HIM?
INSTA-HAREM
A WHILE AGO WE RAN INTO A REALLY CUTE GUY...
But you're really something too!
TEE HEE!
GIRLS UNDER JUN'S SPELL
We just came from the outlet mall.
THE CUTE GUY SAID YOU'D TREAT US TO WHATEVER WE WANTED. IS THAT TRUE?
He said you'd buy anything!
JUN DID THIS!
HEH HEH HEH
THE KEI BLOCK
'Cause we don't mind being treated by you.
SO... HOW ABOUT IT?
HOW ABOUT WHAT?!
GLARE
ACK!
THE SPELL IS BROKEN!
UGH...

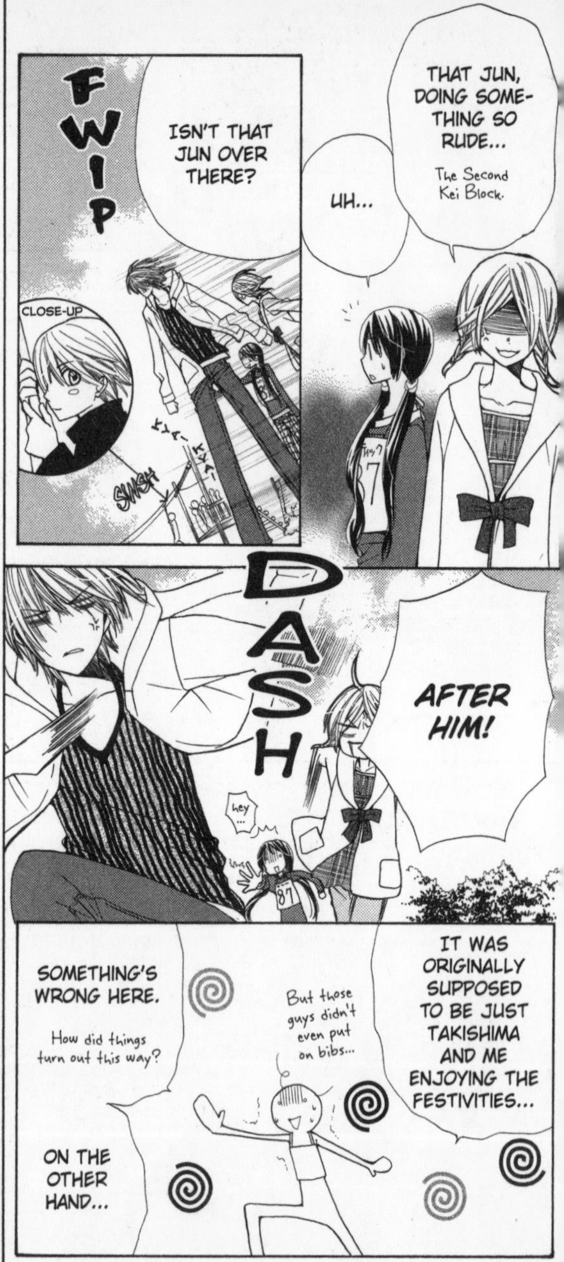
THAT JUN, DOING SOME-THING SO RUDE...
The Second Kei Block.
UH...
ISN'T THAT JUN OVER THERE?
FWIP
CLOSE-UP
SWISH
AFTER HIM!
DASH
hey...
IT WAS ORIGINALLY SUPPOSED TO BE JUST TAKISHIMA AND ME ENJOYING THE FESTIVITIES...
But those guys didn't even put on bibs...
SOMETHING'S WRONG HERE.
How did things turn out this way?
ON THE OTHER HAND...

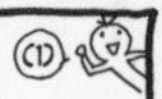
(1)

HOW DO YOU DO & HELLO!!

I'M MAKI MINAMI. THIS IS VOLUME 8. I SAY IT EVERY TIME, SO I'M SORRY IF IT SEEMS LIKE IT'S TURNED INTO A SCRIPT, BUT TIME HAS SURE GONE BY FAST, HASN'T IT? AND I REALLY OWE IT ALL TO YOU!!

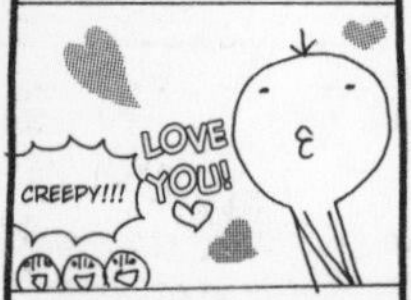
LOVE YOU!
CREEPY!!!

S-SORRY. TRULY I AM!

THIS TIME, AS A BONUS, I'VE INCLUDED A SHORT COMIC THAT RAN IN *HANA TO YUME* MAGAZINE.

IT'S A STORY ABOUT HIKARI AND KEI WHEN THEY WERE LITTLE. IF IT PLEASES YOU, PLEASE STAY WITH ME THROUGH S.A VOLUME 8 AND ENJOY!!!

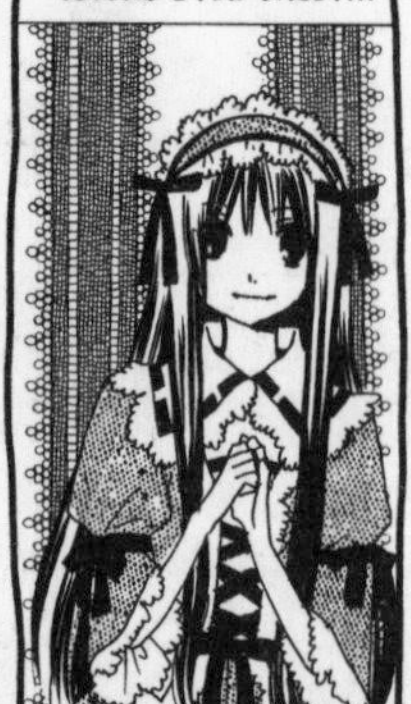

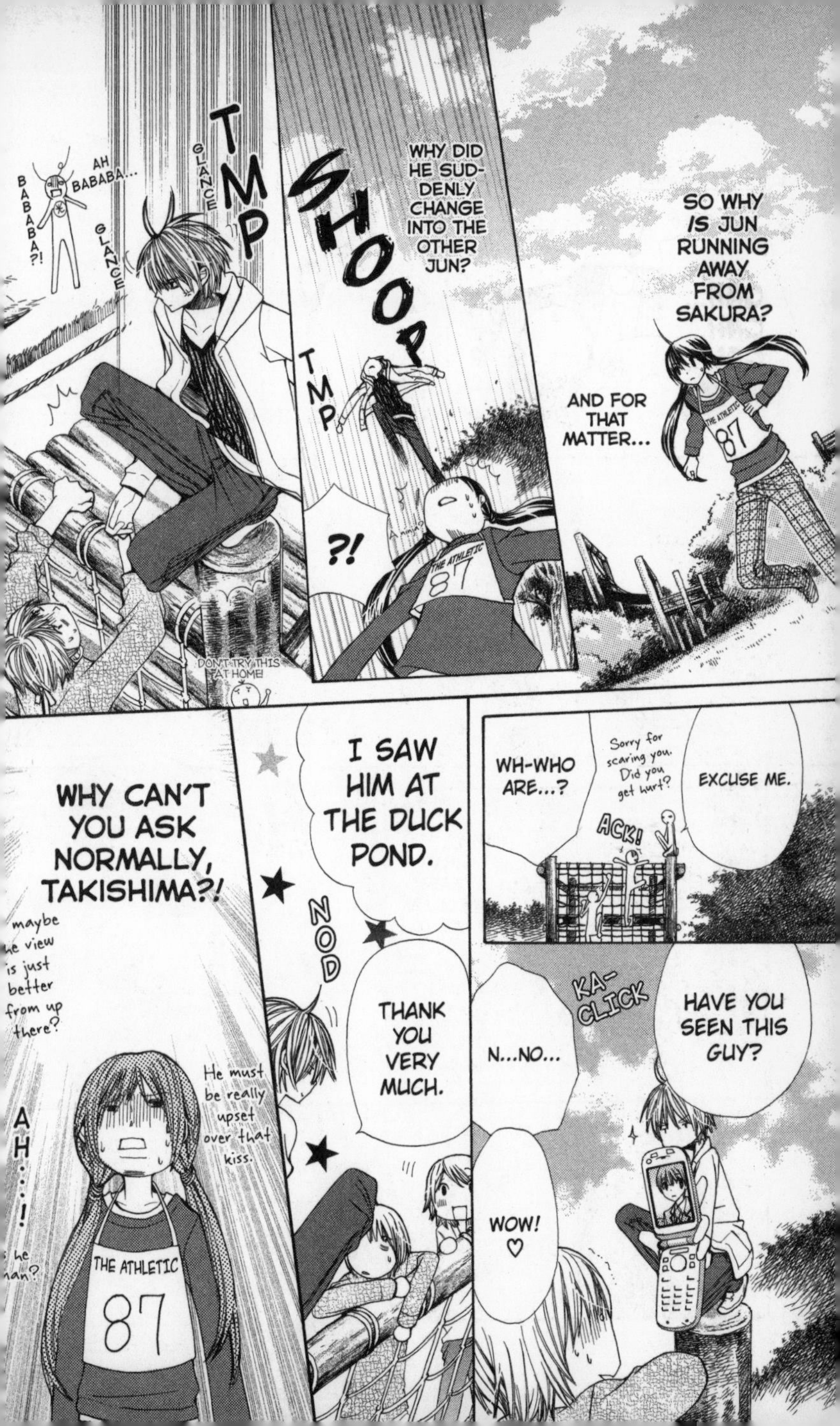
SO WHY IS JUN RUNNING AWAY FROM SAKURA?
AND FOR THAT MATTER...
WHY DID HE SUD-DENLY CHANGE INTO THE OTHER JUN?
SHOOOP
TMP
?!
TMP
GLANCE
GLANCE
AH BABABA...
BABABA?!
DON'T TRY THIS AT HOME!
EXCUSE ME.
Sorry for scaring you. Did you get hurt?
WH-WHO ARE...?
ACK!
HAVE YOU SEEN THIS GUY?
KA-CLICK
N...NO...
WOW! ♡
I SAW HIM AT THE DUCK POND.
NOD
THANK YOU VERY MUCH.
WHY CAN'T YOU ASK NORMALLY, TAKISHIMA?!
maybe the view is just better from up there?
He must be really upset over that kiss.
AH...!

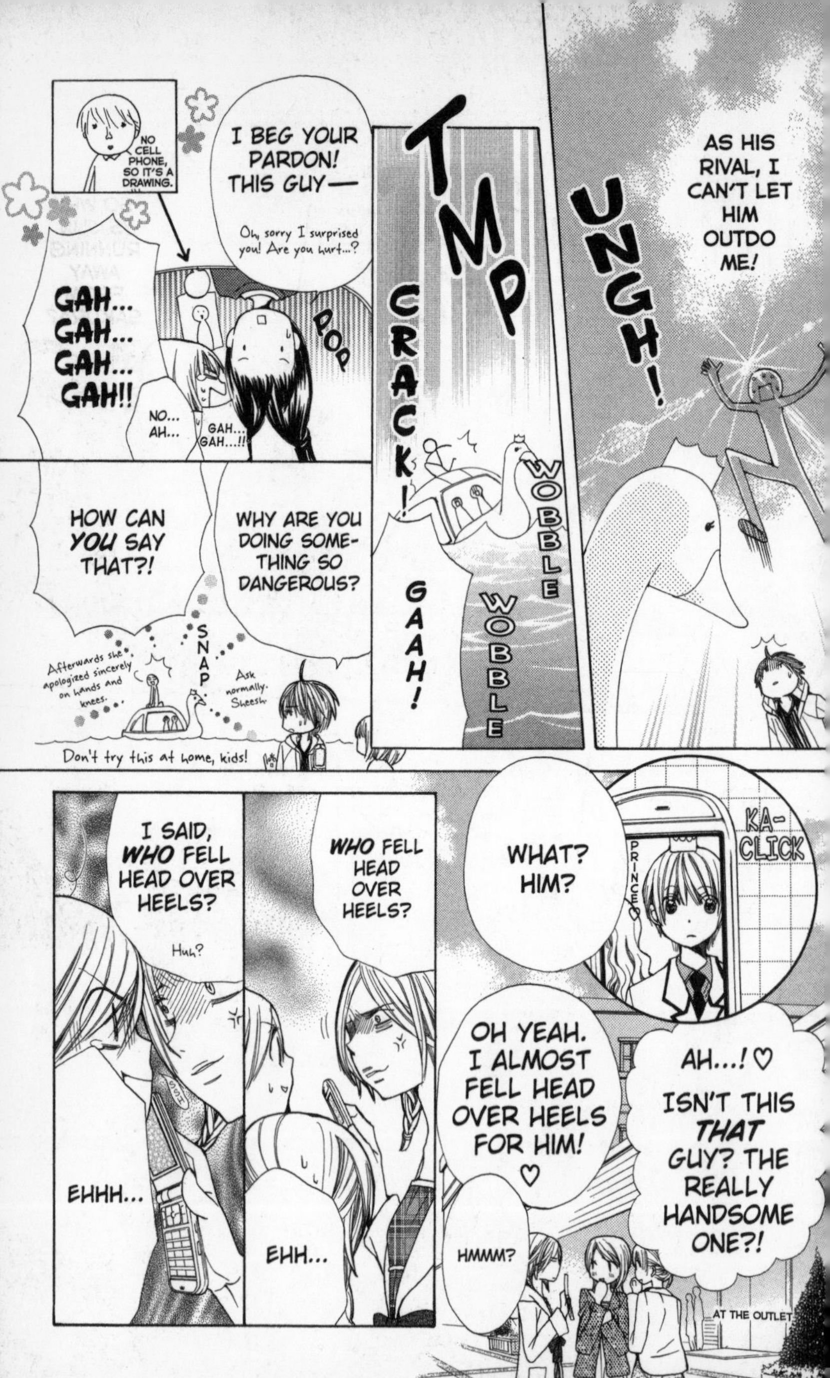
AS HIS RIVAL, I CAN'T LET HIM OUTDO ME!
UNGH!
TMP
CRACK!
WOBBLE
WOBBLE
GAAH!
I BEG YOUR PARDON! THIS GUY—
Oh, sorry I surprised you! Are you hurt...?
POP
NO CELL PHONE, SO IT'S A DRAWING.
GAH... GAH... GAH... GAH!!
NO... AH...
GAH... GAH...!!
WHY ARE YOU DOING SOME-THING SO DANGEROUS?
HOW CAN YOU SAY THAT?!
SNAP
Ask normally. Sheesh.
Afterwards she apologized sincerely on hands and knees.
Don't try this at home, kids!
KA-CLICK
PRINCE
AH...! ♡ ISN'T THIS THAT GUY? THE REALLY HANDSOME ONE?!
WHAT? HIM?
OH YEAH. I ALMOST FELL HEAD OVER HEELS FOR HIM! ♡
HMMM?
AT THE OUTLET
WHO FELL HEAD OVER HEELS?
EHH...
I SAID, WHO FELL HEAD OVER HEELS?
Huh?
EHHH...

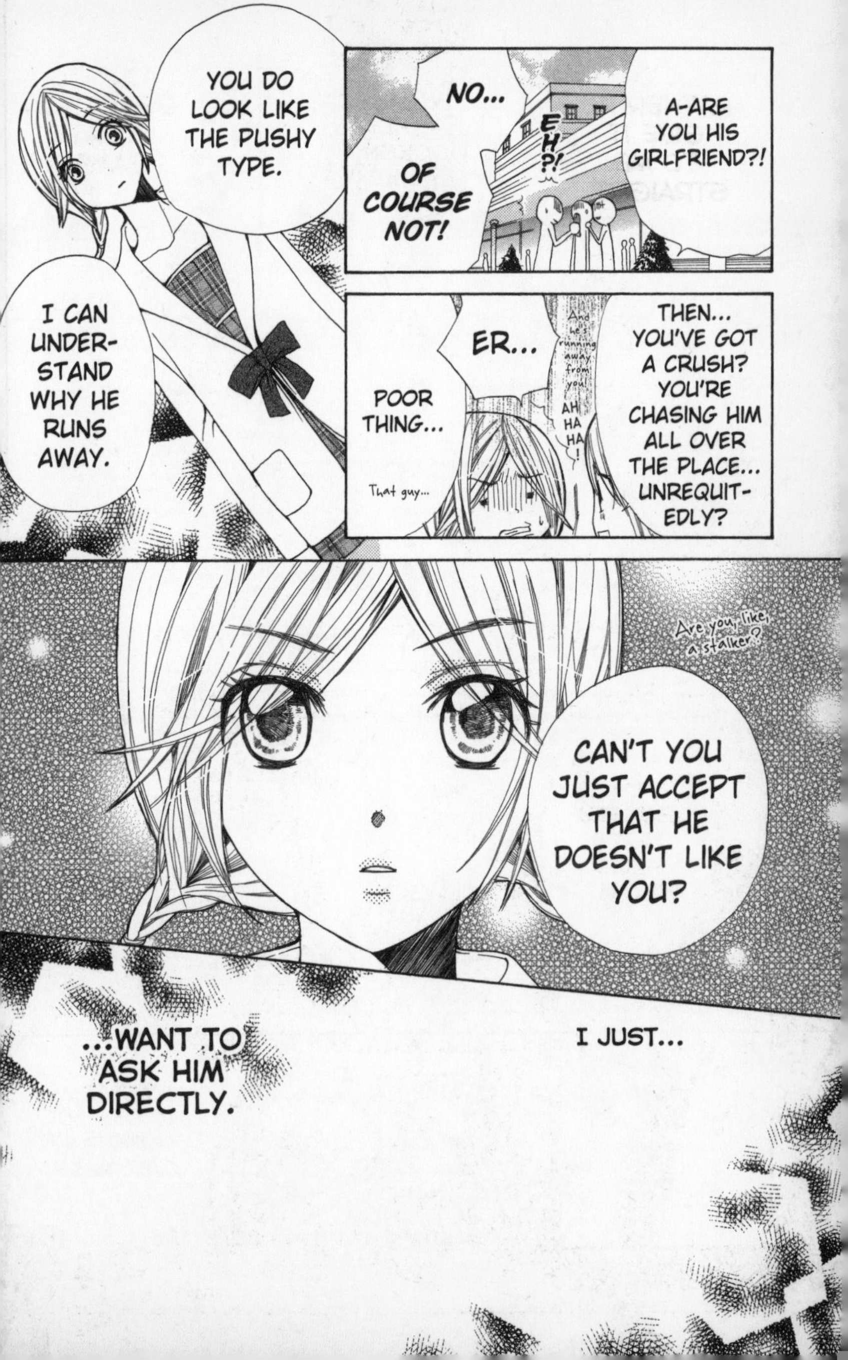
A-ARE YOU HIS GIRLFRIEND?!
EH?!
NO...
OF COURSE NOT!
THEN... YOU'VE GOT A CRUSH? YOU'RE CHASING HIM ALL OVER THE PLACE... UNREQUIT-EDLY?
And he's running away from you!
AH HA HA!
ER...
POOR THING...
That guy...
YOU DO LOOK LIKE THE PUSHY TYPE.
I CAN UNDER-STAND WHY HE RUNS AWAY.
Are you, like, a stalker?
CAN'T YOU JUST ACCEPT THAT HE DOESN'T LIKE YOU?
I JUST...
...WANT TO ASK HIM DIRECTLY.

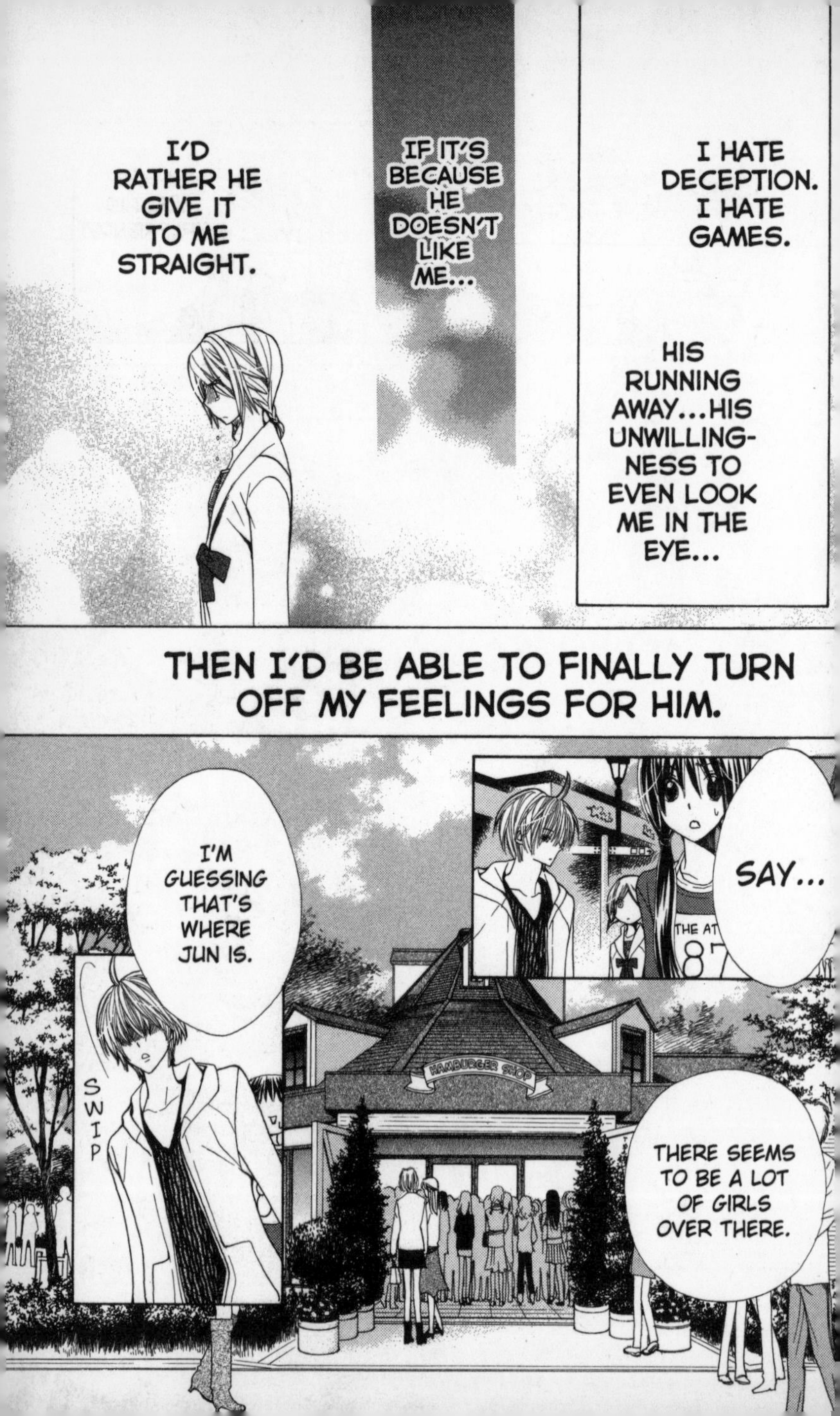
I HATE DECEPTION. I HATE GAMES.
HIS RUNNING AWAY...HIS UNWILLINGNESS TO EVEN LOOK ME IN THE EYE...
IF IT'S BECAUSE HE DOESN'T LIKE ME...
I'D RATHER HE GIVE IT TO ME STRAIGHT.
THEN I'D BE ABLE TO FINALLY TURN OFF MY FEELINGS FOR HIM.
SAY...
THERE SEEMS TO BE A LOT OF GIRLS OVER THERE.
HAMBURGER SHOP
I'M GUESSING THAT'S WHERE JUN IS.
SWIP

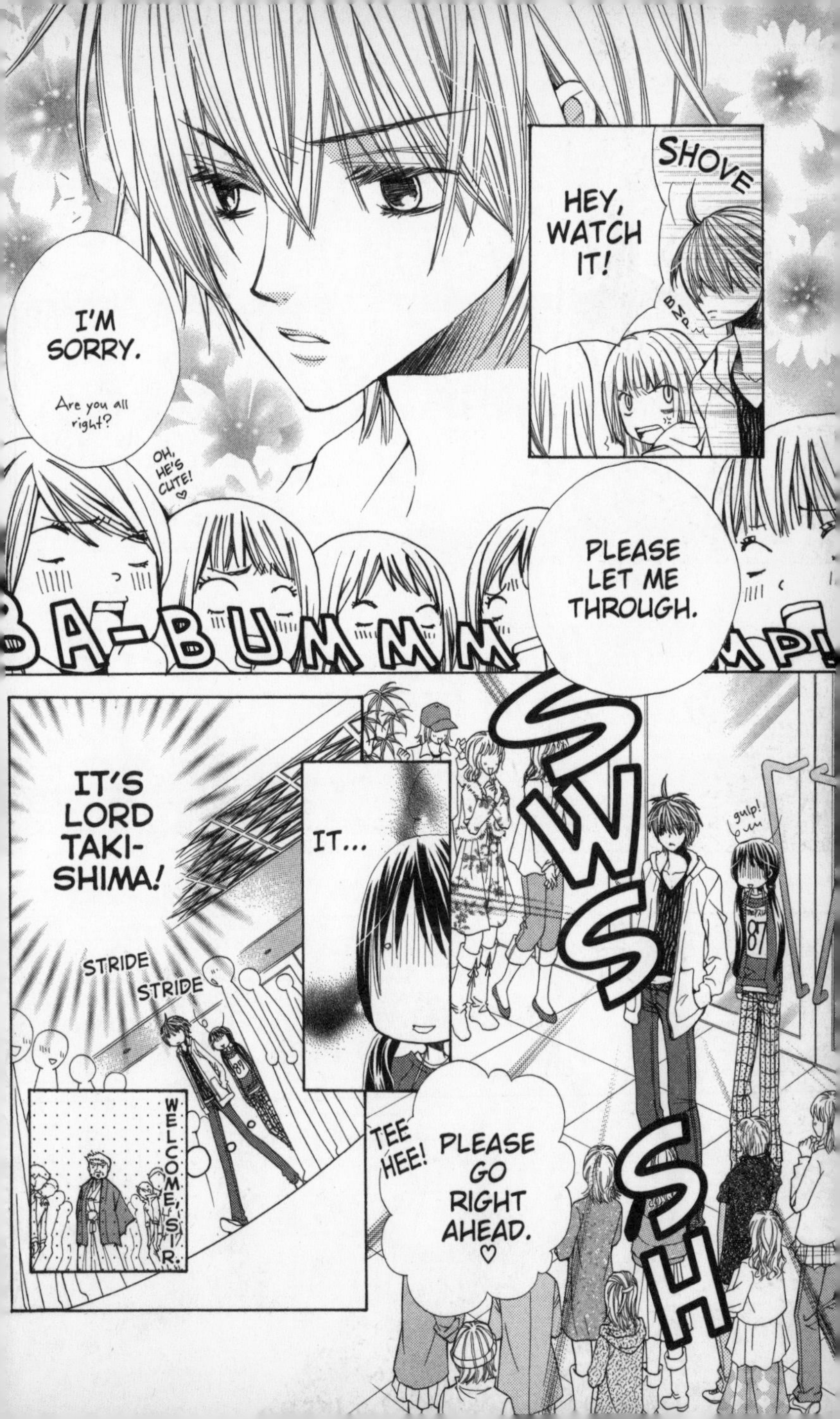
SHOVE
HEY, WATCH IT!
I'M SORRY.
Are you all right?
PLEASE LET ME THROUGH.
OH, HE'S CUTE! ♡
BA-BUMMMM
MP!
SWSSH
gulp!
TEE HEE!
PLEASE GO RIGHT AHEAD. ♡
IT...
IT'S LORD TAKI-SHIMA!
STRIDE
STRIDE
WELCOME, SIR.

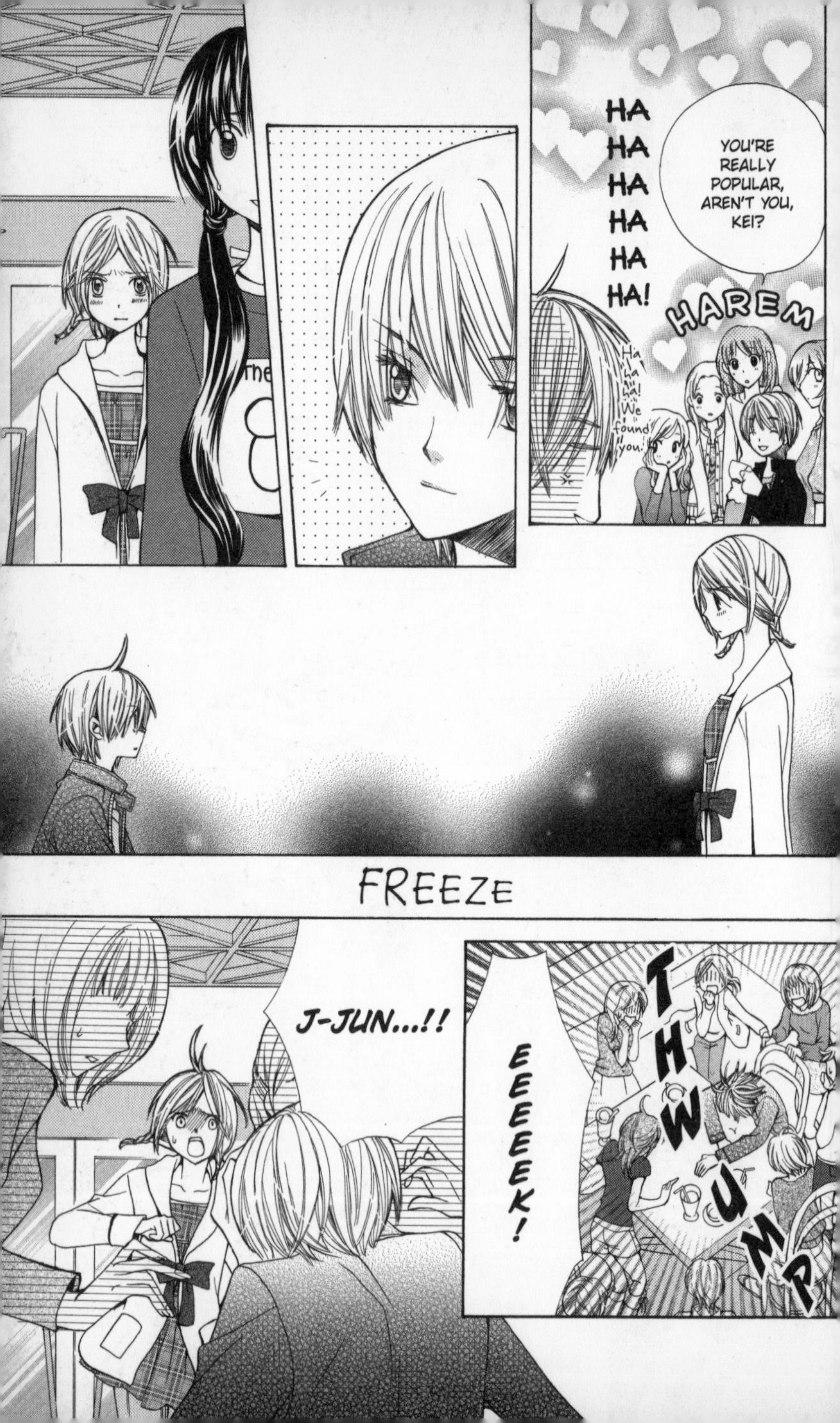
YOU'RE REALLY POPULAR, AREN'T YOU, KEI?
HA HA HA HA HA HA!
HAREM
Ha ha ha! We found you!
FREEZE
THWUMP
EEEEEK!
J-JUN...!!

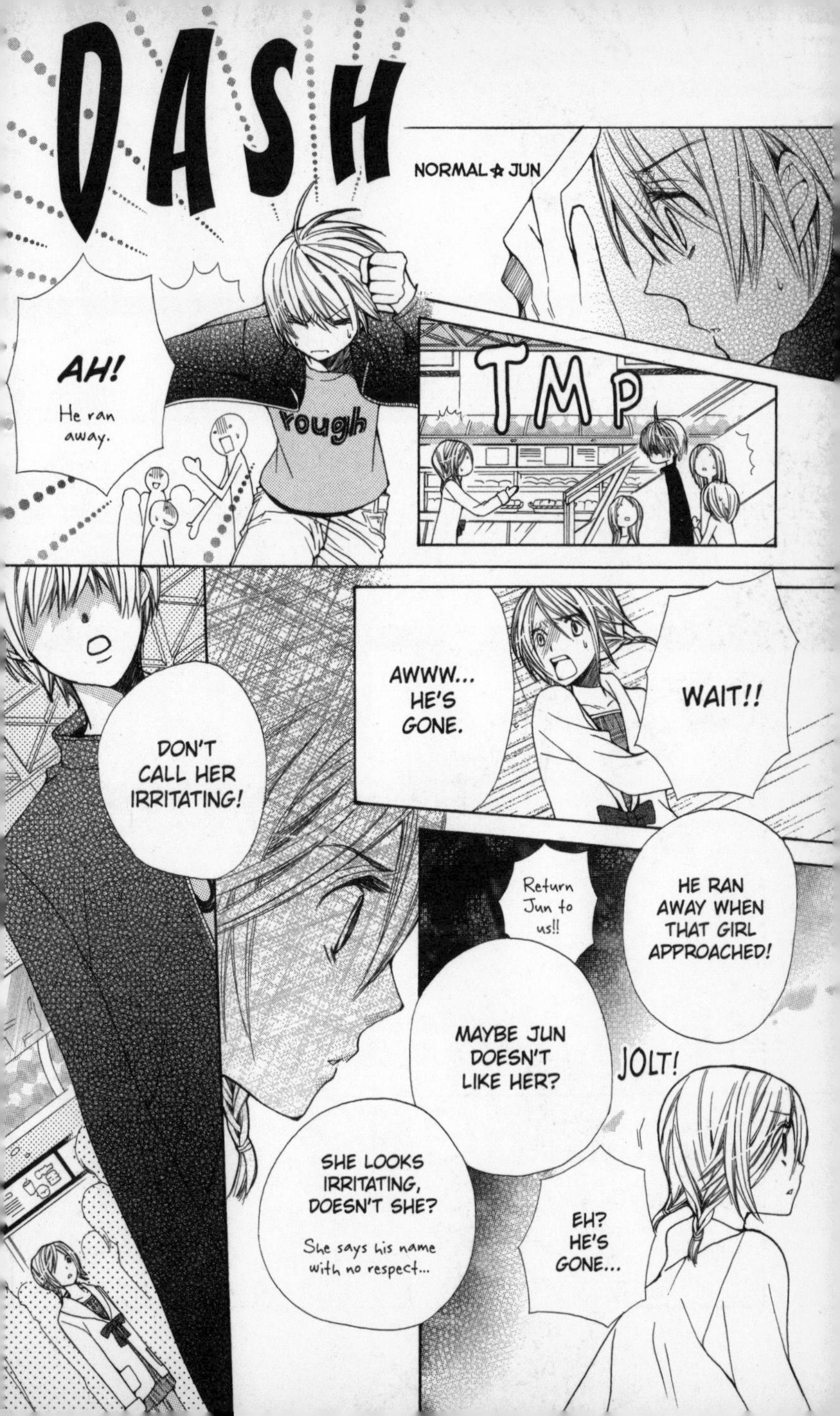
NORMAL☆JUN
TMP
DASH
AH!
He ran away.
WAIT!!
AWWW... HE'S GONE.
HE RAN AWAY WHEN THAT GIRL APPROACHED!
Return Jun to us!!
MAYBE JUN DOESN'T LIKE HER?
JOLT!
EH? HE'S GONE...
SHE LOOKS IRRITATING, DOESN'T SHE?
She says his name with no respect...
DON'T CALL HER IRRITATING!

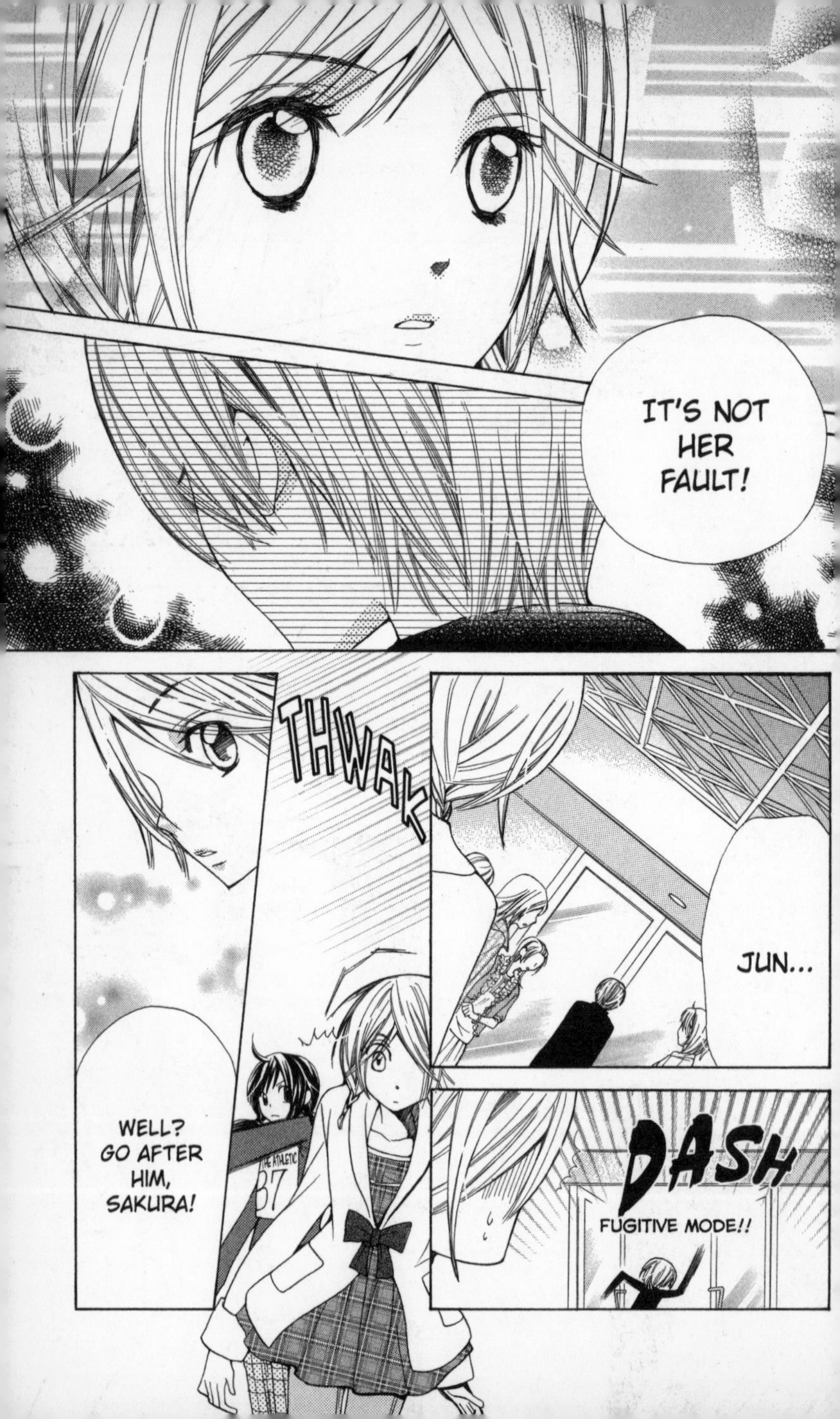
IT'S NOT HER FAULT!
JUN...
DASH
FUGITIVE MODE!!
THWAK
WELL? GO AFTER HIM, SAKURA!

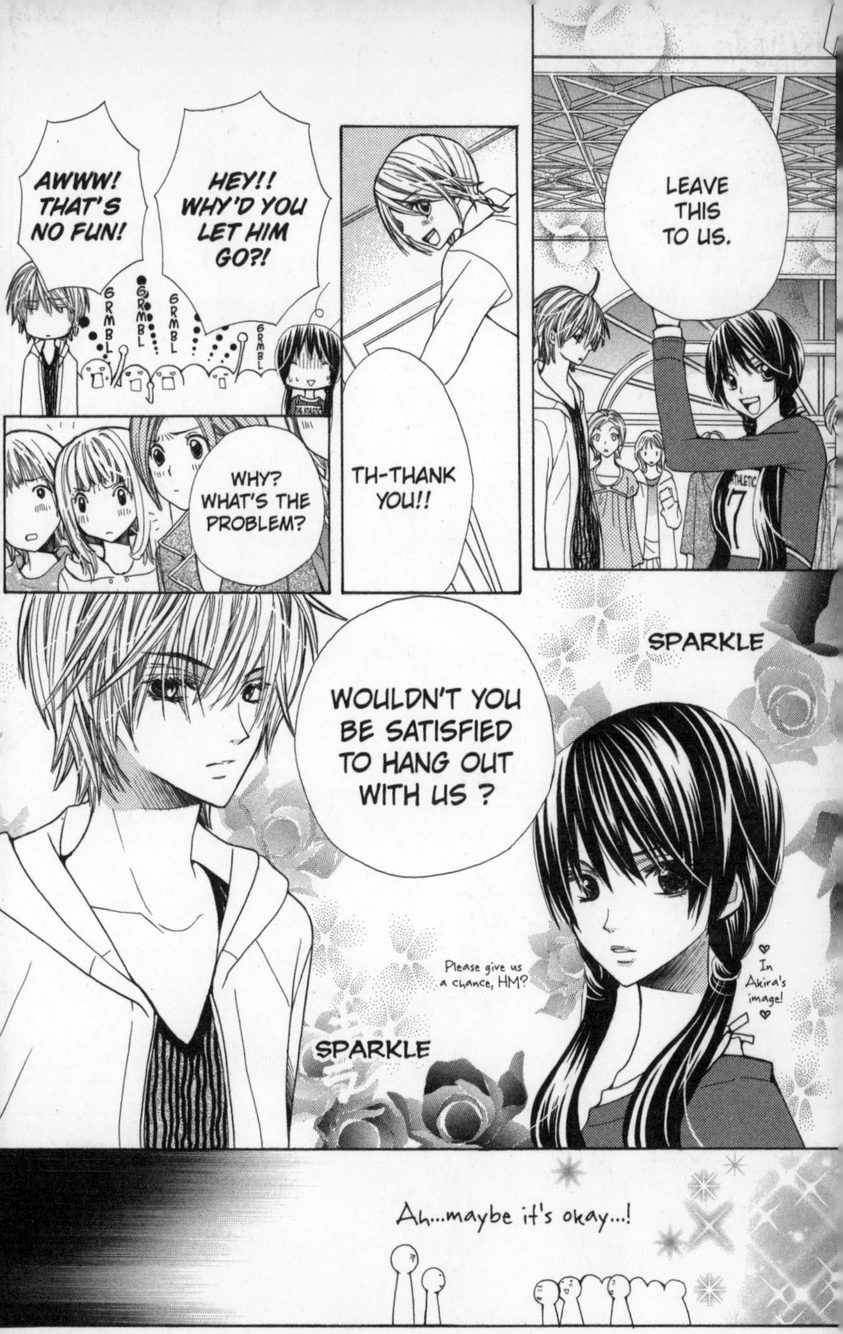
LEAVE THIS TO US.
TH-THANK YOU!!
HEY!! WHY'D YOU LET HIM GO?!
AWWW! THAT'S NO FUN!
GRMBL
GRMBL
GRMBL
GRMBL
WHY? WHAT'S THE PROBLEM?
SPARKLE
WOULDN'T YOU BE SATISFIED TO HANG OUT WITH US ?
In Akira's image!
Please give us a chance, HM?
SPARKLE
Ah...maybe it's okay...!

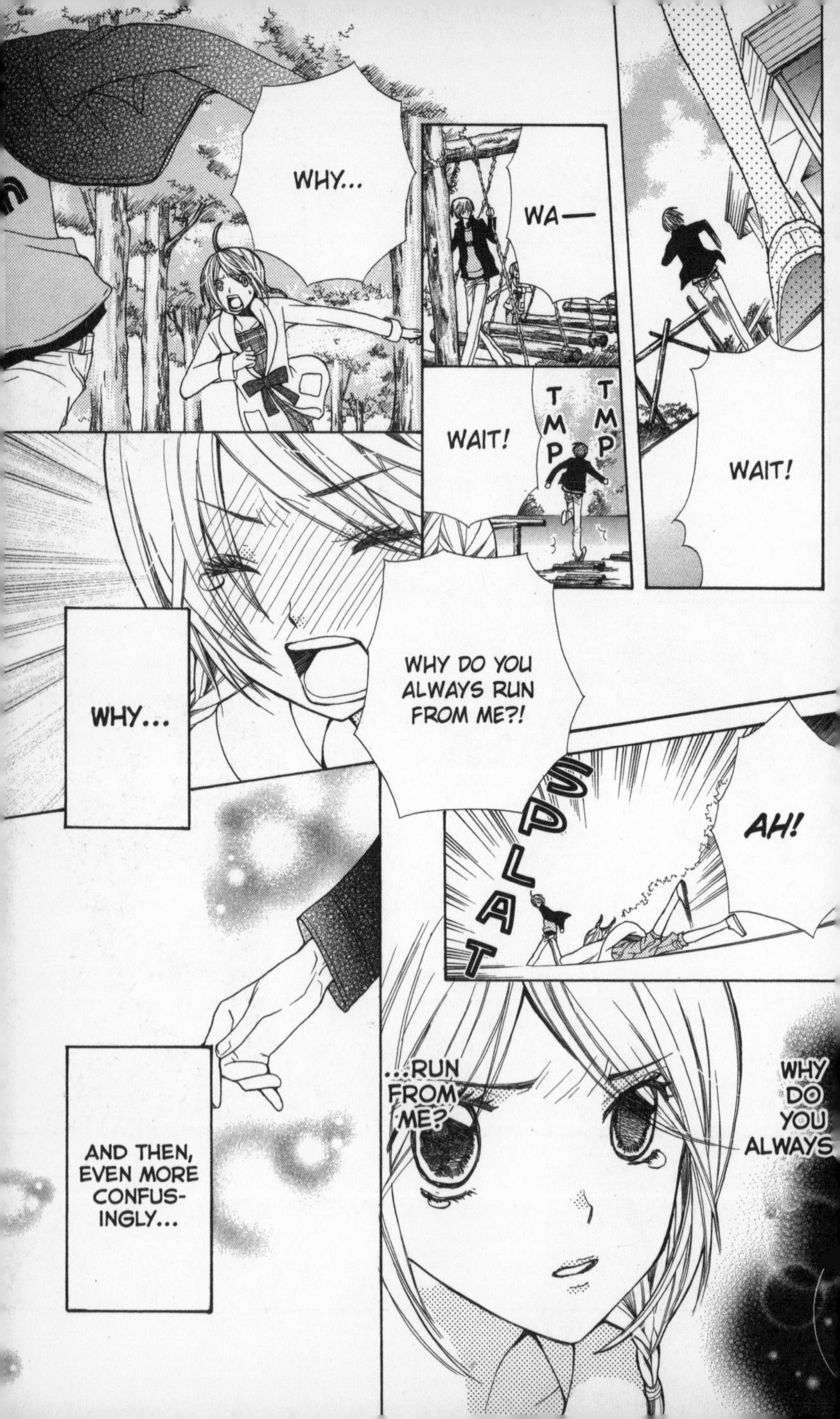

WAIT!
WA—
WAIT!
TMP TMP
WHY...
WHY DO YOU ALWAYS RUN FROM ME?!
SPLAT
AH!
WHY...
WHY DO YOU ALWAYS
...RUN FROM ME?
AND THEN, EVEN MORE CONFUS-INGLY...

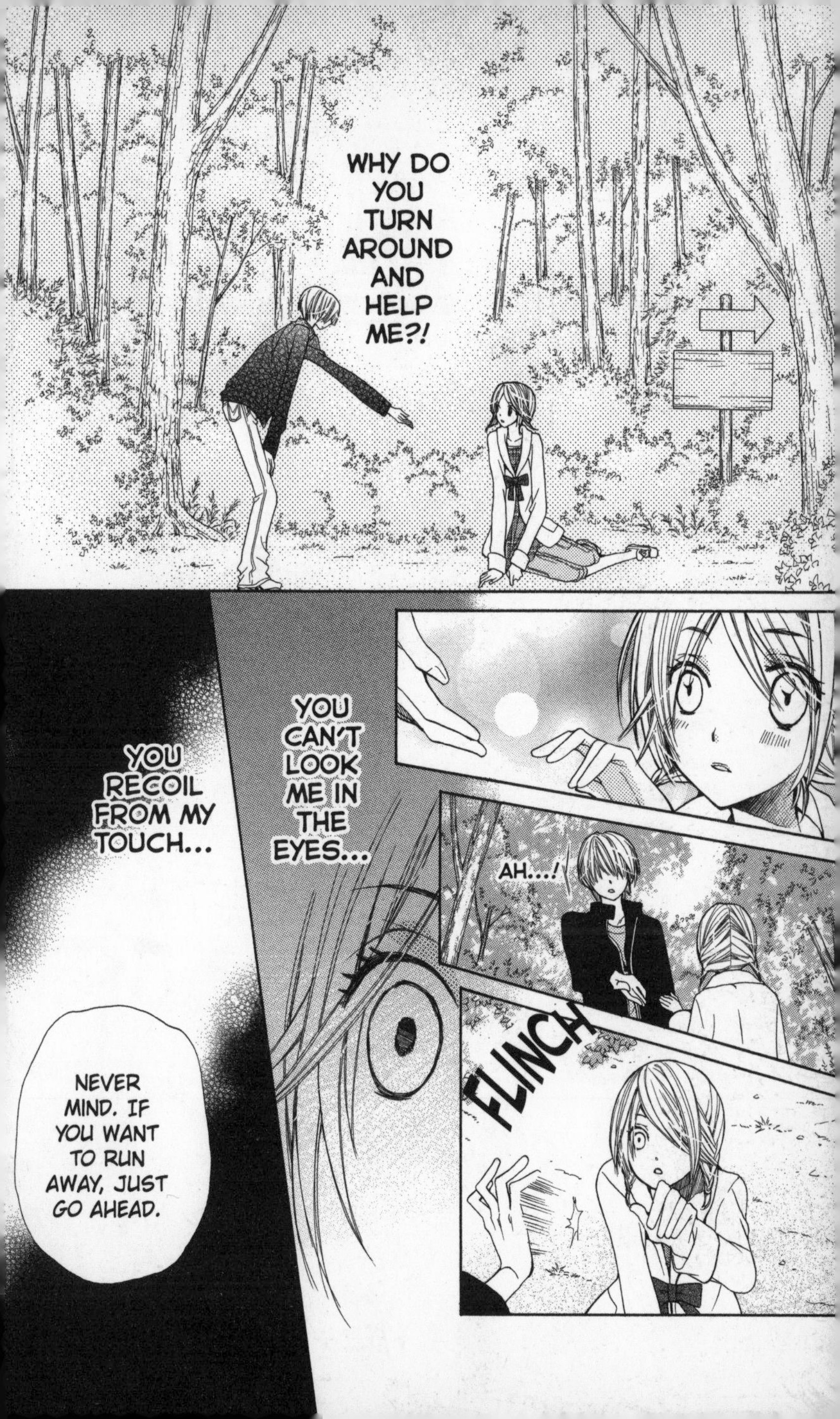
WHY DO YOU TURN AROUND AND HELP ME?!
AH...!
FLINCH
YOU CAN'T LOOK ME IN THE EYES...
YOU RECOIL FROM MY TOUCH...
NEVER MIND. IF YOU WANT TO RUN AWAY, JUST GO AHEAD.

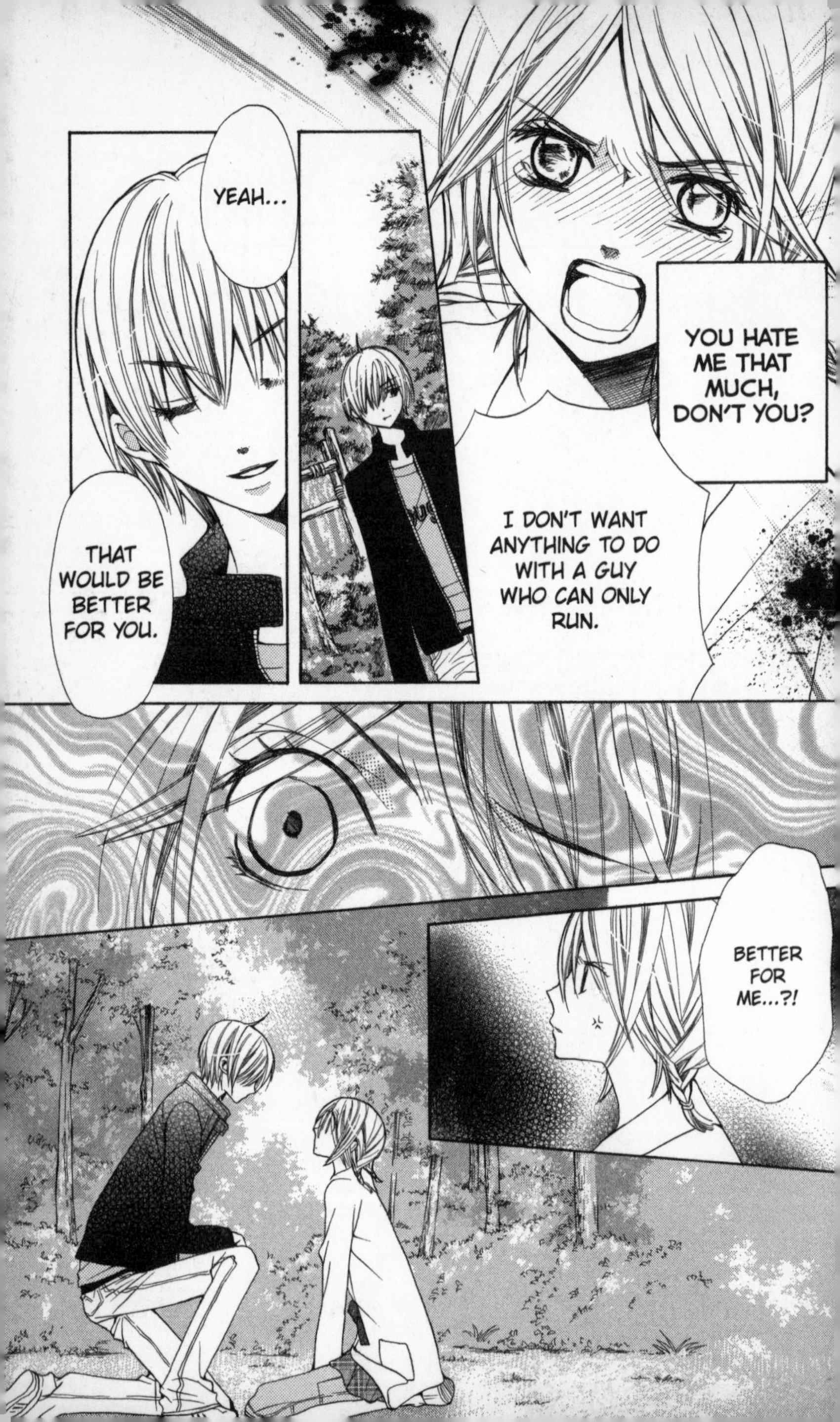
YOU HATE ME THAT MUCH, DON'T YOU?
I DON'T WANT ANYTHING TO DO WITH A GUY WHO CAN ONLY RUN.
YEAH...
THAT WOULD BE BETTER FOR YOU.
BETTER FOR ME...?!

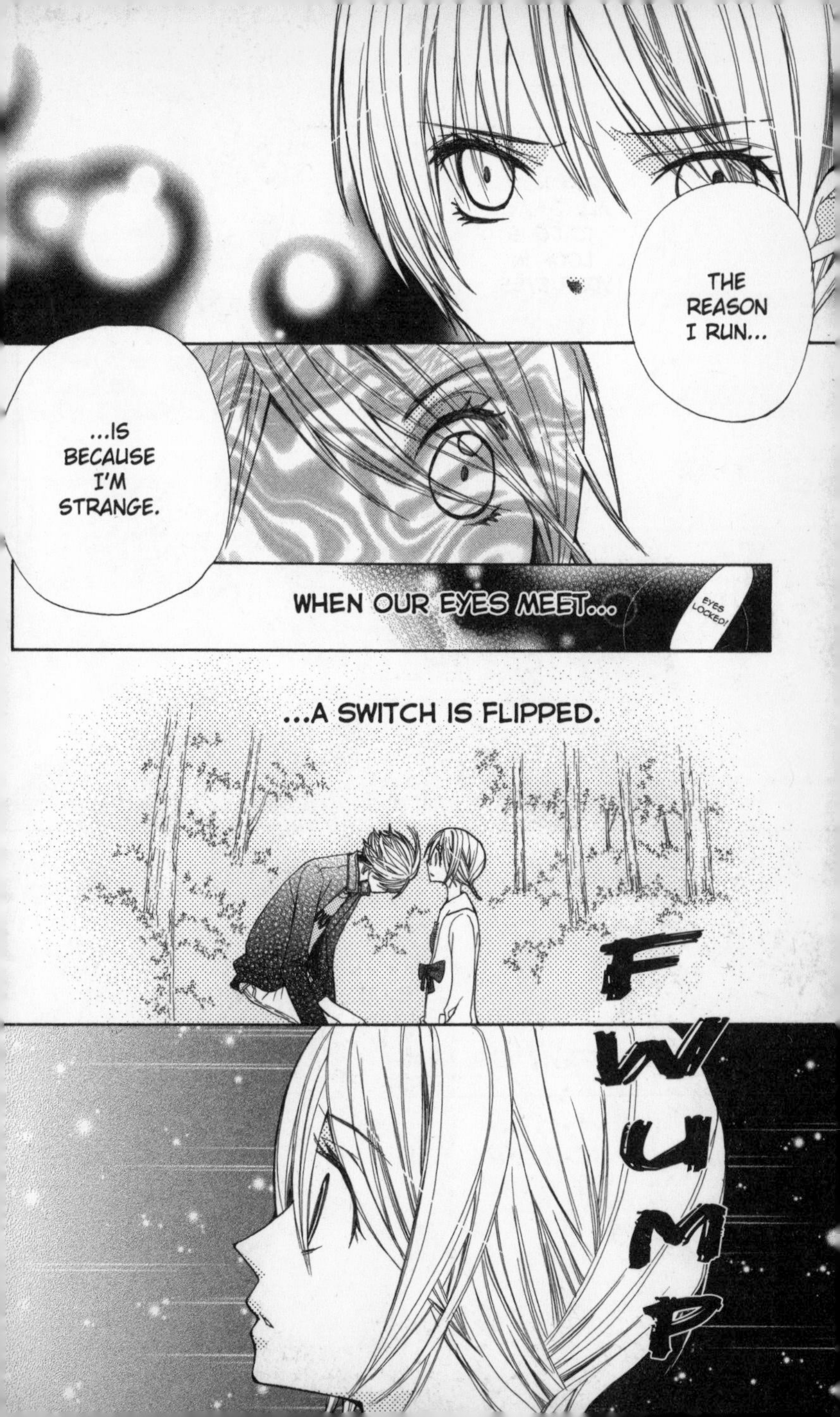
THE REASON I RUN...
...IS BECAUSE I'M STRANGE.
WHEN OUR EYES MEET...
EYES LOCKED!
...A SWITCH IS FLIPPED.
FWUMP

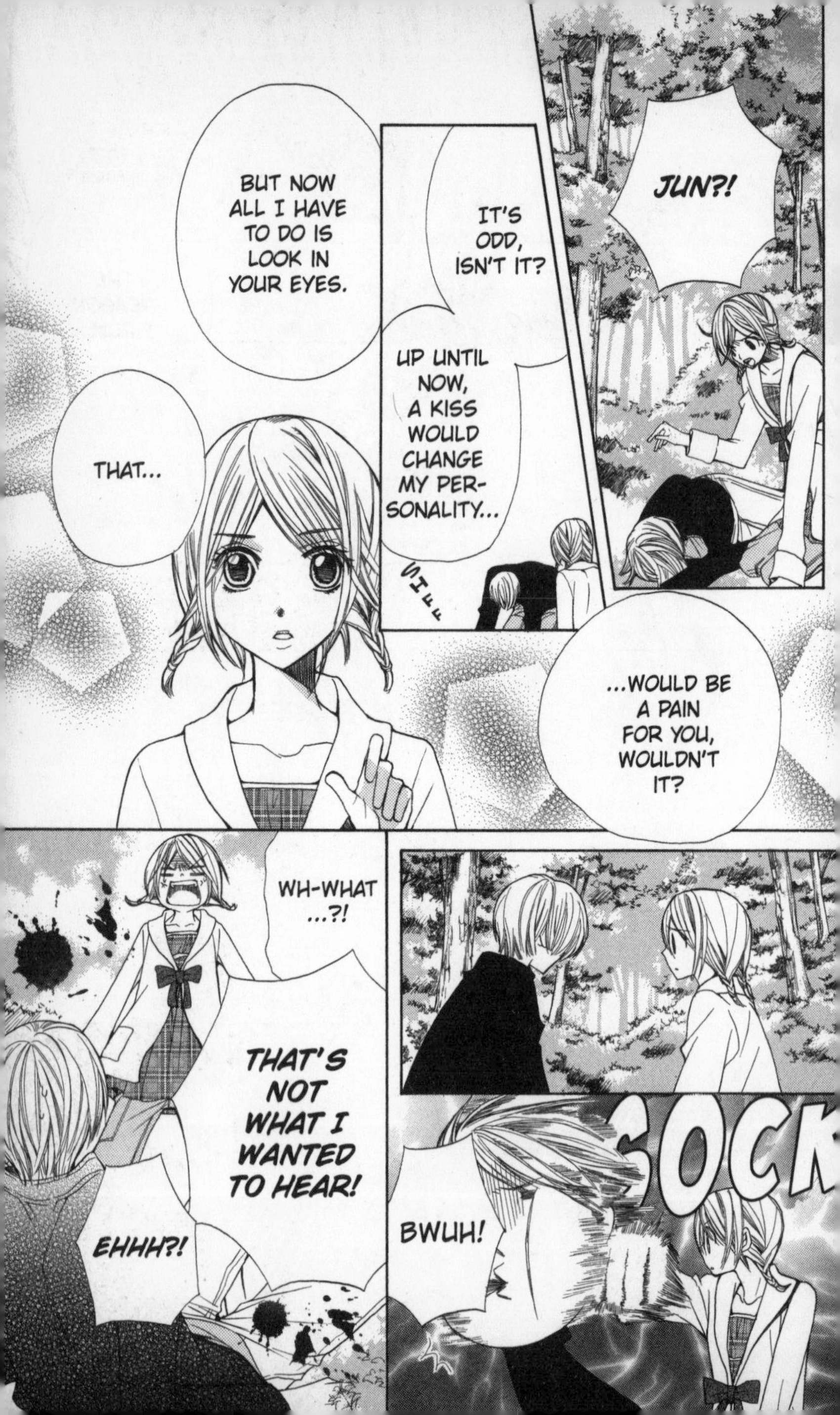
JUN?!
IT'S ODD, ISN'T IT?
UP UNTIL NOW, A KISS WOULD CHANGE MY PER-SONALITY...
BUT NOW ALL I HAVE TO DO IS LOOK IN YOUR EYES.
THAT...
...WOULD BE A PAIN FOR YOU, WOULDN'T IT?
SOCK
BWUH!
WH-WHAT ...?!
THAT'S NOT WHAT I WANTED TO HEAR!
EHHH?!

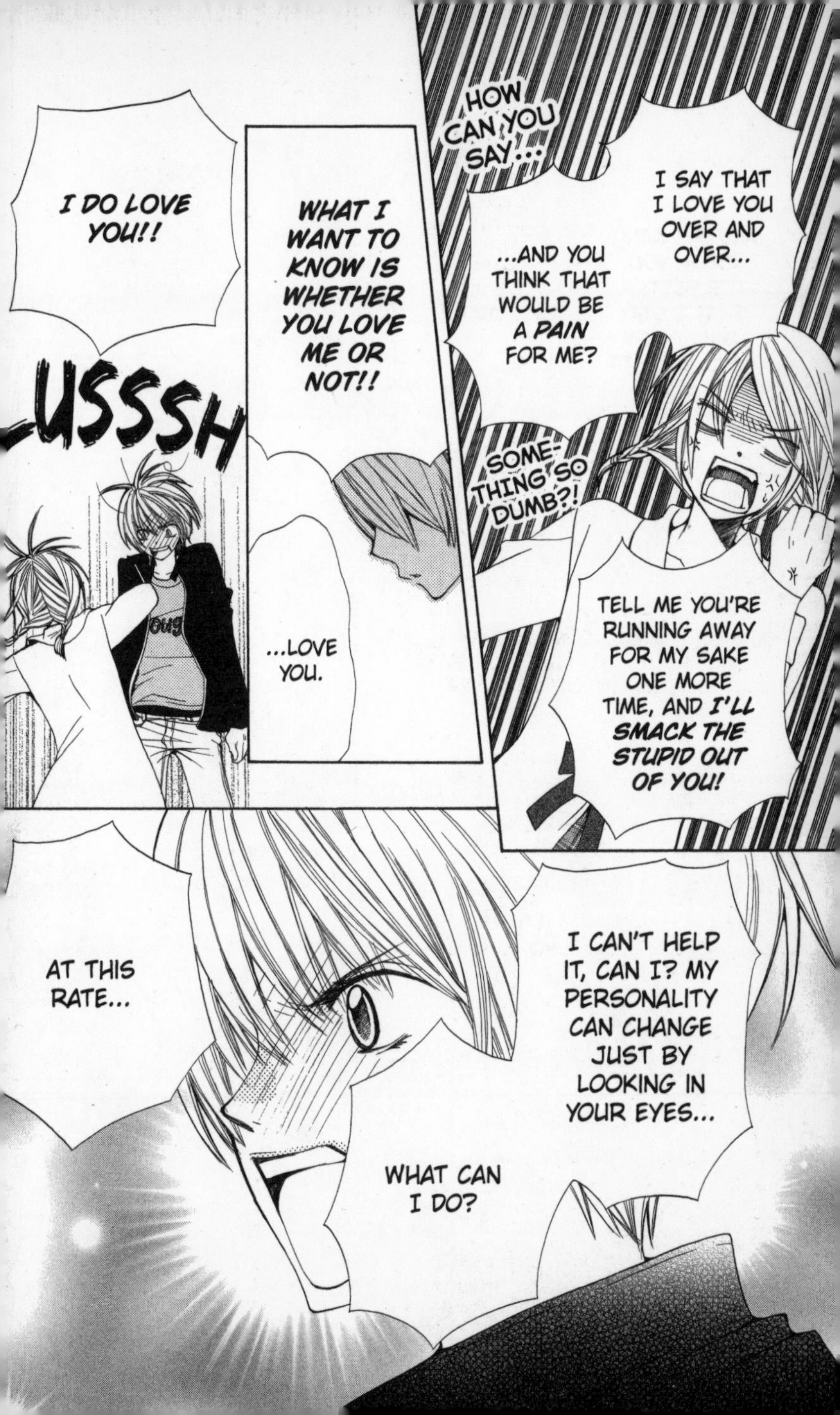
I SAY THAT I LOVE YOU OVER AND OVER...
...AND YOU THINK THAT WOULD BE A PAIN FOR ME?
HOW CAN YOU SAY...
SOME-THING SO DUMB?!
TELL ME YOU'RE RUNNING AWAY FOR MY SAKE ONE MORE TIME, AND I'LL SMACK THE STUPID OUT OF YOU!
WHAT I WANT TO KNOW IS WHETHER YOU LOVE ME OR NOT!!
...LOVE YOU.
I DO LOVE YOU!!
USSSH
I CAN'T HELP IT, CAN I? MY PERSONALITY CAN CHANGE JUST BY LOOKING IN YOUR EYES...
WHAT CAN I DO?
AT THIS RATE...

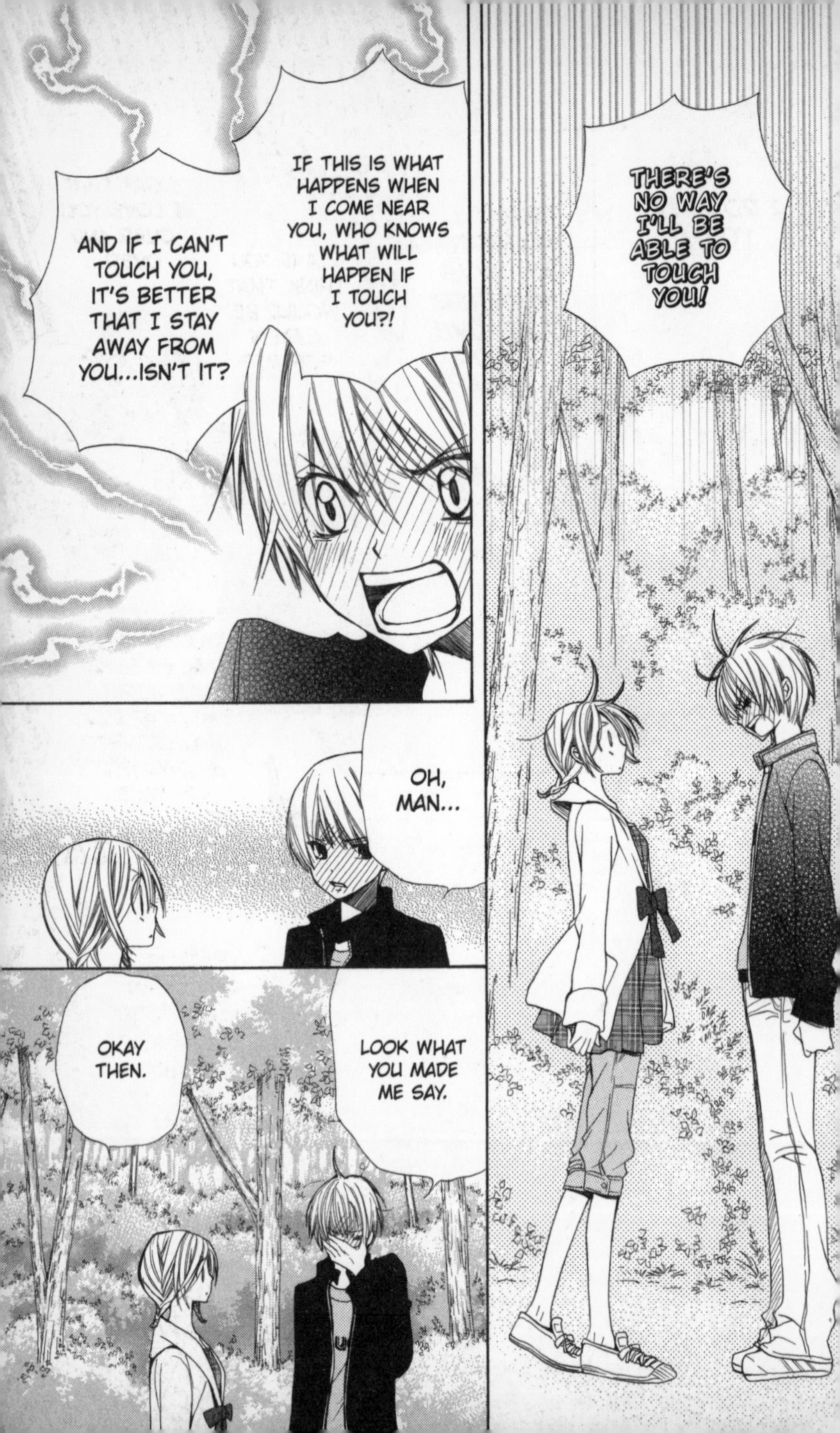
THERE'S NO WAY I'LL BE ABLE TO TOUCH YOU!
IF THIS IS WHAT HAPPENS WHEN I COME NEAR YOU, WHO KNOWS WHAT WILL HAPPEN IF I TOUCH YOU?!
AND IF I CAN'T TOUCH YOU, IT'S BETTER THAT I STAY AWAY FROM YOU...ISN'T IT?
OH, MAN...
LOOK WHAT YOU MADE ME SAY.
OKAY THEN.

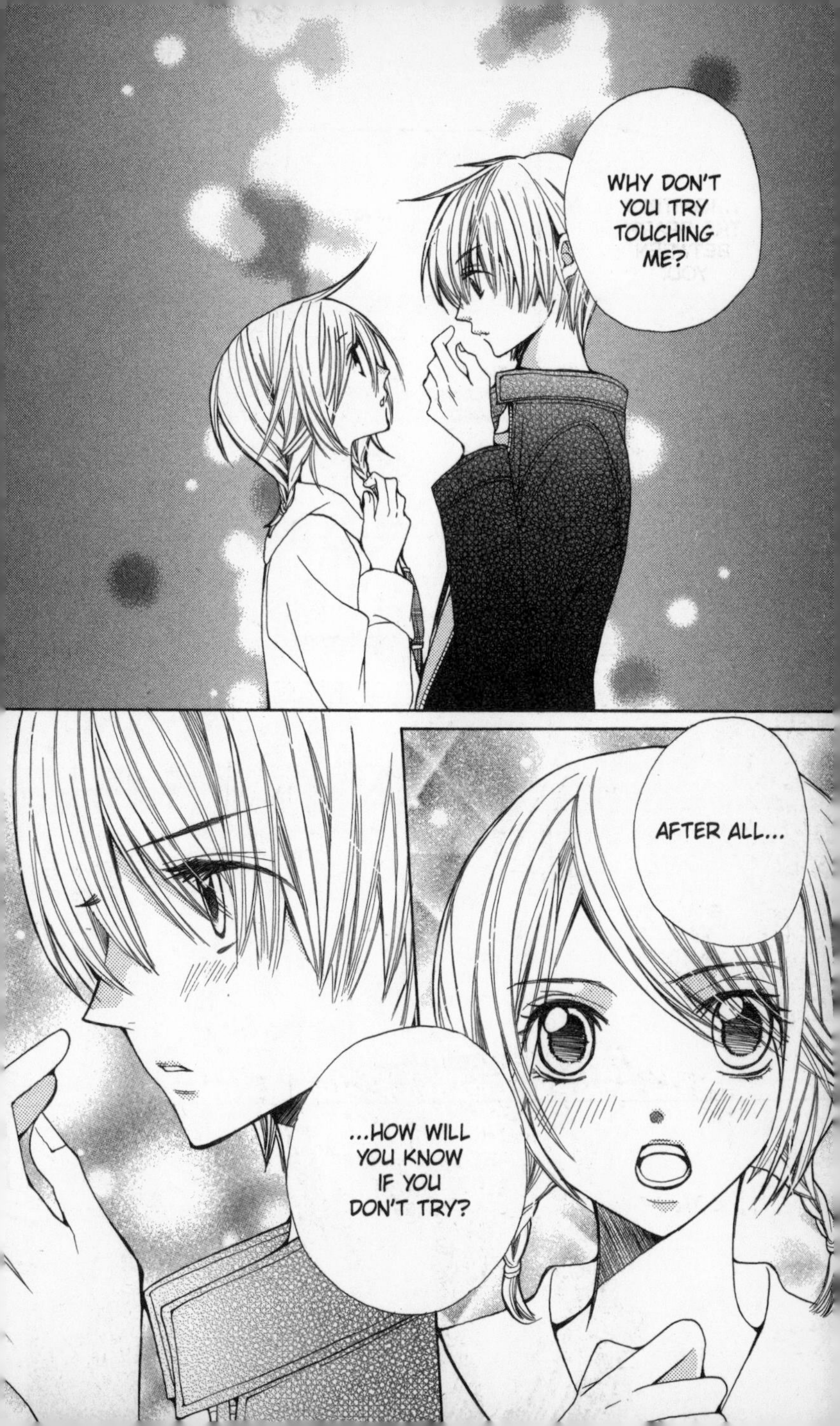
WHY DON'T YOU TRY TOUCHING ME?
AFTER ALL...
...HOW WILL YOU KNOW IF YOU DON'T TRY?

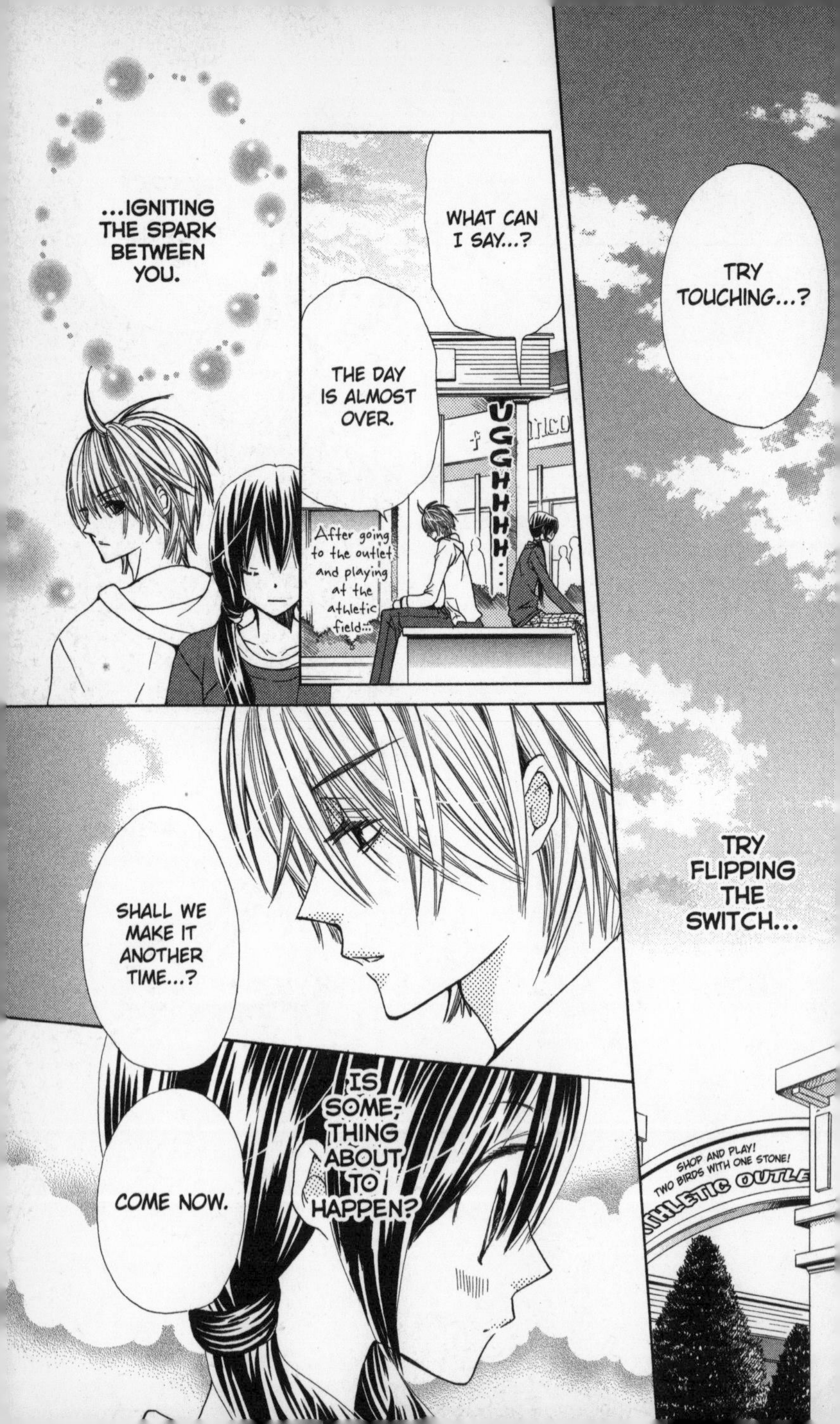
TRY TOUCHING...?
TRY FLIPPING THE SWITCH...
SHOP AND PLAY! TWO BIRDS WITH ONE STONE!
THLETIC OUTLE
WHAT CAN I SAY...?
UGGHHHH...
THE DAY IS ALMOST OVER.
After going to the outlet and playing at the athletic field...
...IGNITING THE SPARK BETWEEN YOU.
SHALL WE MAKE IT ANOTHER TIME...?
IS SOMETHING ABOUT TO HAPPEN?
COME NOW.

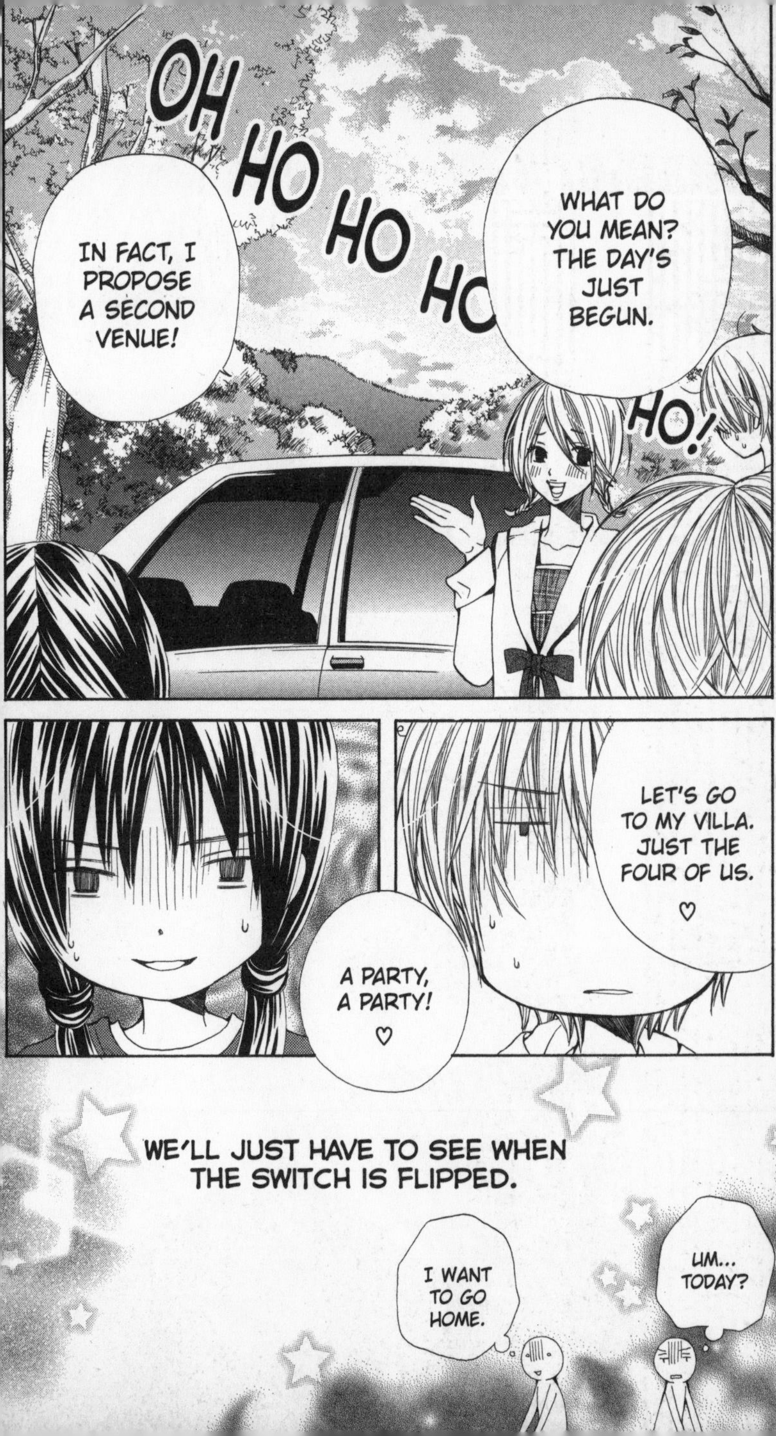
WHAT DO YOU MEAN? THE DAY'S JUST BEGUN.
OH HO HO HO HO!
IN FACT, I PROPOSE A SECOND VENUE!
LET'S GO TO MY VILLA. JUST THE FOUR OF US. ♡
A PARTY, A PARTY! ♡
WE'LL JUST HAVE TO SEE WHEN THE SWITCH IS FLIPPED.
UM... TODAY?
I WANT TO GO HOME.

Chapter 42

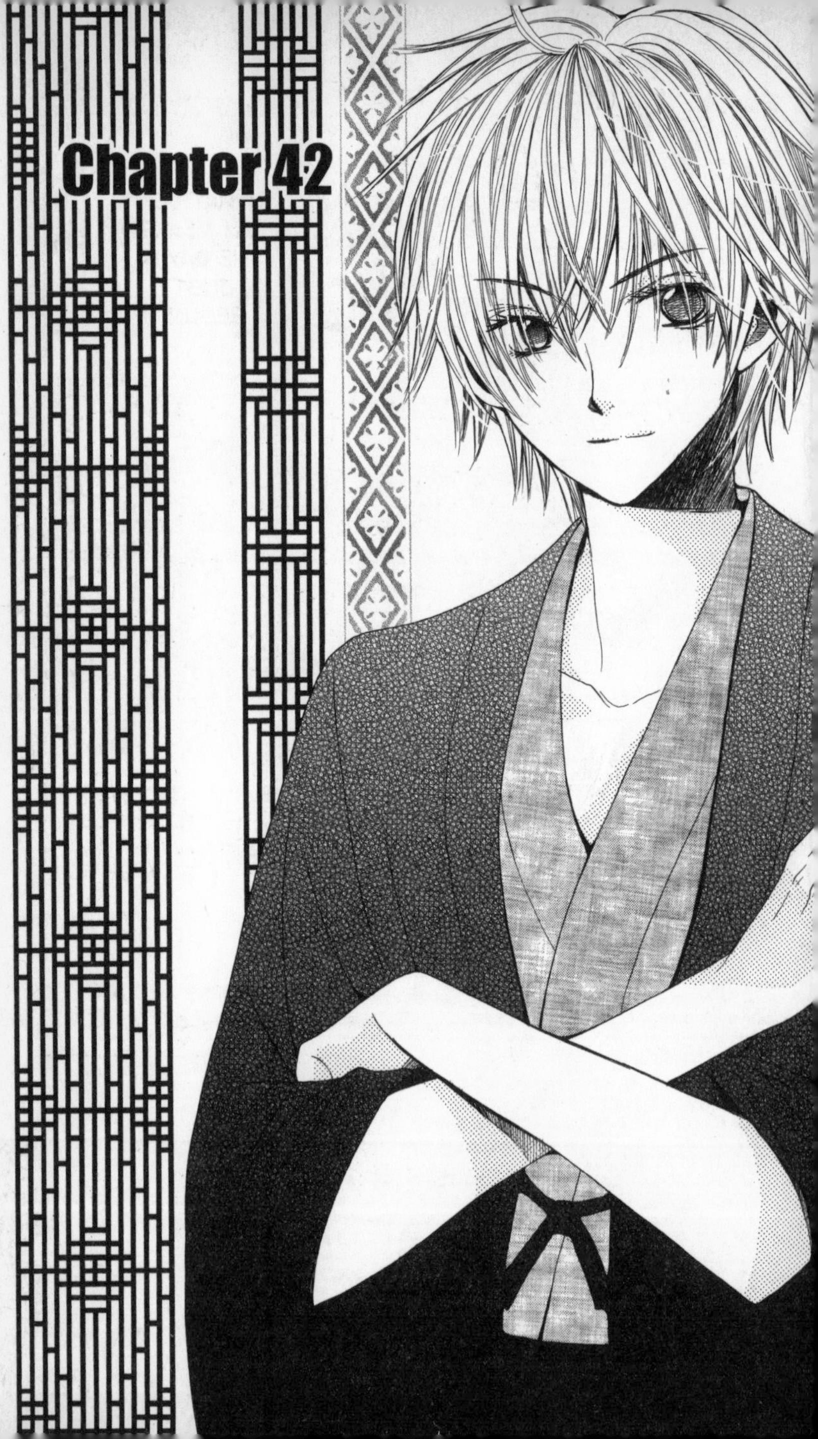

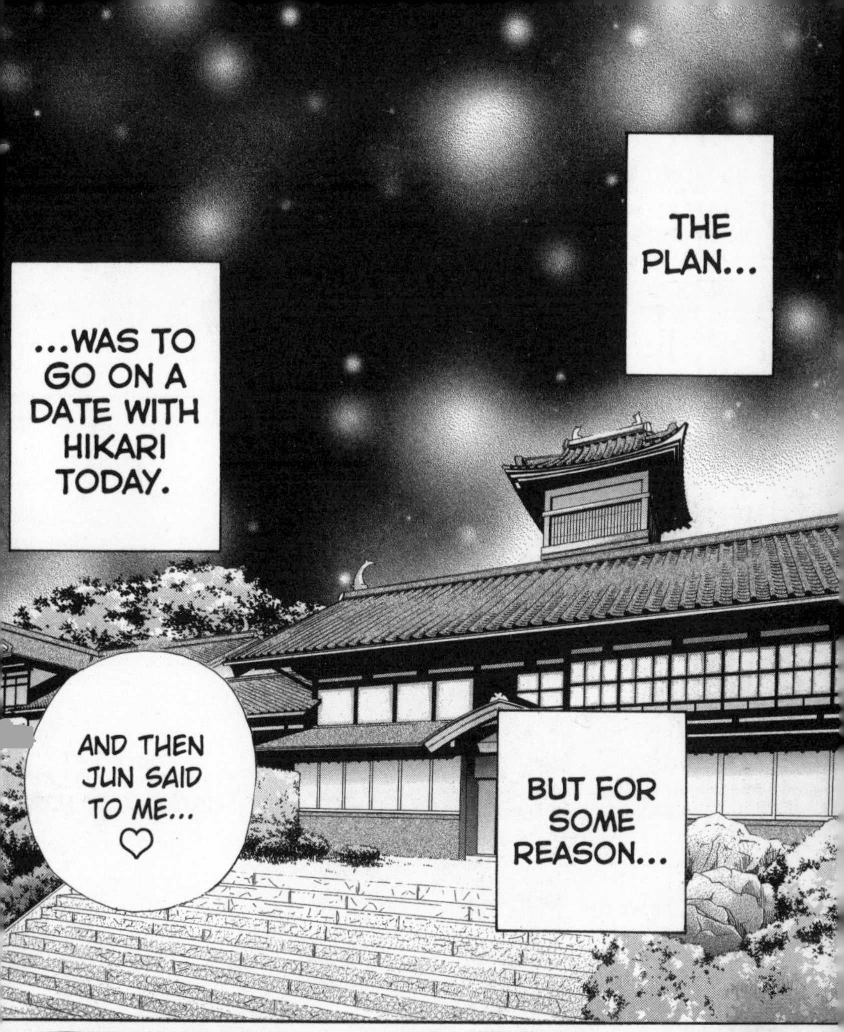
THE PLAN...
...WAS TO GO ON A DATE WITH HIKARI TODAY.
BUT FOR SOME REASON...
AND THEN JUN SAID TO ME... ♡

•QUARTER PAGES IN VOLUME 7•

IN THE LAST VOLUME, SOME WORDS IN YAHIRO'S AND SAKURA'S PROFILES DISAPPEARED, AND PARTS OF THE TEXT SEEMED TO BE IN CODE. SOME OF YOU MAY HAVE THOUGHT IT DIDN'T MAKE SENSE! I'M SORRY FOR ANY INCONVENIENCE.
IT SAID, "ENJOYS DRAWING."
BUT IT SHOULD HAVE SAID "I ENJOY DRAWING THESE TWO." IT SHOULD BE CORRECTED IN THE NEXT PRINTING.
TO THE PRINTERS, I'M SORRY FOR THE TROUBLE. THANK YOU FOR ALWAYS CORRECTING MY ***KANJI***. I TRULY ENJOY DRAWING YAHIRO AND SAKURA. THEY HAVE ALL SORTS OF EVENTS, SO IT'S FUN. I THINK IT WOULD BE GREAT TO WRITE A STORY ABOUT KOKUSEN [NAME OF YAHIRO AND SAKURA'S SCHOOL].

B

Sorry about that.

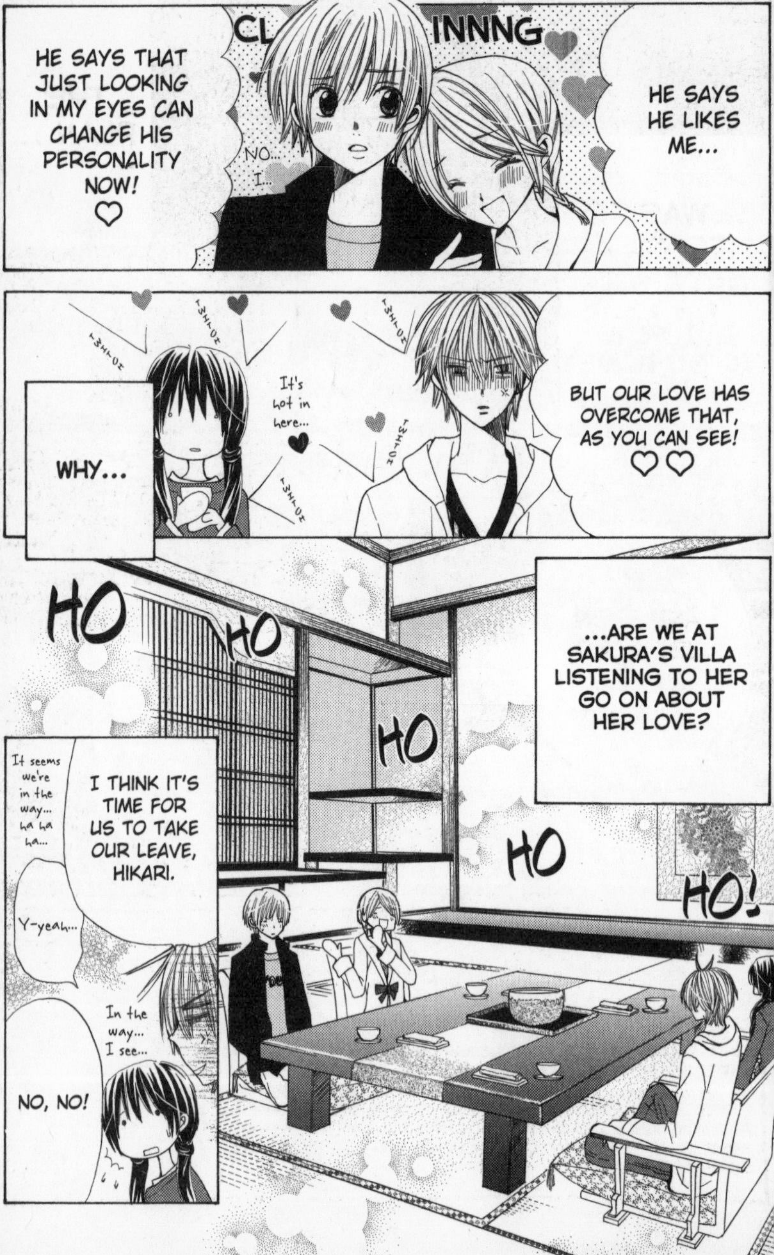
CL INNNG
HE SAYS HE LIKES ME...
NO... I...
HE SAYS THAT JUST LOOKING IN MY EYES CAN CHANGE HIS PERSONALITY NOW! ♡
BUT OUR LOVE HAS OVERCOME THAT, AS YOU CAN SEE! ♡♡
It's hot in here... ♥
WHY...
...ARE WE AT SAKURA'S VILLA LISTENING TO HER GO ON ABOUT HER LOVE?
HO
HO
HO
HO
HO!
I THINK IT'S TIME FOR US TO TAKE OUR LEAVE, HIKARI.
It seems we're in the way... ha ha ha...
Y-yeah...
In the way... I see...
NO, NO!

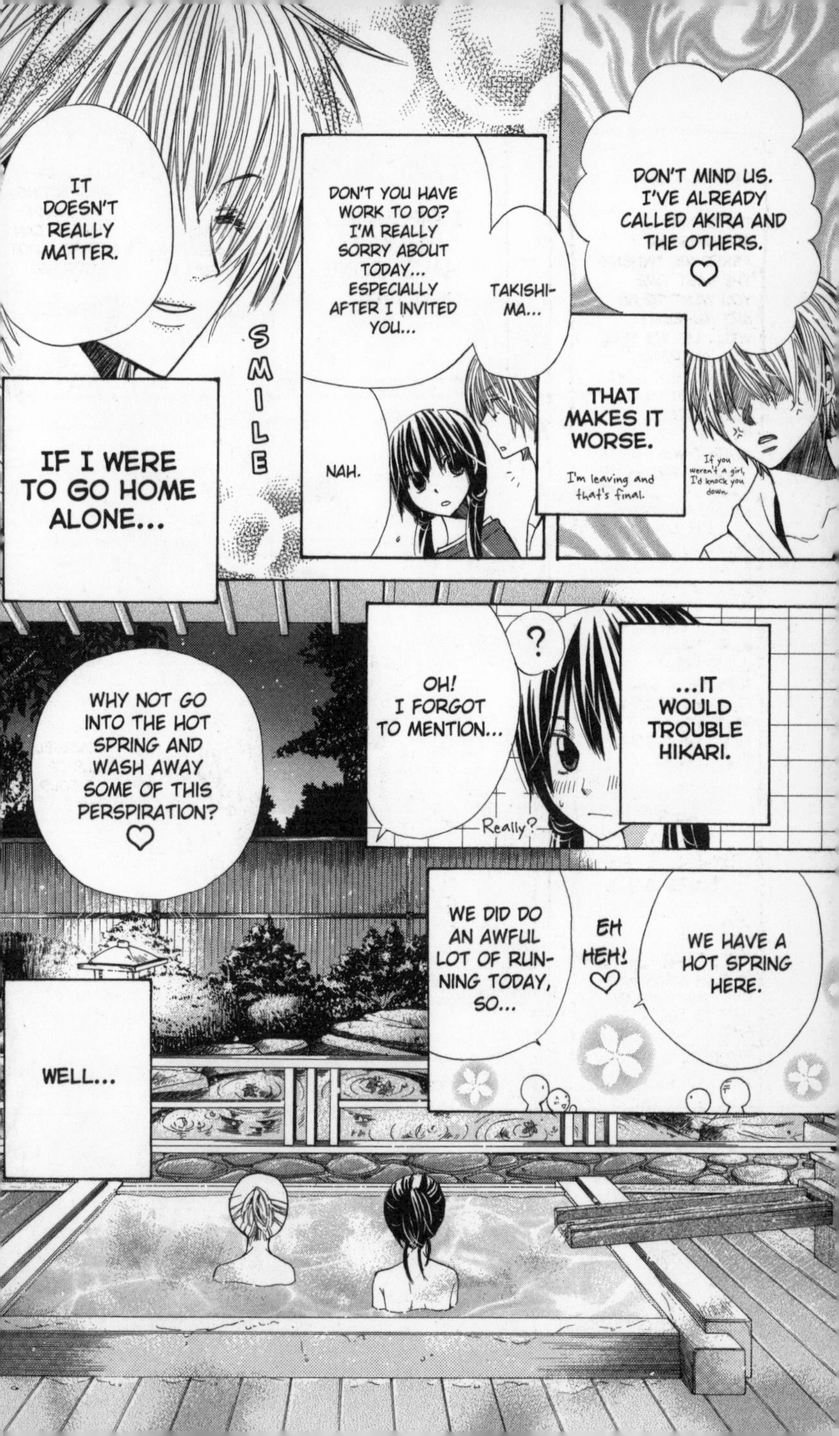
DON'T MIND US. I'VE ALREADY CALLED AKIRA AND THE OTHERS. ♡
THAT MAKES IT WORSE.
I'm leaving and that's final.
If you weren't a girl, I'd knock you down.
TAKISHIMA...
DON'T YOU HAVE WORK TO DO? I'M REALLY SORRY ABOUT TODAY... ESPECIALLY AFTER I INVITED YOU...
NAH.
IT DOESN'T REALLY MATTER.
SMILE
IF I WERE TO GO HOME ALONE...
...IT WOULD TROUBLE HIKARI.
?
OH! I FORGOT TO MENTION...
Really?
WE HAVE A HOT SPRING HERE.
EH HEH! ♡
WE DID DO AN AWFUL LOT OF RUNNING TODAY, SO...
WHY NOT GO INTO THE HOT SPRING AND WASH AWAY SOME OF THIS PERSPIRATION? ♡
WELL...

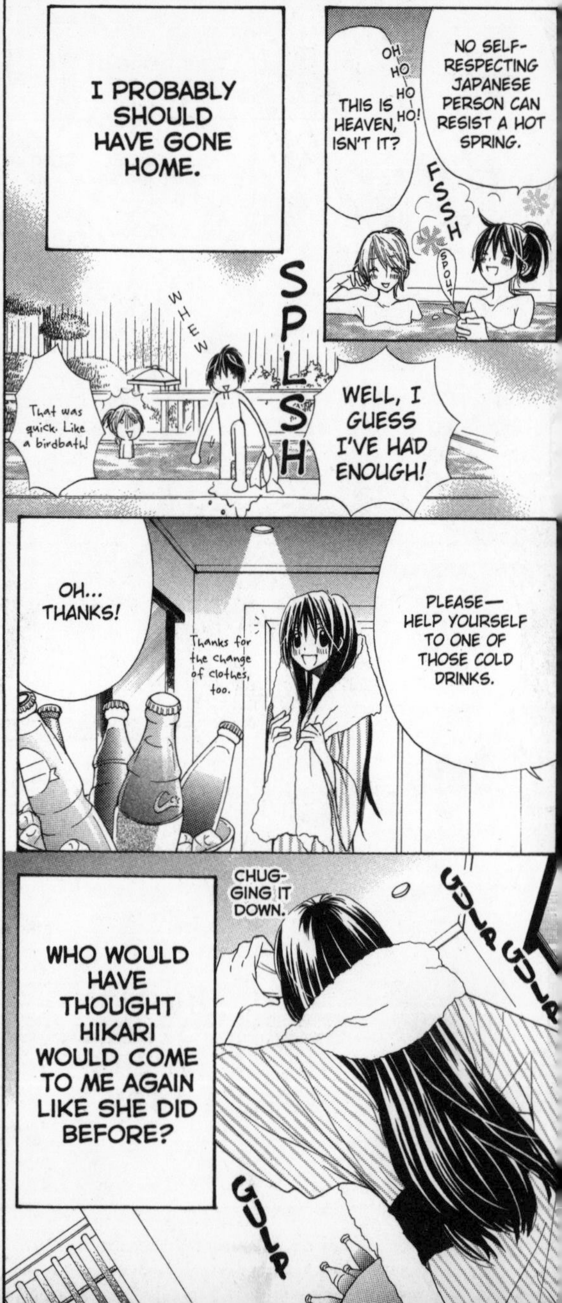
NO SELF-RESPECTING JAPANESE PERSON CAN RESIST A HOT SPRING.
OH HO HO HO!
THIS IS HEAVEN, ISN'T IT?
FSSH
I PROBABLY SHOULD HAVE GONE HOME.
SPLSH
WELL, I GUESS I'VE HAD ENOUGH!
WHEW
That was quick. Like a birdbath!
PLEASE—HELP YOURSELF TO ONE OF THOSE COLD DRINKS.
Thanks for the change of clothes, too.
OH... THANKS!
GULP GULP
CHUG-GING IT DOWN.
GULP
WHO WOULD HAVE THOUGHT HIKARI WOULD COME TO ME AGAIN LIKE SHE DID BEFORE?

2

•ART MUSEUM•

THE OTHER DAY AN ASSISTANT ASKED ME, "WHEN'S THE LAST TIME YOU WENT TO AN ART MUSEUM?" WELL, LET ME TELL YOU. ON RAINY MORNINGS, I LOVE TO LISTEN TO MY FAVORITE SONGS THROUGH EARPHONES AS I WALK LEISURELY THROUGH THE ART MUSEUM LOOKING AT PAINTINGS AND SCULPTURES.IT MAKES ME FEEL LIKE I'M IN A DIFFERENTWORLD... LIKE AN EXTRAORDINARY TRIP TO A DIFFERENT DIMENSION. I LOVE IT....AS I DREAMILY RELATED MY INTEREST, I REALIZED THAT THE LAST

...WAS THE MILLAIS EXHIBIT THREE YEARS AGO.

SORRY FOR GOING OFF ON A TANGENT! I'VE JUST ALWAYS WANTED TO TALK ABOUT IT.

DO YOU LIKE ART MUSEUMS?

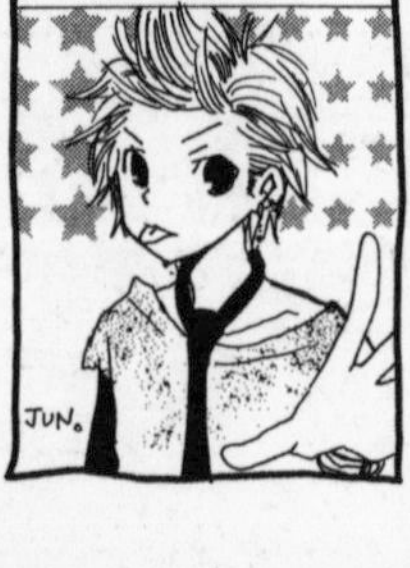
JUN.

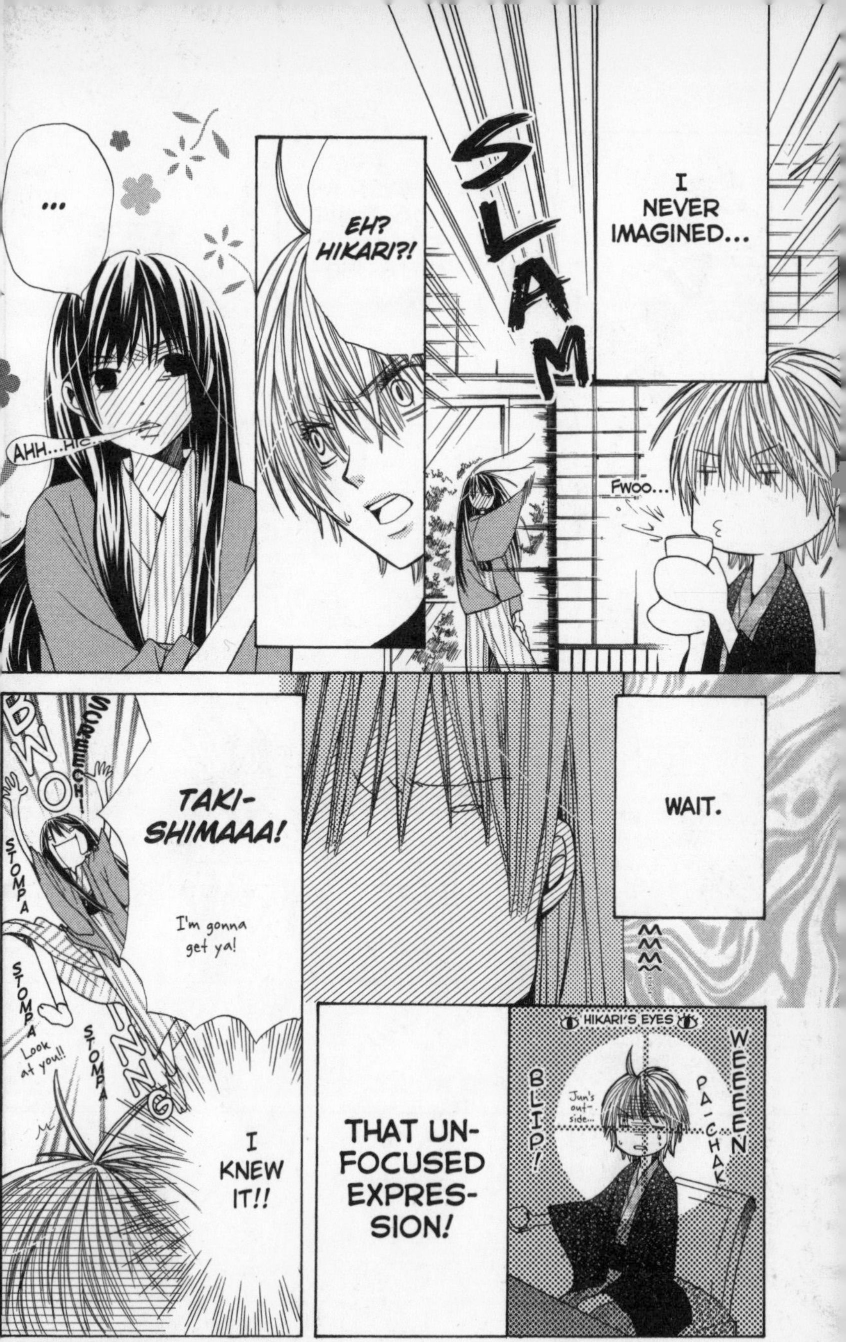
I NEVER IMAGINED...
Fwoo...
SLAM
EH? HIKARI?!
...
AHH...HIC
WAIT.
MMM
HIKARI'S EYES
WEEEEN
PA-CHAK
Jun's out-side...
BLIP!
THAT UN-FOCUSED EXPRES-SION!
TAKI-SHIMAAA!
SCREEECH!
BWOO
I'm gonna get ya!
STOMPA
STOMPA
Look at you!!
STOMPA
ZINNG
I KNEW IT!!

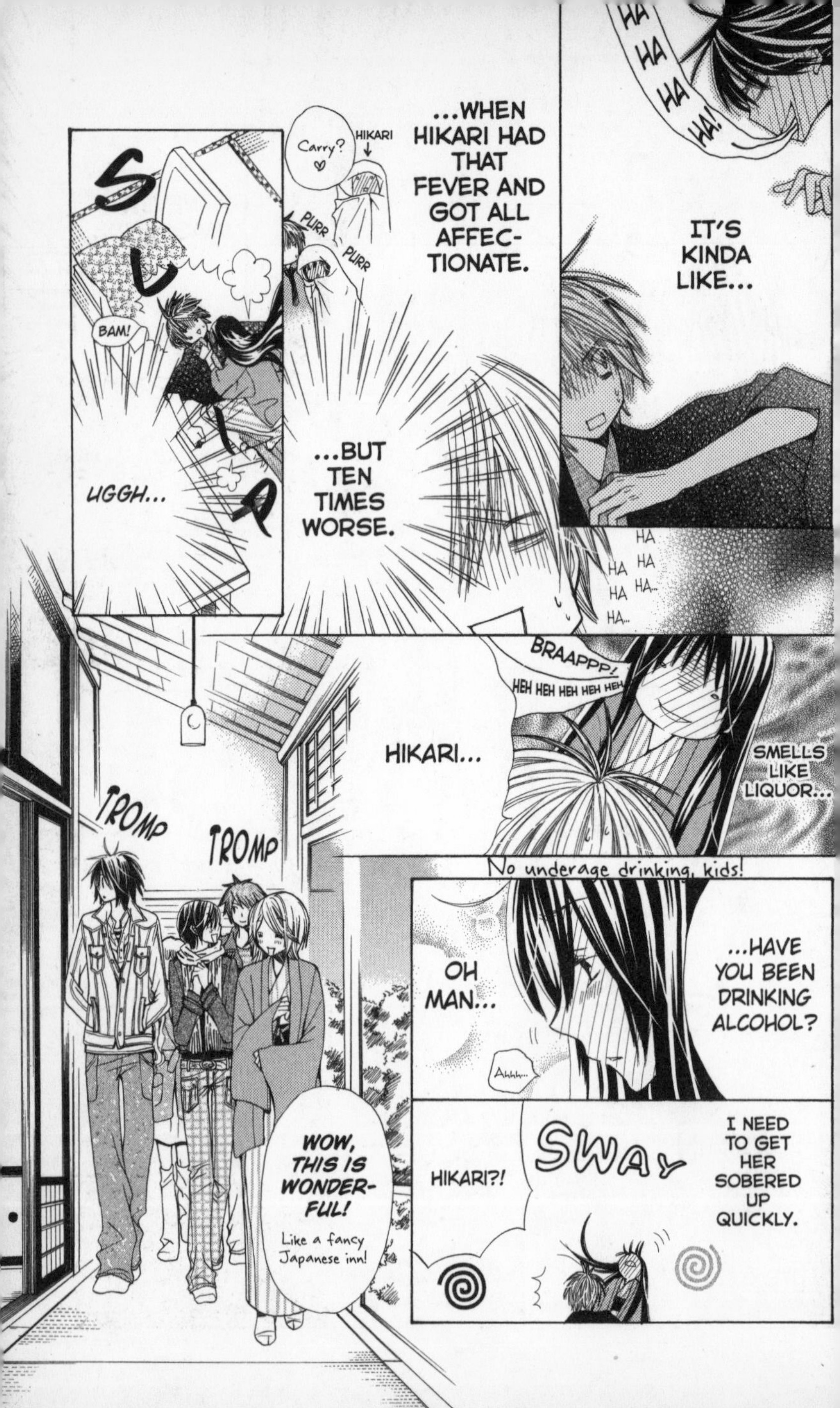
HA HA HA HA!
IT'S KINDA LIKE...
...WHEN HIKARI HAD THAT FEVER AND GOT ALL AFFECTIONATE.
Carry?
HIKARI
PURR PURR
BAM!
UGGH...
...BUT TEN TIMES WORSE.
HA HA HA HA...
HA HA HA...
BRAAPPP!
HEH HEH HEH HEH HEH
HIKARI...
SMELLS LIKE LIQUOR...
No underage drinking, kids!
...HAVE YOU BEEN DRINKING ALCOHOL?
OH MAN...
Ahhh...
I NEED TO GET HER SOBERED UP QUICKLY.
SWAY
HIKARI?!
TROMP
TROMP
WOW, THIS IS WONDERFUL!
Like a fancy Japanese inn!

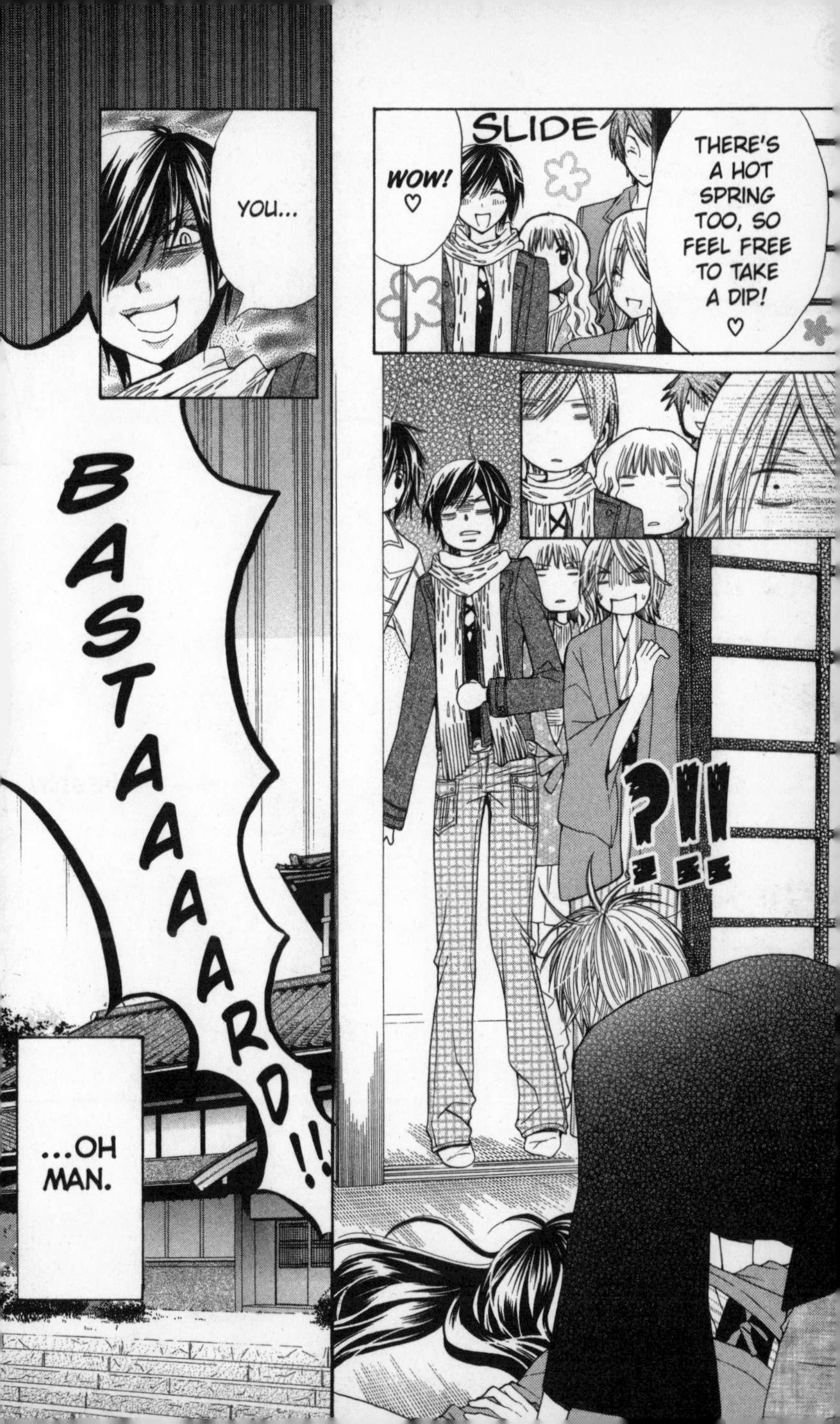
THERE'S A HOT SPRING TOO, SO FEEL FREE TO TAKE A DIP! ♡
SLIDE
WOW! ♡
?!!
YOU...
BASTAAAARD!!
...OH MAN.

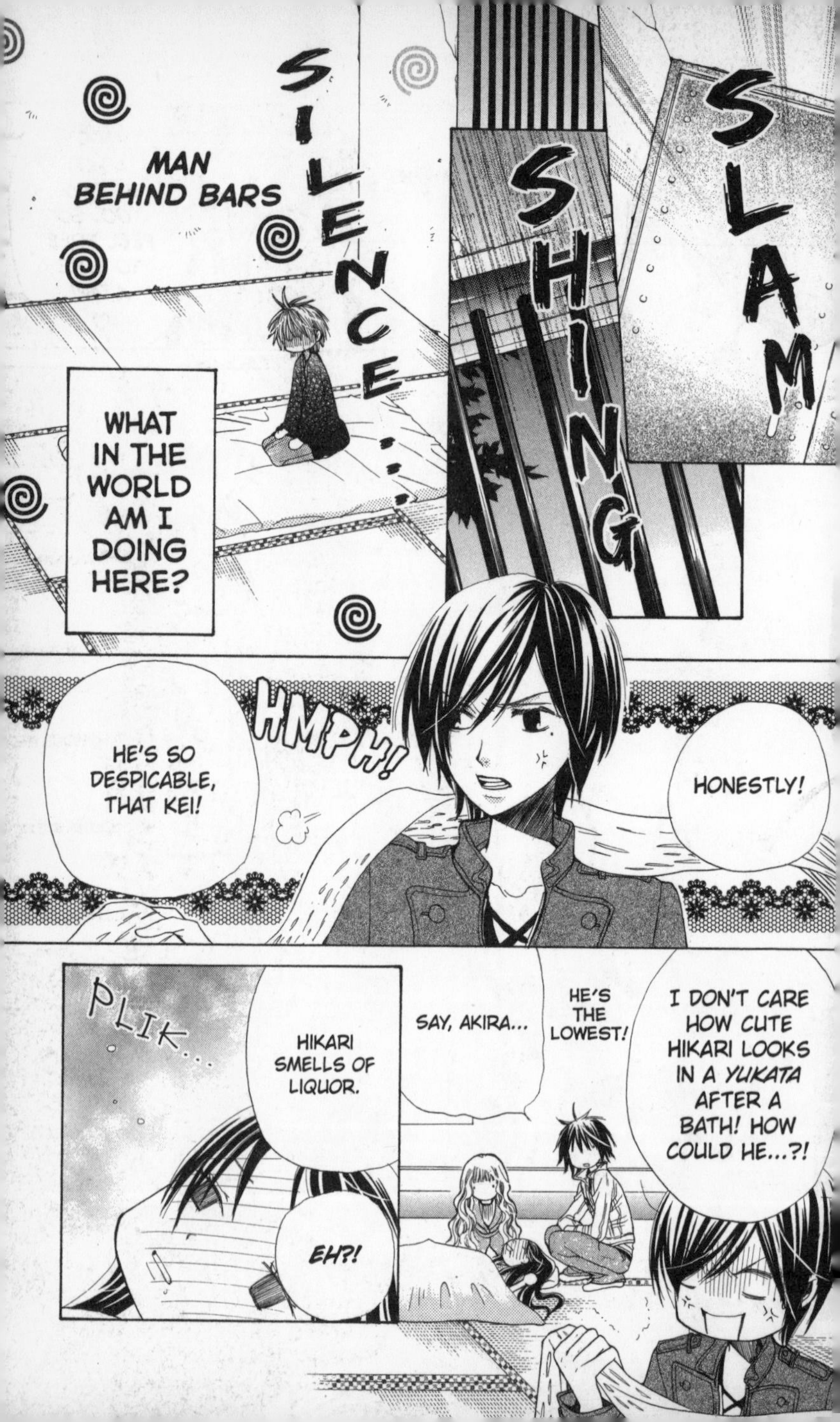
SLAM
SHING
SILENCE...
MAN BEHIND BARS
WHAT IN THE WORLD AM I DOING HERE?
HONESTLY!
HMPH!
HE'S SO DESPICABLE, THAT KEI!
I DON'T CARE HOW CUTE HIKARI LOOKS IN A *YUKATA* AFTER A BATH! HOW COULD HE...?!
HE'S THE LOWEST!
SAY, AKIRA...
HIKARI SMELLS OF LIQUOR.
EH?!
PLIK...

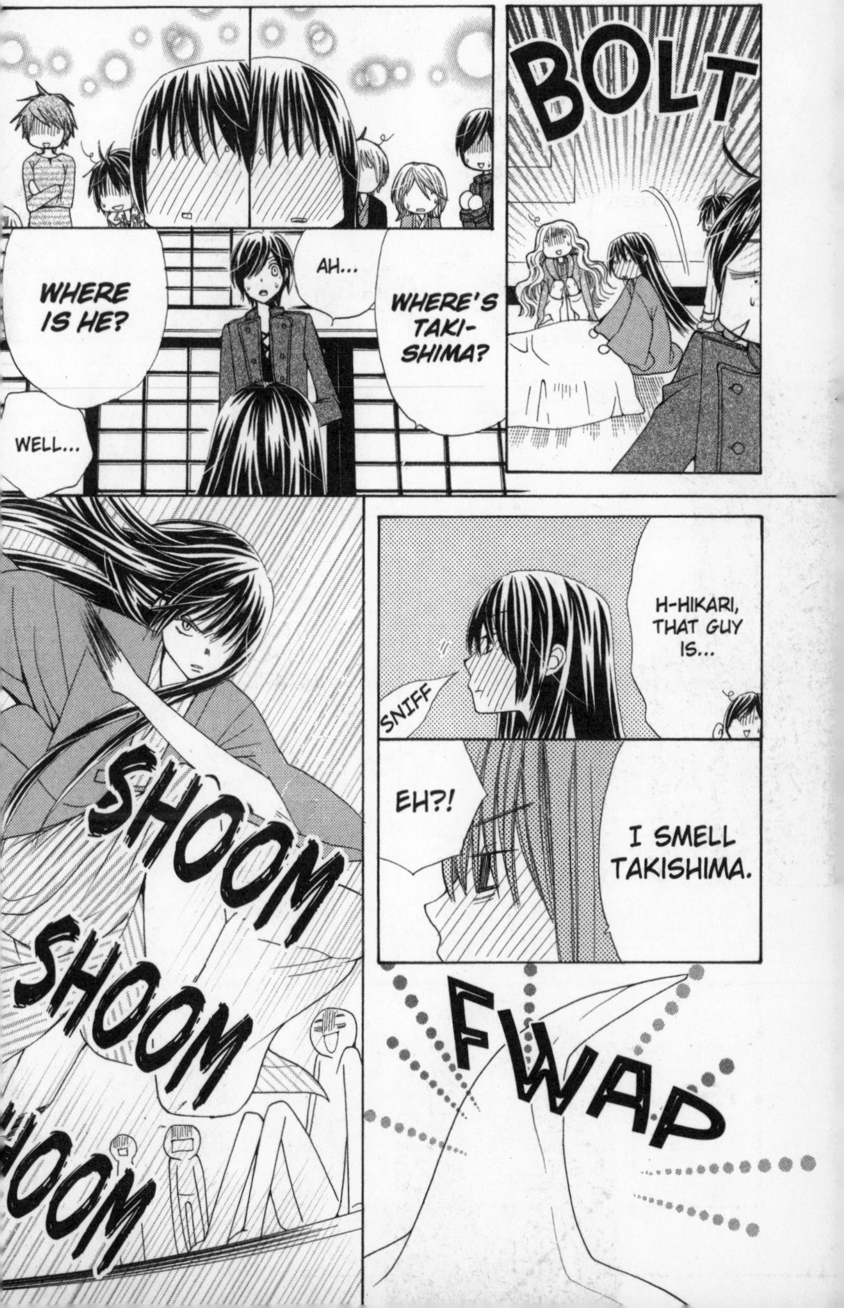
BOLT
WHERE'S TAKI-SHIMA?
AH...
WHERE IS HE?
WELL...
H-HIKARI, THAT GUY IS...
SNIFF
I SMELL TAKISHIMA.
EH?!
FWAP
SHOOM
SHOOM

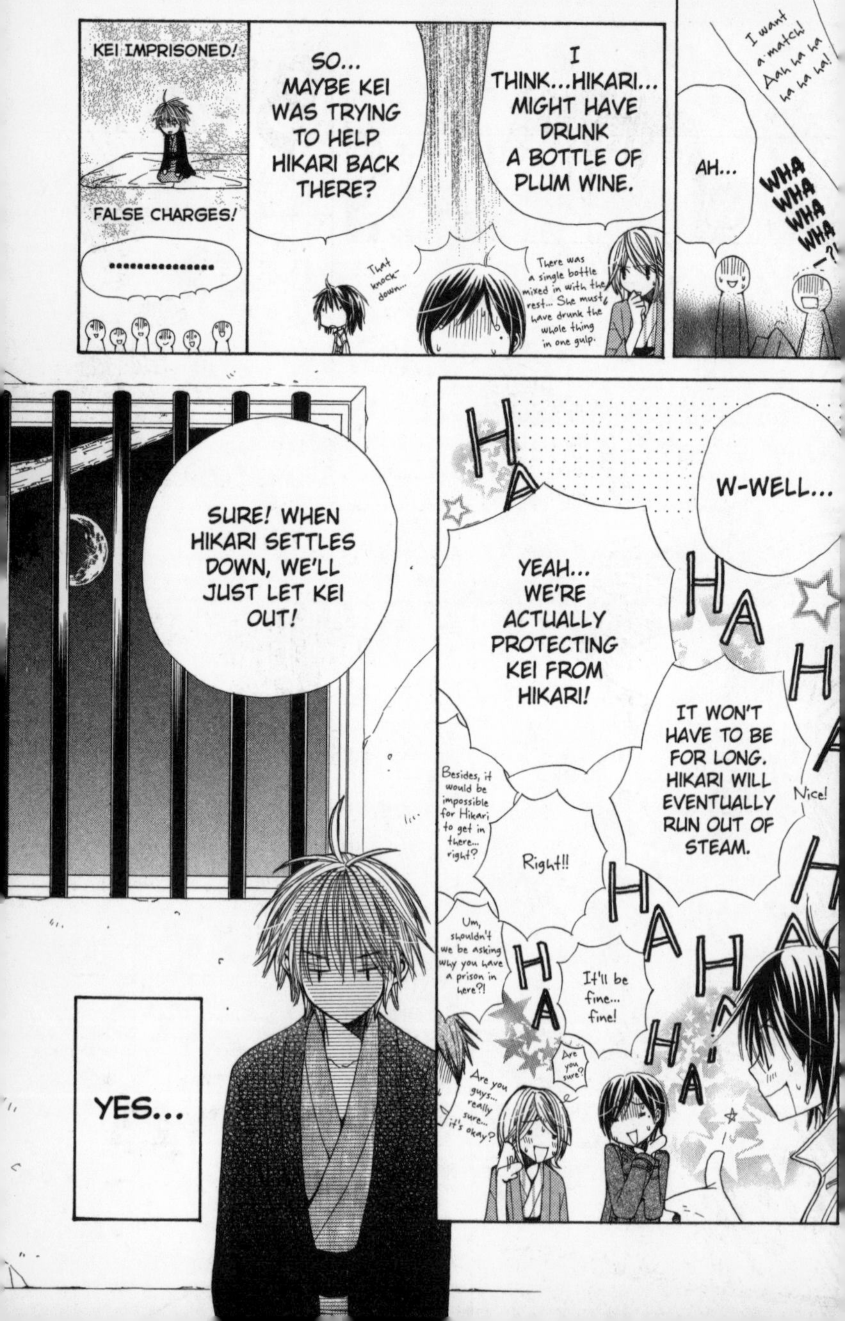
I want a match! Aah ha ha ha ha ha!
AH...
WHA WHA WHA WHA—?!
I THINK...HIKARI... MIGHT HAVE DRUNK A BOTTLE OF PLUM WINE.
There was a single bottle mixed in with the rest... She must have drunk the whole thing in one gulp.
SO... MAYBE KEI WAS TRYING TO HELP HIKARI BACK THERE?
That knock-down...
KEI IMPRISONED!
FALSE CHARGES!
....
W-WELL...
HA HA HA
YEAH... WE'RE ACTUALLY PROTECTING KEI FROM HIKARI!
IT WON'T HAVE TO BE FOR LONG. HIKARI WILL EVENTUALLY RUN OUT OF STEAM.
Nice!
Besides, it would be impossible for Hikari to get in there... right?
Right!!
HA HA HA HA HA HA
Um, shouldn't we be asking why you have a prison in here?!
It'll be fine... fine!
Are you sure?
Are you guys... really sure... it's okay?
SURE! WHEN HIKARI SETTLES DOWN, WE'LL JUST LET KEI OUT!
YES...

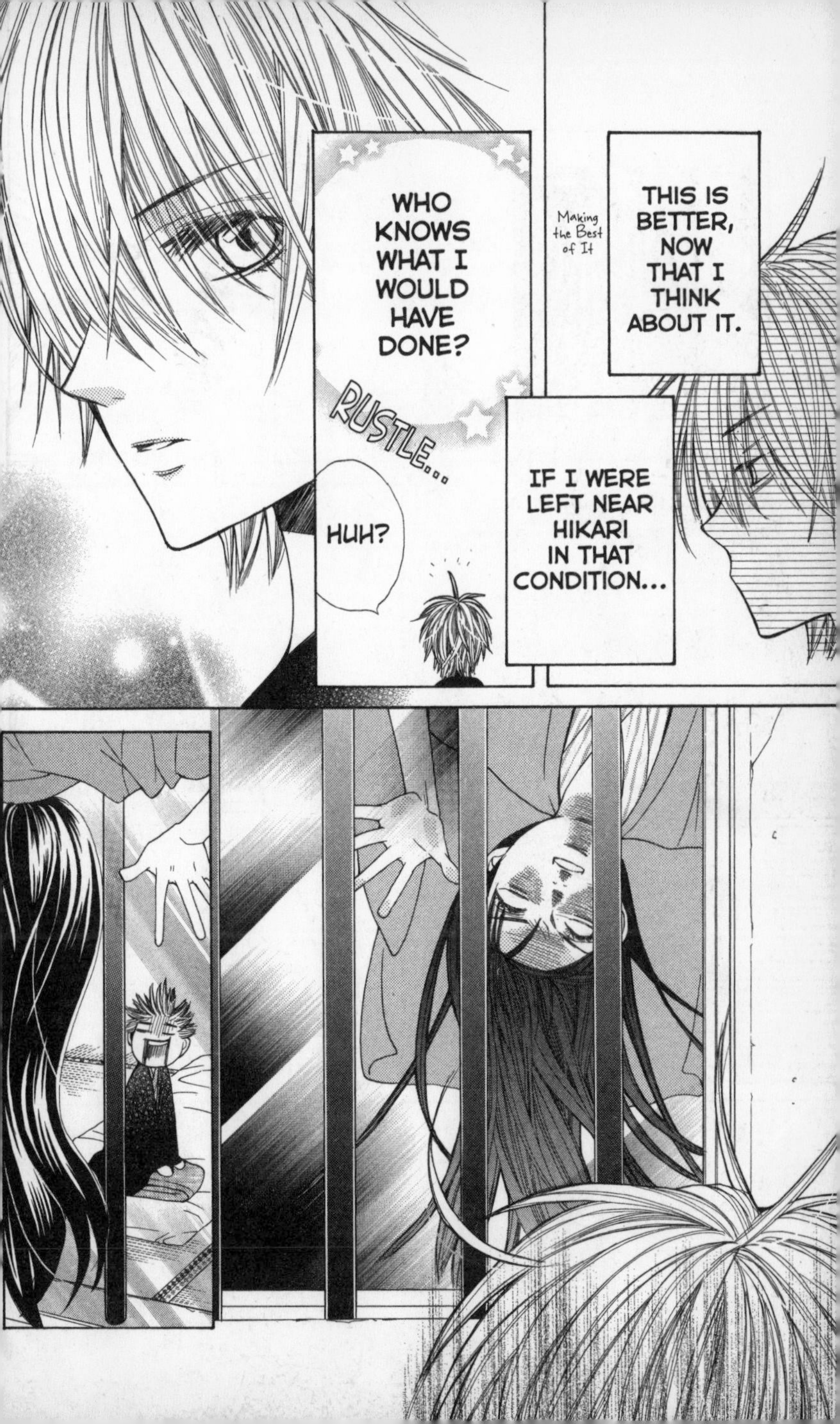
Making the Best of It
THIS IS BETTER, NOW THAT I THINK ABOUT IT.
IF I WERE LEFT NEAR HIKARI IN THAT CONDITION...
WHO KNOWS WHAT I WOULD HAVE DONE?
RUSTLE...
HUH?

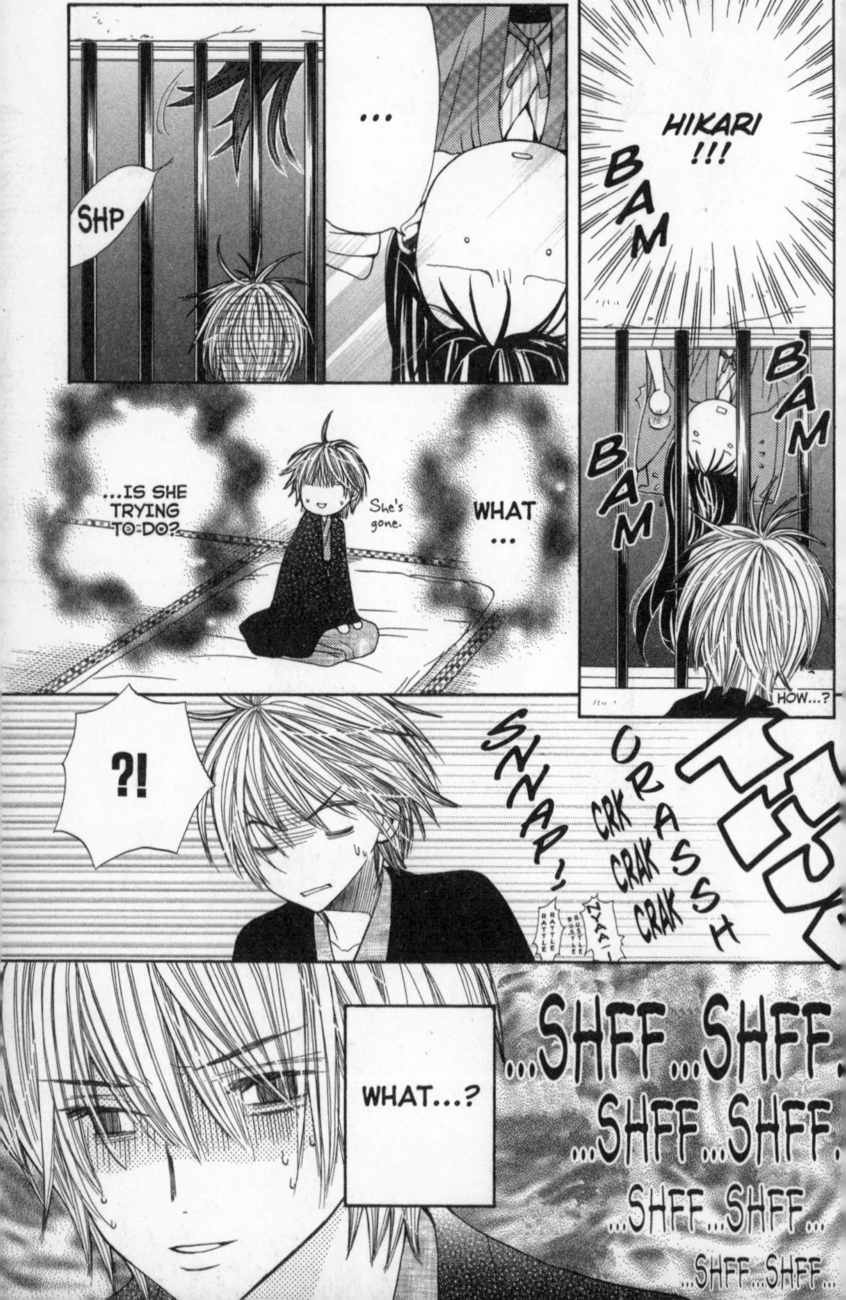
HIKARI !!!
BAM BAM
BAM BAM
BAM BAM
HOW...?
...
SHP
WHAT ...
She's gone.
...IS SHE TRYING TO DO?
CRASSH
CRK CRAK CRAK CRAK
SNNAP!
NYAA!
RUSTLE
RATTLE
?!
...SHFF...SHFF...
...SHFF...SHFF...
...SHFF...SHFF...
...SHFF...SHFF...
WHAT...?

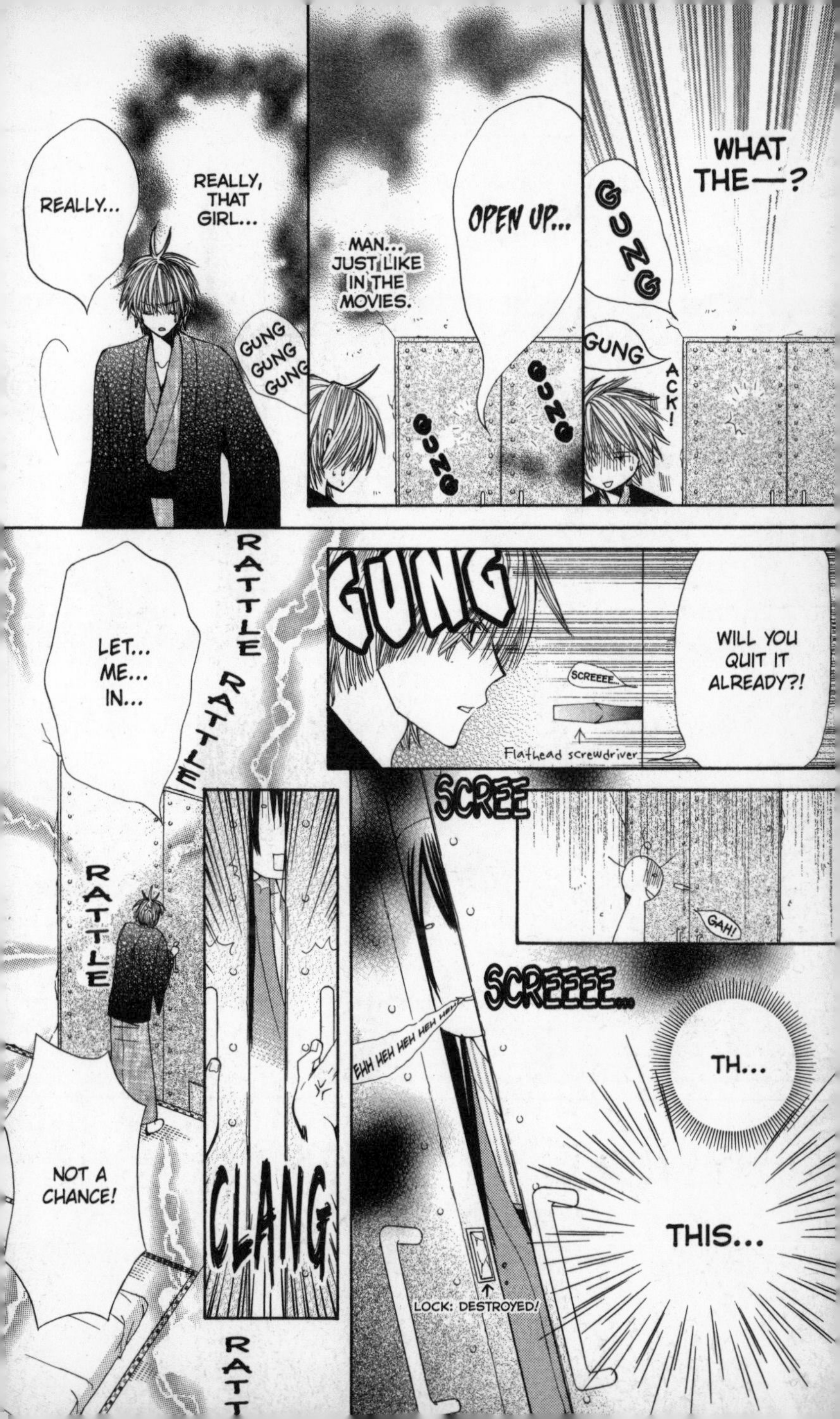
WHAT THE—?
GUNG
GUNG
ACK!
OPEN UP...
MAN... JUST LIKE IN THE MOVIES.
GUNG
GUNG
REALLY, THAT GIRL...
REALLY...
GUNG GUNG GUNG
WILL YOU QUIT IT ALREADY?!
GUNG
SCREEEE...
Flathead screwdriver
SCREE
GAH!
SCREEEEE...
TH...
THIS...
EHH HEH HEH HEH HEH
LOCK: DESTROYED!
LET... ME... IN...
RATTLE
RATTLE
RATTLE
CLANG
NOT A CHANCE!
RATT

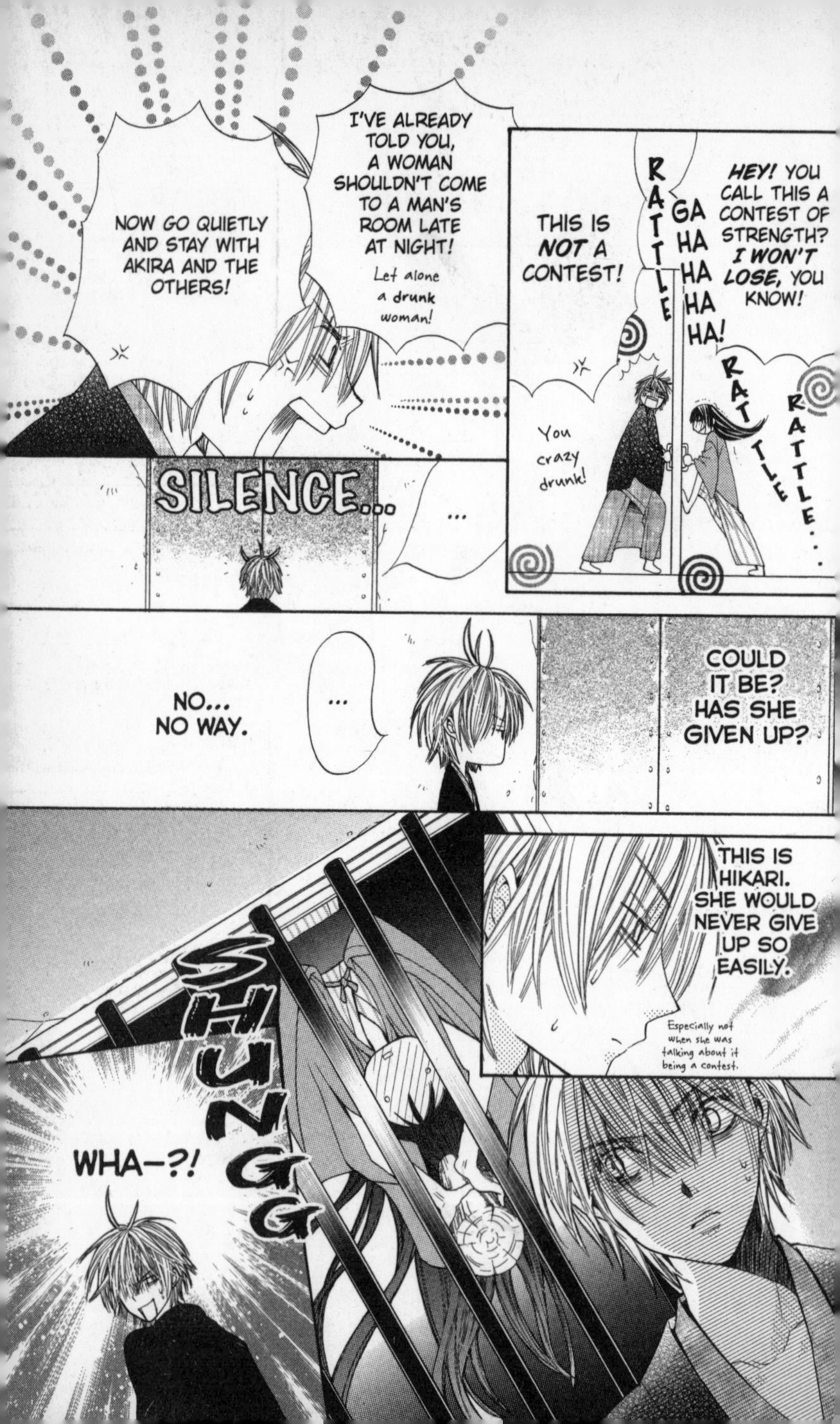
HEY! YOU CALL THIS A CONTEST OF STRENGTH? I WON'T LOSE, YOU KNOW!
GA HA HA HA HA!
RATTLE
THIS IS NOT A CONTEST!
You crazy drunk!
RATTLE
RATTLE...
I'VE ALREADY TOLD YOU, A WOMAN SHOULDN'T COME TO A MAN'S ROOM LATE AT NIGHT!
Let alone a drunk woman!
NOW GO QUIETLY AND STAY WITH AKIRA AND THE OTHERS!
...
SILENCE...
COULD IT BE? HAS SHE GIVEN UP?
...
NO... NO WAY.
THIS IS HIKARI. SHE WOULD NEVER GIVE UP SO EASILY.
Especially not when she was talking about it being a contest.
SHUNGG
WHA-?!

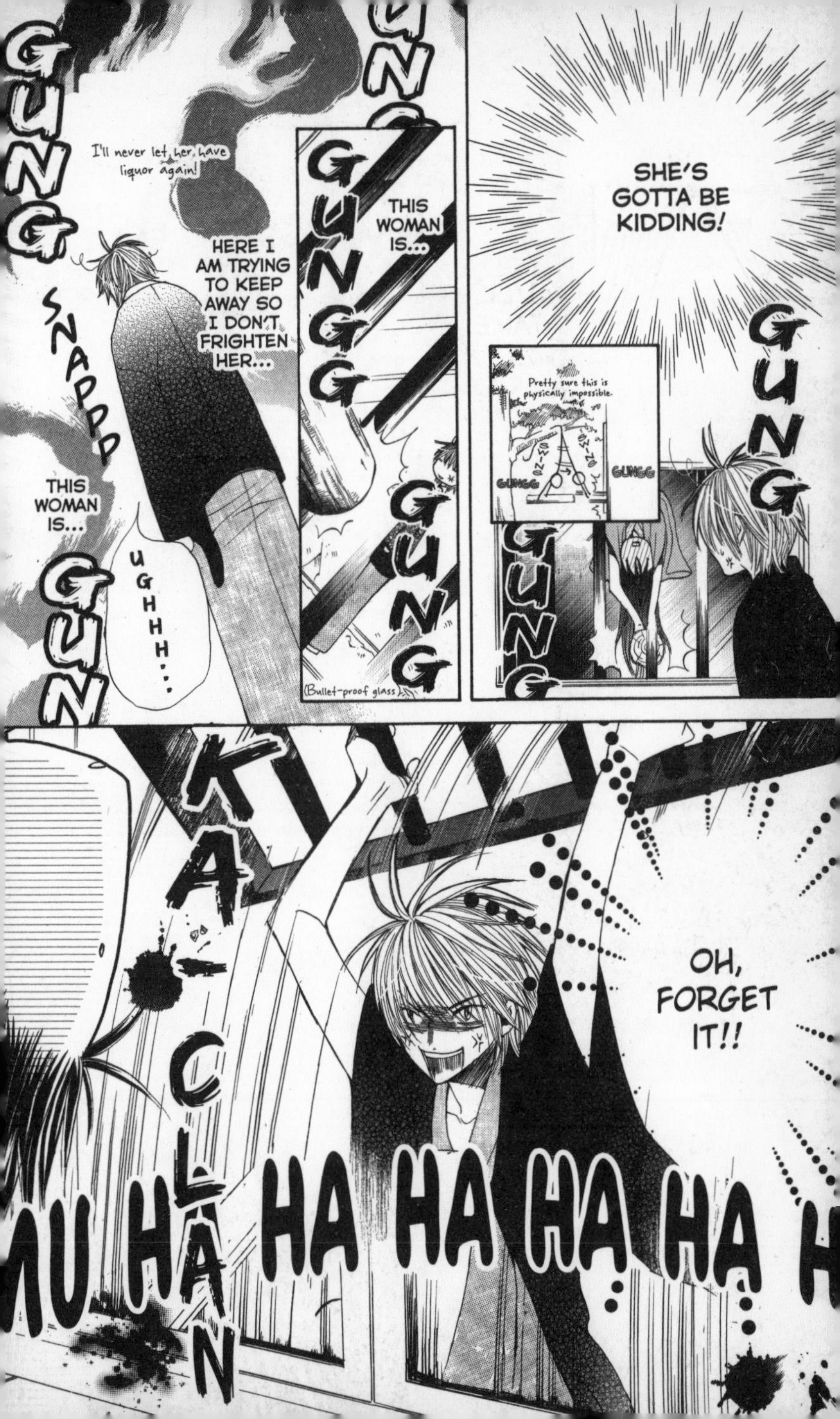
GUNG
SHE'S GOTTA BE KIDDING!
Pretty sure this is physically impossible.
SWING
SWING
GUNGG
GUNGG
GUNG
GUNG
GUNG
THIS WOMAN IS...
GUNG
(Bullet-proof glass
GUNG
I'll never let her have liquor again!
HERE I AM TRYING TO KEEP AWAY SO I DON'T FRIGHTEN HER...
SNAPPP
THIS WOMAN IS...
GUN
UGHHH...
KA
CLLAN
OH, FORGET IT!!
HA HA HA HA HA HA

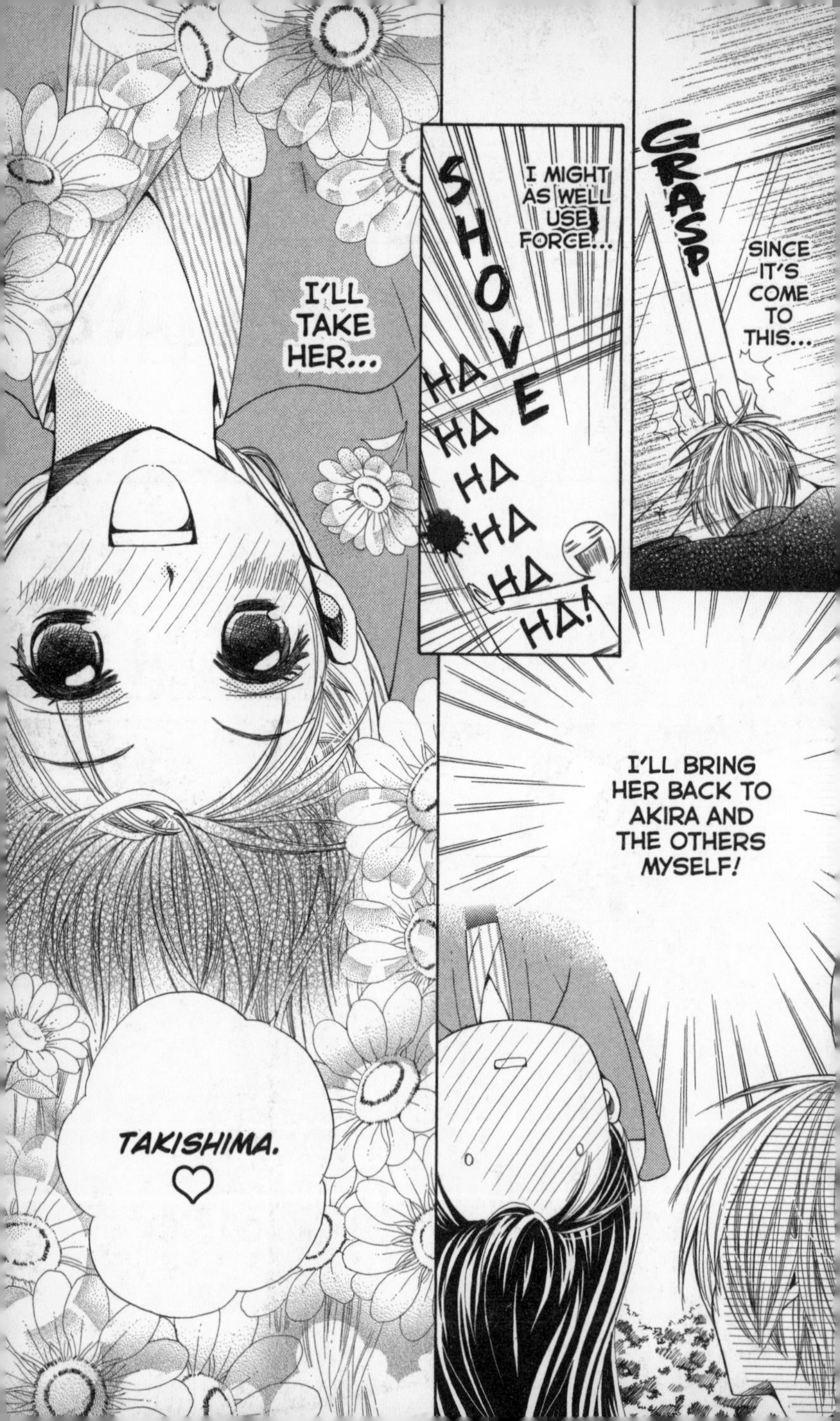

SINCE IT'S COME TO THIS...
GRASP
I MIGHT AS WELL USE FORCE...
SHOVE
HA HA HA HA HA HA!
I'LL BRING HER BACK TO AKIRA AND THE OTHERS MYSELF!
I'LL TAKE HER...
TAKISHIMA. ♡

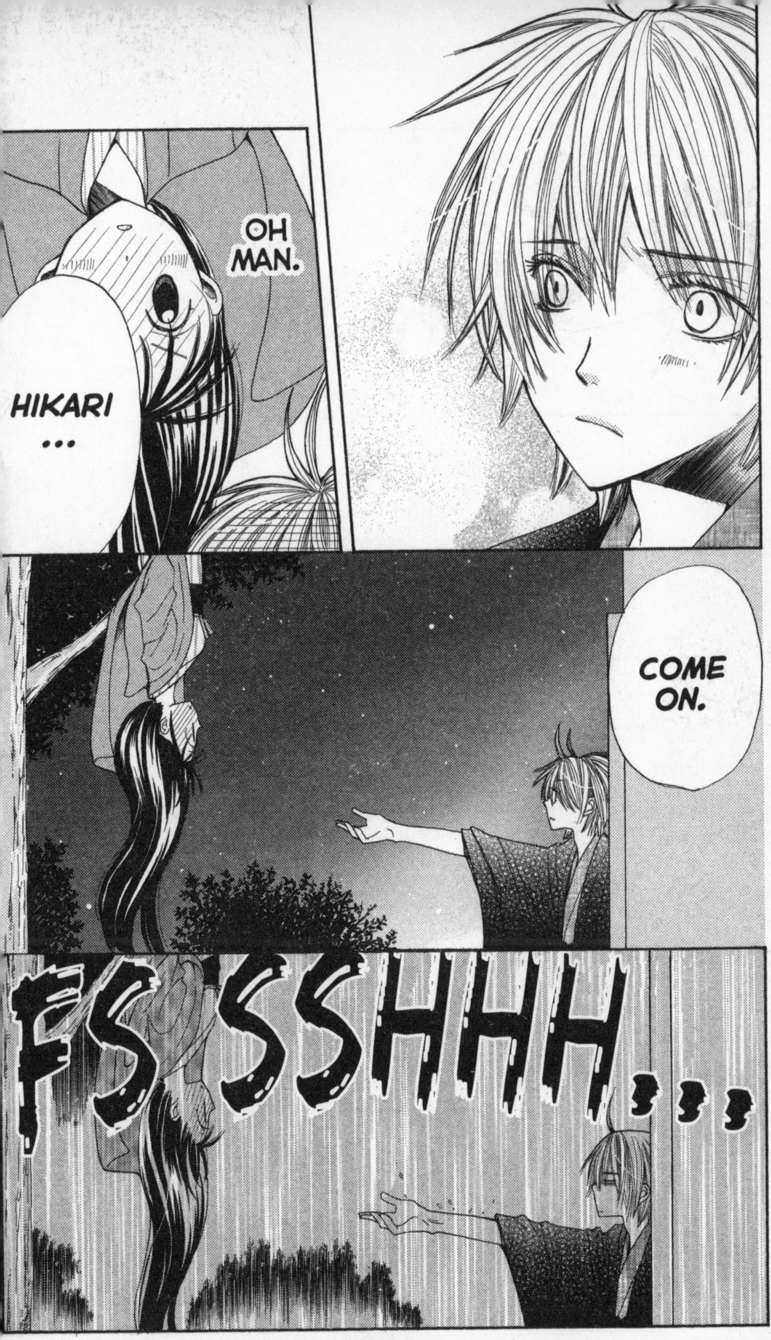
OH MAN.
HIKARI ...
COME ON.
FSSSHHH...

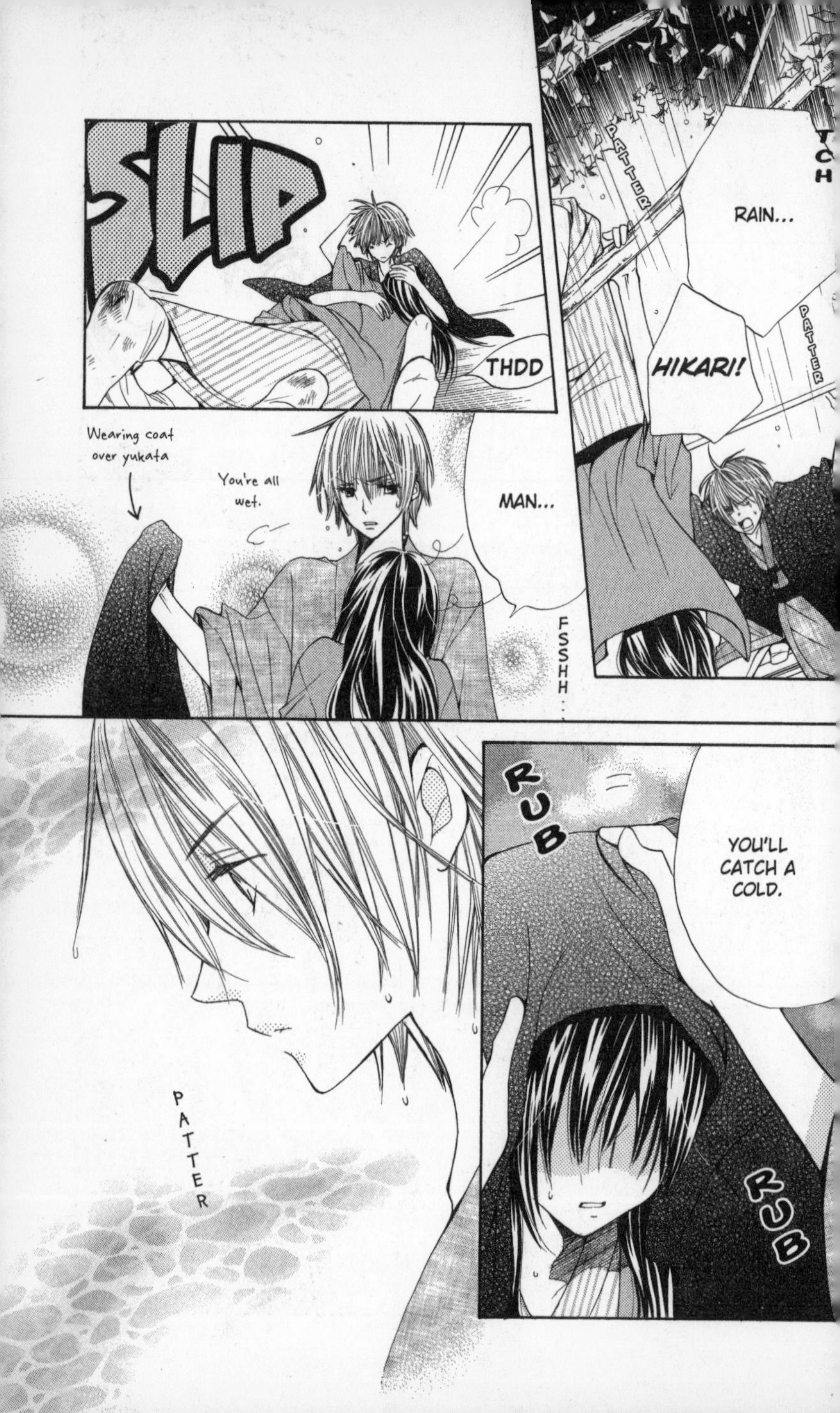
TCH
PATTER
RAIN...
PATTER
HIKARI!
SLIP
THDD
Wearing coat over yukata
You're all wet.
MAN...
FSSHH...
RUB
YOU'LL CATCH A COLD.
RUB
PATTER

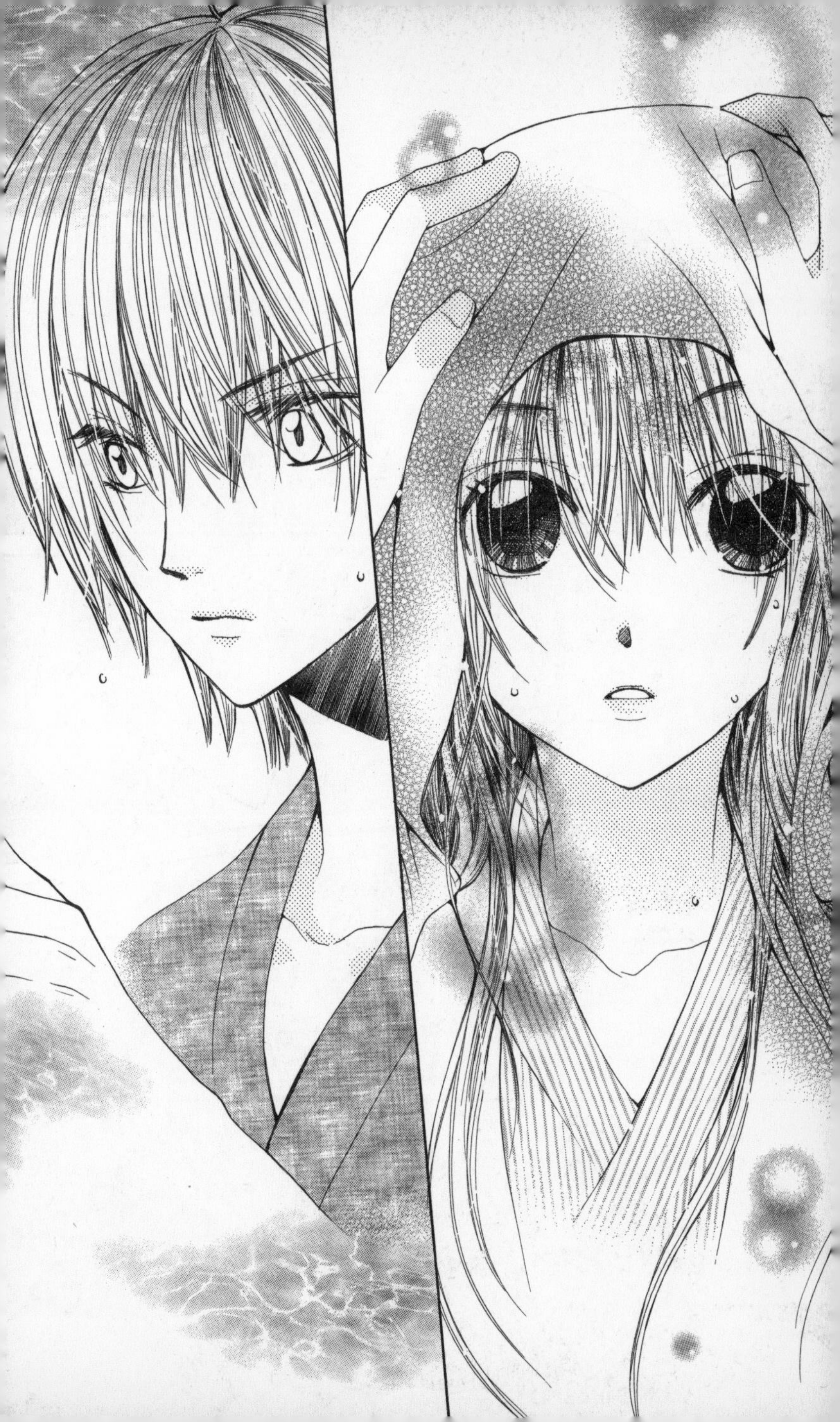

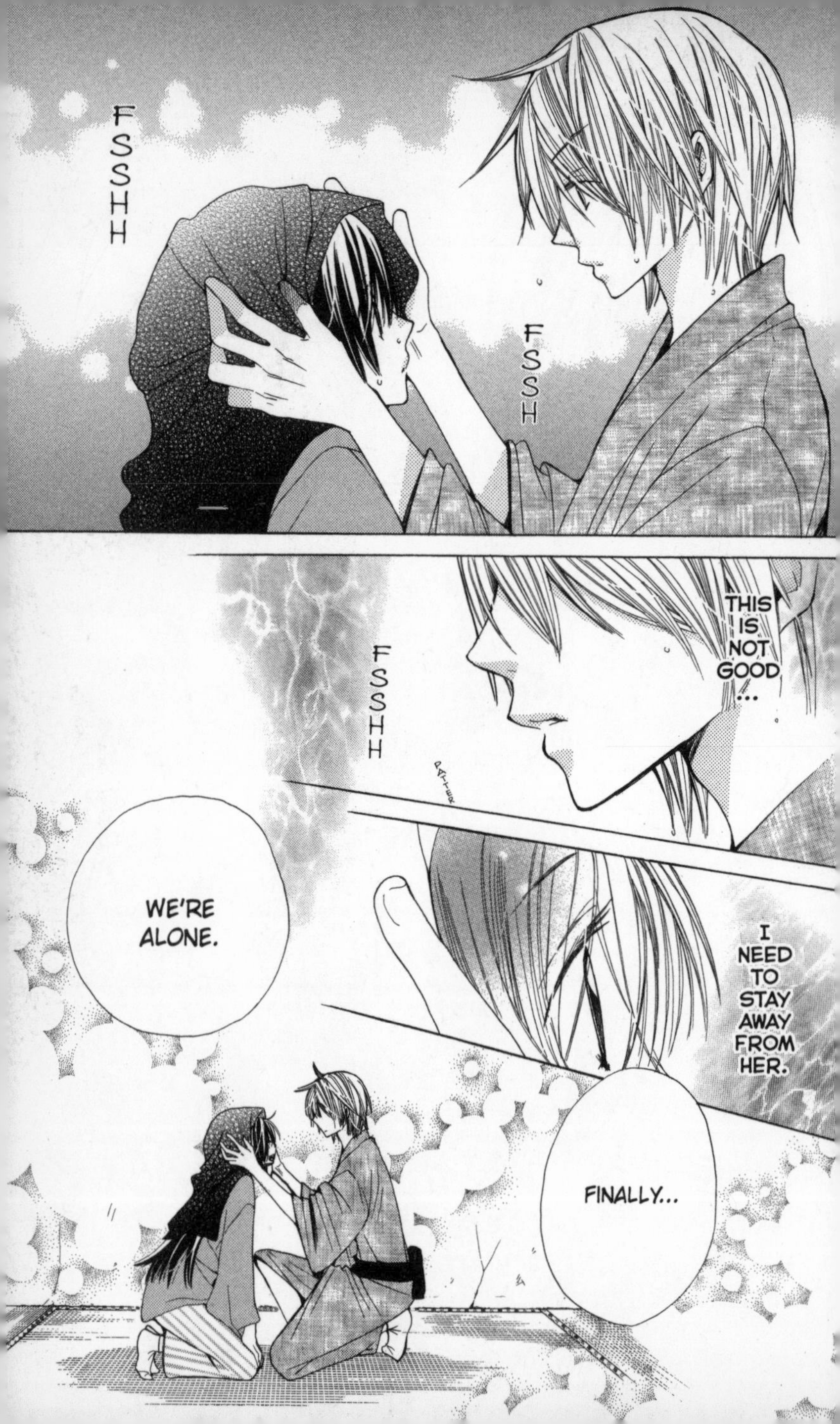
FSSH
FSSHH
THIS IS NOT GOOD...
FSSHH
PATTER
I NEED TO STAY AWAY FROM HER.
FINALLY...
WE'RE ALONE.

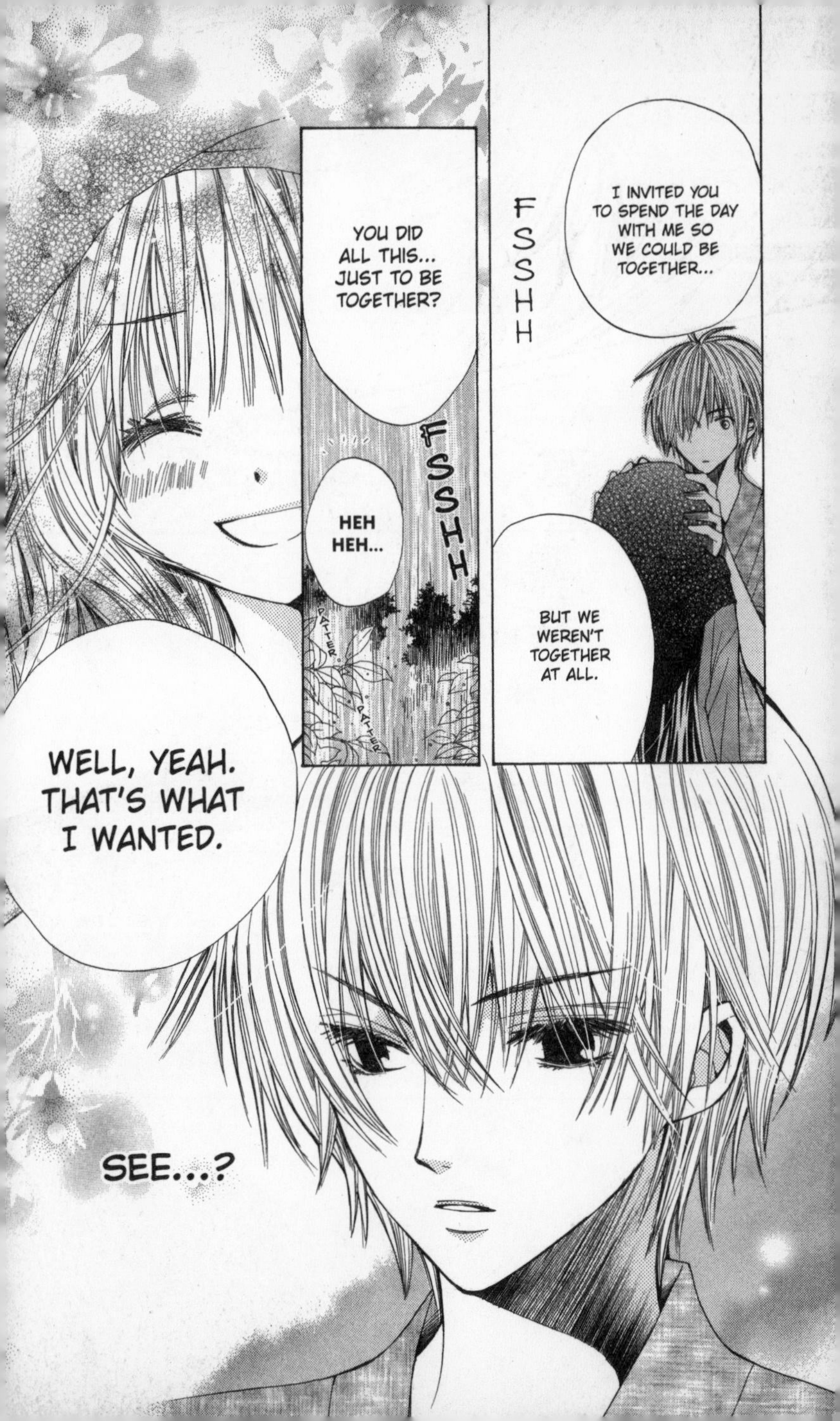

I INVITED YOU TO SPEND THE DAY WITH ME SO WE COULD BE TOGETHER...
FSSHH
BUT WE WEREN'T TOGETHER AT ALL.
YOU DID ALL THIS... JUST TO BE TOGETHER?
FSSHH
HEH HEH...
PATTER
PATTER
WELL, YEAH. THAT'S WHAT I WANTED.
SEE...?

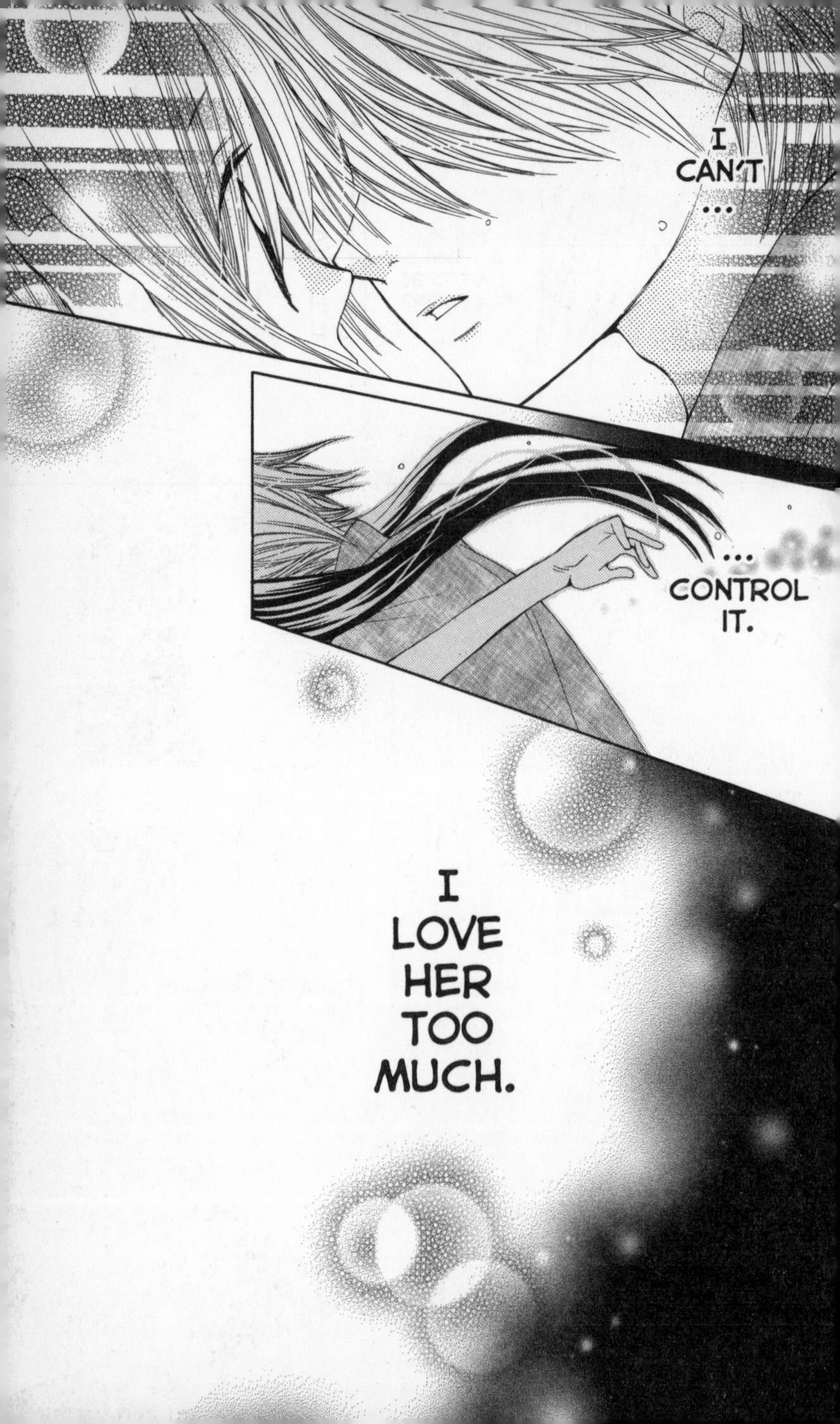
I CAN'T ...
... CONTROL IT.
I LOVE HER TOO MUCH.

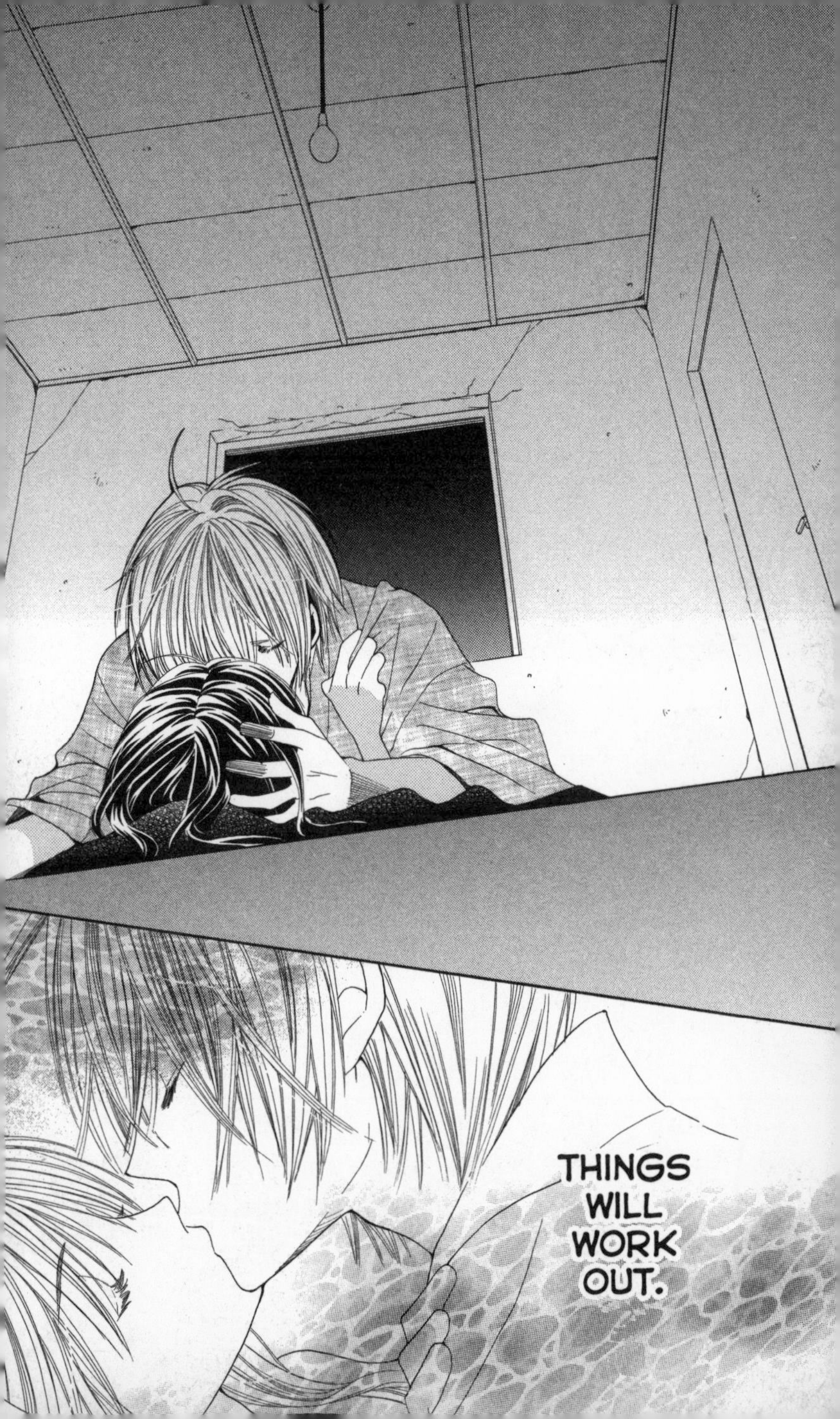
THINGS WILL WORK OUT.

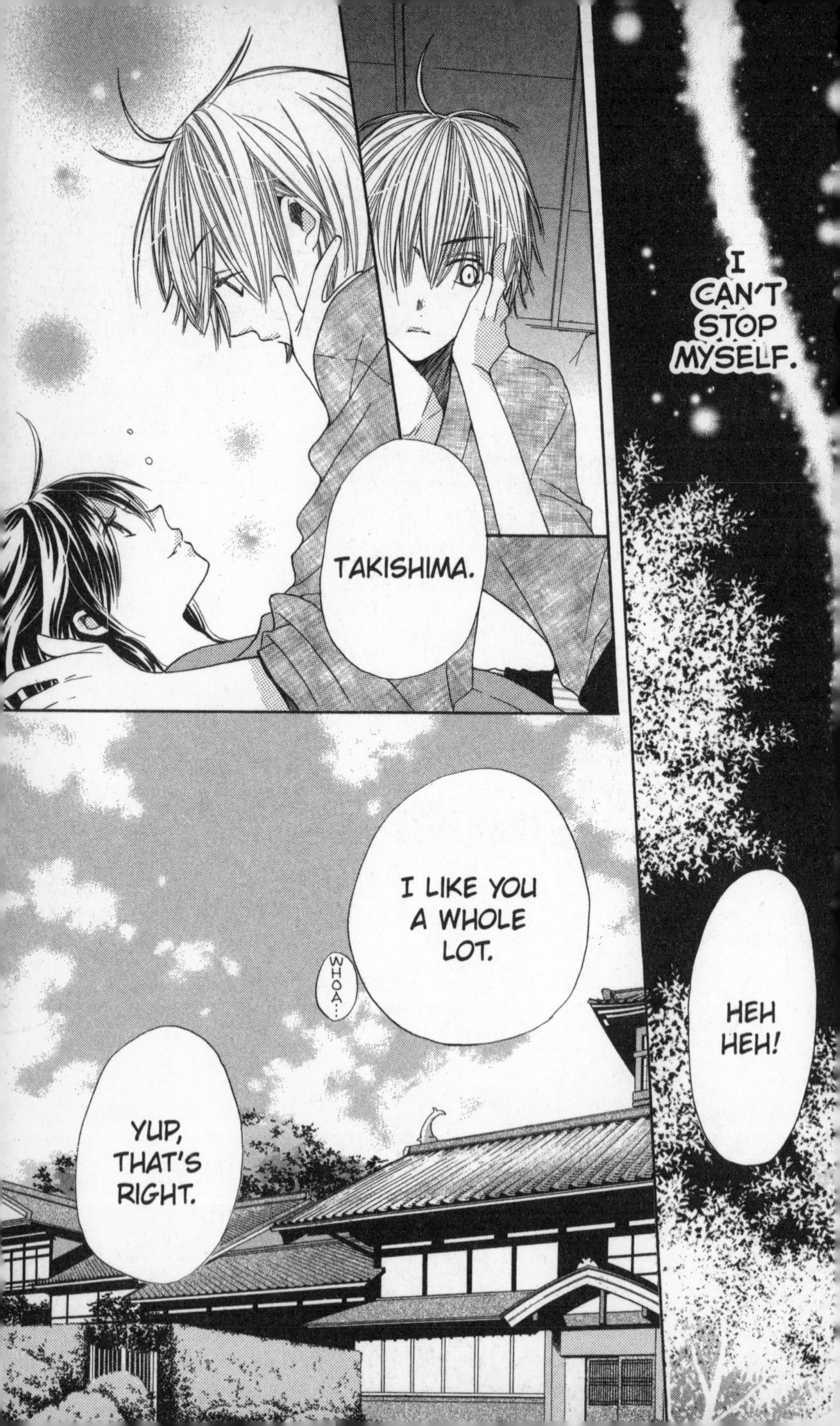
I CAN'T STOP MYSELF.
HEH HEH!
TAKISHIMA.
I LIKE YOU A WHOLE LOT.
WHOA...
YUP, THAT'S RIGHT.

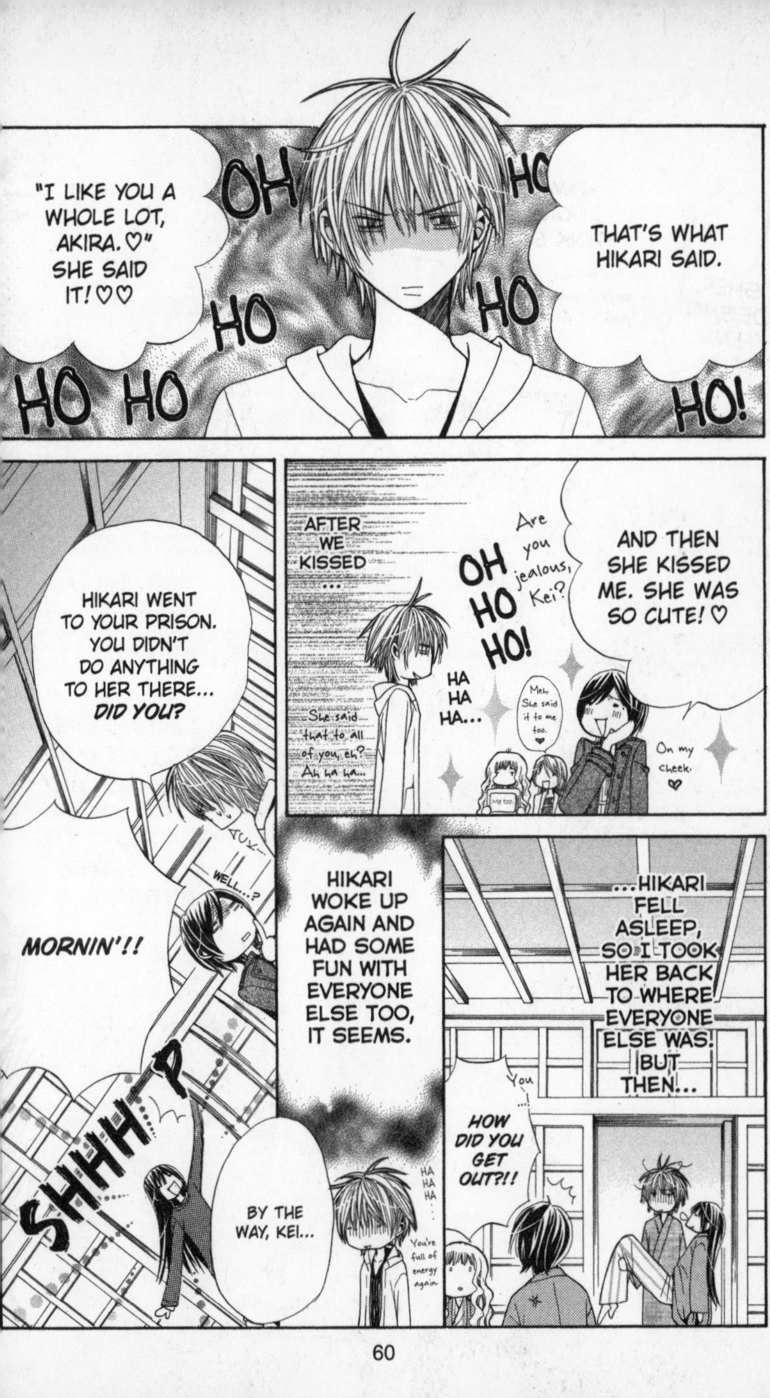
THAT'S WHAT HIKARI SAID.
"I LIKE YOU A WHOLE LOT, AKIRA. ♡" SHE SAID IT! ♡♡
OH HO HO HO HO HO HO!
AND THEN SHE KISSED ME. SHE WAS SO CUTE! ♡
Are you jealous, Kei?
OH HO HO HO!
On my cheek. ♡
Meh. She said it to me too. ♡
Me too.
HA HA HA...
AFTER WE KISSED ...
She said that to all of you, eh? Ah ha ha...
...HIKARI FELL ASLEEP, SO I TOOK HER BACK TO WHERE EVERYONE ELSE WAS. BUT THEN...
You ...!
HOW DID YOU GET OUT?!!
HIKARI WOKE UP AGAIN AND HAD SOME FUN WITH EVERYONE ELSE TOO, IT SEEMS.
HA HA HA...
BY THE WAY, KEI...
You're full of energy again.
HIKARI WENT TO YOUR PRISON. YOU DIDN'T DO ANYTHING TO HER THERE... DID YOU?
WELL...?
MORNIN'!!
SHHHP

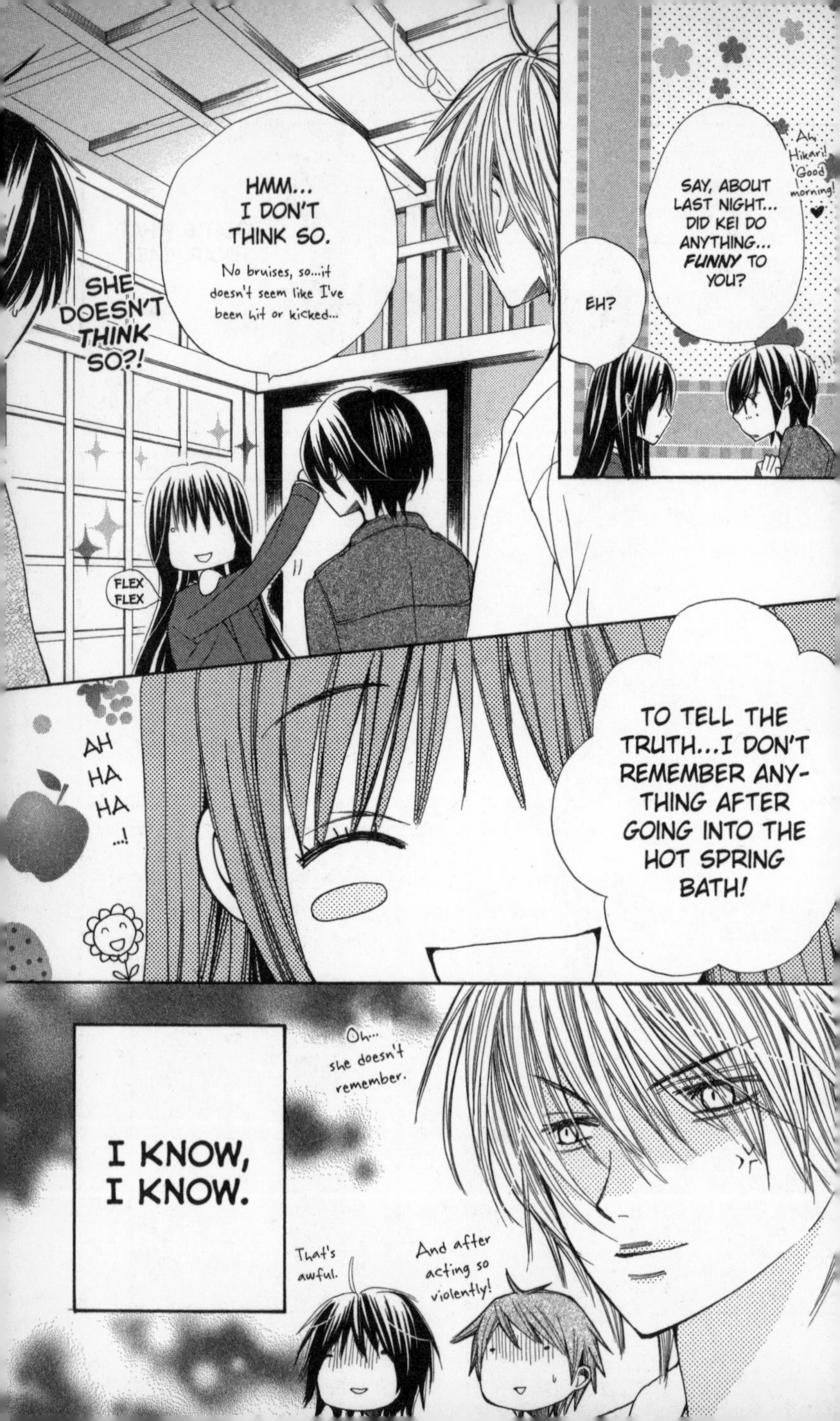
Ah Hikari! Good morning!
SAY, ABOUT LAST NIGHT... DID KEI DO ANYTHING... FUNNY TO YOU?
EH?
HMM... I DON'T THINK SO.
No bruises, so...it doesn't seem like I've been hit or kicked...
SHE DOESN'T THINK SO?!
FLEX FLEX
TO TELL THE TRUTH...I DON'T REMEMBER ANY-THING AFTER GOING INTO THE HOT SPRING BATH!
AH HA HA ...!
Oh... she doesn't remember.
I KNOW, I KNOW.
And after acting so violently!
That's awful.

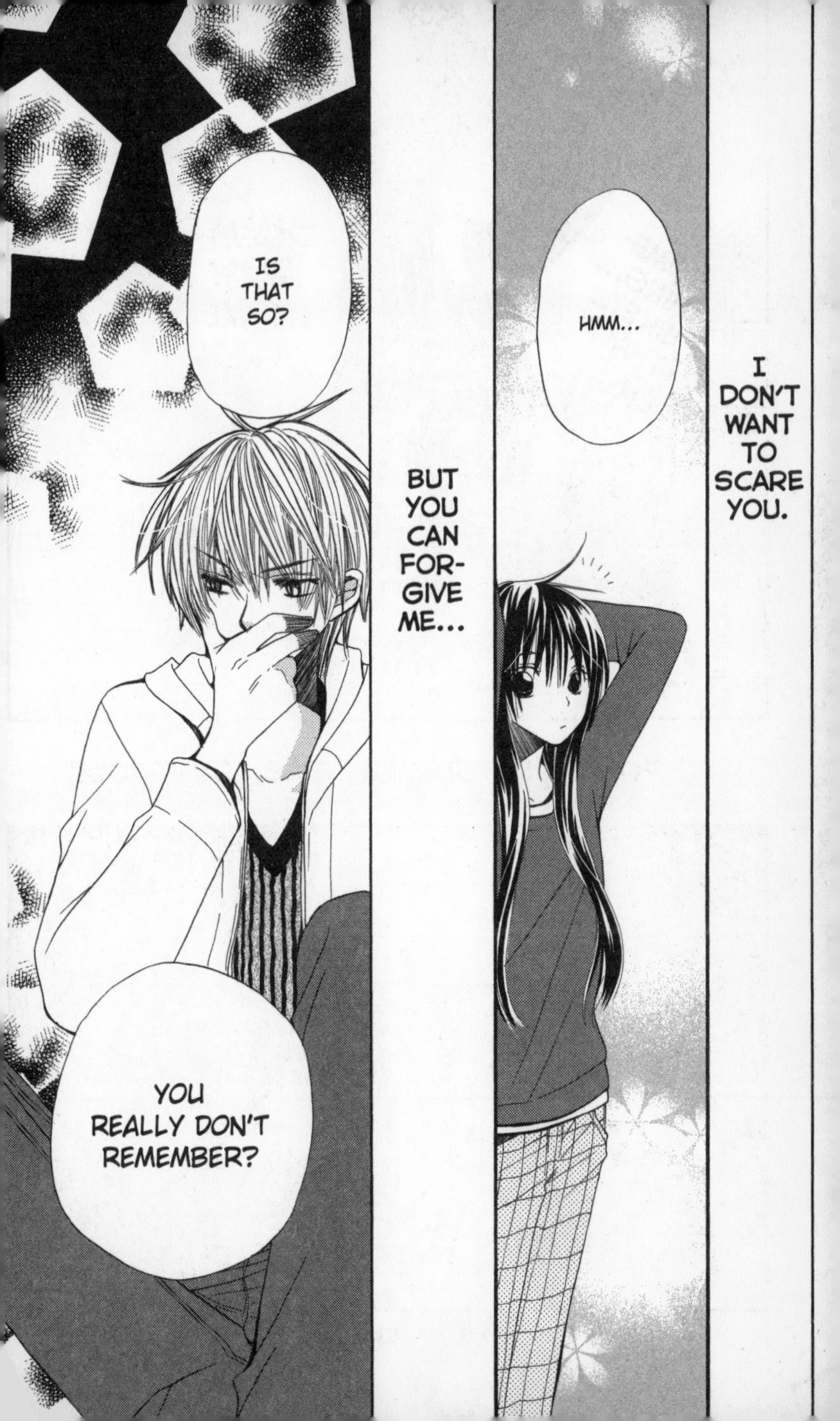
I DON'T WANT TO SCARE YOU.
HMM...
BUT YOU CAN FOR-GIVE ME...
IS THAT SO?
YOU REALLY DON'T REMEMBER?

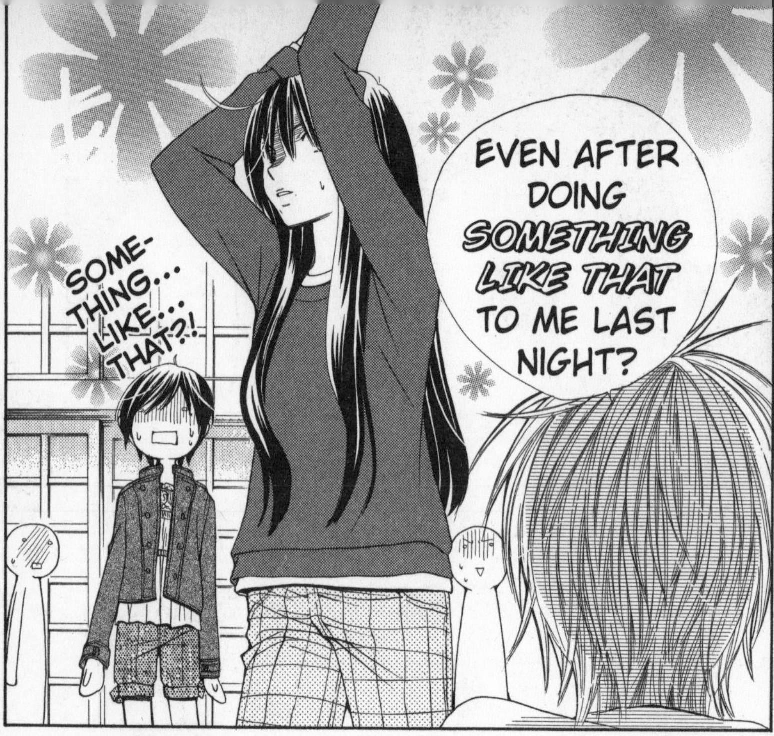
EVEN AFTER DOING SOMETHING LIKE THAT TO ME LAST NIGHT?
SOME-THING... LIKE... THAT?!

...FOR HAVING FUN WITH THIS, CAN'T YOU?

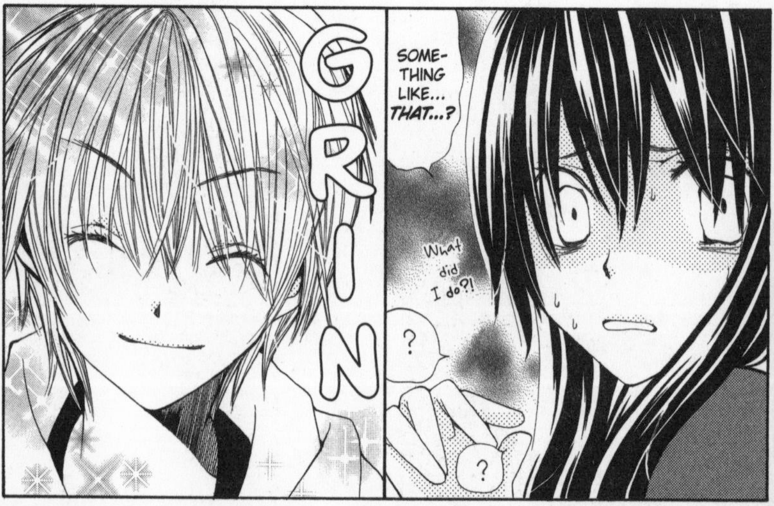
SOME-THING LIKE... THAT...?
What did I do?!
?
?
GRIN

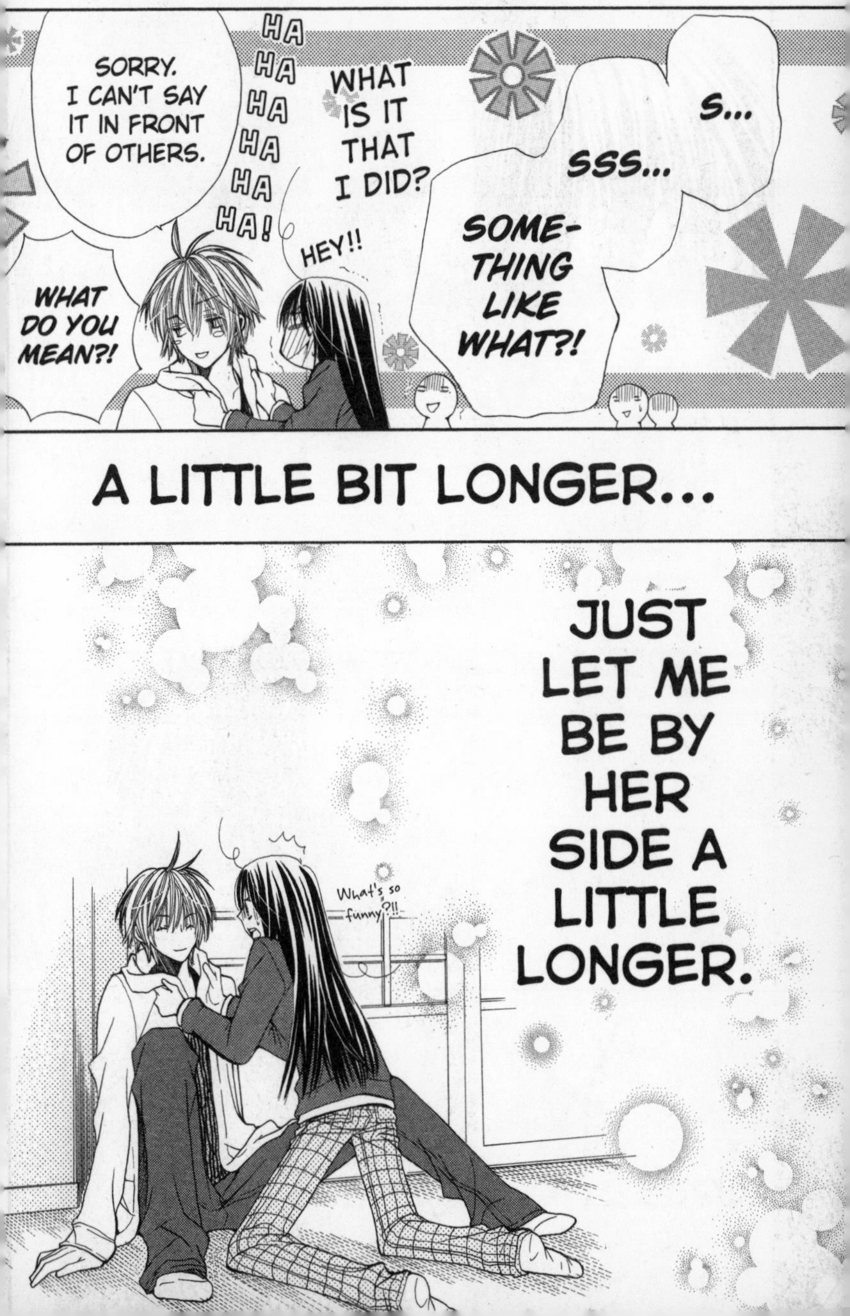
S...
SSS...
SOMETHING LIKE WHAT?!
WHAT IS IT THAT I DID?
HEY!!
HA HA HA HA HA HA!
SORRY. I CAN'T SAY IT IN FRONT OF OTHERS.
WHAT DO YOU MEAN?!
A LITTLE BIT LONGER...
JUST LET ME BE BY HER SIDE A LITTLE LONGER.
What's so funny?!!

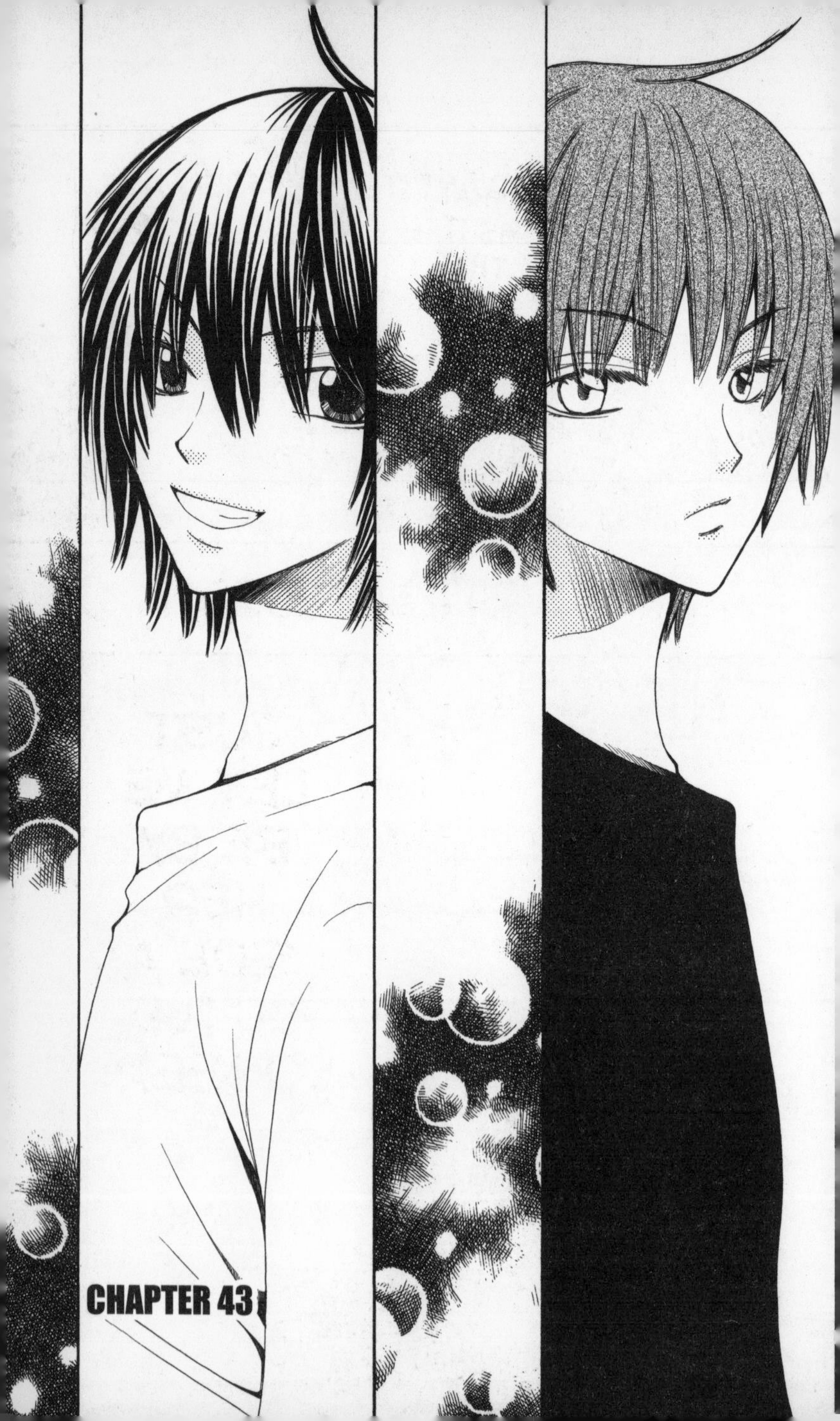
CHAPTER 43

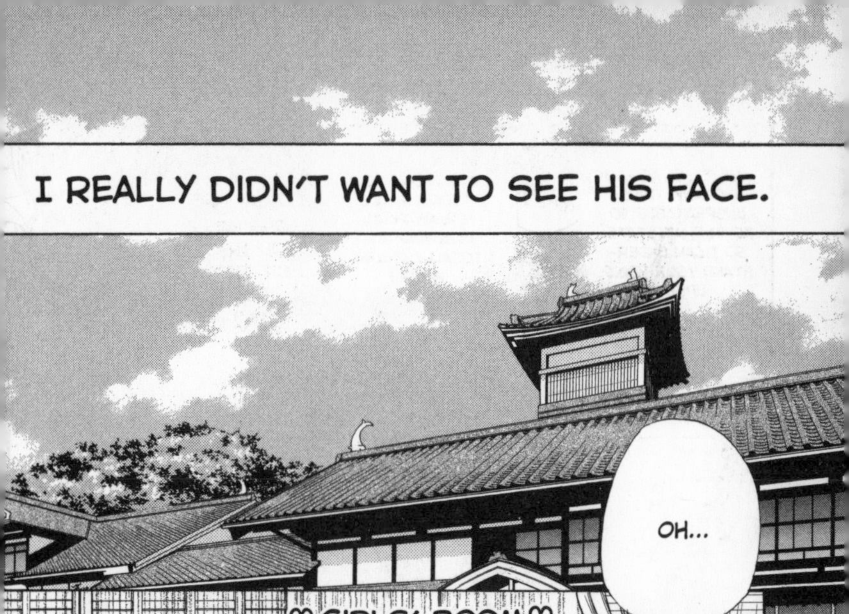
I REALLY DIDN'T WANT TO SEE HIS FACE.
OH...
♡GIRLS' ROOM♡
GLOOM
MMBL
MMBL
MMBL

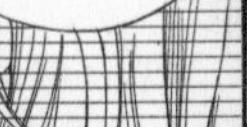

•DRAMA CD•

WELL, WELL, WELL, WELL, WELL! IT'S BEEN DECIDED THAT A DRAMA CD OF *SPECIAL* A WILL BE PRODUCED!! ARE YOU SURE, HAKUSEN PUBLISHING COMPANY? I DIRECT AN ENORMOUS ROLLING BOW ON HANDS AND KNEES TOWARD AWAJI-CHO! AND, OF COURSE, TO ALL OF YOU WHO SUPPORT ME—A ***JUMPING*** AND ***ROLLING*** AND ***DANCING*** BOW ON HANDS AND KNEES! I CAN ALREADY TELL YOU THAT THE DRAMA CD WILL BE COMPLETELY ORIGINAL, AND THAT THE VOICE ACTORS ARE TRULY SPLENDID!! THE ONLY ONE I WORRY ABOUT IS MEGUMI. I WONDER HOW THEY'LL HANDLE THE SKETCHBOOK CONVERSATIONS...ANYWAY, I'M REALLY LOOKING FORWARD TO THIS. IT'S SCHEDULED TO COME OUT IN FEBRUARY. I HOPE ALL OF YOU GIVE IT A LISTEN!

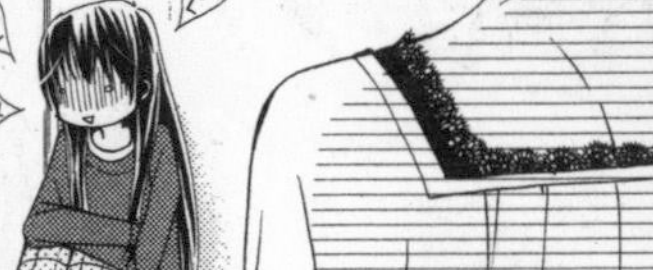
A DREAM?
IT'S NOT A DREAM! HOW DARE YOU?!
IT'S A DREAM.
...IS IT?

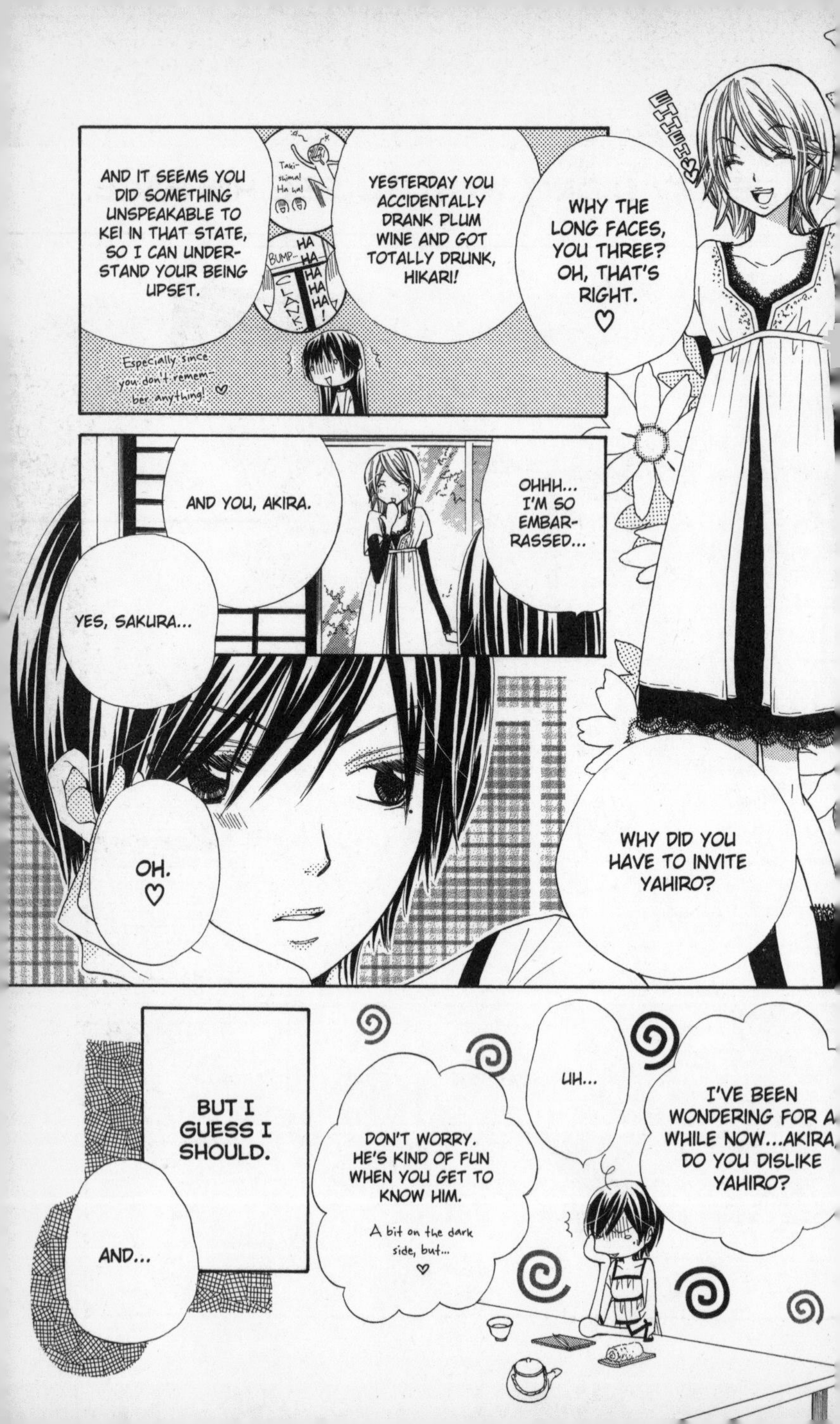

WHY THE LONG FACES, YOU THREE? OH, THAT'S RIGHT. ♡
YESTERDAY YOU ACCIDENTALLY DRANK PLUM WINE AND GOT TOTALLY DRUNK, HIKARI!
Taki-shima! Ha ha!
HA HA HA HA!
BUMP...
CLANK
AND IT SEEMS YOU DID SOMETHING UNSPEAKABLE TO KEI IN THAT STATE, SO I CAN UNDER-STAND YOUR BEING UPSET.
Especially since you don't remem-ber anything! ♡
OHHH... I'M SO EMBAR-RASSED...
AND YOU, AKIRA.
YES, SAKURA...
WHY DID YOU HAVE TO INVITE YAHIRO?
OH. ♡
I'VE BEEN WONDERING FOR A WHILE NOW...AKIRA, DO YOU DISLIKE YAHIRO?
UH...
DON'T WORRY. HE'S KIND OF FUN WHEN YOU GET TO KNOW HIM.
A bit on the dark side, but... ♡
BUT I GUESS I SHOULD.
AND...

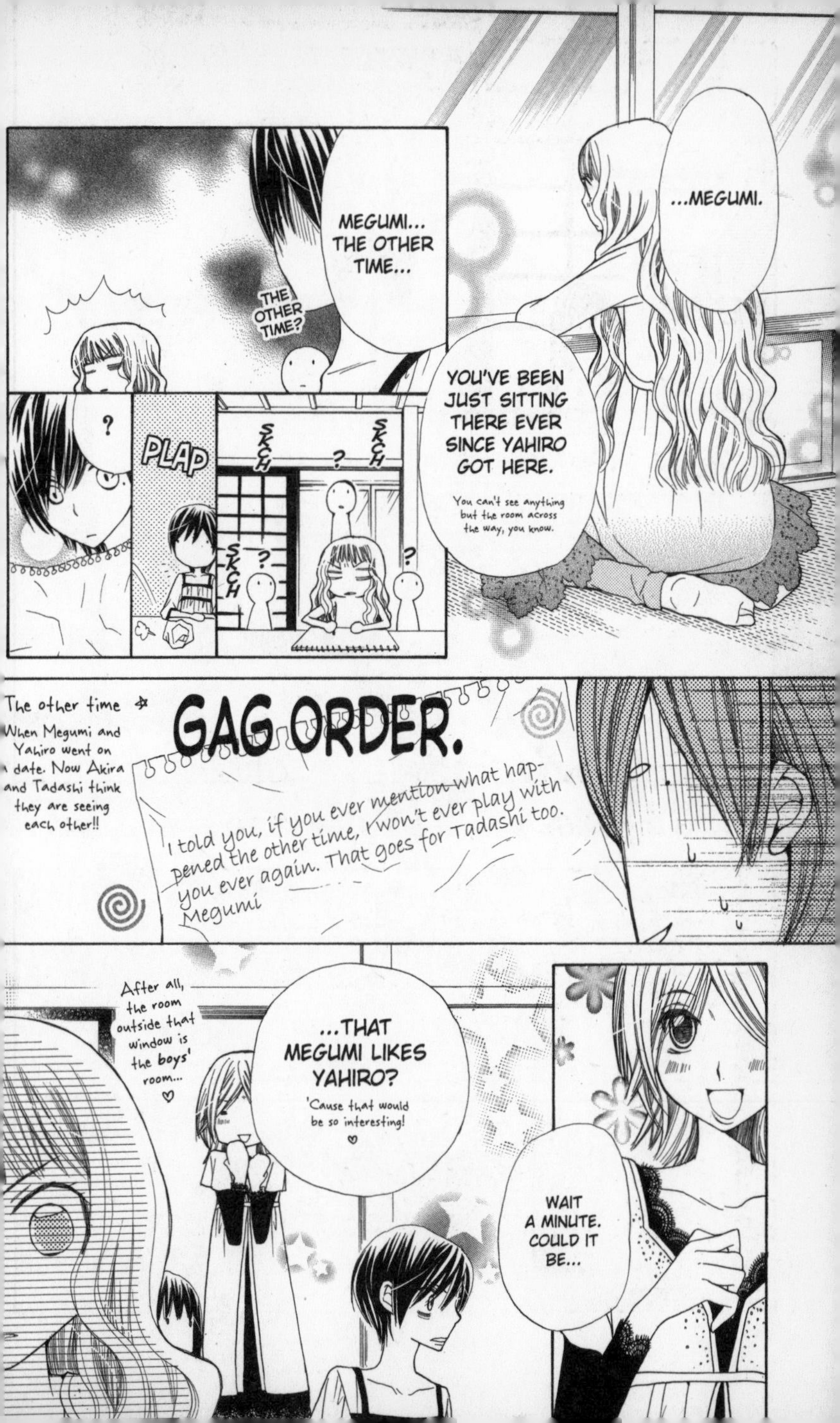

...MEGUMI.
YOU'VE BEEN JUST SITTING THERE EVER SINCE YAHIRO GOT HERE.
You can't see anything but the room across the way, you know.
MEGUMI... THE OTHER TIME...
THE OTHER TIME?
SKCH
?
SKCH
?
SKCH
?
PLAP
?
GAG ORDER.
I told you, if you ever mention what happened the other time, I won't ever play with you ever again. That goes for Tadashi too.
Megumi
The other time ☆
When Megumi and Yahiro went on a date. Now Akira and Tadashi think they are seeing each other!!
WAIT A MINUTE. COULD IT BE...
...THAT MEGUMI LIKES YAHIRO?
'Cause that would be so interesting! ♡
After all, the room outside that window is the boys' room... ♡

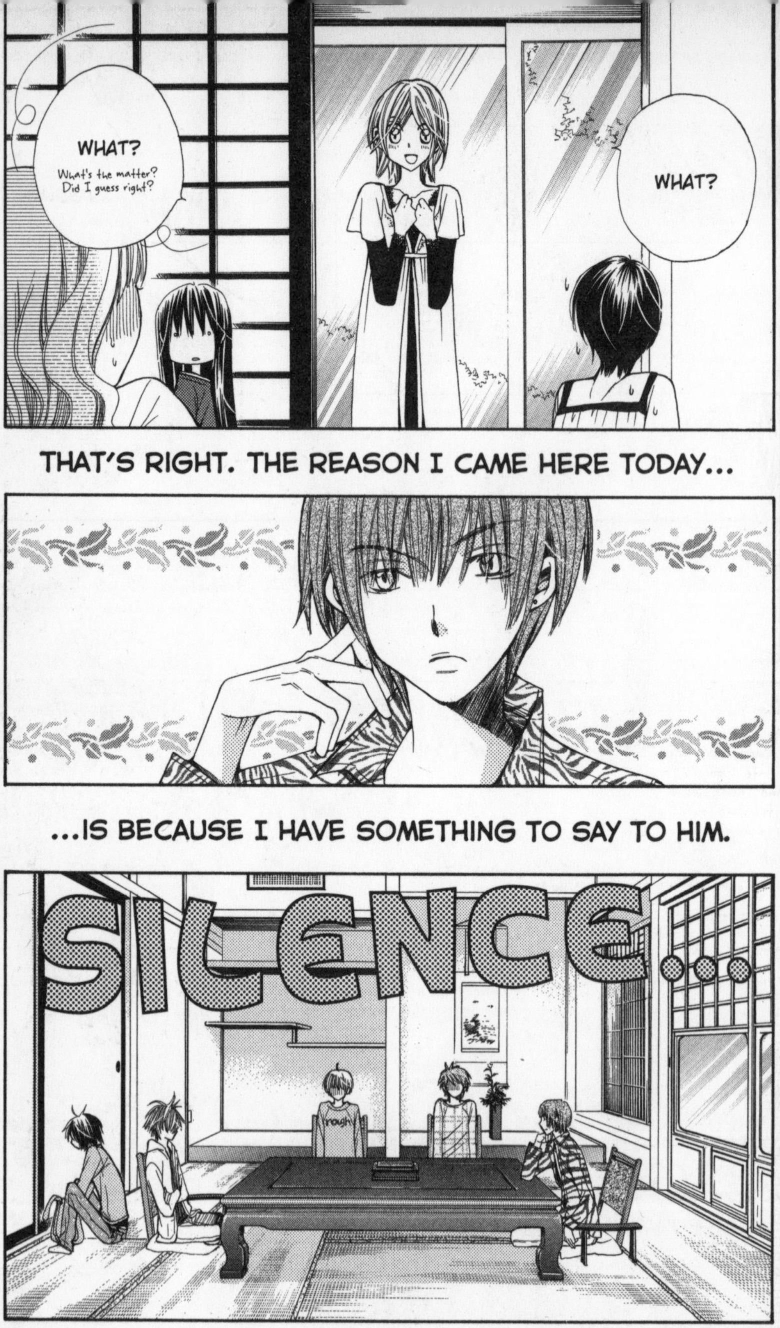
WHAT?
WHAT?
What's the matter? Did I guess right?
THAT'S RIGHT. THE REASON I CAME HERE TODAY...
...IS BECAUSE I HAVE SOMETHING TO SAY TO HIM.
SILENCE...
rough

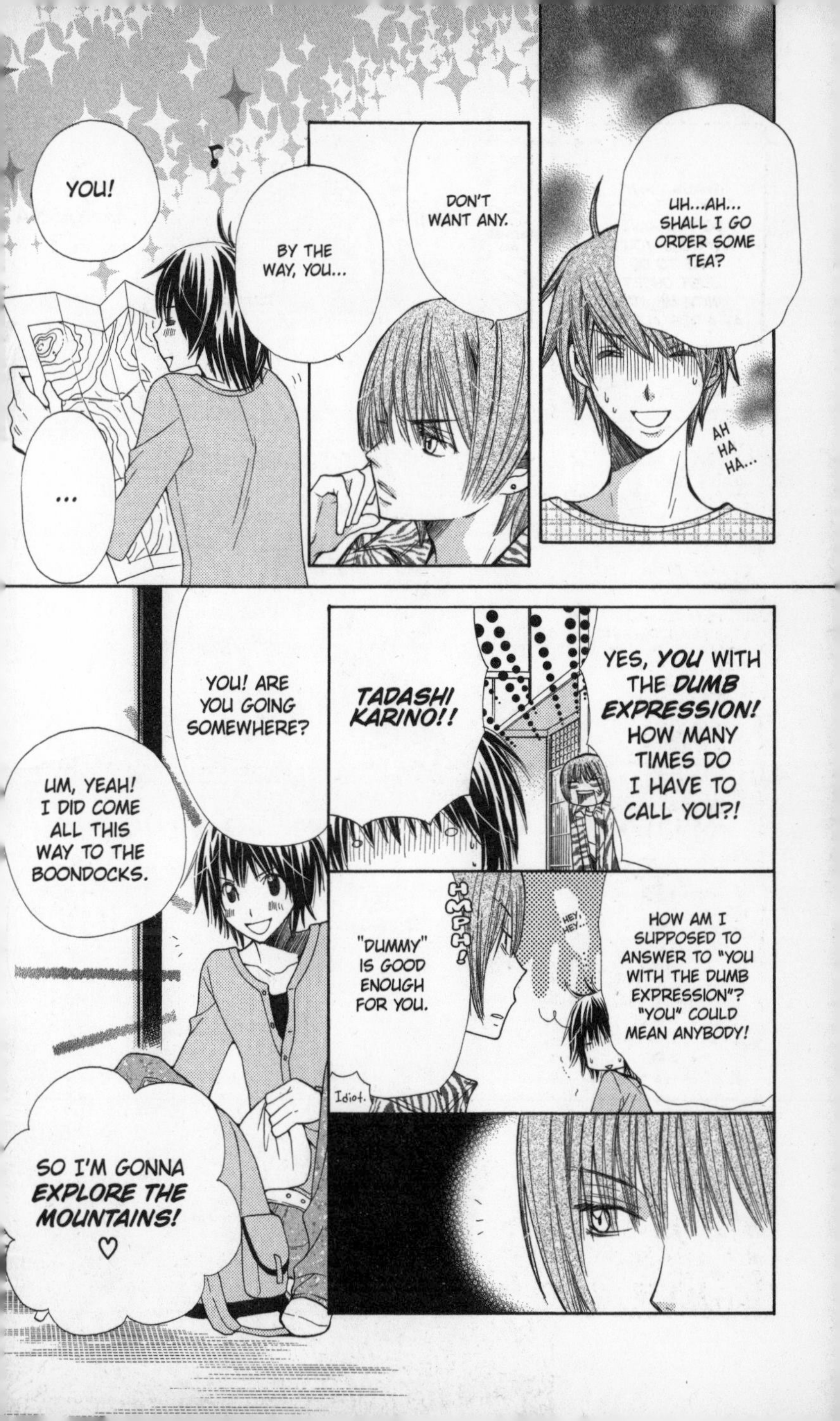
UH...AH... SHALL I GO ORDER SOME TEA?
AH HA HA...
DON'T WANT ANY.
BY THE WAY, YOU...
YOU!
...
YES, *YOU* WITH THE *DUMB EXPRESSION!* HOW MANY TIMES DO I HAVE TO CALL YOU?!
TADASHI KARINO!!
HOW AM I SUPPOSED TO ANSWER TO "YOU WITH THE DUMB EXPRESSION"? "YOU" COULD MEAN ANYBODY!
HEY, HEY...
HMPH!
"DUMMY" IS GOOD ENOUGH FOR YOU.
Idiot.
YOU! ARE YOU GOING SOMEWHERE?
UM, YEAH! I DID COME ALL THIS WAY TO THE BOONDOCKS.
SO I'M GONNA *EXPLORE THE MOUNTAINS!* ♡

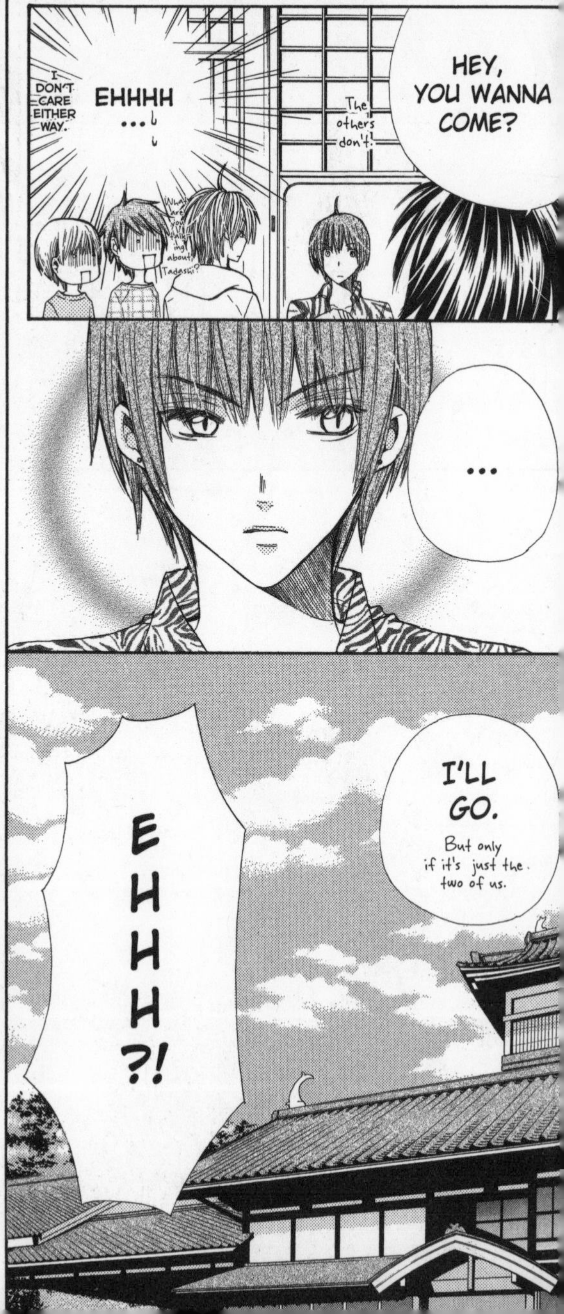

HEY, YOU WANNA COME?
The others don't.
What are you talking about, Tadashi?
EHHHH...
I DON'T CARE EITHER WAY.
...
I'LL GO.
But only if it's just the two of us.
EHHHH?!

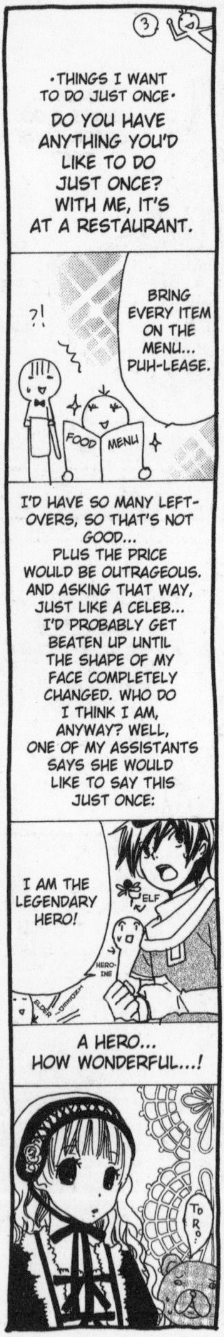

3
•THINGS I WANT TO DO JUST ONCE•
DO YOU HAVE ANYTHING YOU'D LIKE TO DO JUST ONCE? WITH ME, IT'S AT A RESTAURANT.
BRING EVERY ITEM ON THE MENU... PUH-LEASE.
?!
FOOD MENU
I'D HAVE SO MANY LEFT-OVERS, SO THAT'S NOT GOOD... PLUS THE PRICE WOULD BE OUTRAGEOUS. AND ASKING THAT WAY, JUST LIKE A CELEB... I'D PROBABLY GET BEATEN UP UNTIL THE SHAPE OF MY FACE COMPLETELY CHANGED. WHO DO I THINK I AM, ANYWAY? WELL, ONE OF MY ASSISTANTS SAYS SHE WOULD LIKE TO SAY THIS JUST ONCE:
I AM THE LEGENDARY HERO!
ELF
HERO-INE
A HERO... HOW WONDERFUL...!
TORO

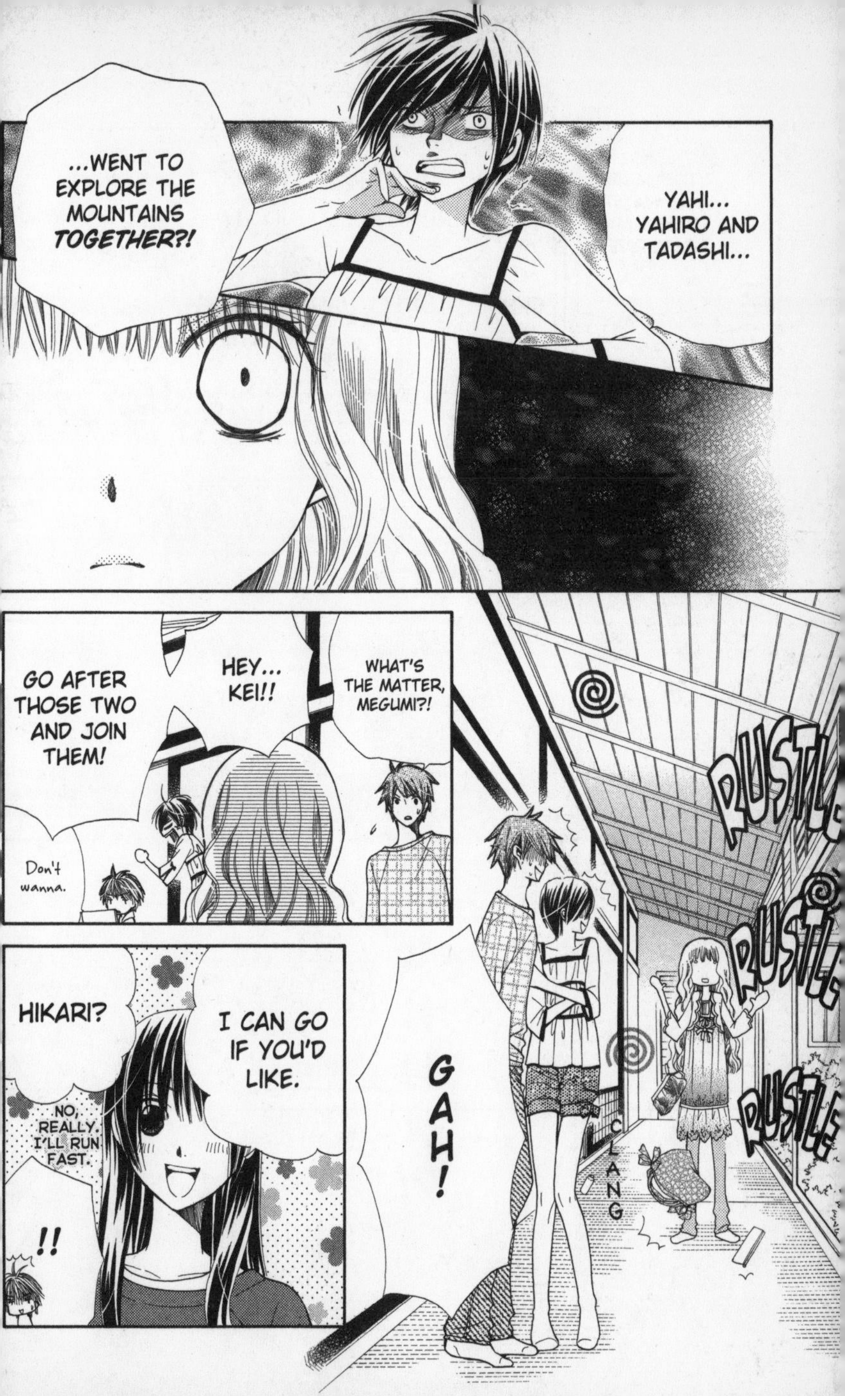
YAHI... YAHIRO AND TADASHI...
...WENT TO EXPLORE THE MOUNTAINS TOGETHER?!
RUSTLE
RUSTLE
RUSTLE
GAH!
CLANG
WHAT'S THE MATTER, MEGUMI?!
HEY... KEI!!
GO AFTER THOSE TWO AND JOIN THEM!
Don't wanna.
I CAN GO IF YOU'D LIKE.
HIKARI?
NO, REALLY. I'LL RUN FAST.
!!

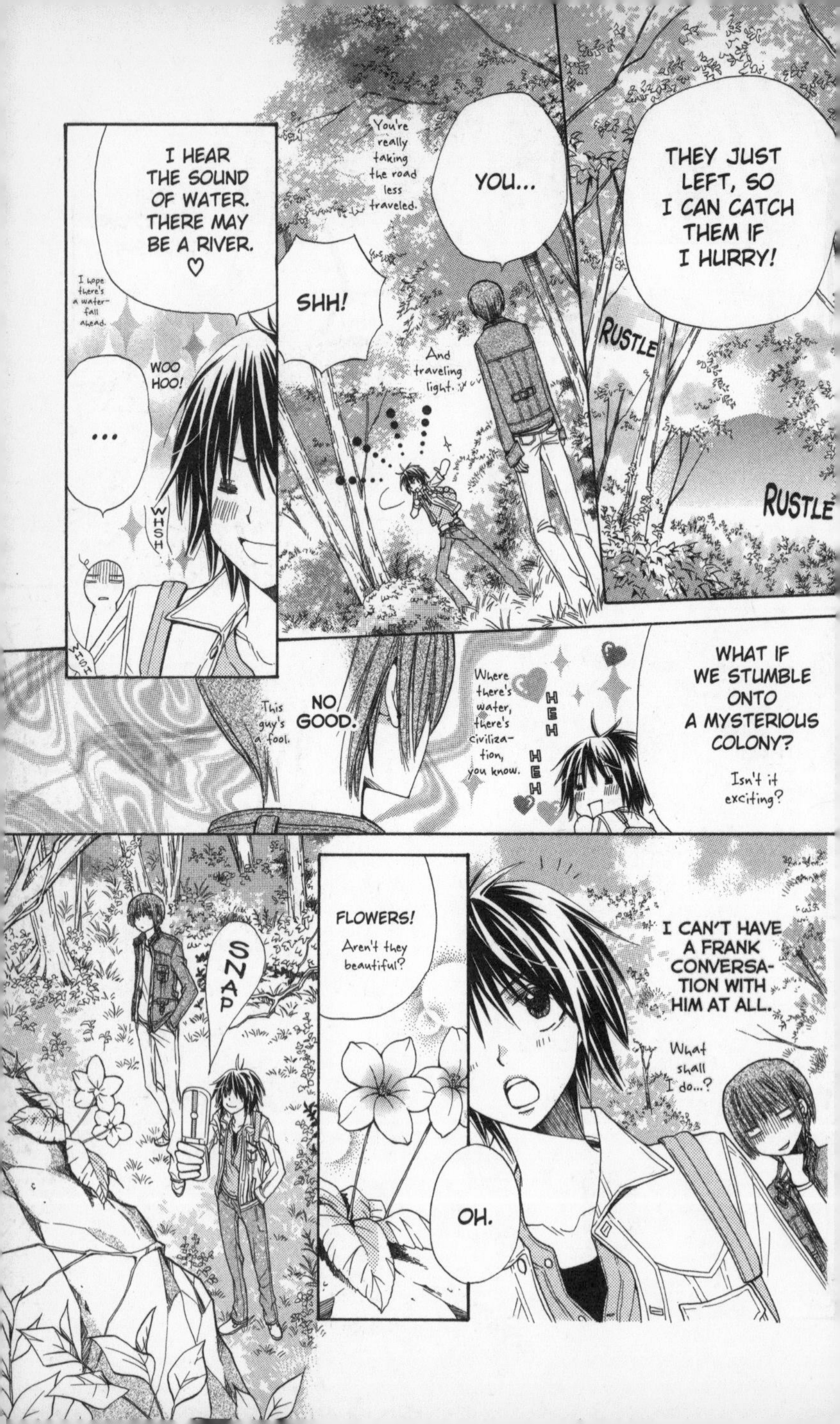

THEY JUST LEFT, SO I CAN CATCH THEM IF I HURRY!
RUSTLE
RUSTLE
YOU...
You're really taking the road less traveled.
SHH!
And traveling light.
I HEAR THE SOUND OF WATER. THERE MAY BE A RIVER. ♡
I hope there's a water-fall ahead.
WOO HOO!
...
WHSH
WHSH
WHAT IF WE STUMBLE ONTO A MYSTERIOUS COLONY?
Isn't it exciting?
HEH HEH
Where there's water, there's civiliza-tion, you know.
NO GOOD.
This guy's a fool.
I CAN'T HAVE A FRANK CONVERSA-TION WITH HIM AT ALL.
What shall I do...?
FLOWERS!
Aren't they beautiful?
OH.
SNAP

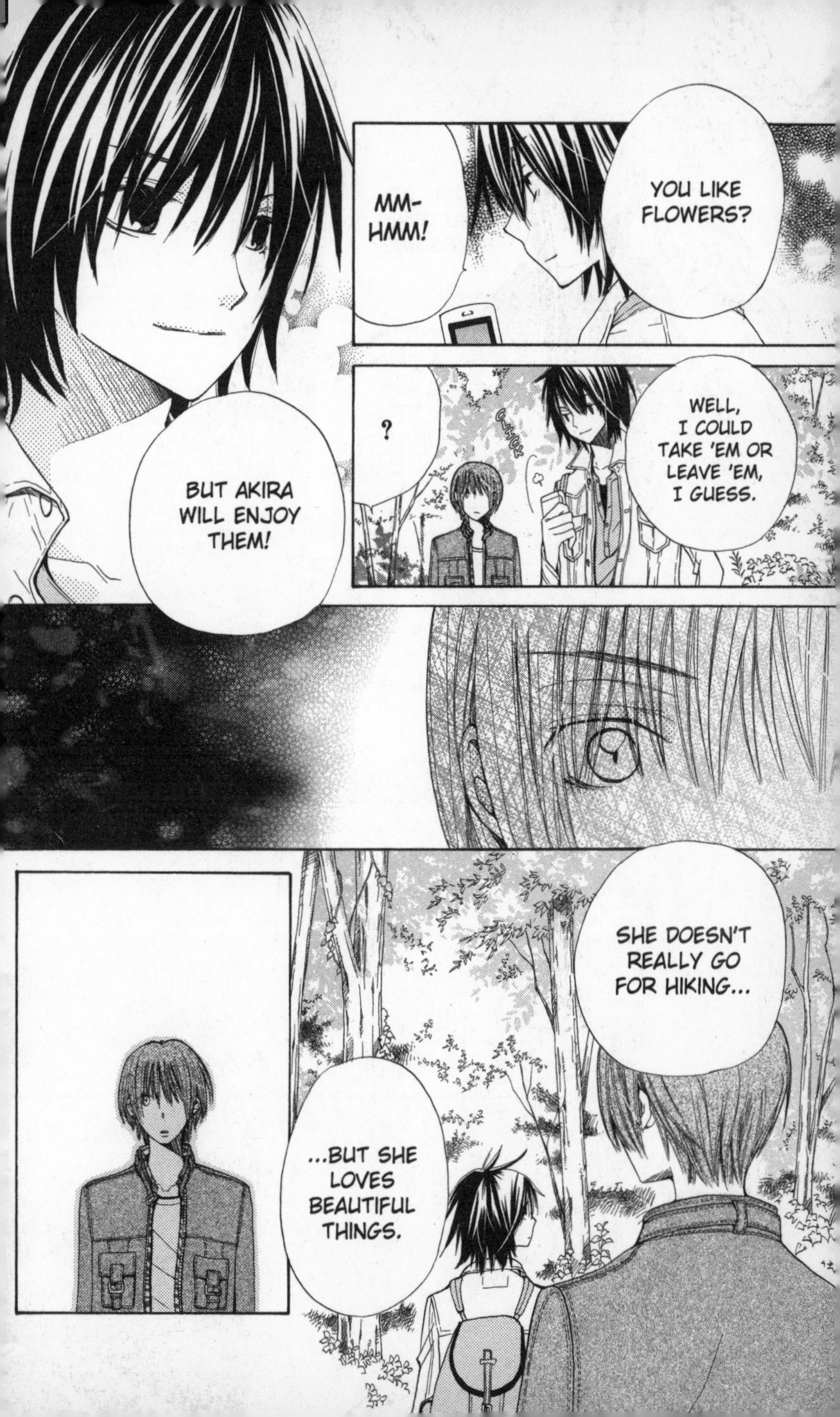
YOU LIKE FLOWERS?
MM-HMM!
CLICK
WELL, I COULD TAKE 'EM OR LEAVE 'EM, I GUESS.
?
BUT AKIRA WILL ENJOY THEM!
SHE DOESN'T REALLY GO FOR HIKING...
...BUT SHE LOVES BEAUTIFUL THINGS.

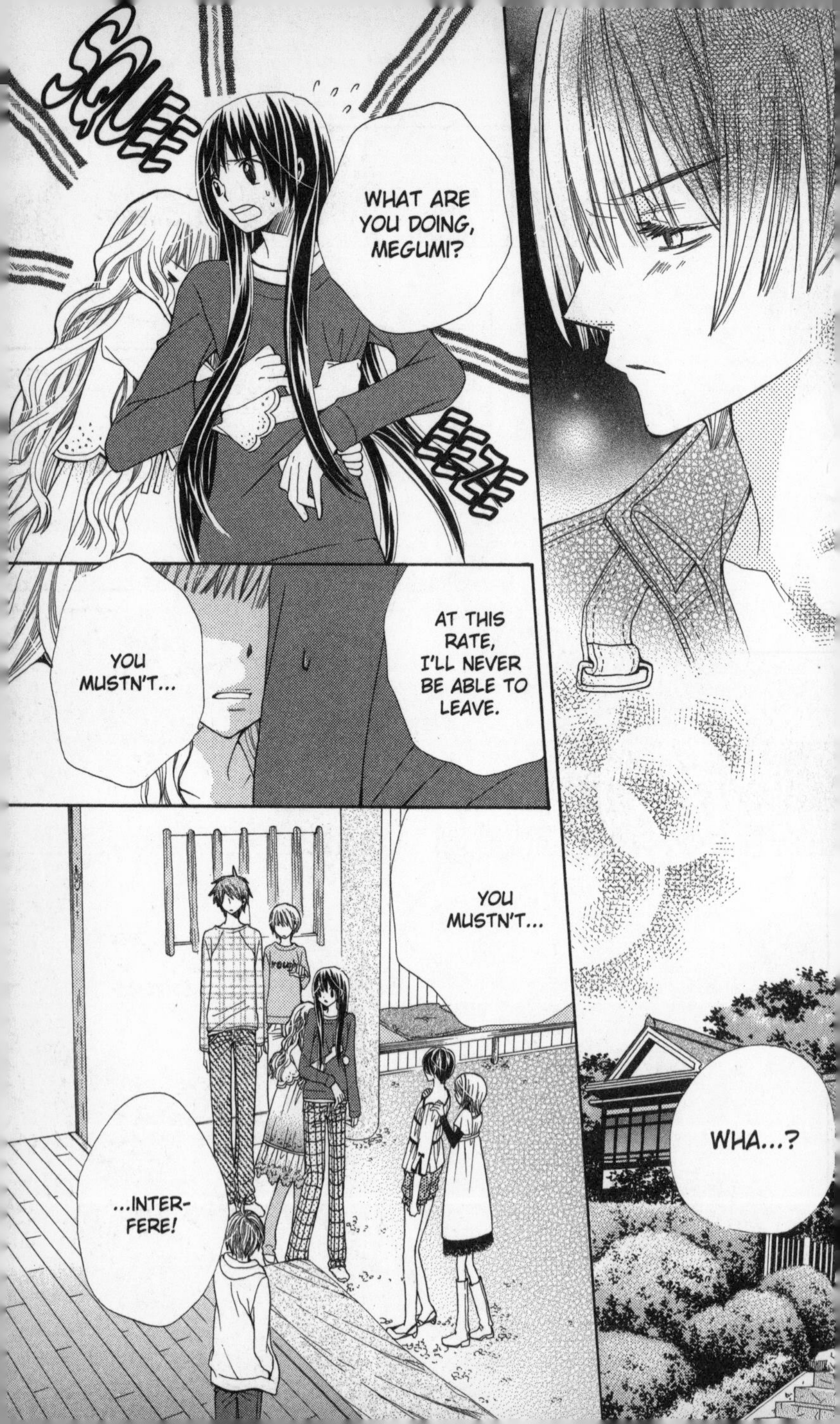
WHA...?
WHAT ARE YOU DOING, MEGUMI?
SQUEEE
EEEE
AT THIS RATE, I'LL NEVER BE ABLE TO LEAVE.
YOU MUSTN'T...
YOU MUSTN'T...
...INTER-FERE!

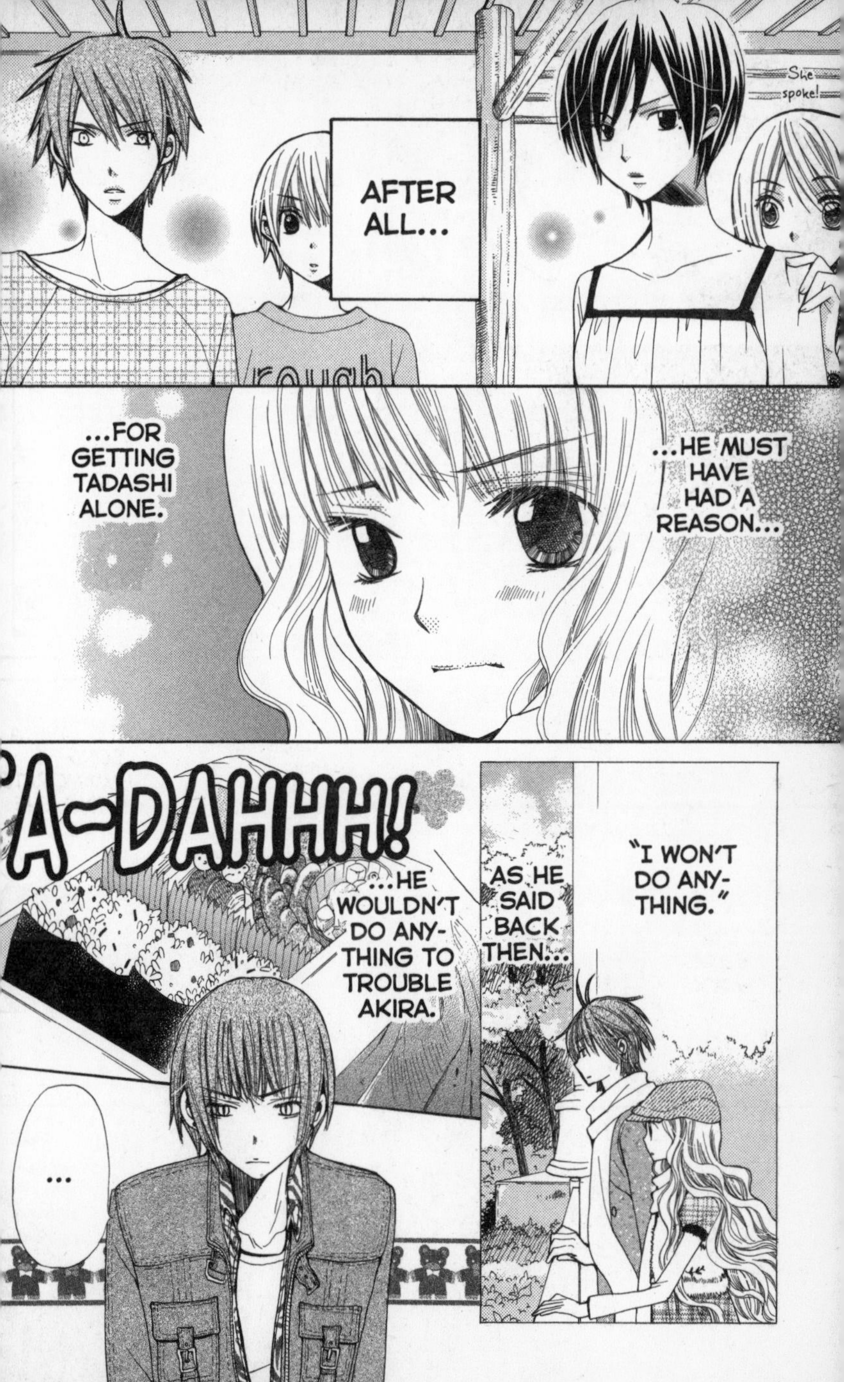
She spoke!
AFTER ALL...
...HE MUST HAVE HAD A REASON...
...FOR GETTING TADASHI ALONE.
"I WON'T DO ANY-THING."
AS HE SAID BACK THEN...
...HE WOULDN'T DO ANY-THING TO TROUBLE AKIRA.
A-DAHHH!
...

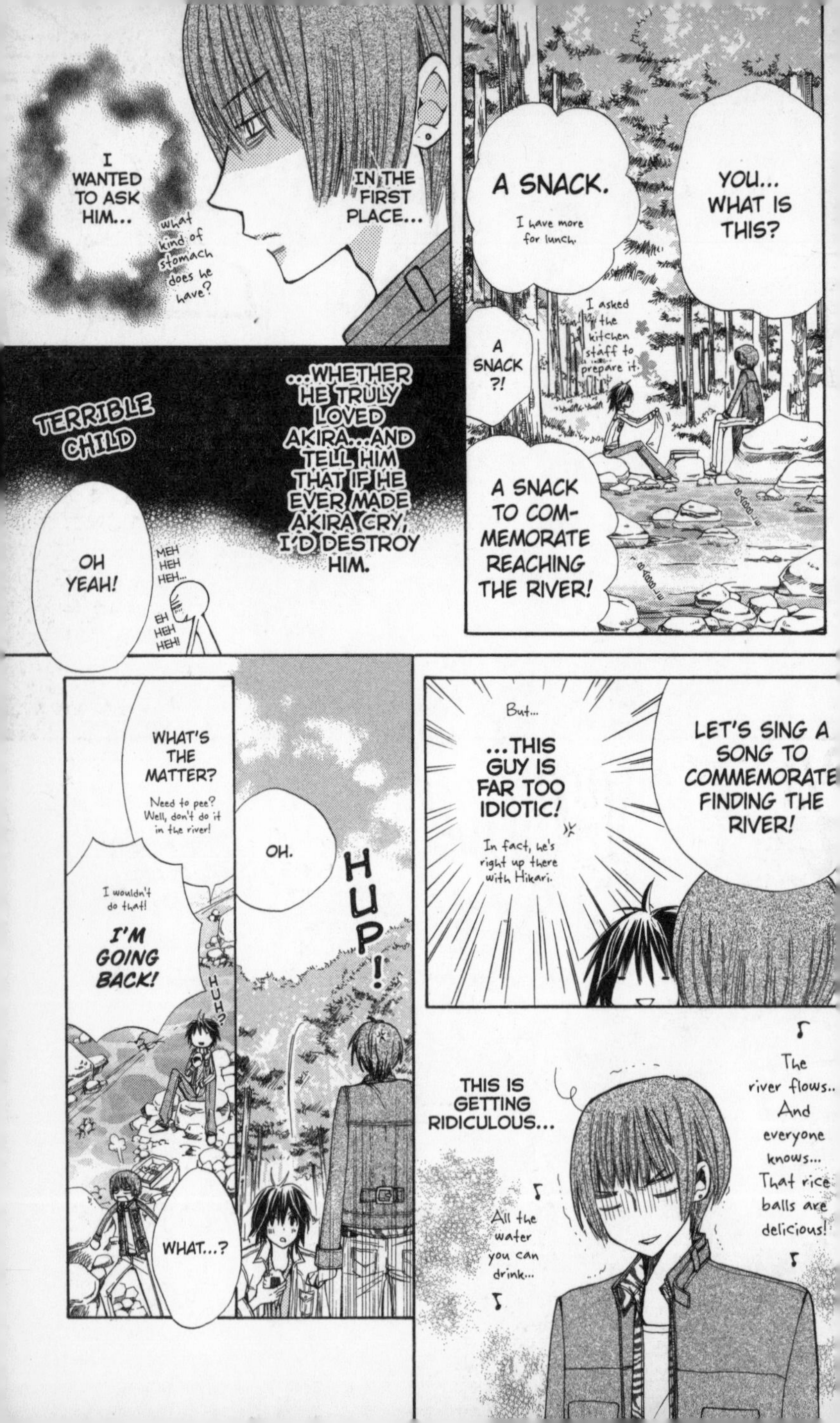

YOU... WHAT IS THIS?
A SNACK.
I have more for lunch.
A SNACK?!
I asked the kitchen staff to prepare it.
A SNACK TO COMMEMORATE REACHING THE RIVER!
I WANTED TO ASK HIM...
IN THE FIRST PLACE...
what kind of stomach does he have?
...WHETHER HE TRULY LOVED AKIRA...AND TELL HIM THAT IF HE EVER MADE AKIRA CRY, I'D DESTROY HIM.
TERRIBLE CHILD
MEH HEH HEH...
OH YEAH!
EH HEH HEH!
LET'S SING A SONG TO COMMEMORATE FINDING THE RIVER!
But...
...THIS GUY IS FAR TOO IDIOTIC!
In fact, he's right up there with Hikari.
The river flows... And everyone knows... That rice balls are delicious!
THIS IS GETTING RIDICULOUS...
All the water you can drink...
WHAT'S THE MATTER?
Need to pee? Well, don't do it in the river!
OH.
HUP!
I wouldn't do that!
I'M GOING BACK!
HUH?
WHAT...?

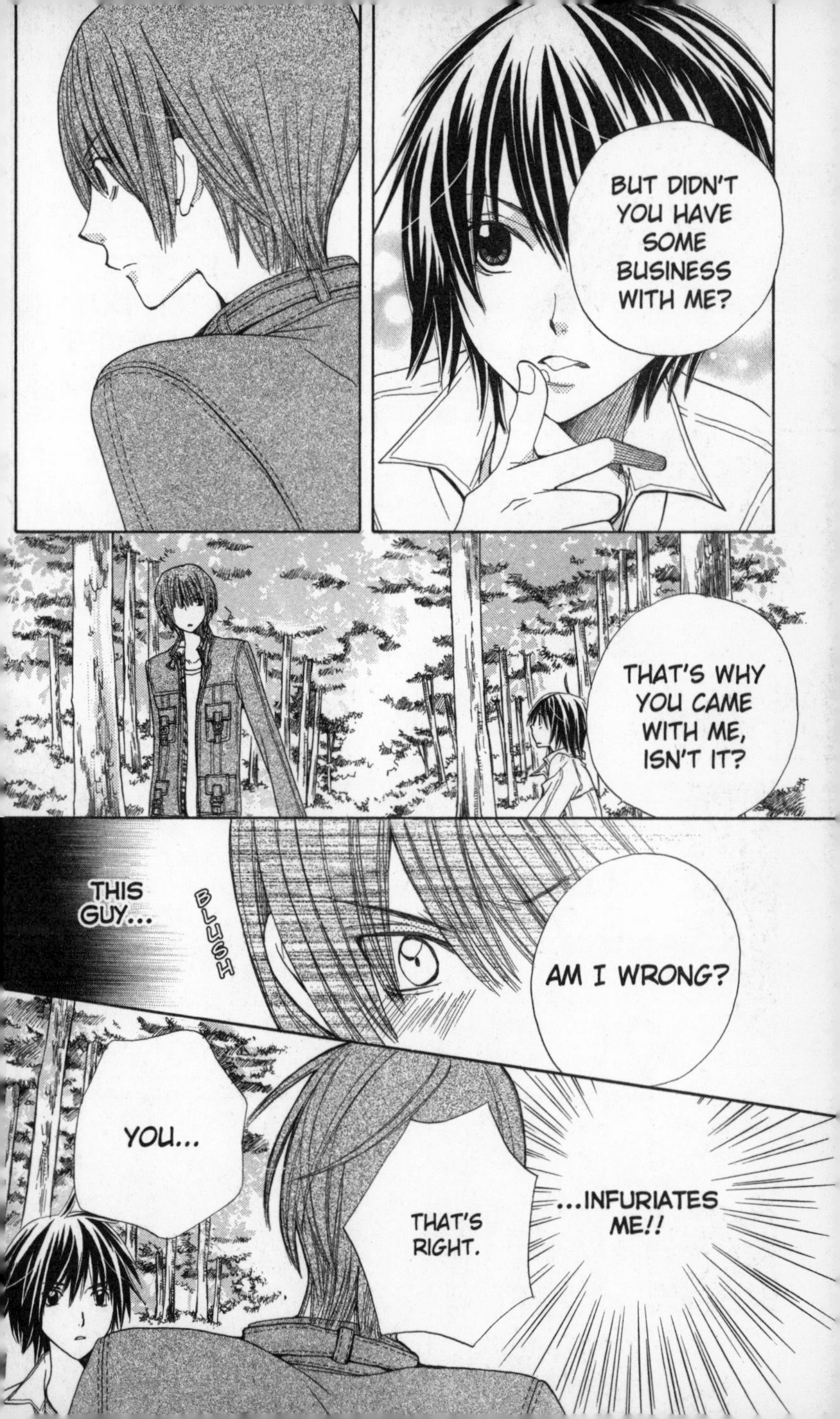
BUT DIDN'T YOU HAVE SOME BUSINESS WITH ME?
THAT'S WHY YOU CAME WITH ME, ISN'T IT?
AM I WRONG?
BLUSH
THIS GUY...
THAT'S RIGHT.
YOU...
...INFURIATES ME!!

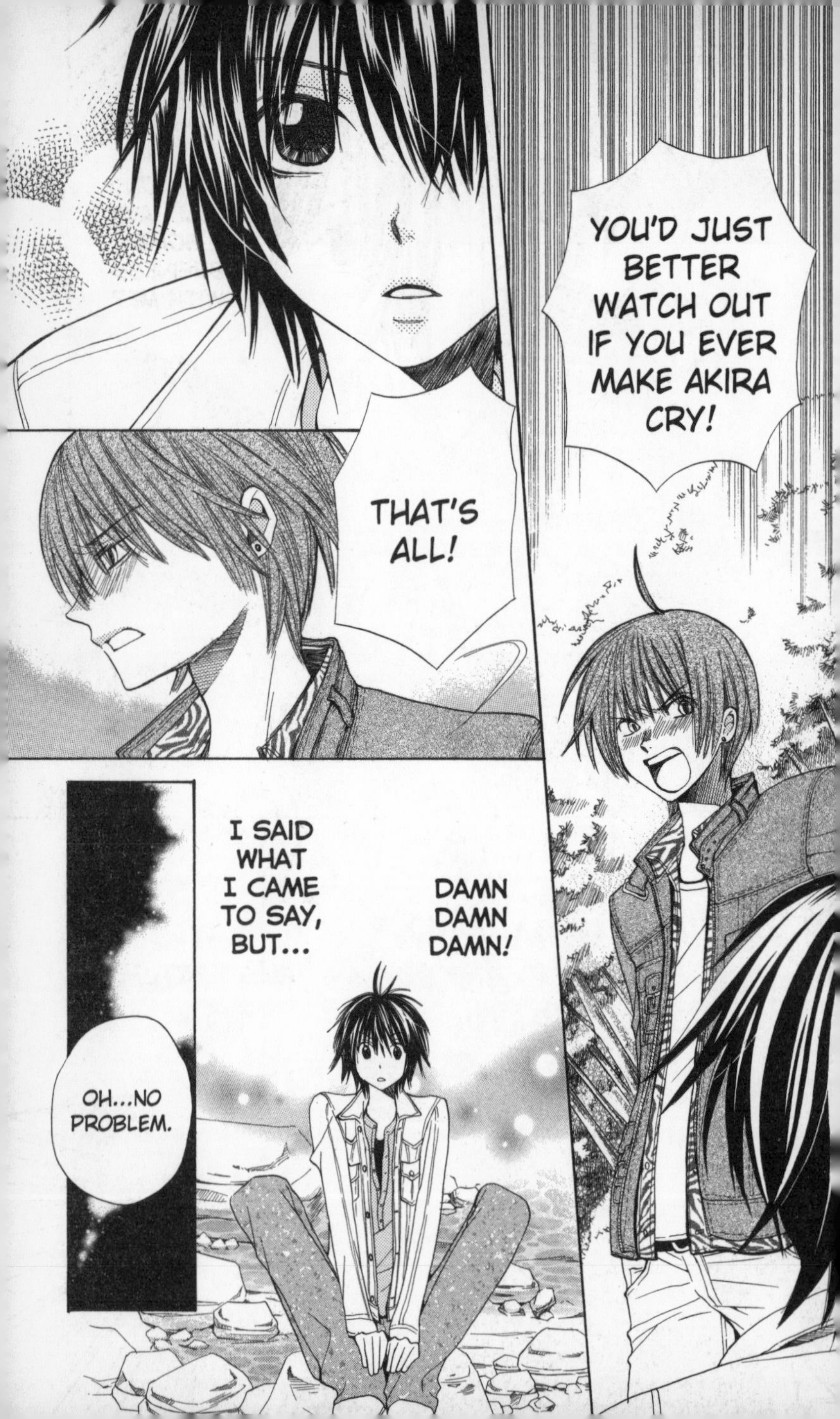
YOU'D JUST BETTER WATCH OUT IF YOU EVER MAKE AKIRA CRY!
THAT'S ALL!
DAMN DAMN DAMN!
I SAID WHAT I CAME TO SAY, BUT...
OH...NO PROBLEM.

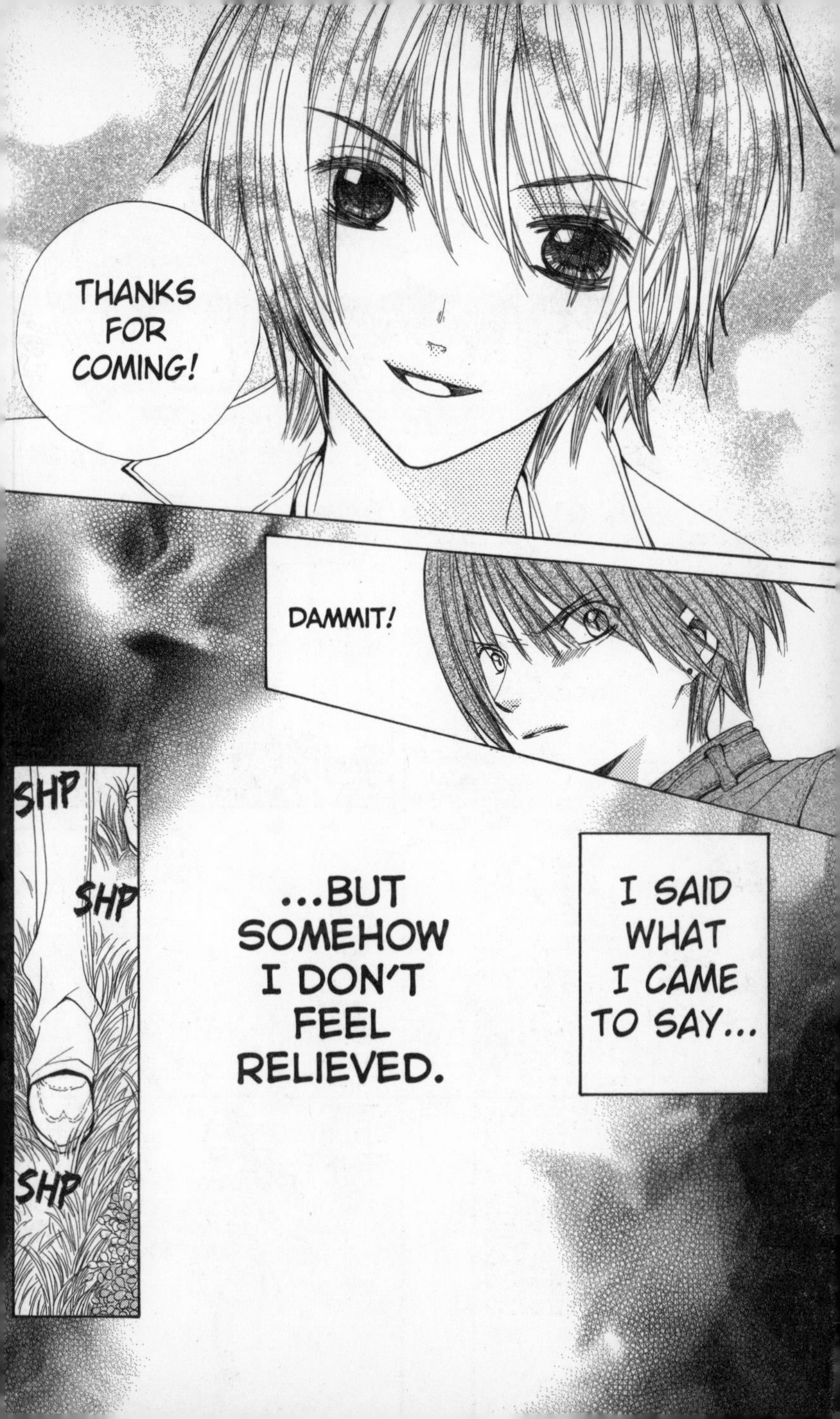
THANKS FOR COMING!
DAMMIT!
I SAID WHAT I CAME TO SAY...
...BUT SOMEHOW I DON'T FEEL RELIEVED.
SHP
SHP
SHP

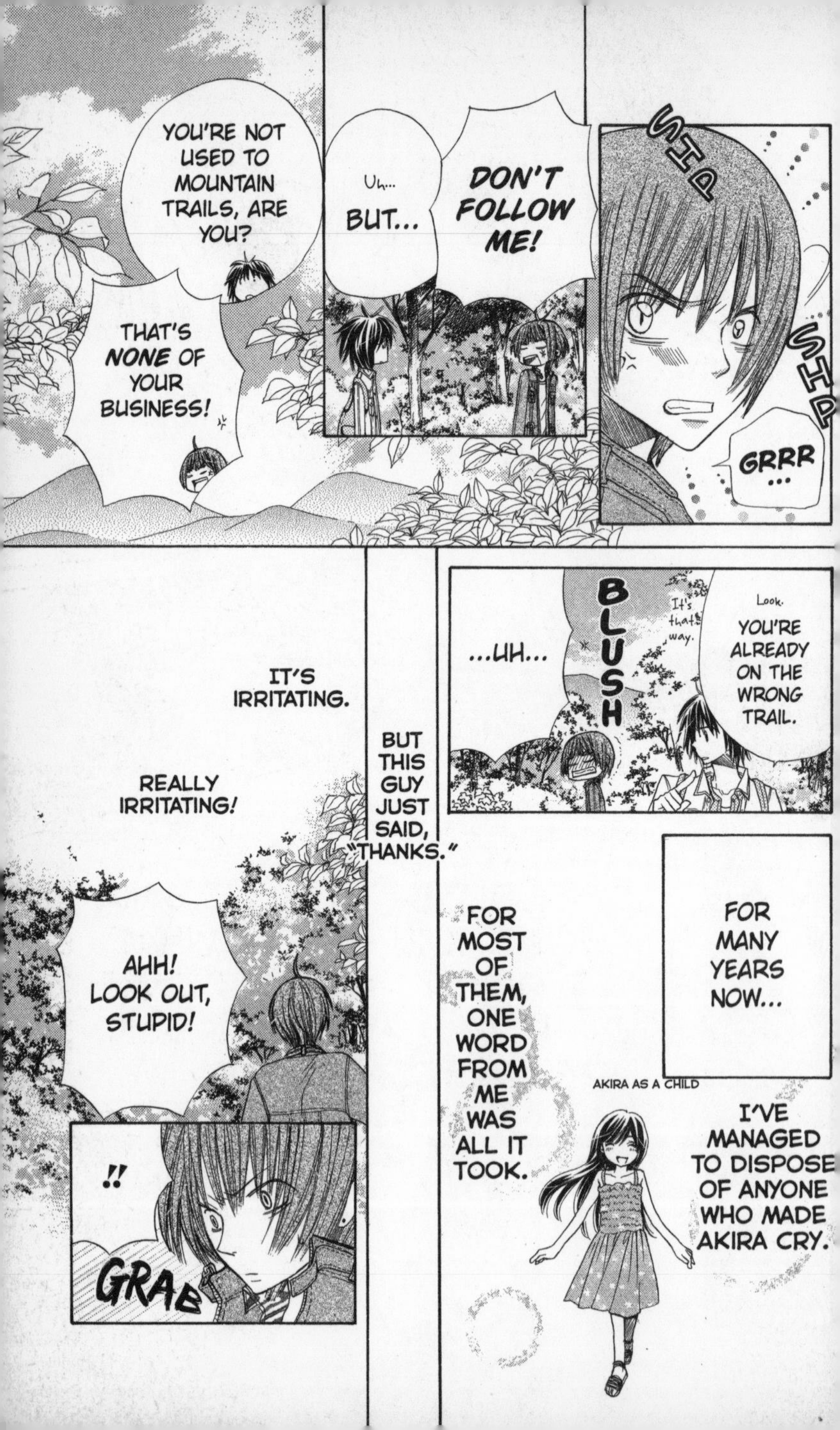
SHP
SHP
GRRR...
DON'T FOLLOW ME!
Uh...
BUT...
YOU'RE NOT USED TO MOUNTAIN TRAILS, ARE YOU?
THAT'S *NONE* OF YOUR BUSINESS!
Look.
YOU'RE ALREADY ON THE WRONG TRAIL.
It's that way.
BLUSH
...UH...
FOR MANY YEARS NOW...
I'VE MANAGED TO DISPOSE OF ANYONE WHO MADE AKIRA CRY.
AKIRA AS A CHILD
FOR MOST OF THEM, ONE WORD FROM ME WAS ALL IT TOOK.
BUT THIS GUY JUST SAID, "THANKS."
IT'S IRRITATING.
REALLY IRRITATING!
AHH! LOOK OUT, STUPID!
!!
GRAB

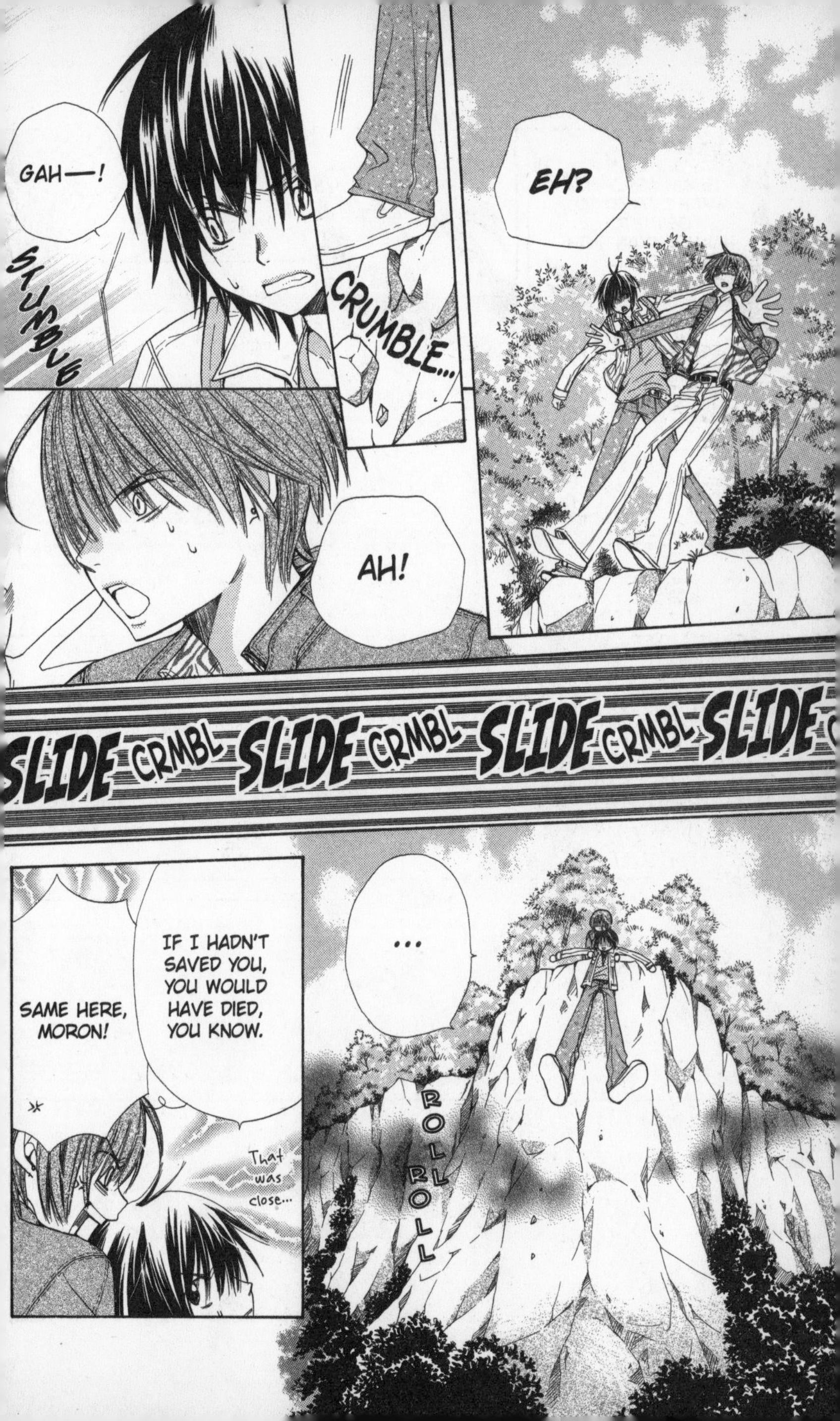
EH?
CRUMBLE...
GAH—!
STUMBLE
AH!
SLIDE CRMBL SLIDE CRMBL SLIDE CRMBL SLIDE
...
ROLL ROLL
IF I HADN'T SAVED YOU, YOU WOULD HAVE DIED, YOU KNOW.
SAME HERE, MORON!
That was close...

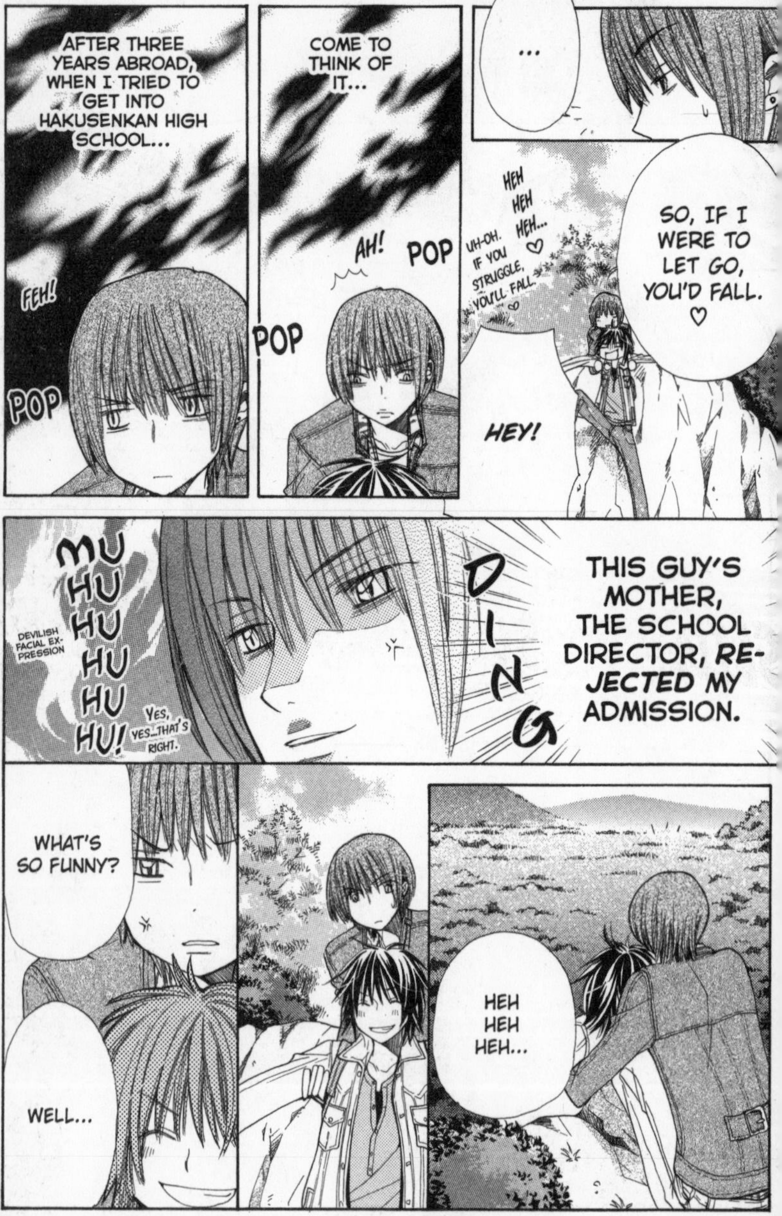
...
SO, IF I WERE TO LET GO, YOU'D FALL. ♡
HEH HEH HEH... ♡
UH-OH. IF YOU STRUGGLE, YOU'LL FALL. ♡
HEY!
COME TO THINK OF IT...
AH!
POP
POP
AFTER THREE YEARS ABROAD, WHEN I TRIED TO GET INTO HAKUSENKAN HIGH SCHOOL...
FEH!
POP
THIS GUY'S MOTHER, THE SCHOOL DIRECTOR, *REJECTED* MY ADMISSION.
DING
MUHUHUHUHUHU!
DEVILISH FACIAL EXPRESSION
YES, YES...THAT'S RIGHT.
HEH HEH HEH...
WHAT'S SO FUNNY?
WELL...

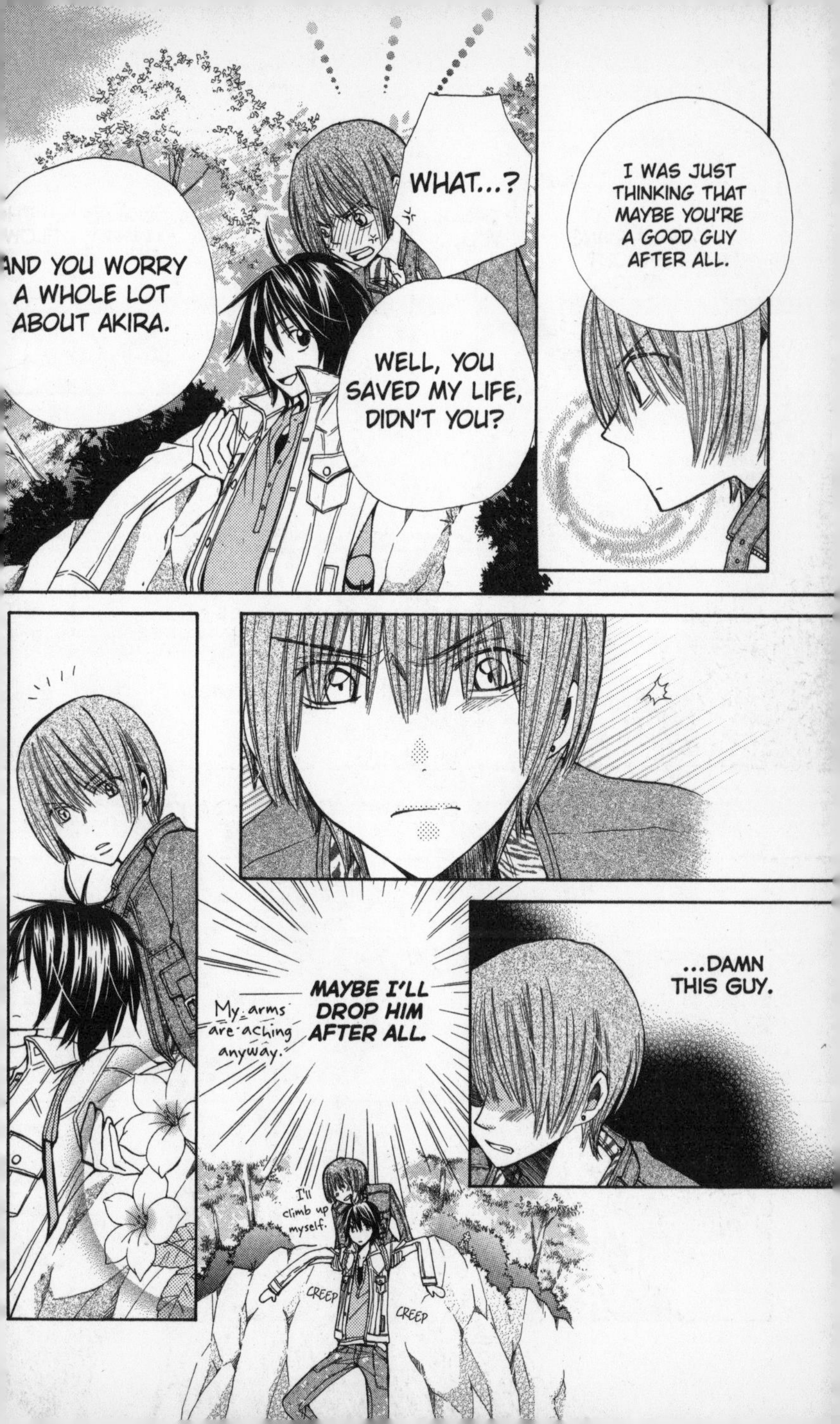
I WAS JUST THINKING THAT MAYBE YOU'RE A GOOD GUY AFTER ALL.
WHAT...?
WELL, YOU SAVED MY LIFE, DIDN'T YOU?
AND YOU WORRY A WHOLE LOT ABOUT AKIRA.
...DAMN THIS GUY.
MAYBE I'LL DROP HIM AFTER ALL.
My arms are aching anyway.
I'll climb up myself.
CREEP
CREEP

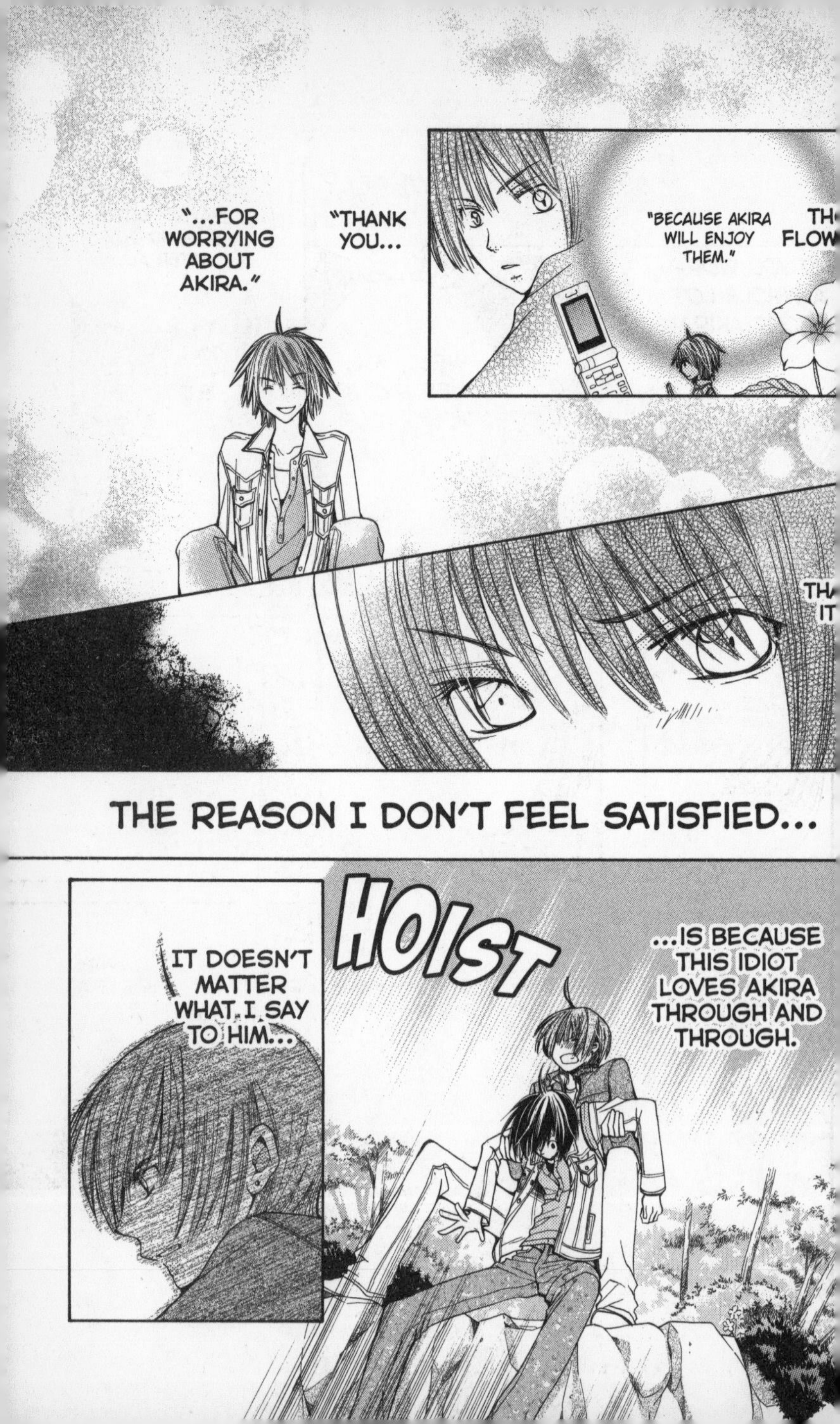
TH FLOW
"BECAUSE AKIRA WILL ENJOY THEM."
"THANK YOU...
"...FOR WORRYING ABOUT AKIRA."
THA IT
THE REASON I DON'T FEEL SATISFIED...
...IS BECAUSE THIS IDIOT LOVES AKIRA THROUGH AND THROUGH.
HOIST
IT DOESN'T MATTER WHAT I SAY TO HIM...

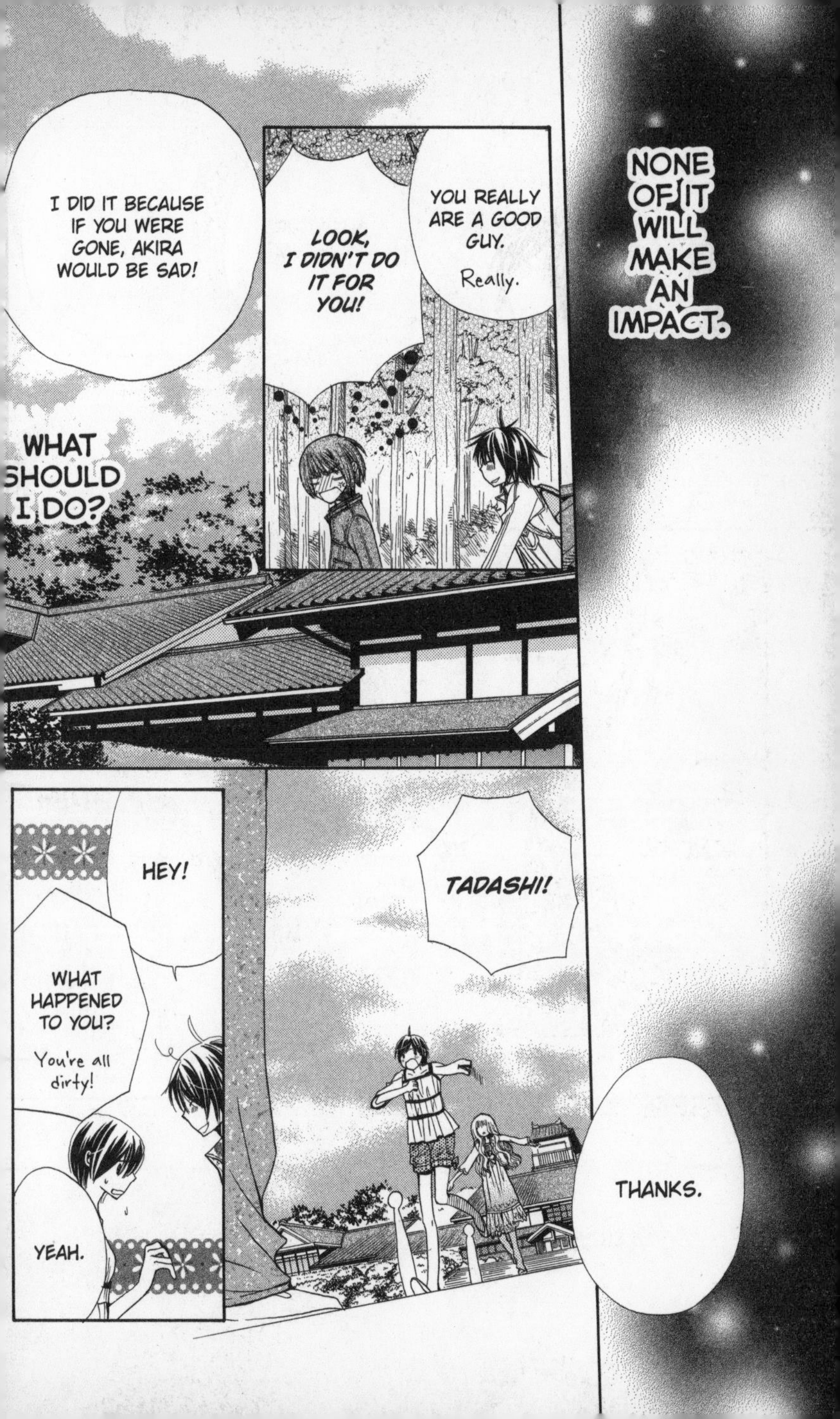
NONE OF IT WILL MAKE AN IMPACT.
THANKS.
YOU REALLY ARE A GOOD GUY.
Really.
LOOK, I DIDN'T DO IT FOR YOU!
I DID IT BECAUSE IF YOU WERE GONE, AKIRA WOULD BE SAD!
WHAT SHOULD I DO?
TADASHI!
HEY!
WHAT HAPPENED TO YOU?
You're all dirty!
YEAH.

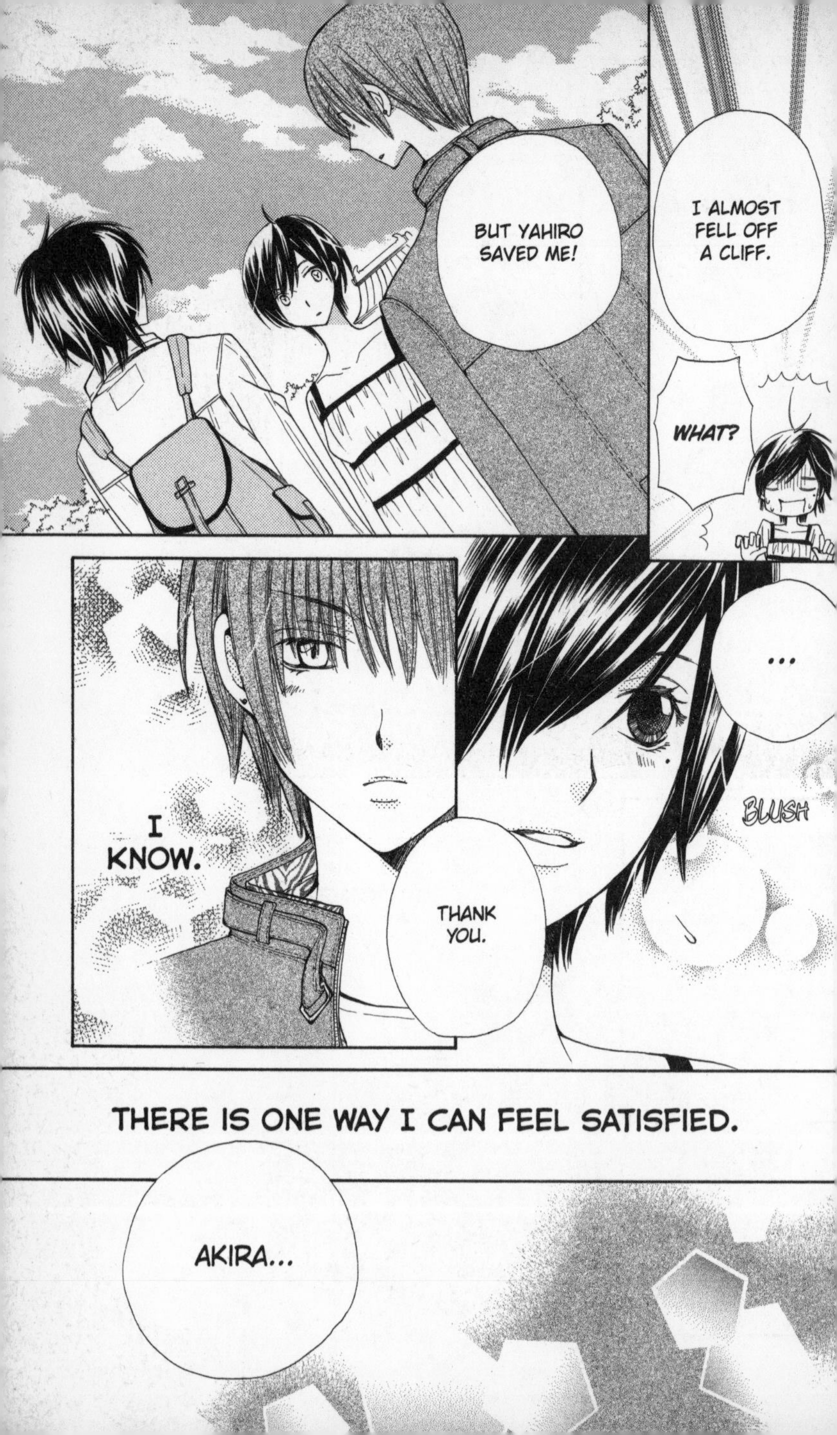
I ALMOST FELL OFF A CLIFF.
WHAT?
BUT YAHIRO SAVED ME!
...
BLUSH
THANK YOU.
I KNOW.
THERE IS ONE WAY I CAN FEEL SATISFIED.
AKIRA...

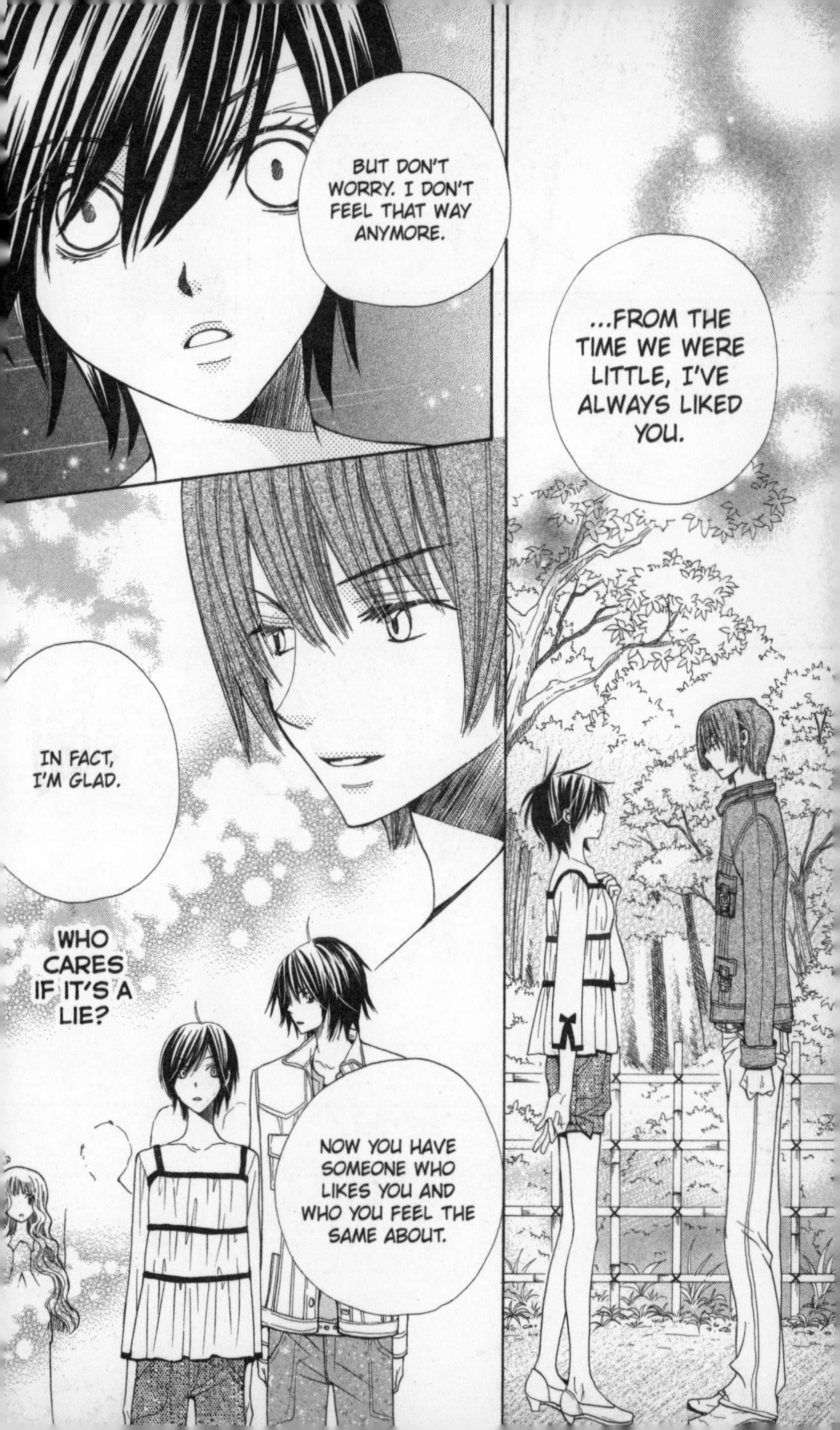
...FROM THE TIME WE WERE LITTLE, I'VE ALWAYS LIKED YOU.
BUT DON'T WORRY. I DON'T FEEL THAT WAY ANYMORE.
IN FACT, I'M GLAD.
NOW YOU HAVE SOMEONE WHO LIKES YOU AND WHO YOU FEEL THE SAME ABOUT.
WHO CARES IF IT'S A LIE?

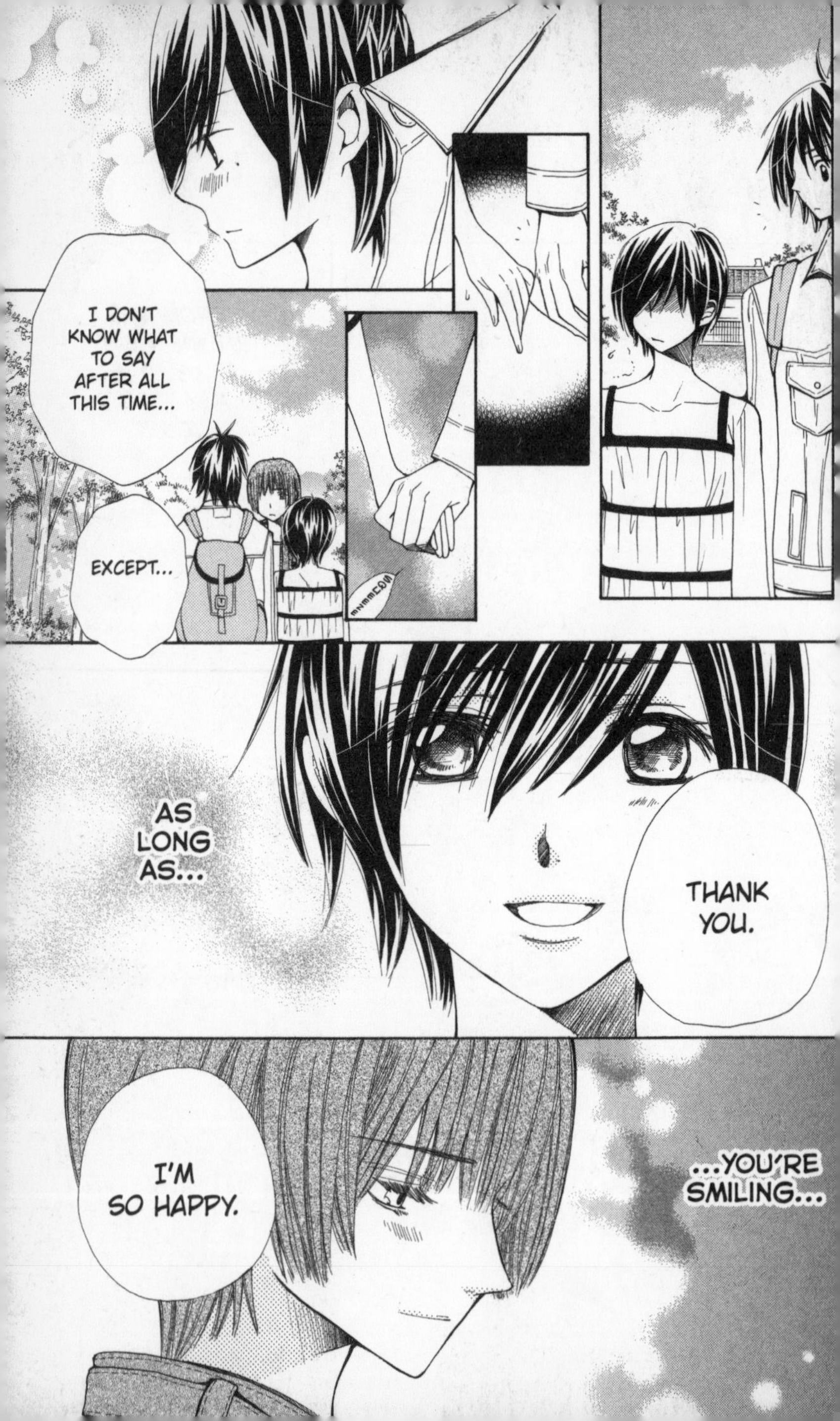
I DON'T KNOW WHAT TO SAY AFTER ALL THIS TIME...
EXCEPT...
THANK YOU.
AS LONG AS...
...YOU'RE SMILING...
I'M SO HAPPY.

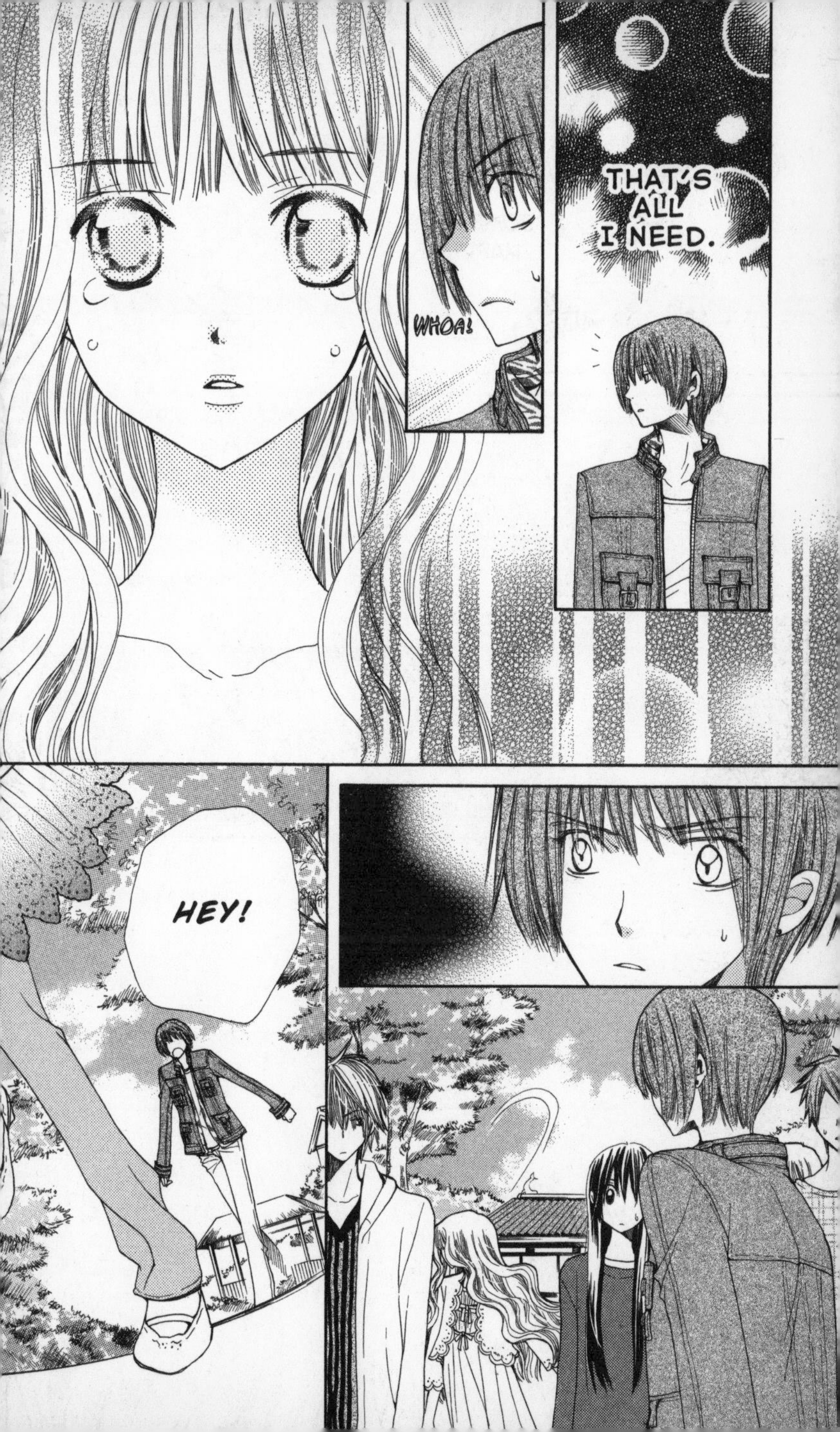
THAT'S ALL I NEED.
WHOA!
HEY!

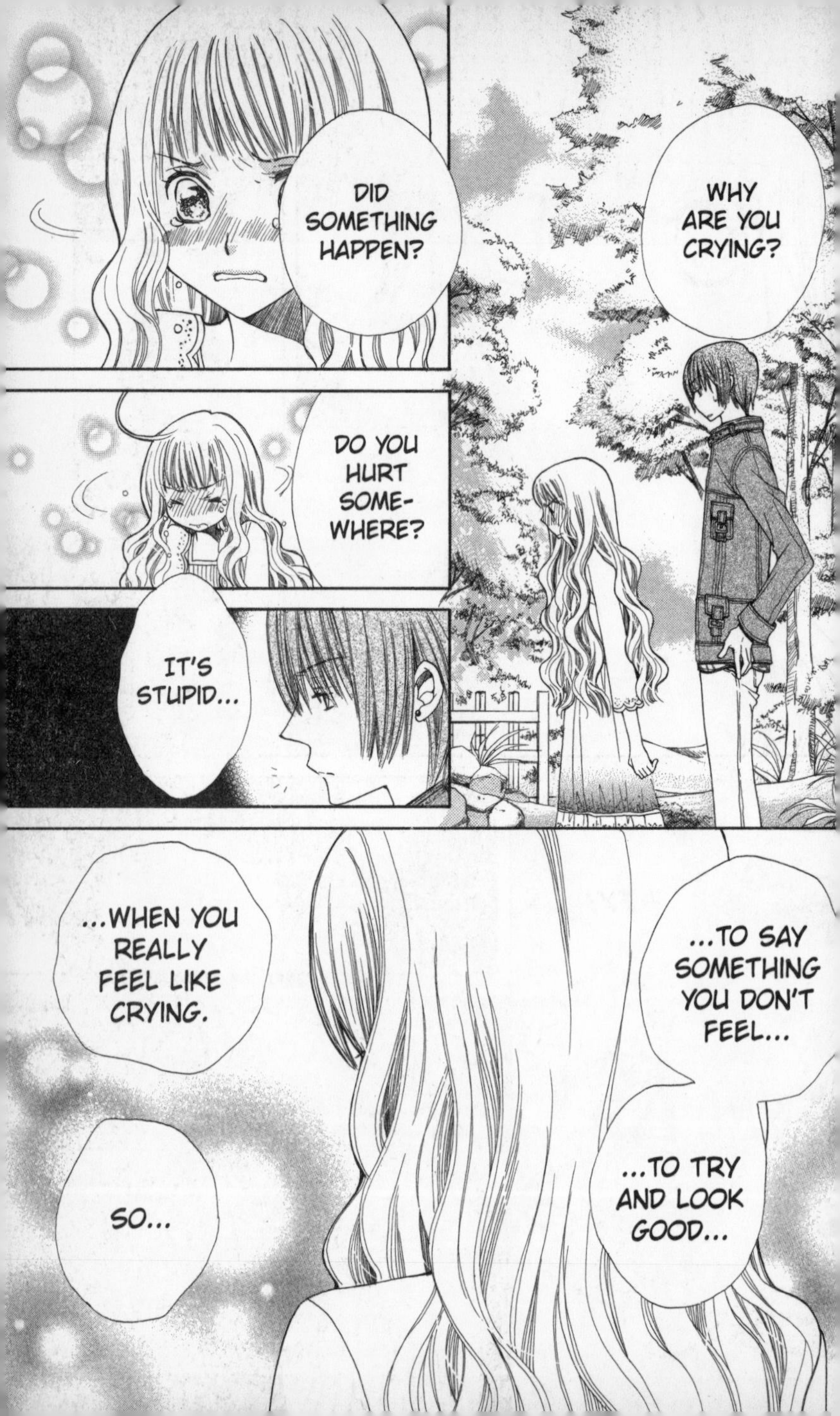
WHY ARE YOU CRYING?
DID SOMETHING HAPPEN?
DO YOU HURT SOME-WHERE?
IT'S STUPID...
...TO SAY SOMETHING YOU DON'T FEEL...
...TO TRY AND LOOK GOOD...
...WHEN YOU REALLY FEEL LIKE CRYING.
SO...

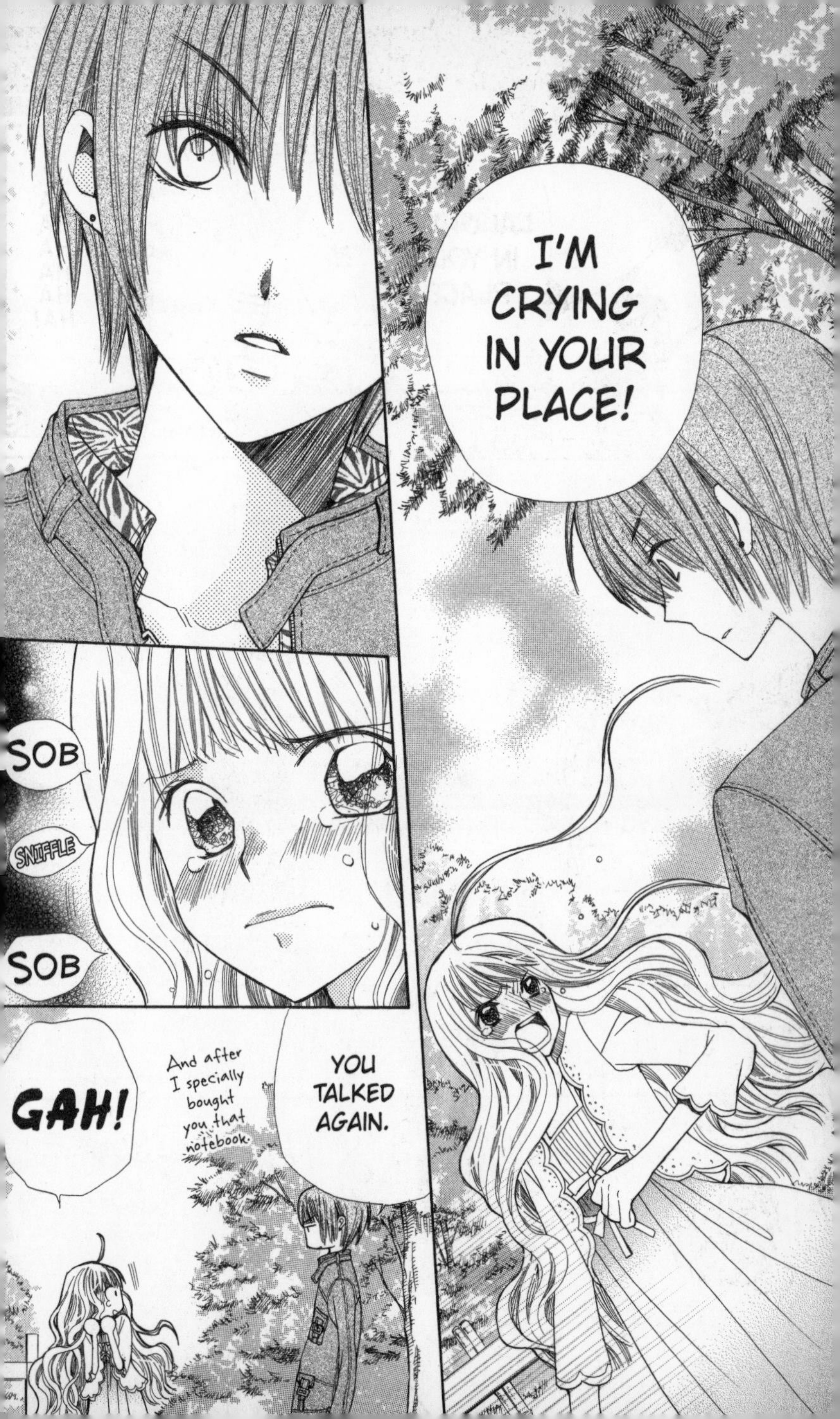
I'M CRYING IN YOUR PLACE!
SOB
SNIFFLE
SOB
YOU TALKED AGAIN.
And after I specially bought you that notebook.
GAH!

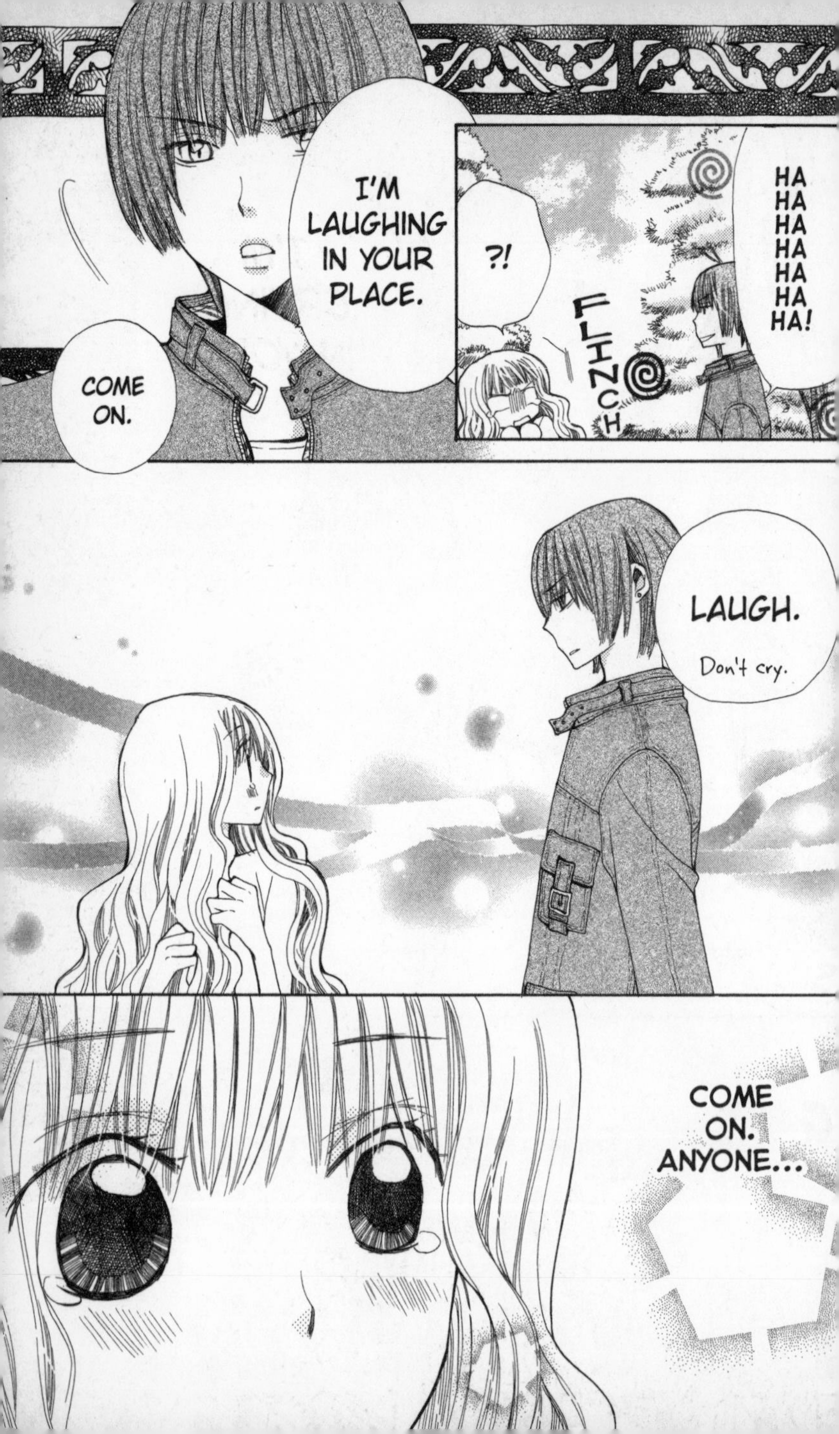
HA HA HA HA HA HA HA!
FLINCH
?!
I'M LAUGHING IN YOUR PLACE.
COME ON.
LAUGH.
Don't cry.
COME ON. ANYONE...

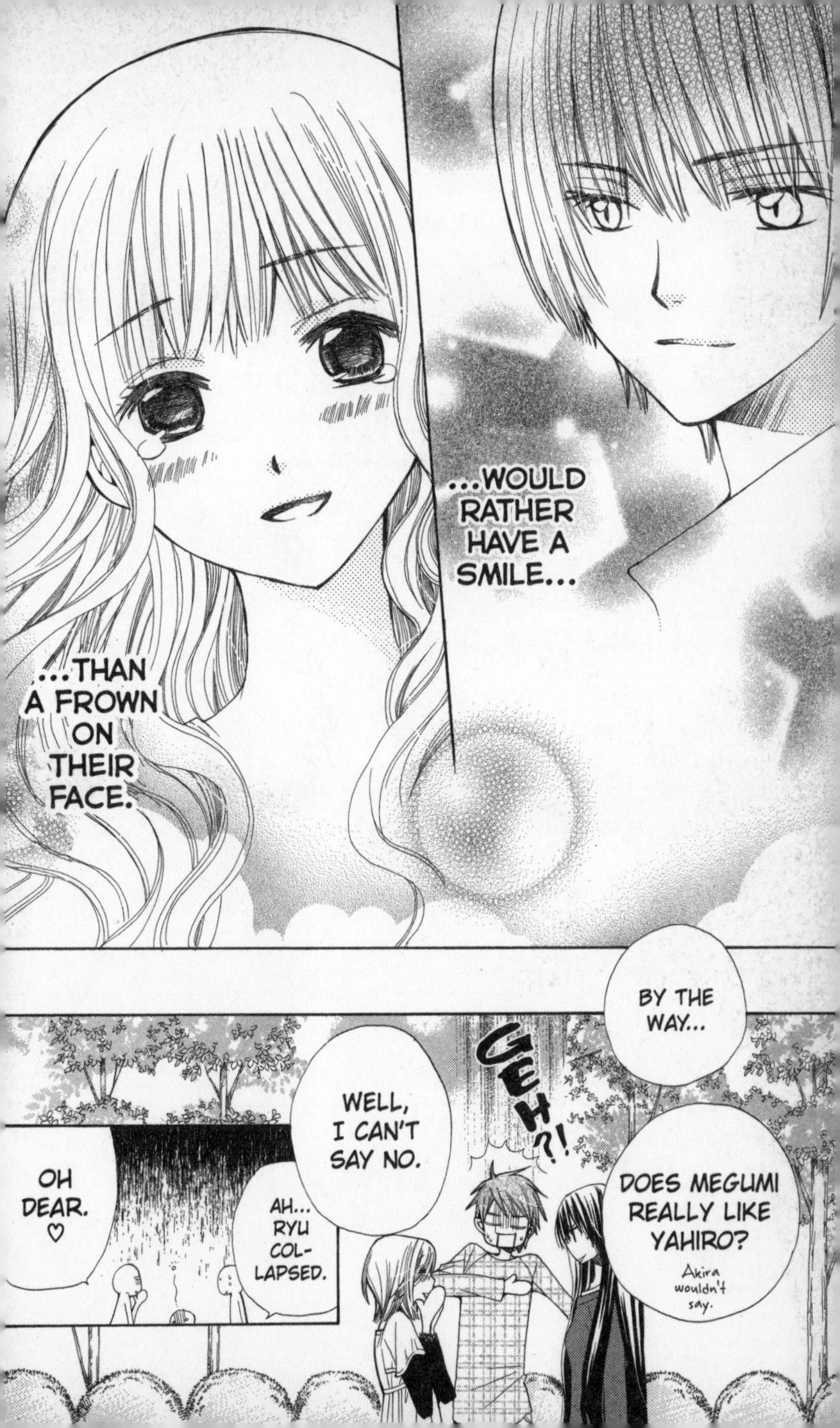
...WOULD RATHER HAVE A SMILE...
...THAN A FROWN ON THEIR FACE.
BY THE WAY...
GEH?!
DOES MEGUMI REALLY LIKE YAHIRO?
Akira wouldn't say.
WELL, I CAN'T SAY NO.
AH... RYU COL-LAPSED.
OH DEAR. ♡

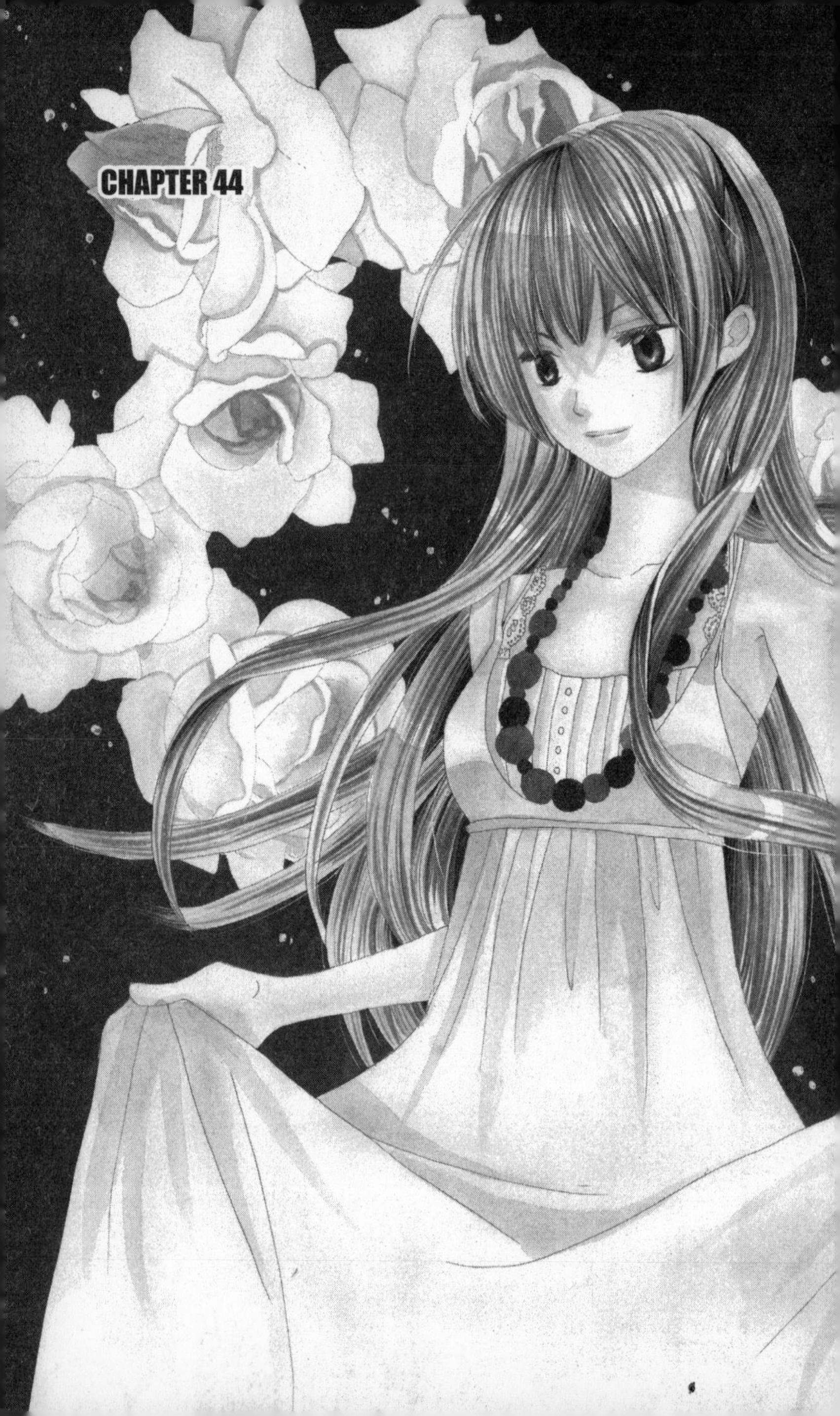
CHAPTER 44

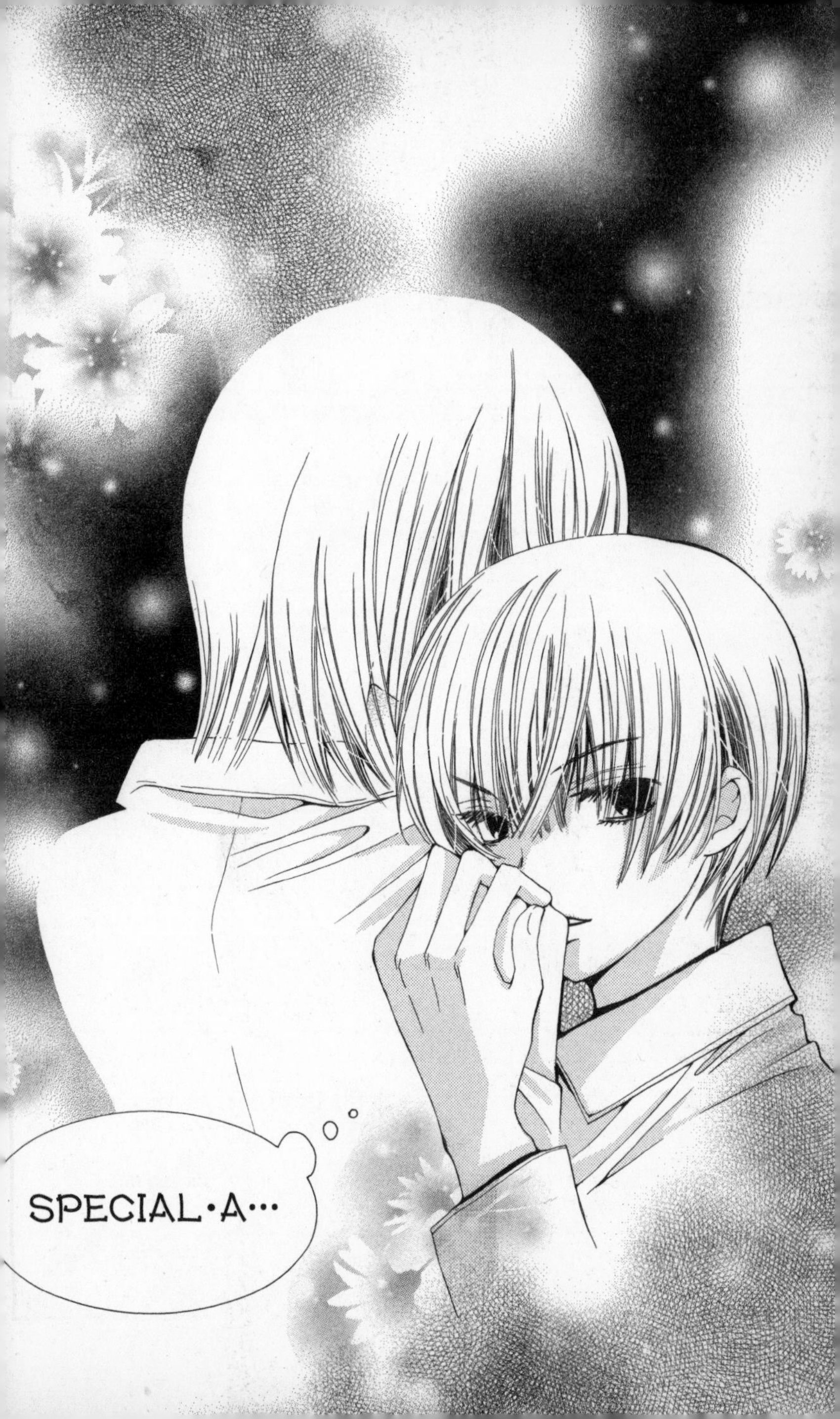
SPECIAL·A…

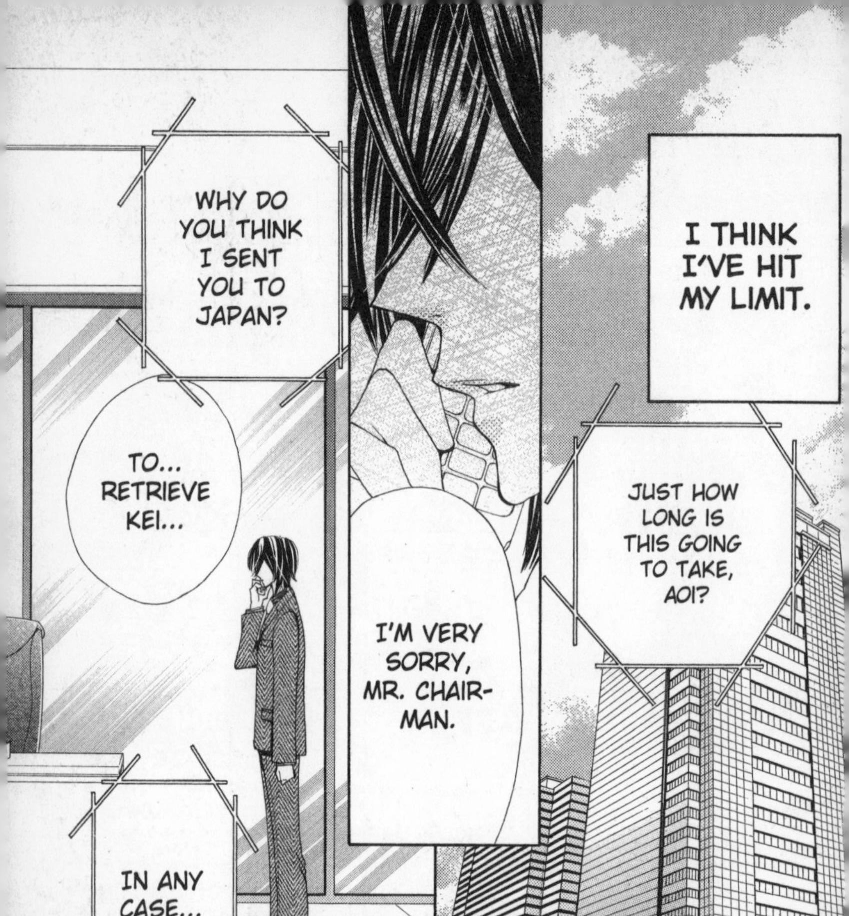
I THINK I'VE HIT MY LIMIT.
JUST HOW LONG IS THIS GOING TO TAKE, AOI?
I'M VERY SORRY, MR. CHAIR-MAN.
WHY DO YOU THINK I SENT YOU TO JAPAN?
TO... RETRIEVE KEI...
IN ANY CASE...

•BACKGROUNDS•

THE BEAUTIFUL BACKGROUNDS THAT ENHANCE THESE COMICS ARE DRAWN BY MY ASSISTANTS. I'M TREMENDOUSLY GRATEFUL FOR THE WAY THEY DRAW THE MINUTE DETAILS OF PLACES THAT MANY TIMES WON'T EVEN BE SHOWN. I THINK SOMEDAY I'LL INCLUDE THOSE SECTIONS IN THE BONUS PAGES.

AFTER ALL, IT WOULD BE A WASTE TO NEVER SHOW THEM! THANK YOU FOR ALL YOUR HARD WORK! IF YOU WEREN'T HERE, I WOULD NEVER BE ABLE TO FINISH PRODUCTION! BOW
AND TO ALL OF YOU WHO LOOK AT THE ART: BOW
THANK YOU VERY MUCH TOO!

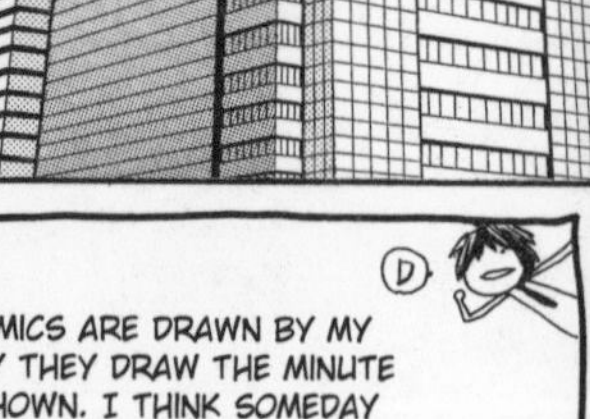
"SOME TOWN"...?
SORRY MY SPECIFICA-TIONS ARE ALWAYS SO VAGUE.
SOME TOWN
...

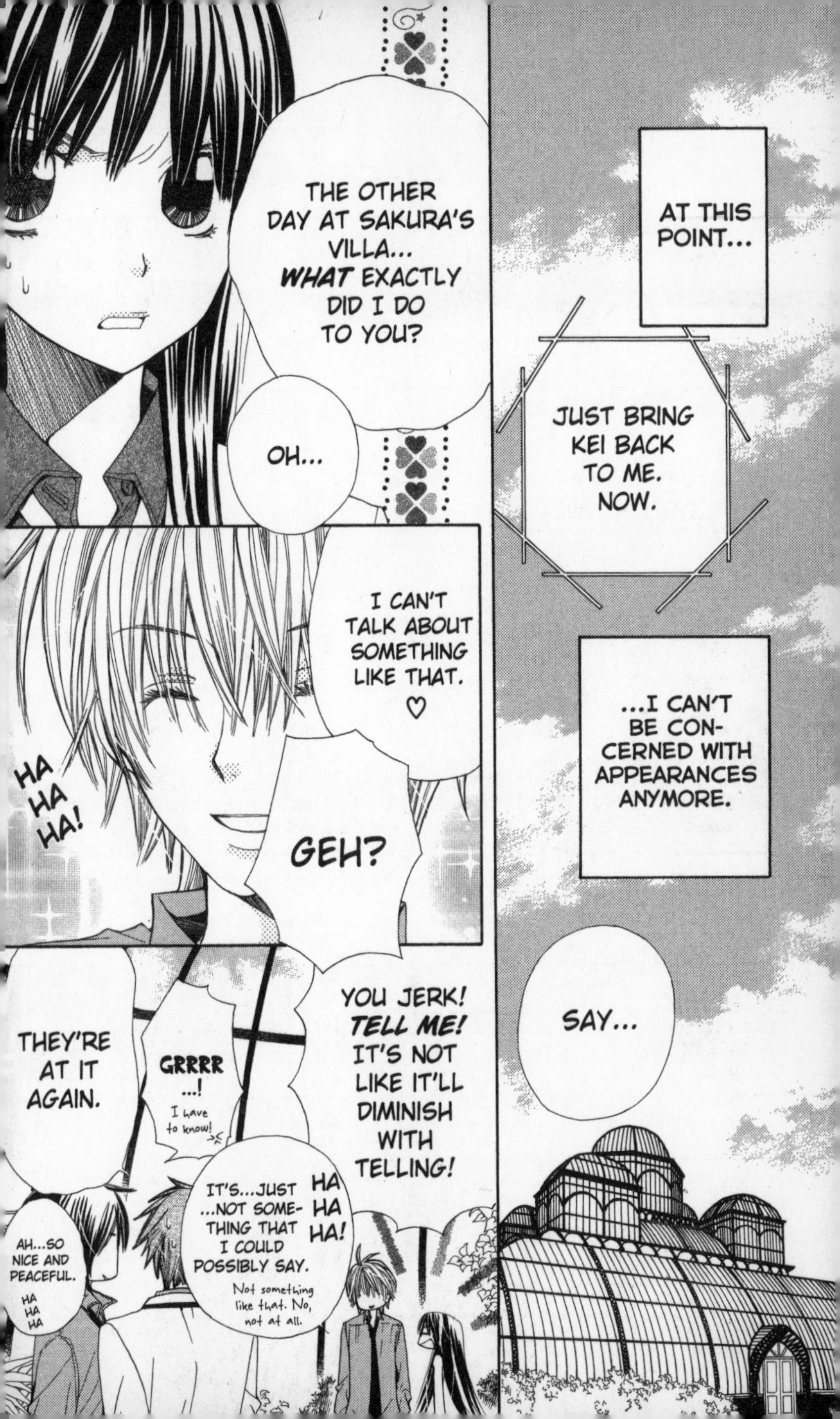
AT THIS POINT...
JUST BRING KEI BACK TO ME. NOW.
...I CAN'T BE CONCERNED WITH APPEARANCES ANYMORE.
SAY...
THE OTHER DAY AT SAKURA'S VILLA... *WHAT* EXACTLY DID I DO TO YOU?
OH...
I CAN'T TALK ABOUT SOMETHING LIKE THAT. ♡
GEH?
HA HA HA!
YOU JERK! *TELL ME!* IT'S NOT LIKE IT'LL DIMINISH WITH TELLING!
GRRRR ...!
I have to know!
IT'S...JUST ...NOT SOMETHING THAT I COULD POSSIBLY SAY.
HA HA HA!
Not something like that. No, not at all.
THEY'RE AT IT AGAIN.
AH...SO NICE AND PEACEFUL.
HA HA HA

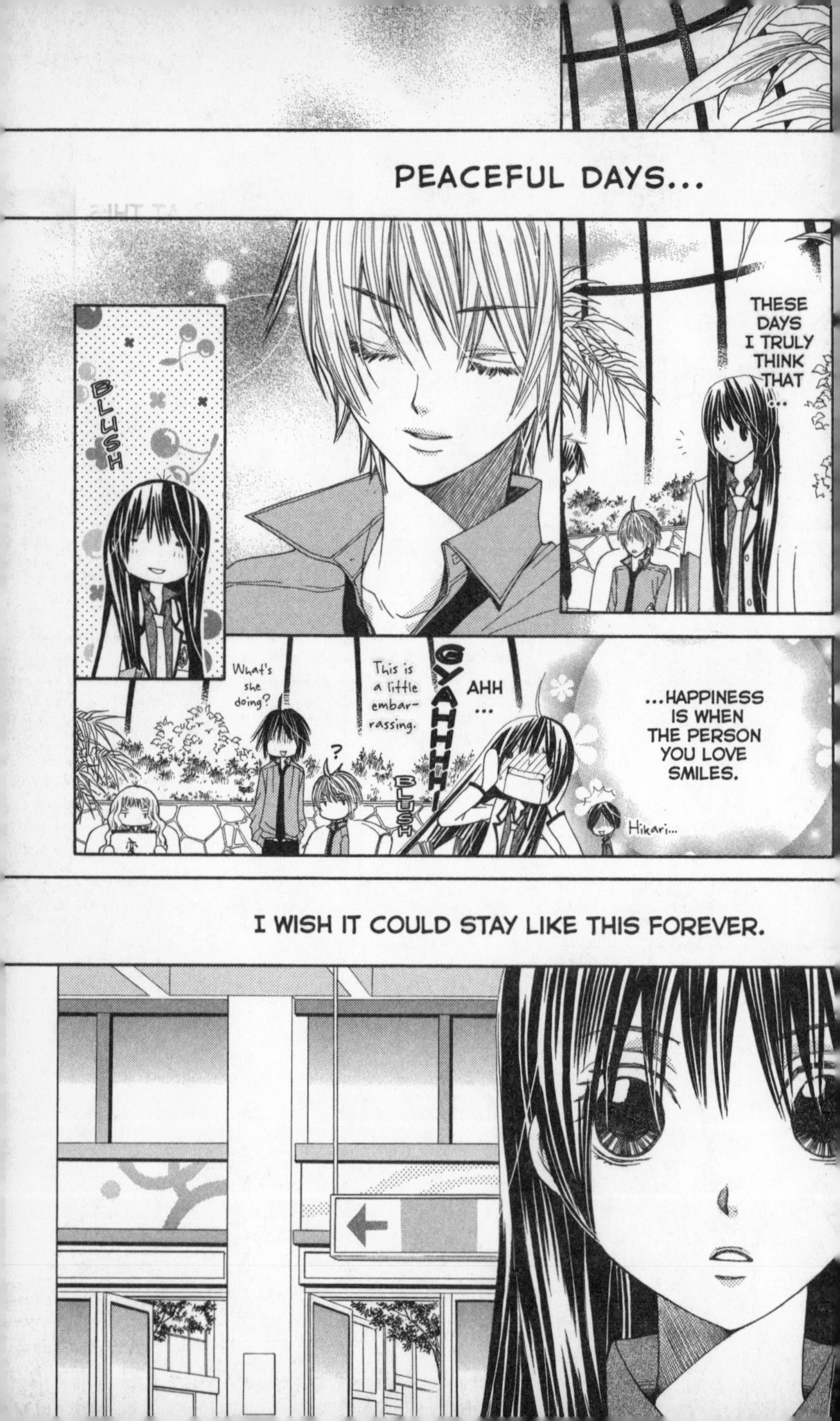
PEACEFUL DAYS...
THESE DAYS I TRULY THINK THAT...
BLUSH
...HAPPINESS IS WHEN THE PERSON YOU LOVE SMILES.
Hikari...
AHH...
GYAHHH!
BLUSH
This is a little embarrassing.
?
What's she doing?
I WISH IT COULD STAY LIKE THIS FOREVER.

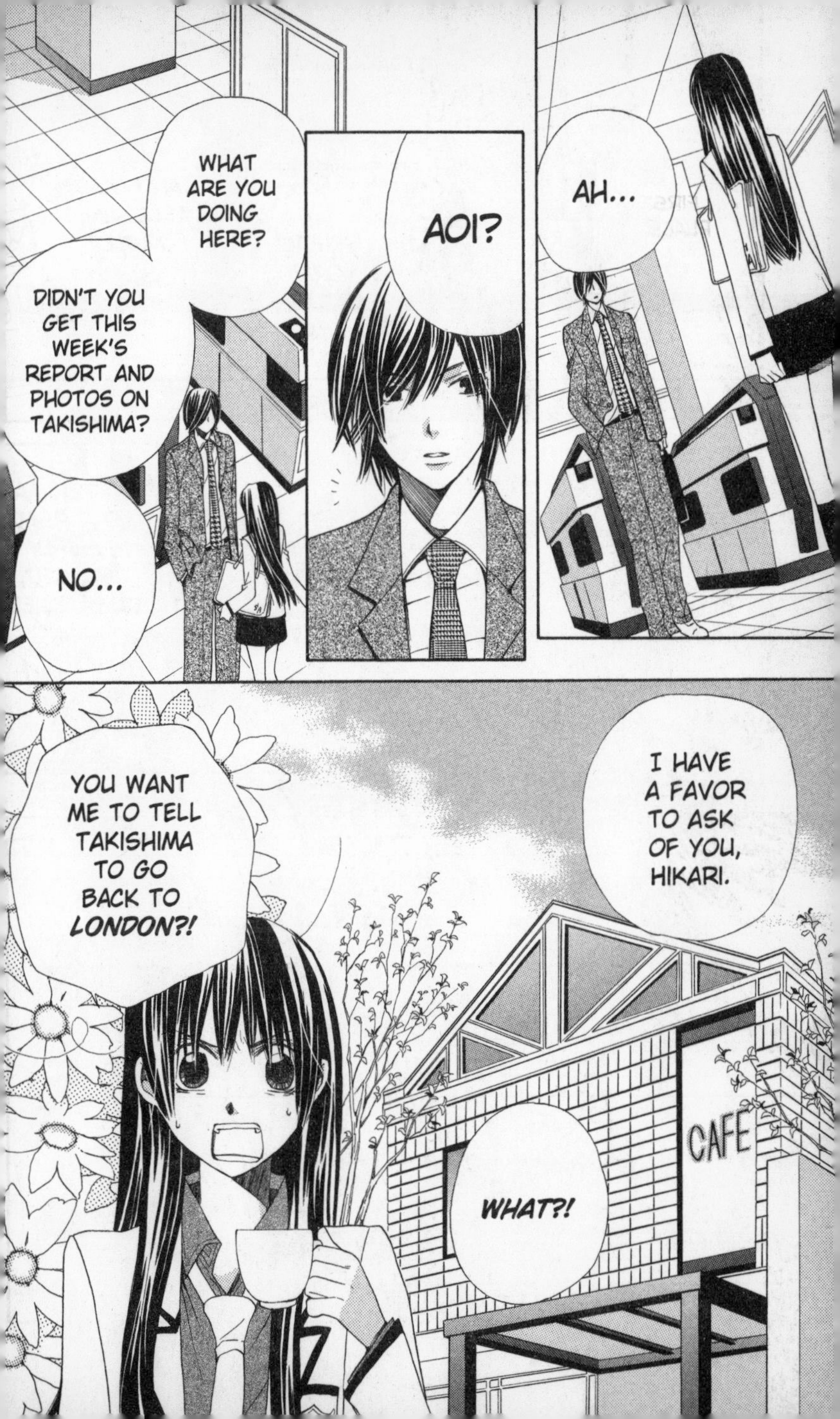
AH...
AOI?
WHAT ARE YOU DOING HERE?
DIDN'T YOU GET THIS WEEK'S REPORT AND PHOTOS ON TAKISHIMA?
NO...
I HAVE A FAVOR TO ASK OF YOU, HIKARI.
YOU WANT ME TO TELL TAKISHIMA TO GO BACK TO *LONDON?!*
CAFE
WHAT?!

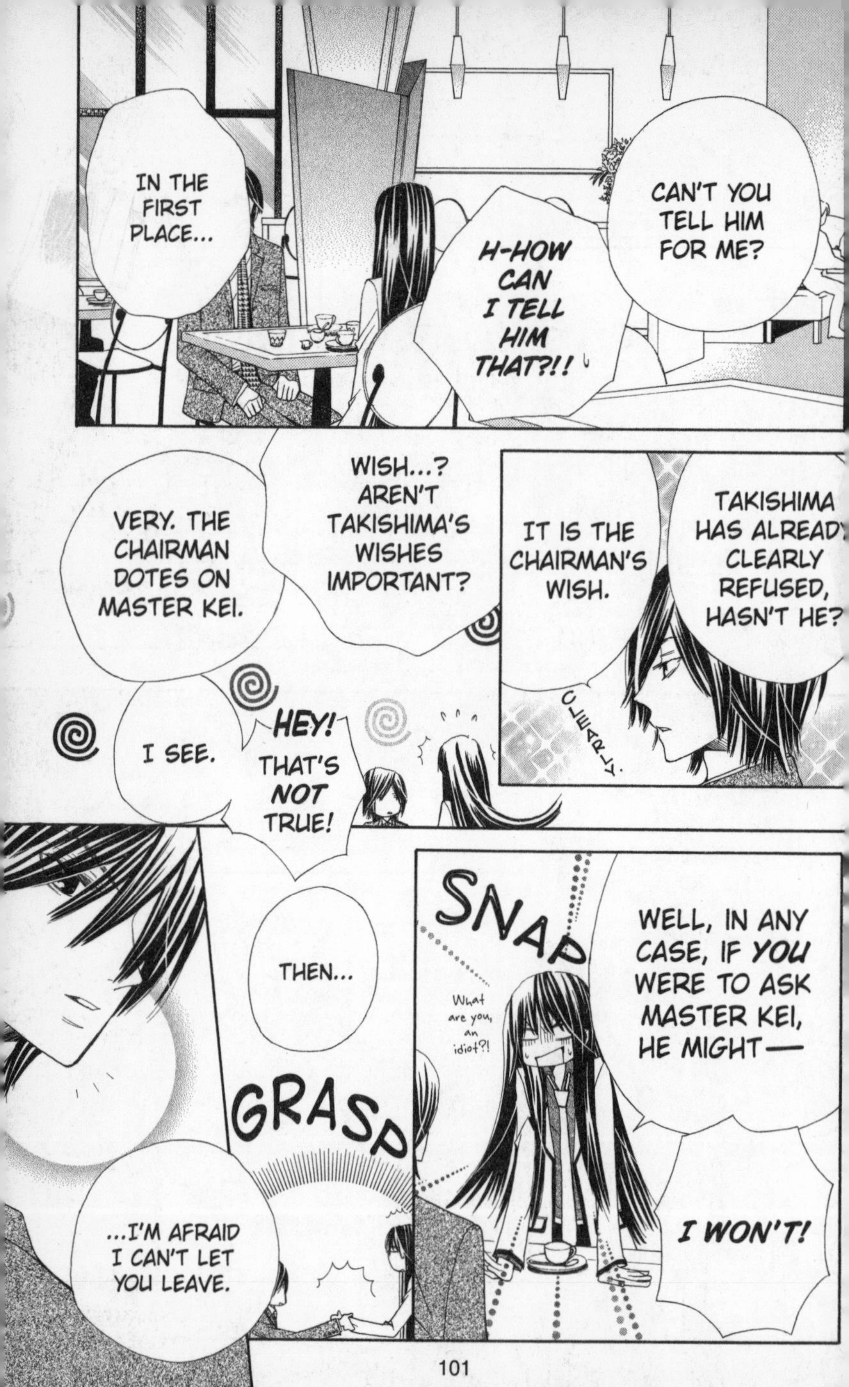

CAN'T YOU TELL HIM FOR ME?
H-HOW CAN I TELL HIM THAT?!!
IN THE FIRST PLACE...
TAKISHIMA HAS ALREADY CLEARLY REFUSED, HASN'T HE?
CLEARLY
IT IS THE CHAIRMAN'S WISH.
WISH...? AREN'T TAKISHIMA'S WISHES IMPORTANT?
VERY. THE CHAIRMAN DOTES ON MASTER KEI.
HEY! THAT'S NOT TRUE!
I SEE.
WELL, IN ANY CASE, IF YOU WERE TO ASK MASTER KEI, HE MIGHT—
SNAP
What are you, an idiot?!
I WON'T!
THEN...
GRASP
...I'M AFRAID I CAN'T LET YOU LEAVE.

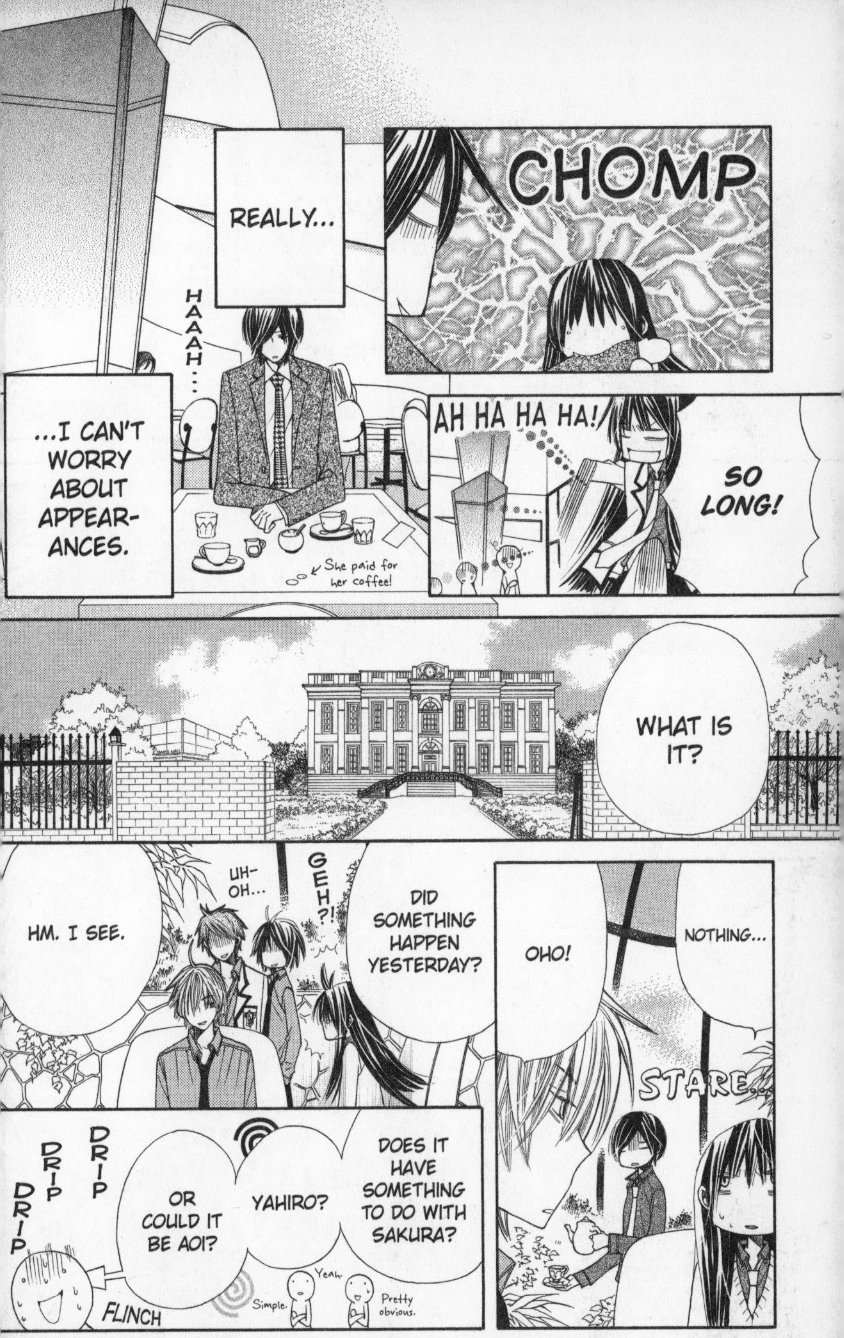
CHOMP
SO LONG!
AH HA HA HA!
REALLY...
HAAAH...
...I CAN'T WORRY ABOUT APPEARANCES.
She paid for her coffee!
WHAT IS IT?
NOTHING...
OHO!
STARE...
DID SOMETHING HAPPEN YESTERDAY?
GEH?!
UH-OH...
HM. I SEE.
DOES IT HAVE SOMETHING TO DO WITH SAKURA?
YAHIRO?
OR COULD IT BE AOI?
DRIP DRIP DRIP
FLINCH
Pretty obvious.
Yeah.
Simple.

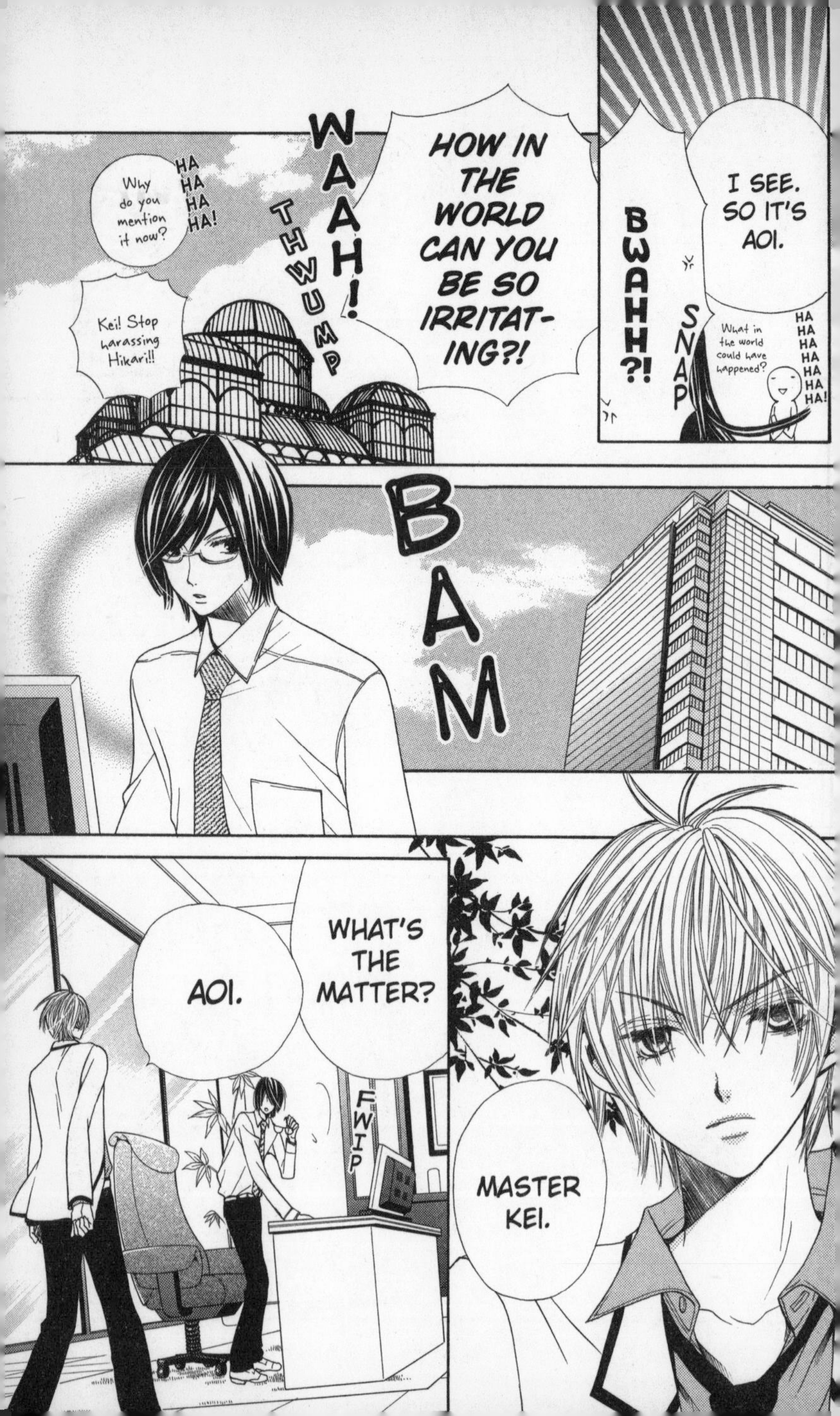
I SEE. SO IT'S AOI.
BWAHH?!
SNAP
What in the world could have happened?
HA HA HA HA HA HA HA!
HOW IN THE WORLD CAN YOU BE SO IRRITAT-ING?!
WAAH!
THWUMP
Why do you mention it now?
HA HA HA HA!
Kei! Stop harassing Hikari!!
BAM
MASTER KEI.
WHAT'S THE MATTER?
AOI.
FWIP

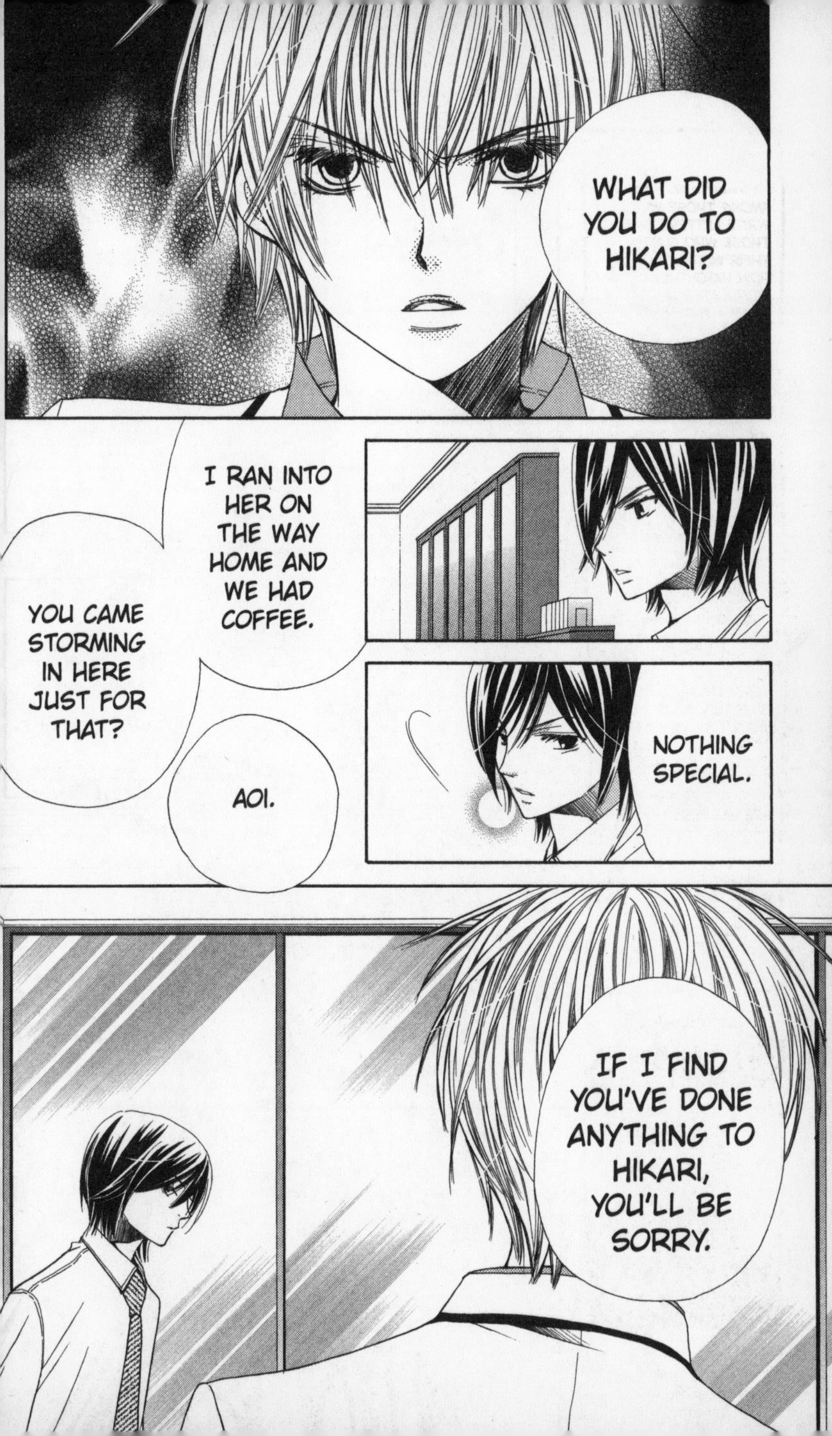
WHAT DID YOU DO TO HIKARI?
NOTHING SPECIAL.
I RAN INTO HER ON THE WAY HOME AND WE HAD COFFEE.
YOU CAME STORMING IN HERE JUST FOR THAT?
AOI.
IF I FIND YOU'VE DONE ANYTHING TO HIKARI, YOU'LL BE SORRY.

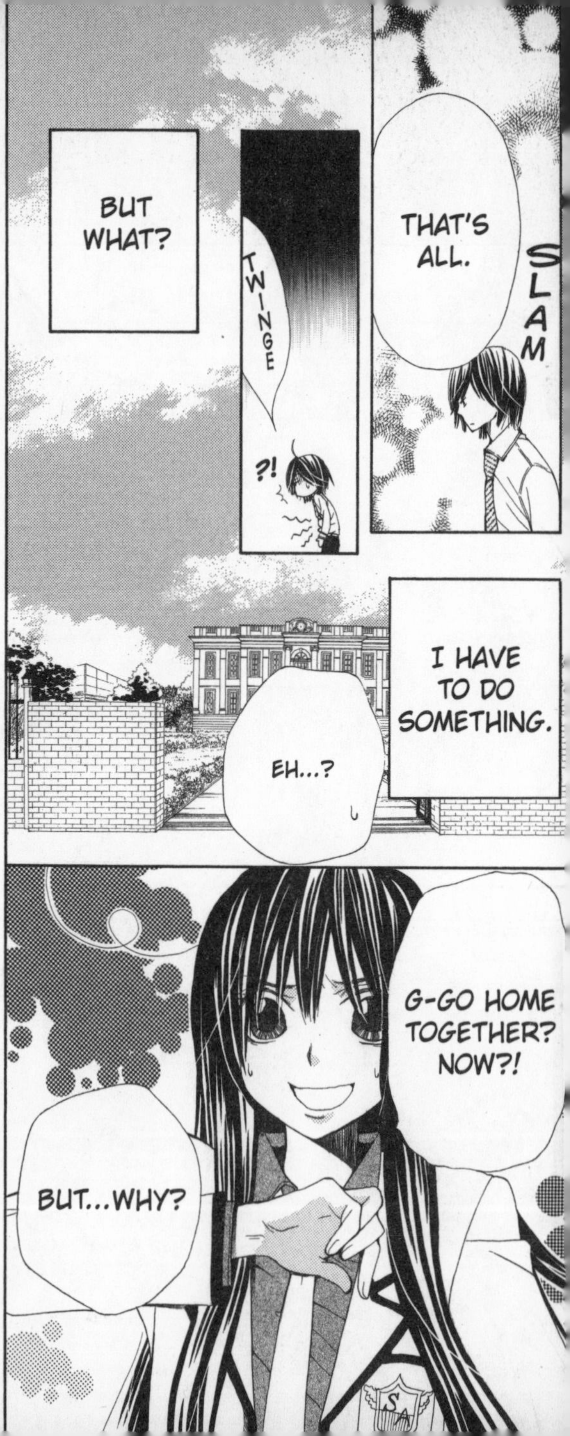
THAT'S ALL.
SLAM
TWINGE
?!
BUT WHAT?
I HAVE TO DO SOMETHING.
EH...?
G-GO HOME TOGETHER? NOW?!
BUT...WHY?

4

• SUBMISSIONS •

AMONG THOSE WHO WRITE LETTERS ARE THOSE WHO SUBMIT THEIR WORK. SEEING HOW HARD THEY WORK STIMULATES *ME* TO WORK HARDER, AND MAKES ME WONDER WHAT I CAN GIVE THEM IN RETURN. BUT I HAVE NOTHING DECENT, SO INSTEAD I WILL TELL YOU ABOUT MY OWN EXPERIENCES SUBMITTING WORK...

(WHAT? YOU DON'T WANT TO HEAR IT?!)

- 6 PROPOSALS
- 11 SUBMISSIONS

I THINK THOSE WERE THE NUMBERS. I WAS ROUTINELY REJECTED.

THE FIRST TIME A CUT WAS PUBLISHED, I WAS SO HAPPY, I CUT IT OUT AND PUT IT IN MY CLEAR PLASTIC COMMUTER PASS HOLDER SO I WOULD ALWAYS SEE IT. I THINK IT WAS FOURTH PLACE IN HMC. I THOUGHT I WAS HAVING A BLISSFUL DREAM...YES...

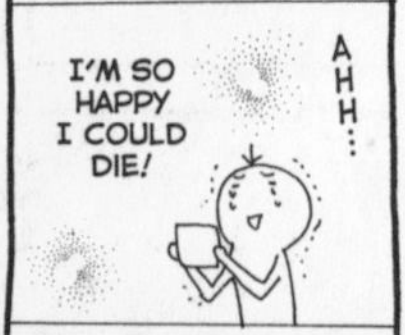
I'M SO HAPPY I COULD DIE!
AHH...

CONTINUED IN (5) →

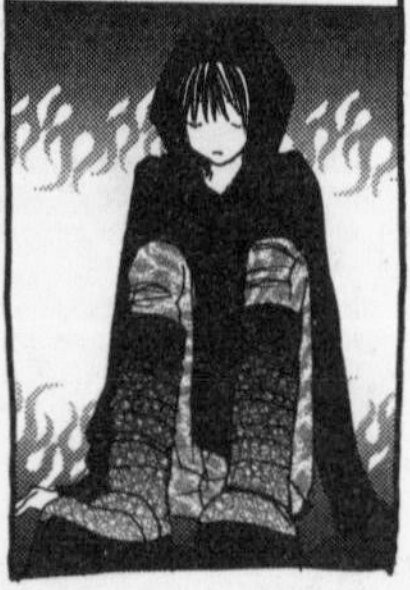

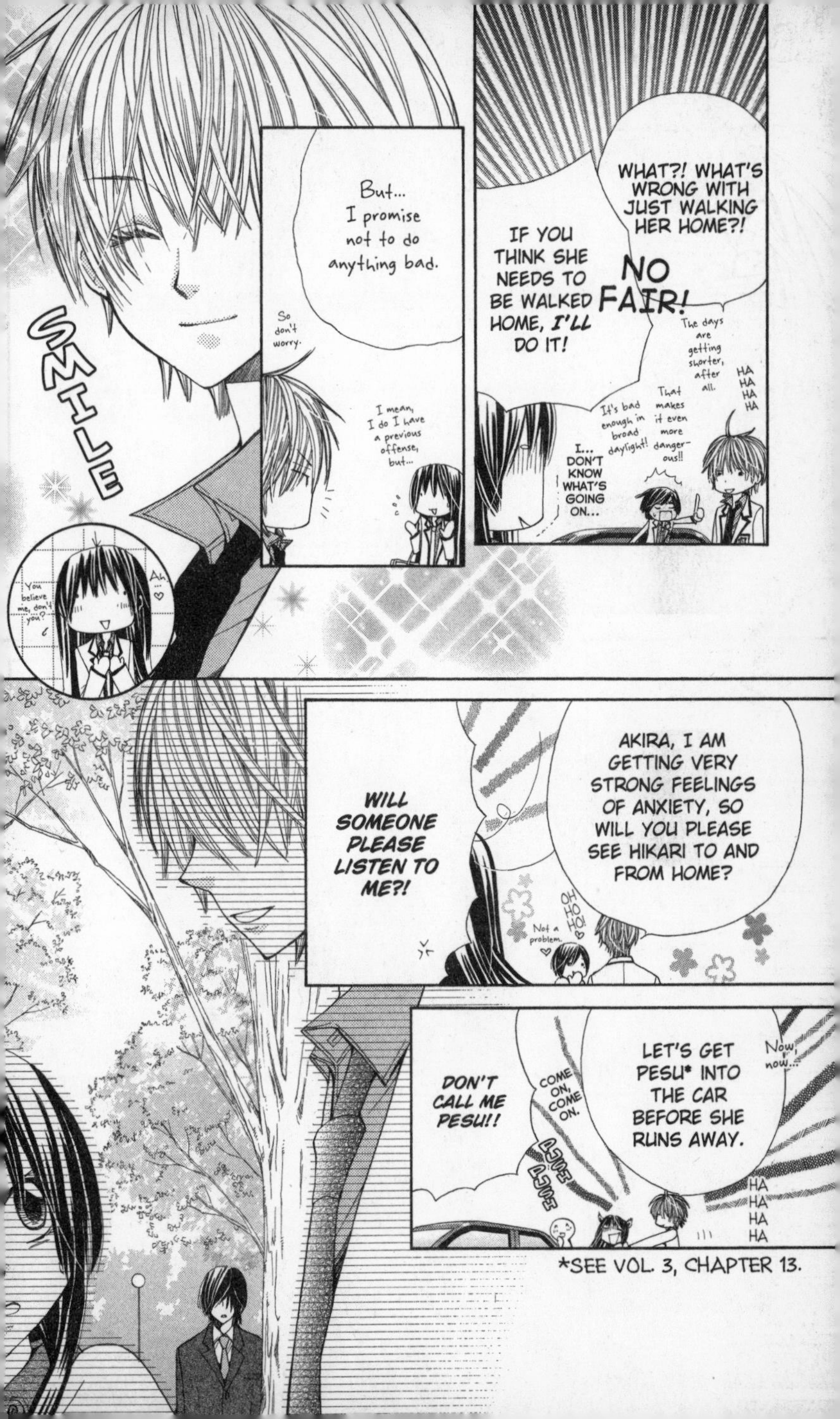
WHAT?! WHAT'S WRONG WITH JUST WALKING HER HOME?!
NO FAIR!
IF YOU THINK SHE NEEDS TO BE WALKED HOME, I'LL DO IT!
The days are getting shorter, after all.
HA HA HA HA
That makes it even more danger-ous!!
It's bad enough in broad daylight!
I... DON'T KNOW WHAT'S GOING ON...
But... I promise not to do anything bad.
So don't worry.
I mean, I do I have a previous offense, but...
SMILE
Ah... ♡
You believe me, don't you?
AKIRA, I AM GETTING VERY STRONG FEELINGS OF ANXIETY, SO WILL YOU PLEASE SEE HIKARI TO AND FROM HOME?
OH HO HO!
Not a problem. ♡
WILL SOMEONE PLEASE LISTEN TO ME?!
Now, now...
LET'S GET PESU* INTO THE CAR BEFORE SHE RUNS AWAY.
HA HA HA HA
COME ON, COME ON.
DON'T CALL ME PESU!!

*SEE VOL. 3, CHAPTER 13.

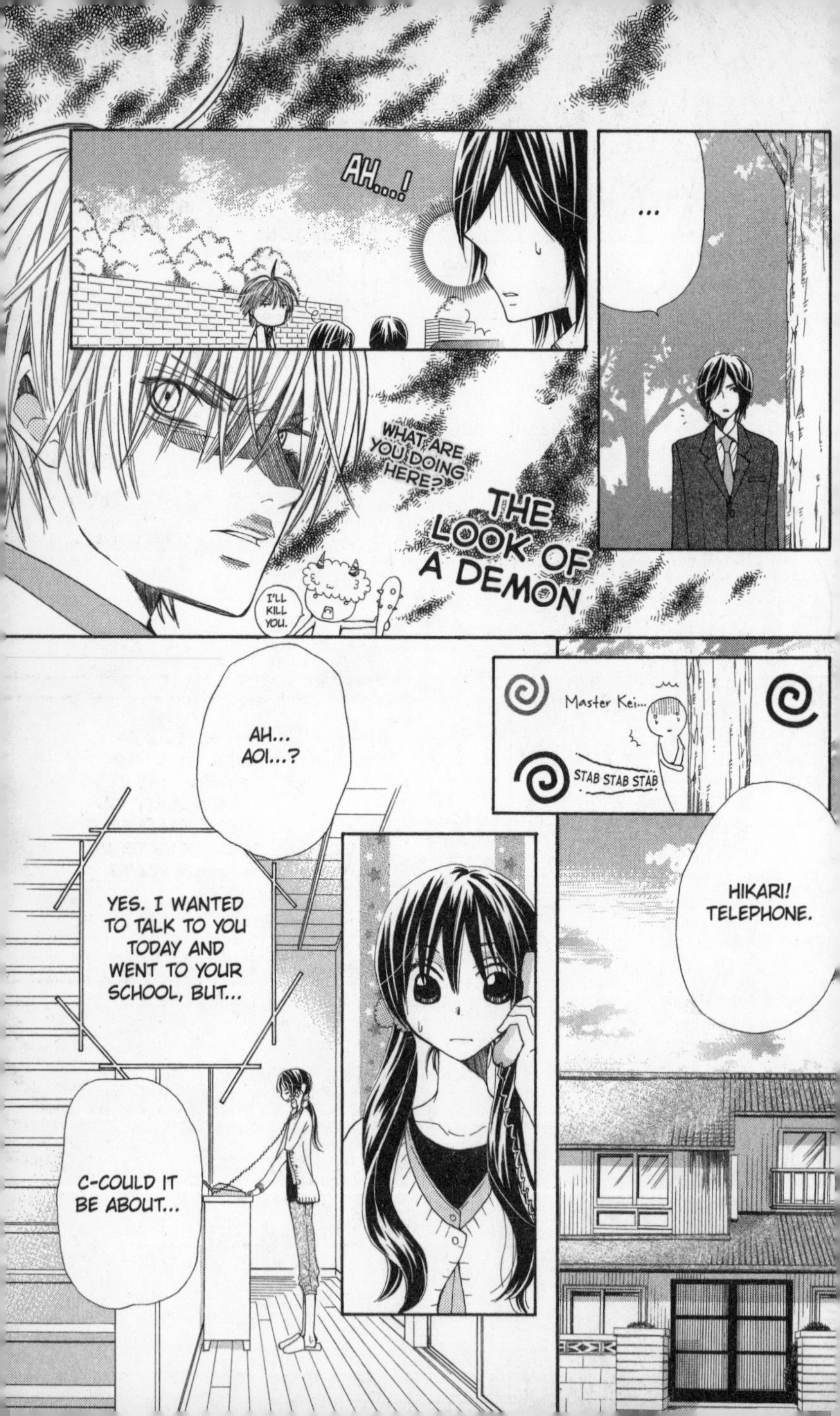
...
AH...!
WHAT ARE YOU DOING HERE?
THE LOOK OF A DEMON
I'LL KILL YOU.
Master Kei...
STAB STAB STAB
HIKARI! TELEPHONE.
AH... AOI...?
YES. I WANTED TO TALK TO YOU TODAY AND WENT TO YOUR SCHOOL, BUT...
C-COULD IT BE ABOUT...

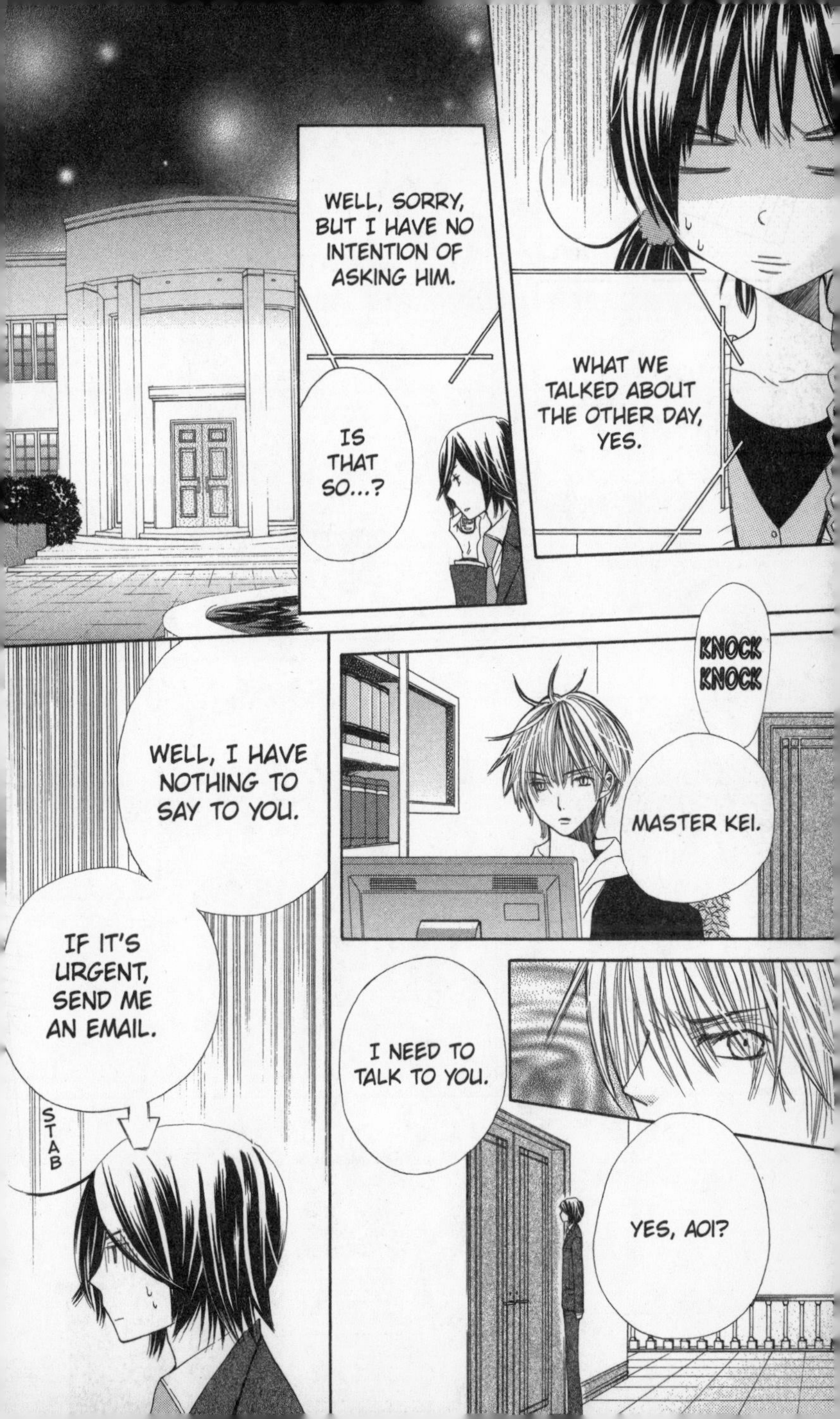
WHAT WE TALKED ABOUT THE OTHER DAY, YES.
WELL, SORRY, BUT I HAVE NO INTENTION OF ASKING HIM.
IS THAT SO...?
KNOCK KNOCK
MASTER KEI.
YES, AOI?
I NEED TO TALK TO YOU.
WELL, I HAVE NOTHING TO SAY TO YOU.
IF IT'S URGENT, SEND ME AN EMAIL.
STAB

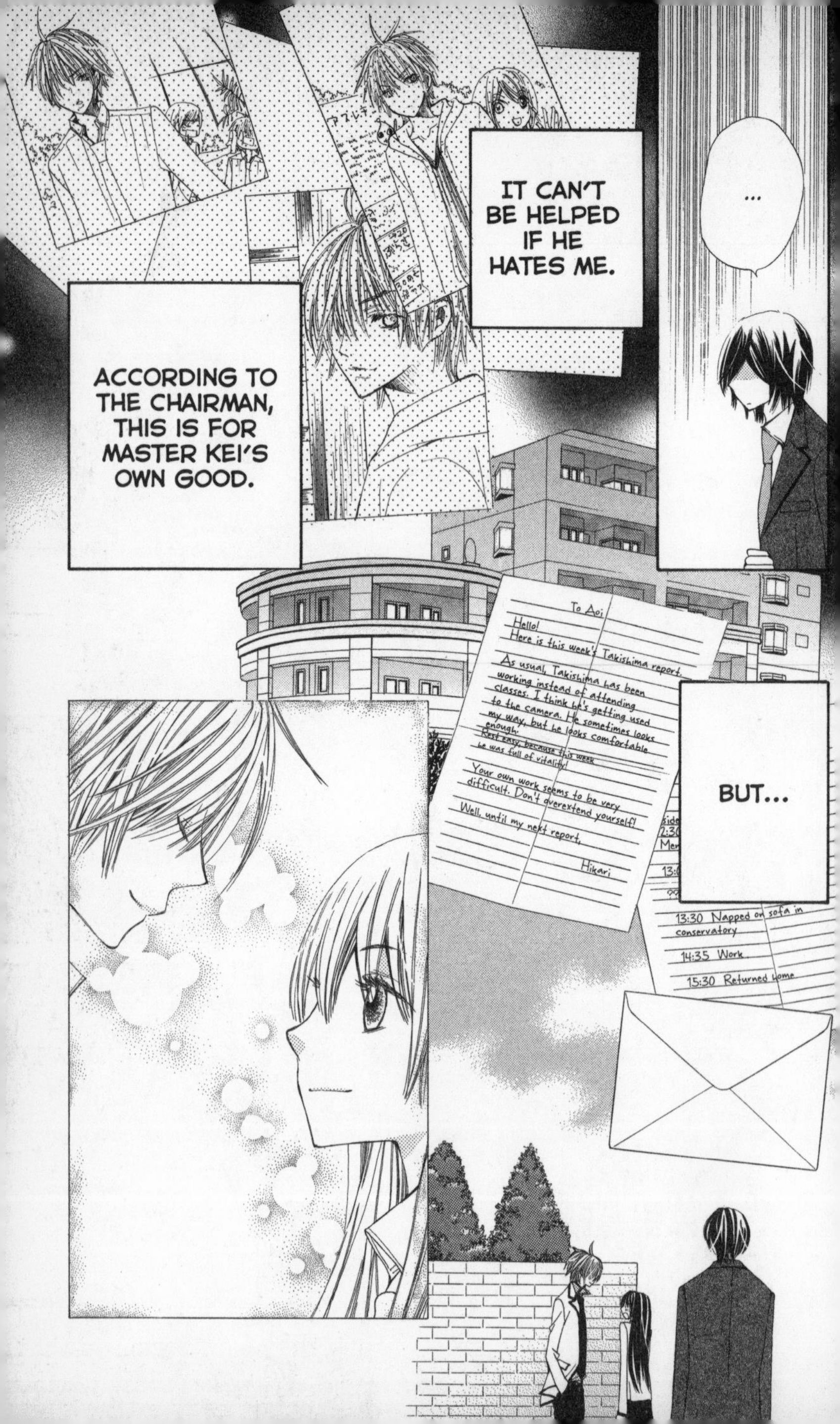
...
IT CAN'T BE HELPED IF HE HATES ME.
ACCORDING TO THE CHAIRMAN, THIS IS FOR MASTER KEI'S OWN GOOD.
BUT...
To Aoi
Hello!
Here is this week's Takishima report.
As usual, Takishima has been working instead of attending classes. I think he's getting used to the camera. He sometimes looks my way, but he looks comfortable enough.
Rest easy, because this week he was full of vitality!
Your own work seems to be very difficult. Don't overextend yourself!
Well, until my next report,
Hikari
13:30 Napped on sofa in conservatory
14:35 Work
15:30 Returned home

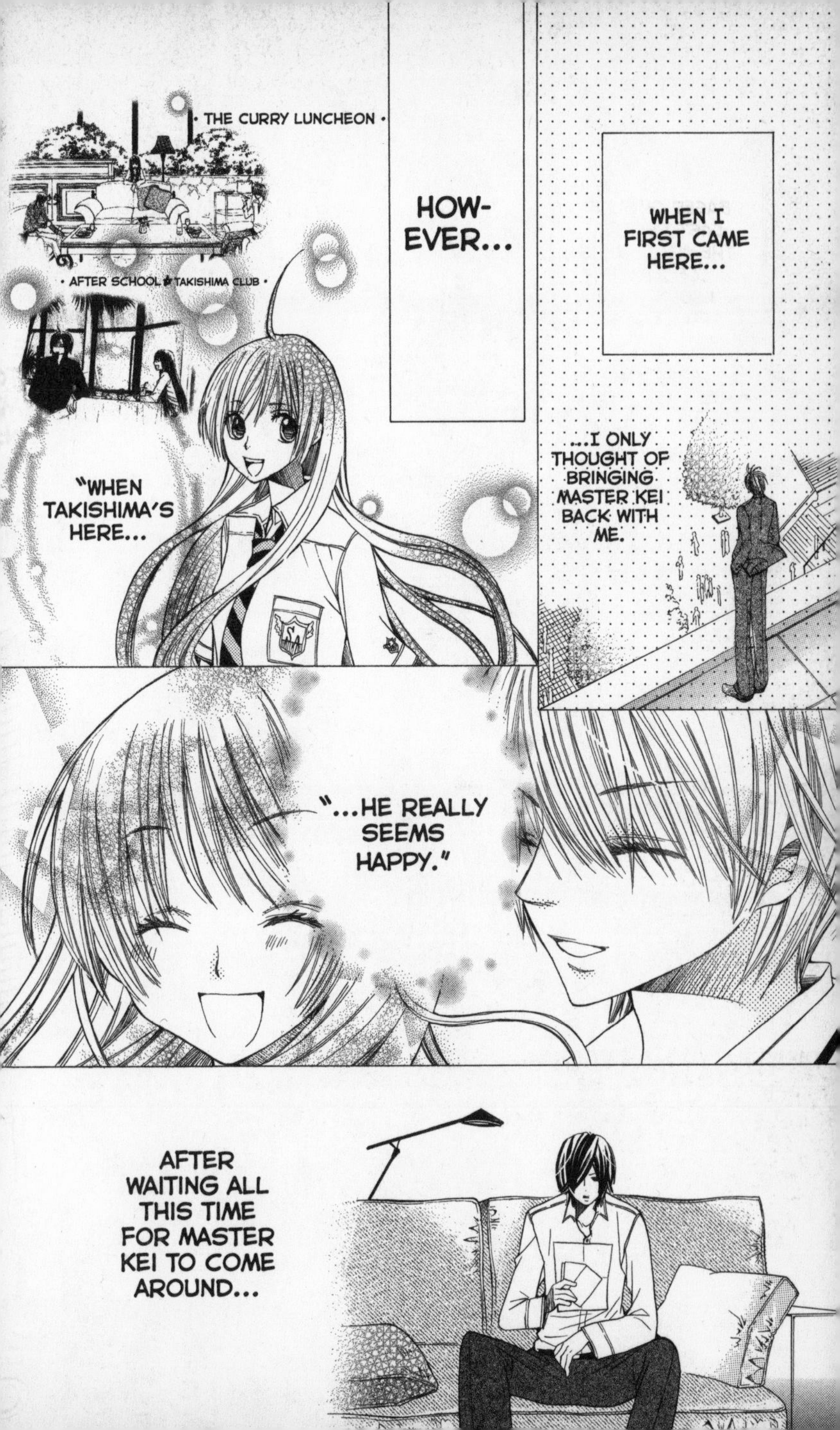
WHEN I FIRST CAME HERE...
...I ONLY THOUGHT OF BRINGING MASTER KEI BACK WITH ME.
HOW-EVER...
• THE CURRY LUNCHEON •
• AFTER SCHOOL & TAKISHIMA CLUB •
"WHEN TAKISHIMA'S HERE...
"...HE REALLY SEEMS HAPPY."
AFTER WAITING ALL THIS TIME FOR MASTER KEI TO COME AROUND...

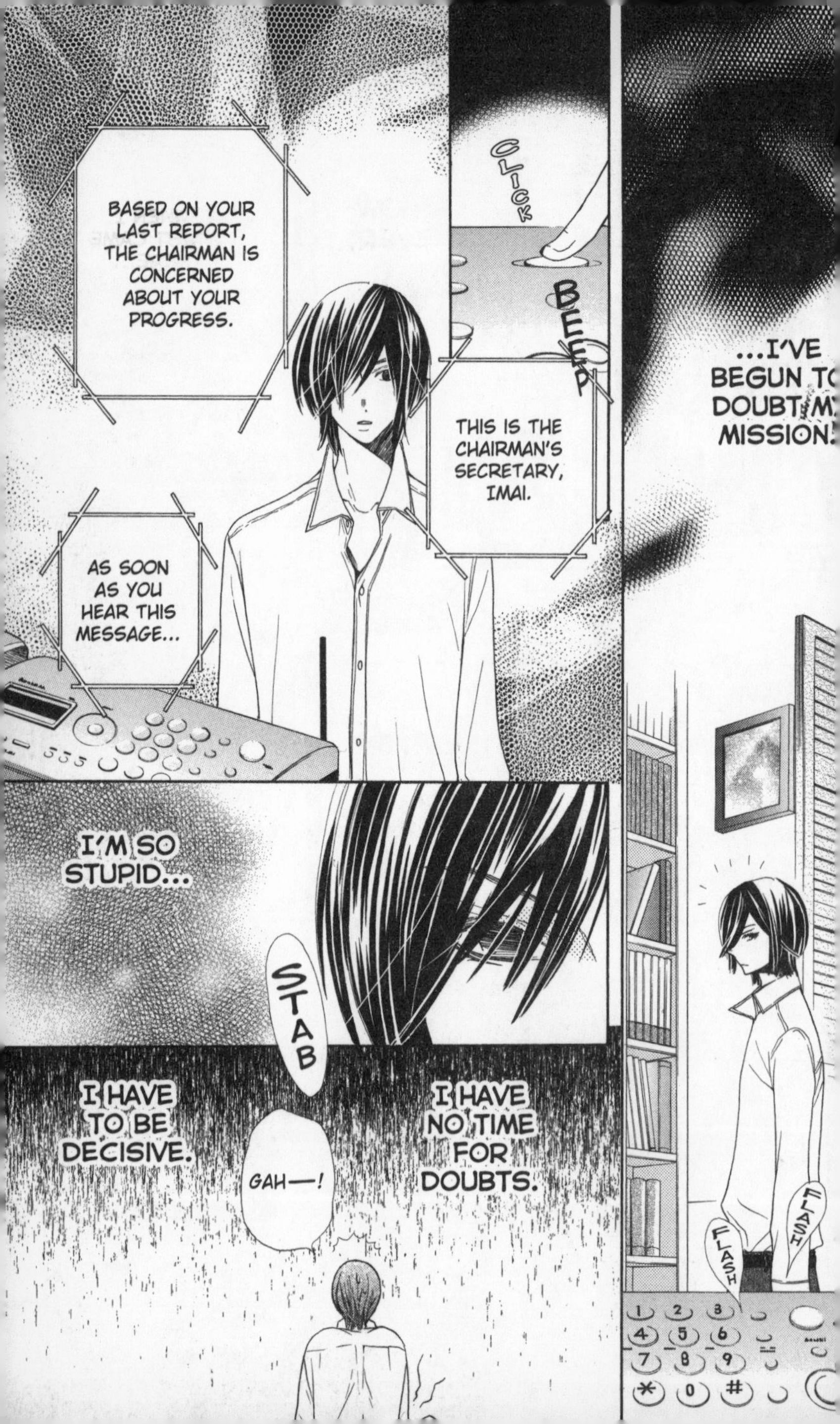

...I'VE BEGUN TO DOUBT MY MISSION.
FLASH
FLASH
CLICK
BEEP
THIS IS THE CHAIRMAN'S SECRETARY, IMAI.
BASED ON YOUR LAST REPORT, THE CHAIRMAN IS CONCERNED ABOUT YOUR PROGRESS.
AS SOON AS YOU HEAR THIS MESSAGE...
I'M SO STUPID...
STAB
I HAVE NO TIME FOR DOUBTS.
GAH—!
I HAVE TO BE DECISIVE.

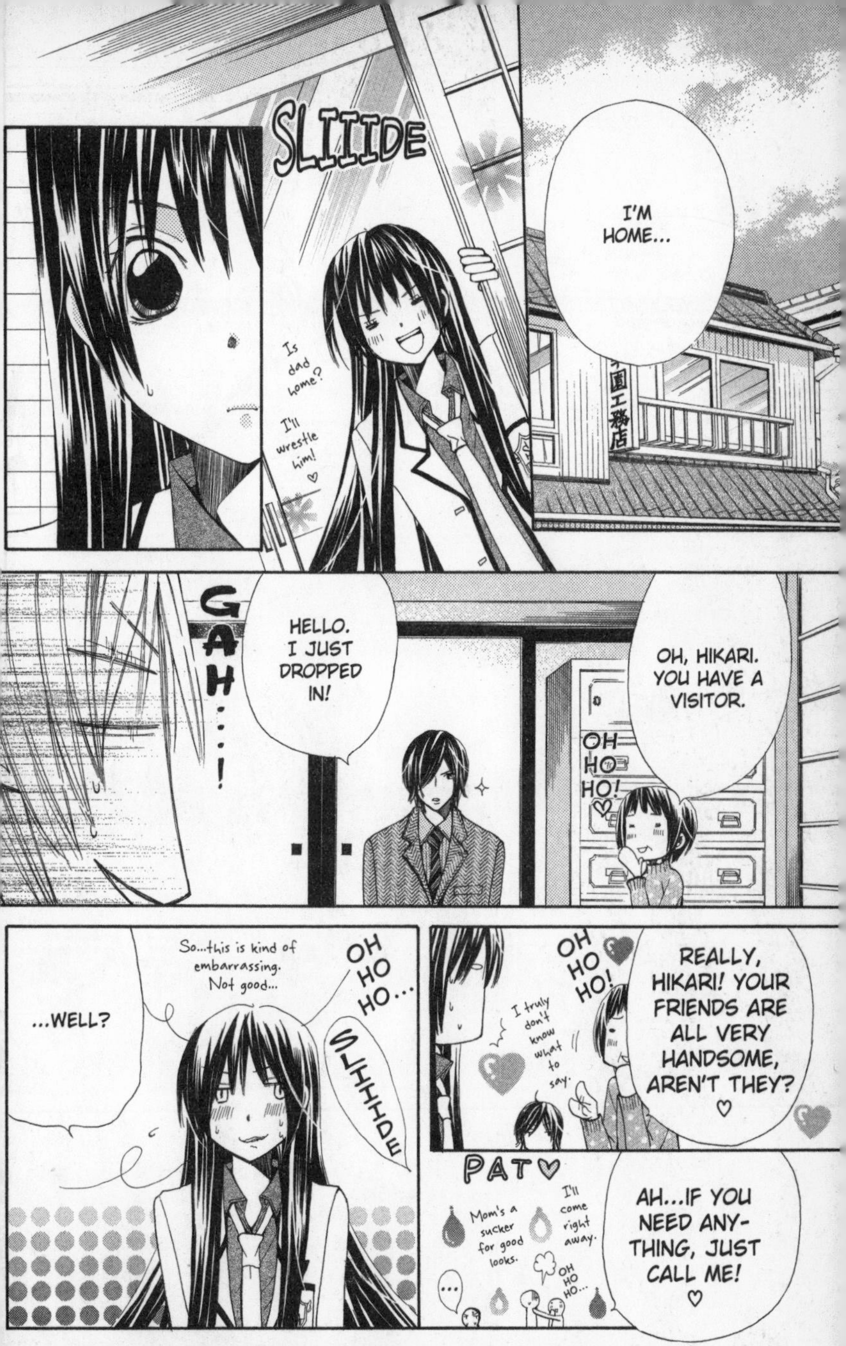
I'M HOME...
SLIIIDE
Is dad home?
I'll wrestle him! ♡
OH, HIKARI. YOU HAVE A VISITOR.
OH HO HO! ♡
HELLO. I JUST DROPPED IN!
GAH...!
OH HO HO!
REALLY, HIKARI! YOUR FRIENDS ARE ALL VERY HANDSOME, AREN'T THEY? ♡
I truly don't know what to say.
PAT ♡
AH...IF YOU NEED ANY-THING, JUST CALL ME! ♡
I'll come right away.
Mom's a sucker for good looks.
OH HO HO...
...
OH HO HO...
SLIIIDE
So...this is kind of embarrassing. Not good...
...WELL?

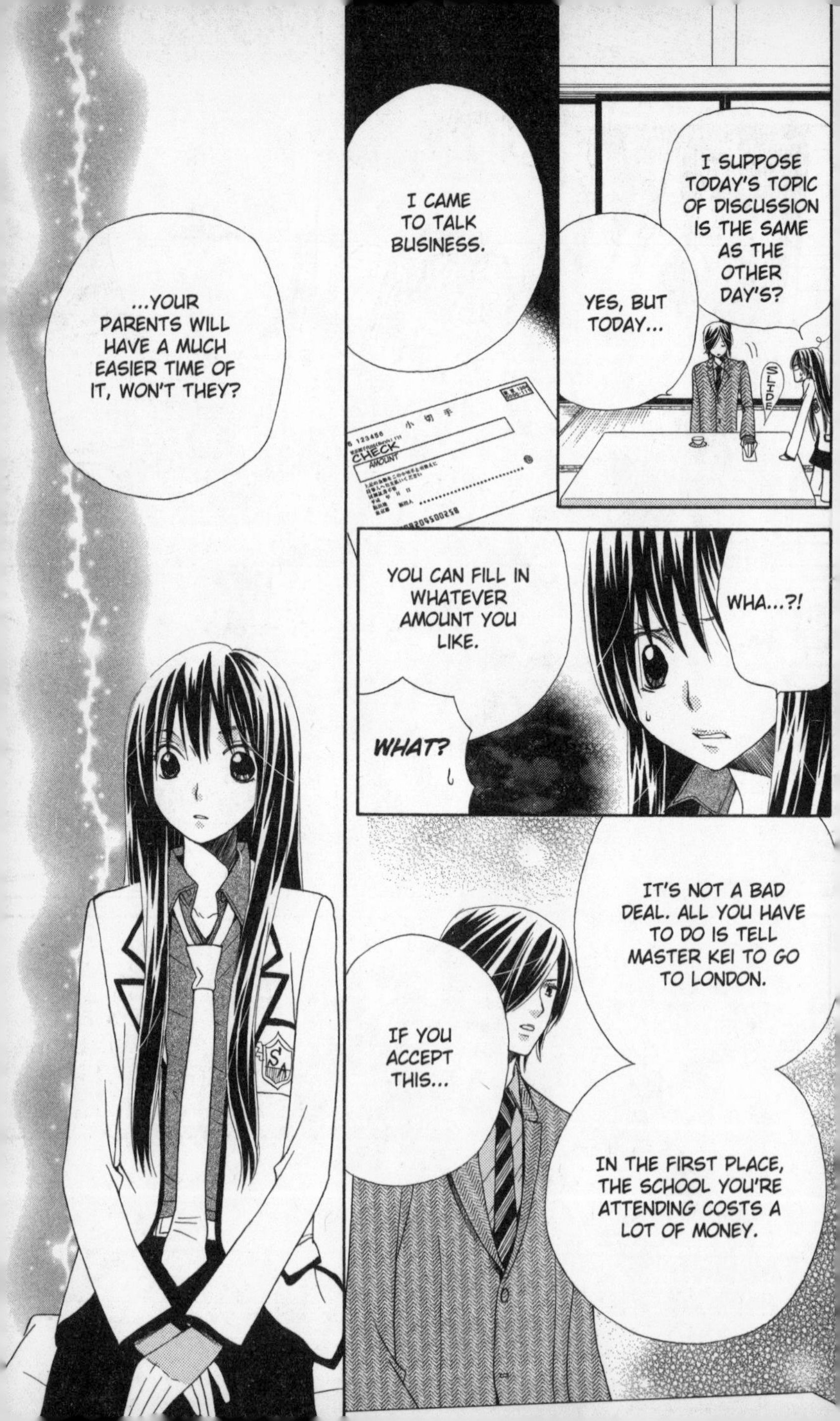
I SUPPOSE TODAY'S TOPIC OF DISCUSSION IS THE SAME AS THE OTHER DAY'S?
YES, BUT TODAY...
SLIDE
I CAME TO TALK BUSINESS.
CHECK
AMOUNT
WHA...?!
YOU CAN FILL IN WHATEVER AMOUNT YOU LIKE.
WHAT?
IT'S NOT A BAD DEAL. ALL YOU HAVE TO DO IS TELL MASTER KEI TO GO TO LONDON.
IF YOU ACCEPT THIS...
IN THE FIRST PLACE, THE SCHOOL YOU'RE ATTENDING COSTS A LOT OF MONEY.
...YOUR PARENTS WILL HAVE A MUCH EASIER TIME OF IT, WON'T THEY?

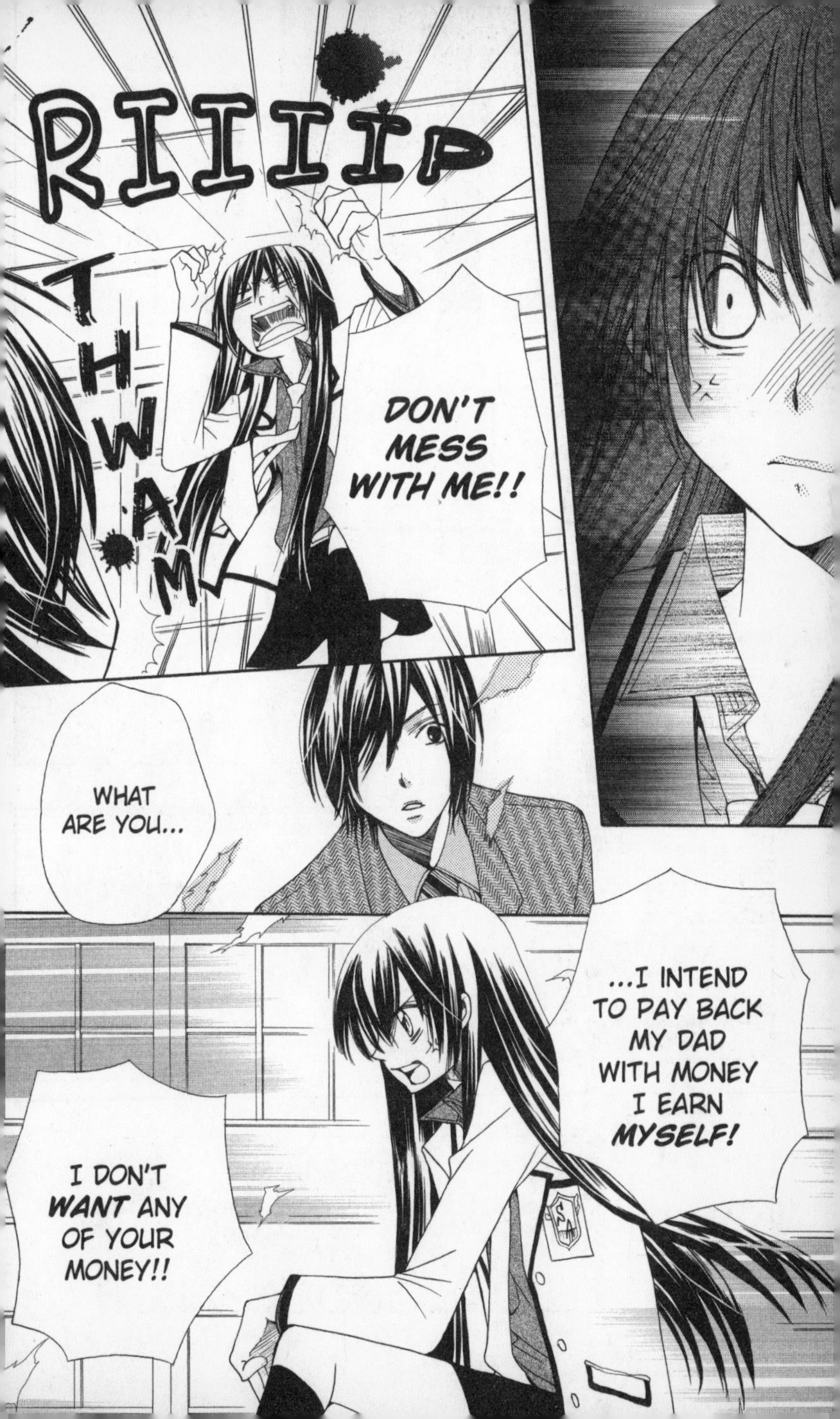
RIIIIP
THWAM
DON'T MESS WITH ME!!
WHAT ARE YOU...
...I INTEND TO PAY BACK MY DAD WITH MONEY I EARN *MYSELF*!
I DON'T *WANT* ANY OF YOUR MONEY!!

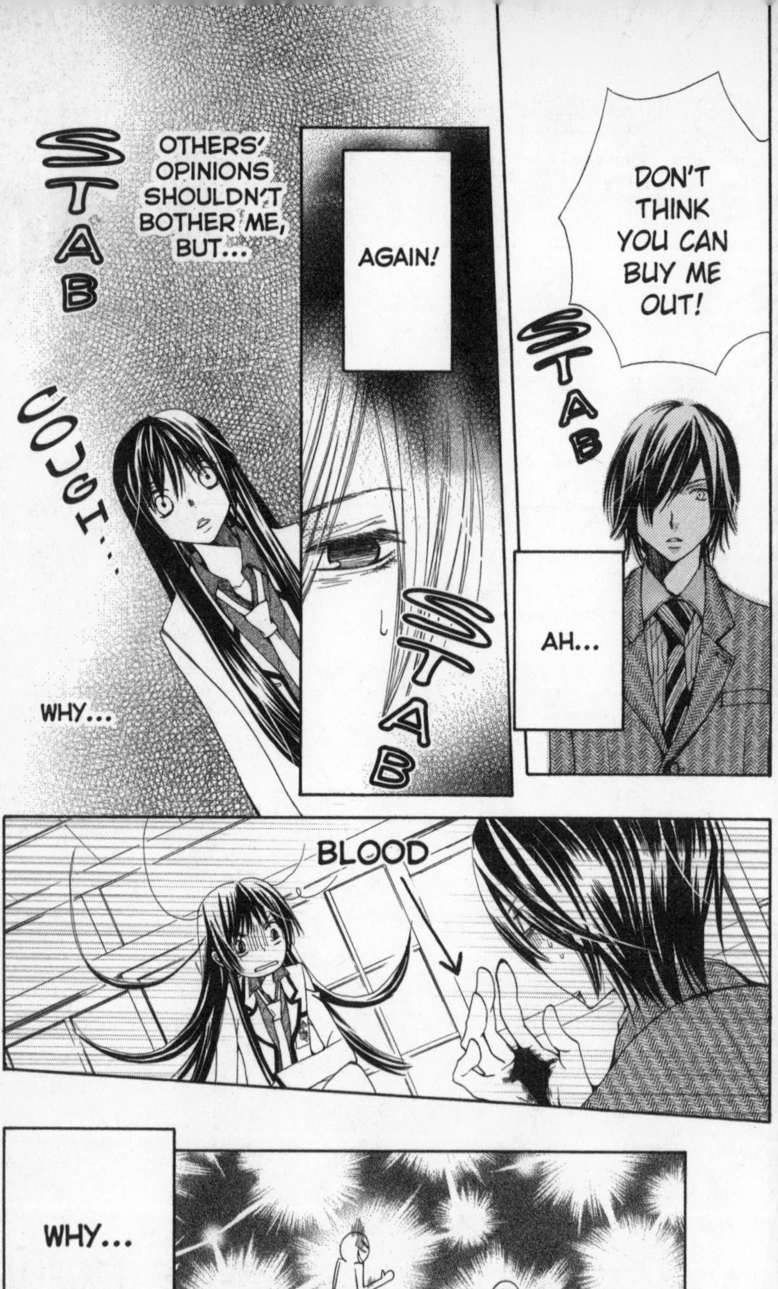
DON'T THINK YOU CAN BUY ME OUT!
STAB
AH...
AGAIN!
STAB
OTHERS' OPINIONS SHOULDN'T BOTHER ME, BUT...
STAB
OOJIGI...
WHY...
BLOOD
WHY...

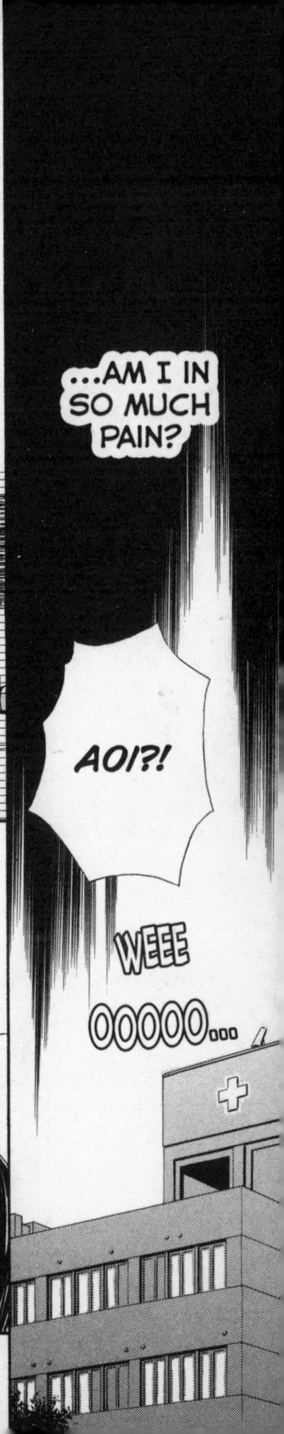
...AM I IN SO MUCH PAIN?
AOI?!
WEEE
OOOOO...

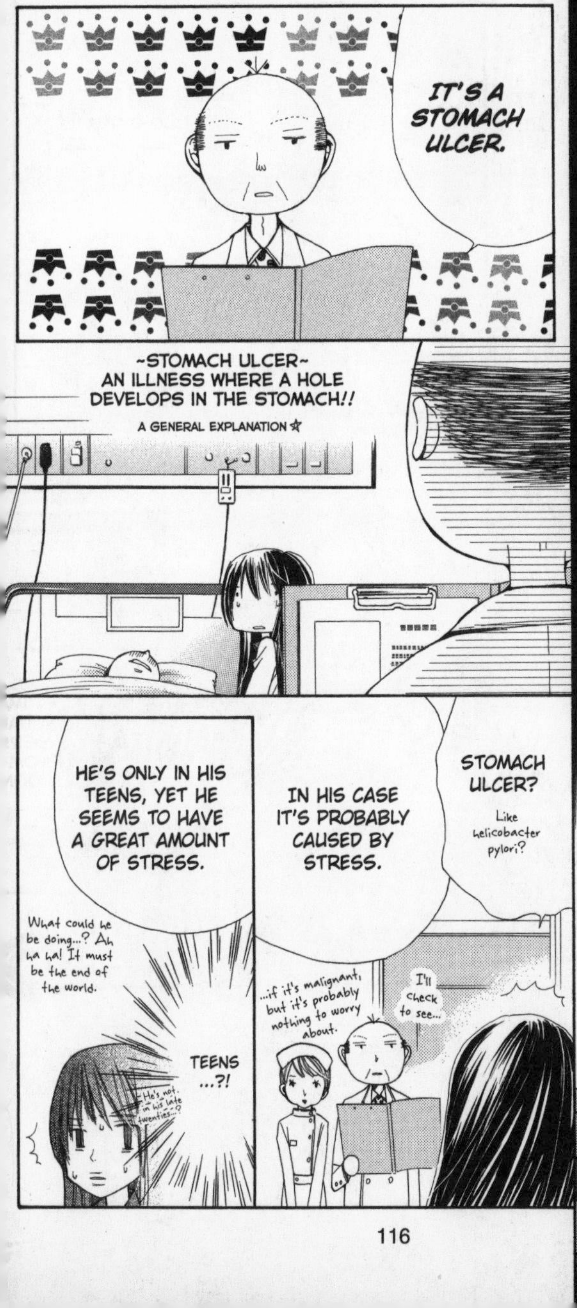
IT'S A STOMACH ULCER.
~STOMACH ULCER~ AN ILLNESS WHERE A HOLE DEVELOPS IN THE STOMACH!!
A GENERAL EXPLANATION ☆
STOMACH ULCER?
Like helicobacter pylori?
IN HIS CASE IT'S PROBABLY CAUSED BY STRESS.
I'll check to see...
...if it's malignant, but it's probably nothing to worry about.
HE'S ONLY IN HIS TEENS, YET HE SEEMS TO HAVE A GREAT AMOUNT OF STRESS.
What could he be doing...? Ah ha ha! It must be the end of the world.
TEENS ...?!
He's not in his late twenties...?

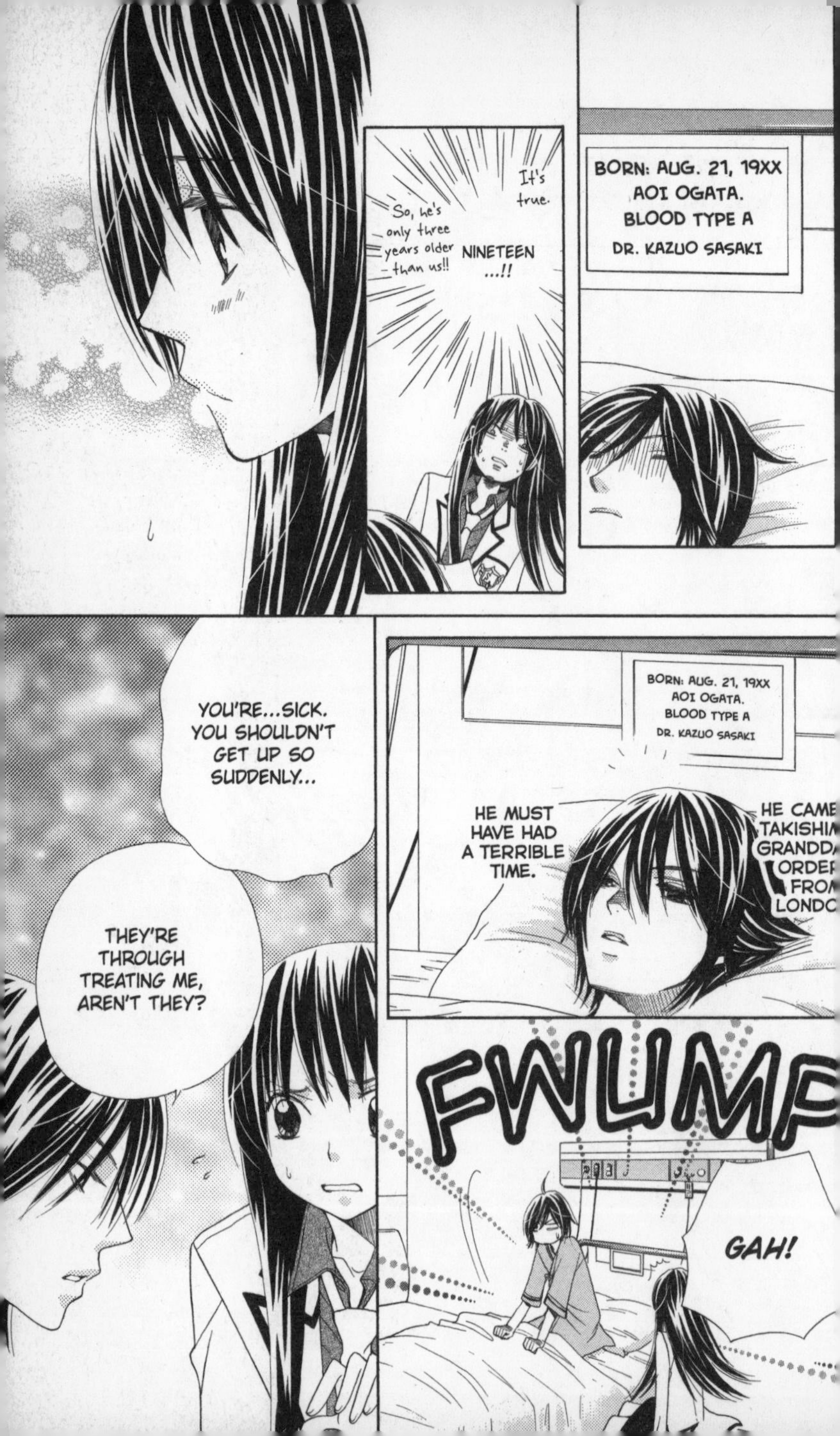
BORN: AUG. 21, 19XX
AOI OGATA.
BLOOD TYPE A
DR. KAZUO SASAKI
It's true.
NINETEEN ...!!
So, he's only three years older than us!!
BORN: AUG. 21, 19XX
AOI OGATA.
BLOOD TYPE A
DR. KAZUO SASAKI
HE CAME
TAKISHIM
GRANDD
ORDER
FROM
LONDO
HE MUST HAVE HAD A TERRIBLE TIME.
FWUMP
GAH!
YOU'RE...SICK. YOU SHOULDN'T GET UP SO SUDDENLY...
THEY'RE THROUGH TREATING ME, AREN'T THEY?

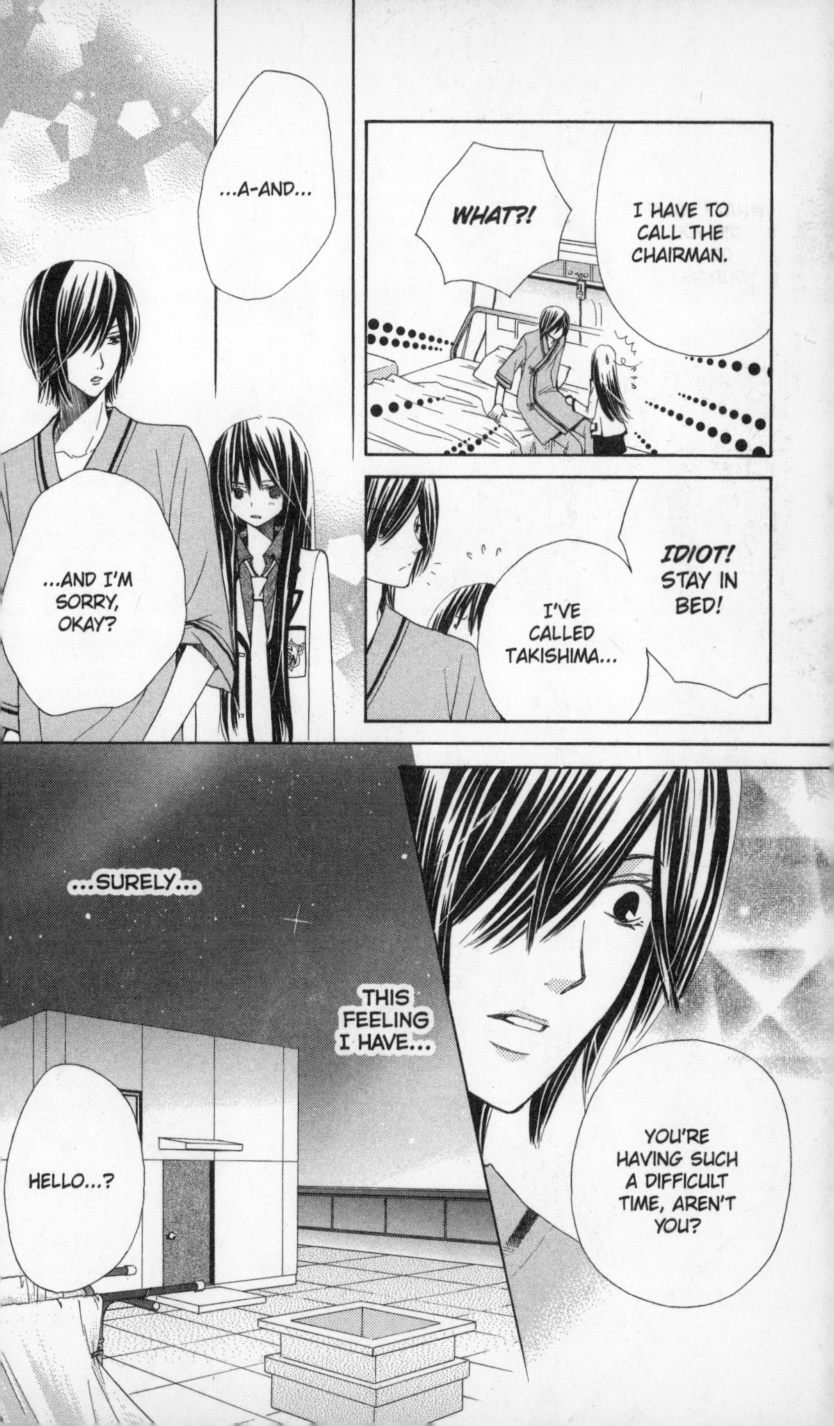
I HAVE TO CALL THE CHAIRMAN.
WHAT?!
IDIOT! STAY IN BED!
I'VE CALLED TAKISHIMA...
...A-AND...
...AND I'M SORRY, OKAY?
YOU'RE HAVING SUCH A DIFFICULT TIME, AREN'T YOU?
...SURELY...
THIS FEELING I HAVE...
HELLO...?

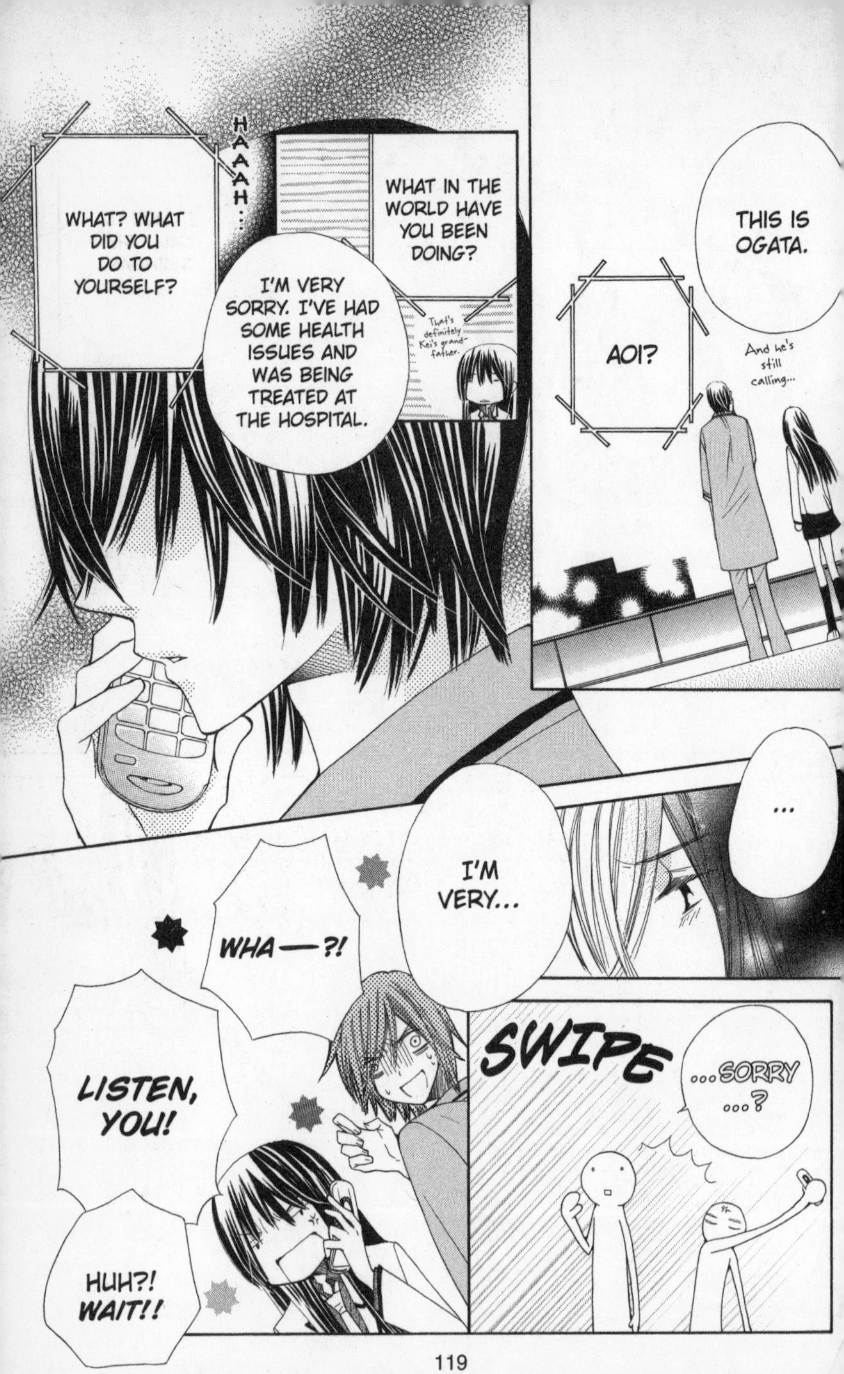
THIS IS OGATA.
And he's still calling...
AOI?
WHAT IN THE WORLD HAVE YOU BEEN DOING?
HAAAAH...
That's definitely Kei's grand-father.
WHAT? WHAT DID YOU DO TO YOURSELF?
I'M VERY SORRY. I'VE HAD SOME HEALTH ISSUES AND WAS BEING TREATED AT THE HOSPITAL.
...
I'M VERY...
SWIPE
...SORRY...?
WHA—?!
LISTEN, YOU!
HUH?! WAIT!!

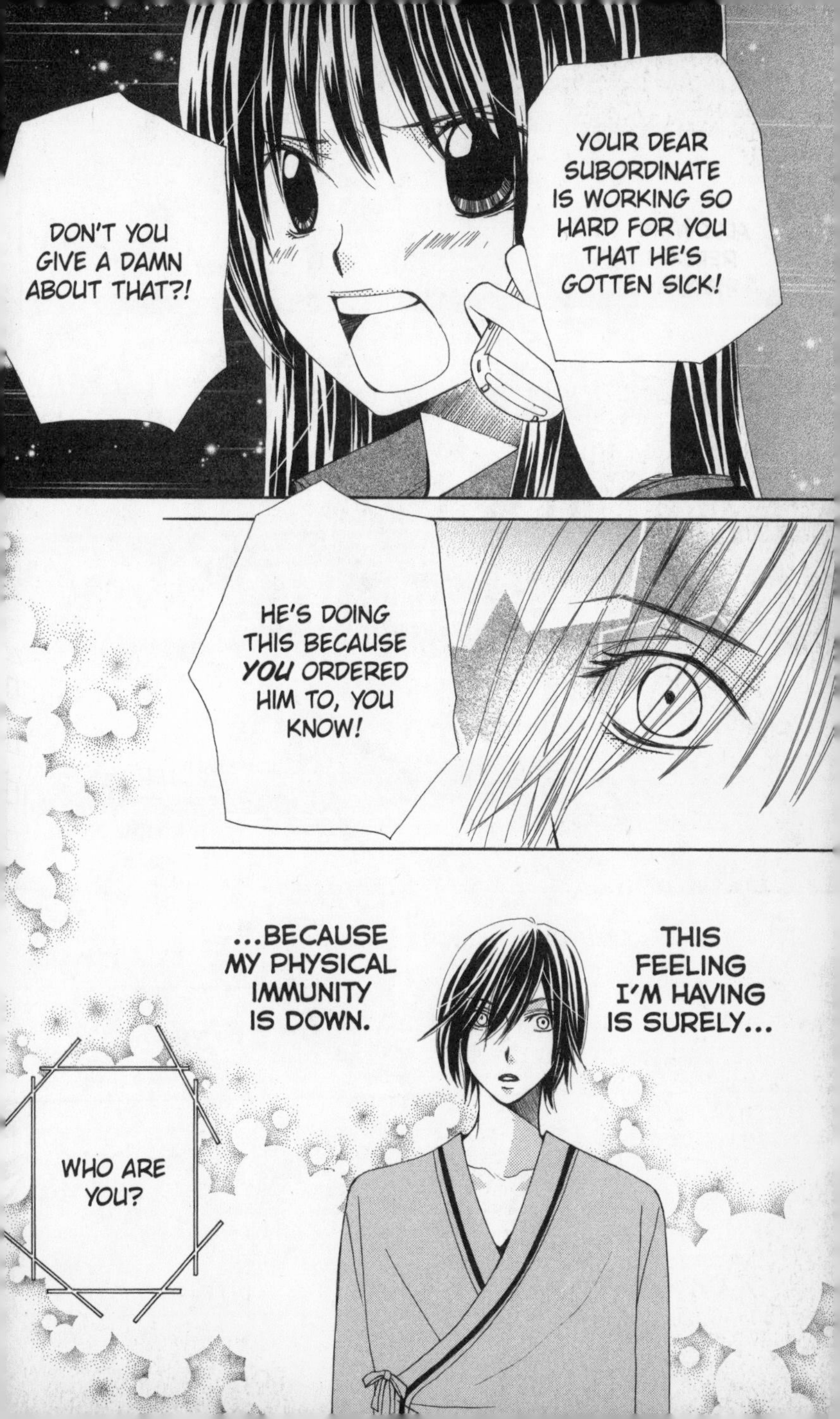
YOUR DEAR SUBORDINATE IS WORKING SO HARD FOR YOU THAT HE'S GOTTEN SICK!
DON'T YOU GIVE A DAMN ABOUT THAT?!
HE'S DOING THIS BECAUSE *YOU* ORDERED HIM TO, YOU KNOW!
THIS FEELING I'M HAVING IS SURELY...
...BECAUSE MY PHYSICAL IMMUNITY IS DOWN.
WHO ARE YOU?

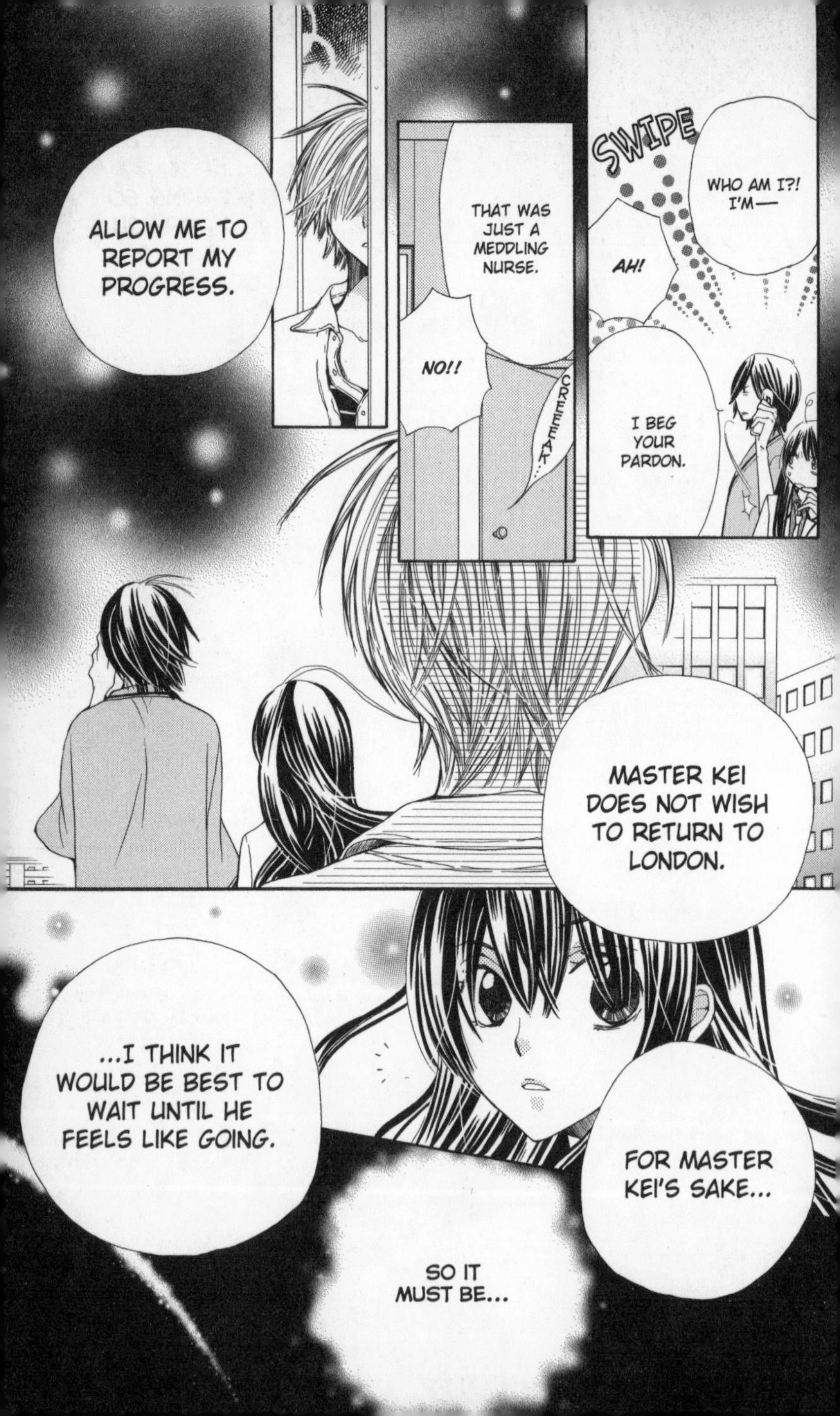
SWIPE
WHO AM I?! I'M—
AH!
I BEG YOUR PARDON.
THAT WAS JUST A MEDDLING NURSE.
NO!!
CREEEAK...
ALLOW ME TO REPORT MY PROGRESS.
MASTER KEI DOES NOT WISH TO RETURN TO LONDON.
FOR MASTER KEI'S SAKE...
...I THINK IT WOULD BE BEST TO WAIT UNTIL HE FEELS LIKE GOING.
SO IT MUST BE...

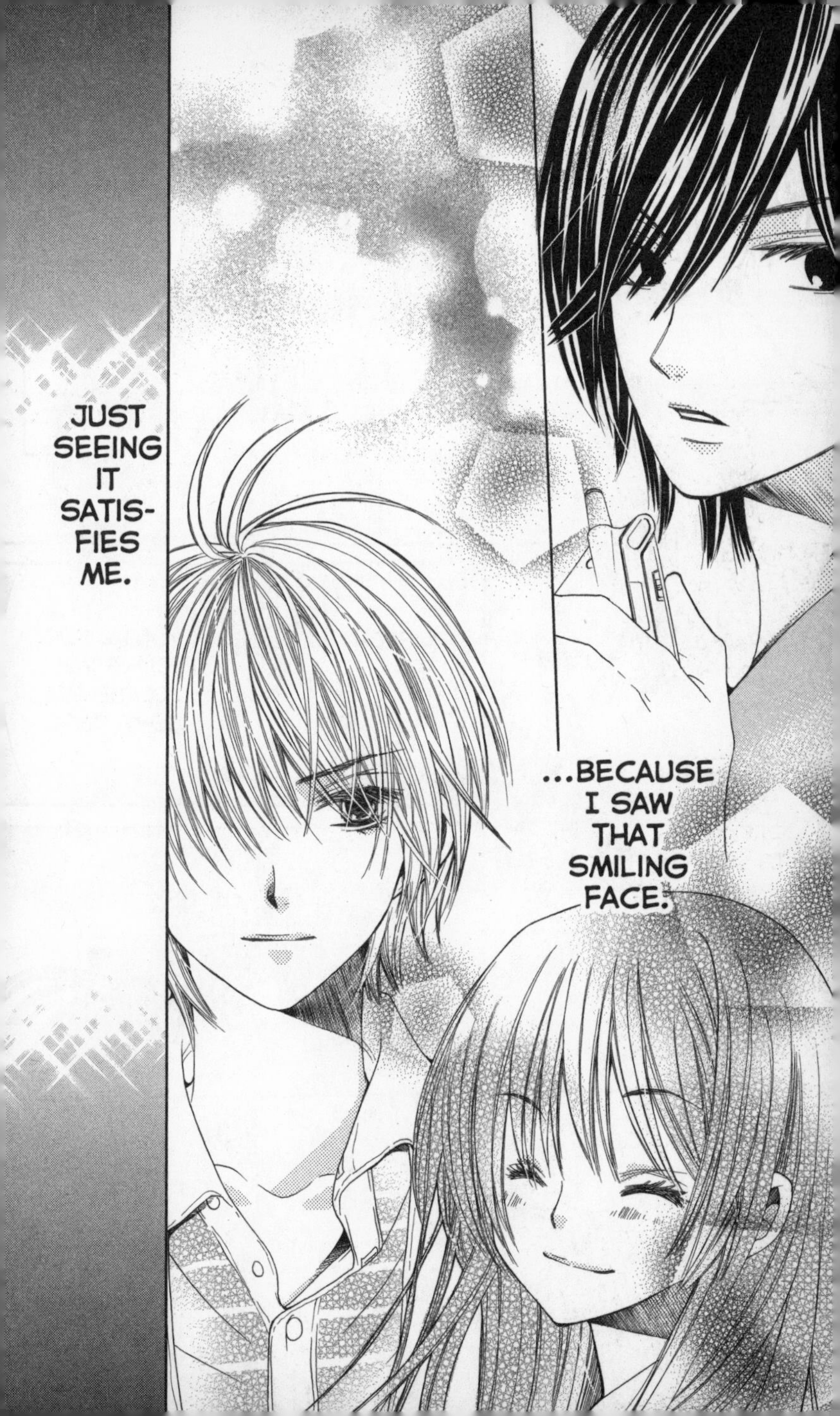
...BECAUSE I SAW THAT SMILING FACE.
JUST SEEING IT SATIS-FIES ME.

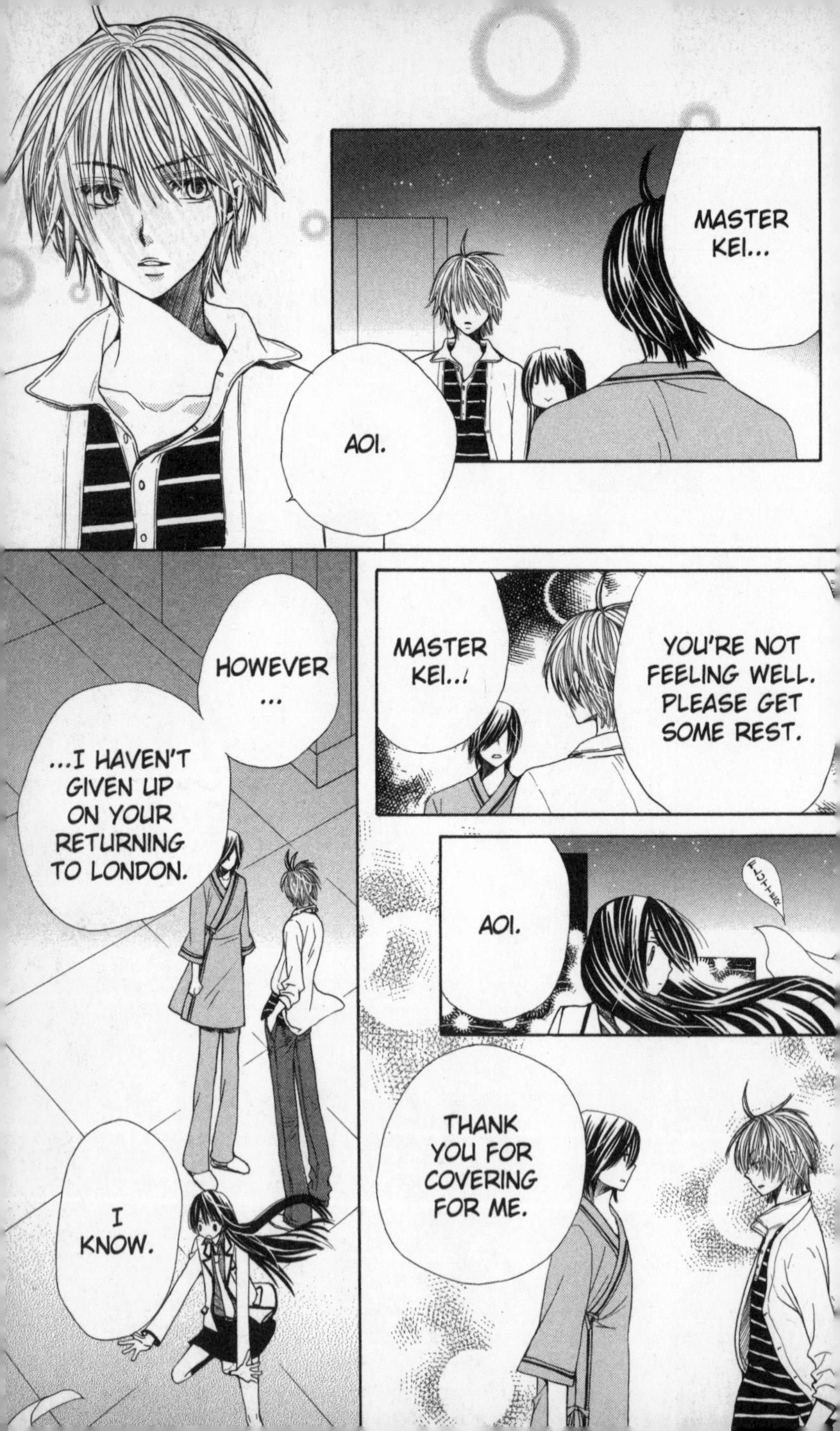
MASTER KEI...
AOI.
YOU'RE NOT FEELING WELL. PLEASE GET SOME REST.
MASTER KEI...!
AOI.
THANK YOU FOR COVERING FOR ME.
HOWEVER...
...I HAVEN'T GIVEN UP ON YOUR RETURNING TO LONDON.
I KNOW.

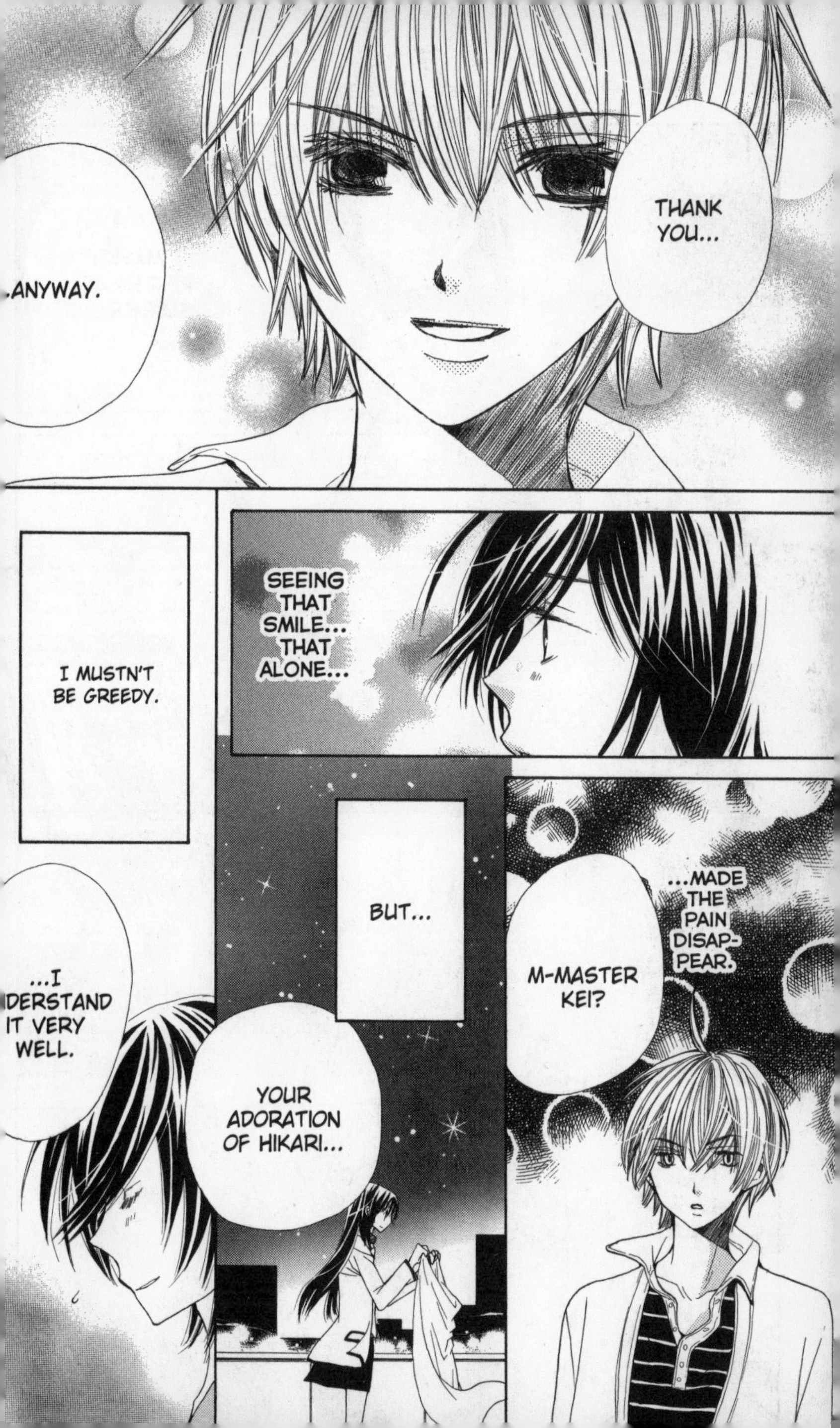
THANK YOU...
.ANYWAY.
SEEING THAT SMILE... THAT ALONE...
...MADE THE PAIN DISAP-PEAR.
M-MASTER KEI?
BUT...
YOUR ADORATION OF HIKARI...
I MUSTN'T BE GREEDY.
...I DERSTAND IT VERY WELL.

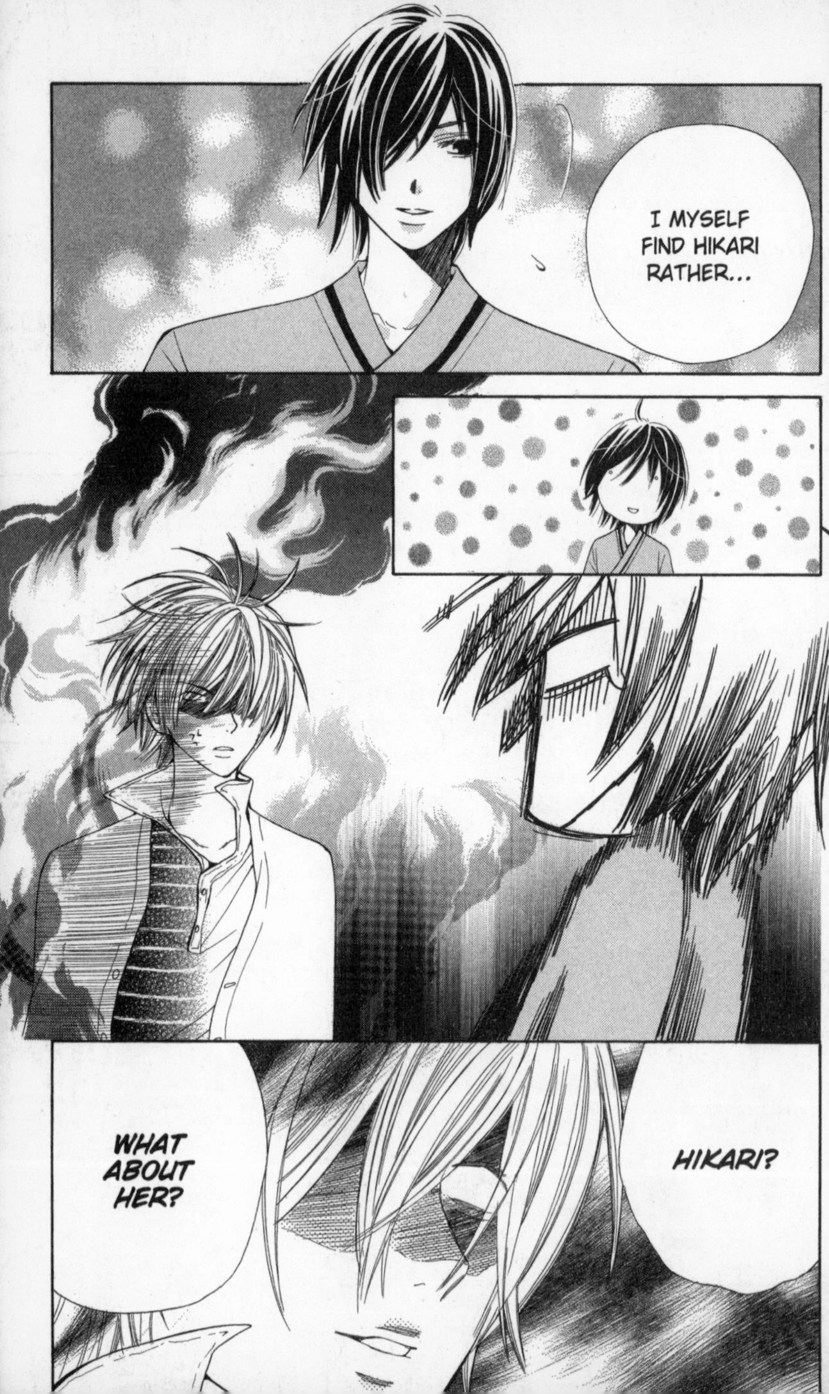
I MYSELF FIND HIKARI RATHER...
HIKARI?
WHAT ABOUT HER?

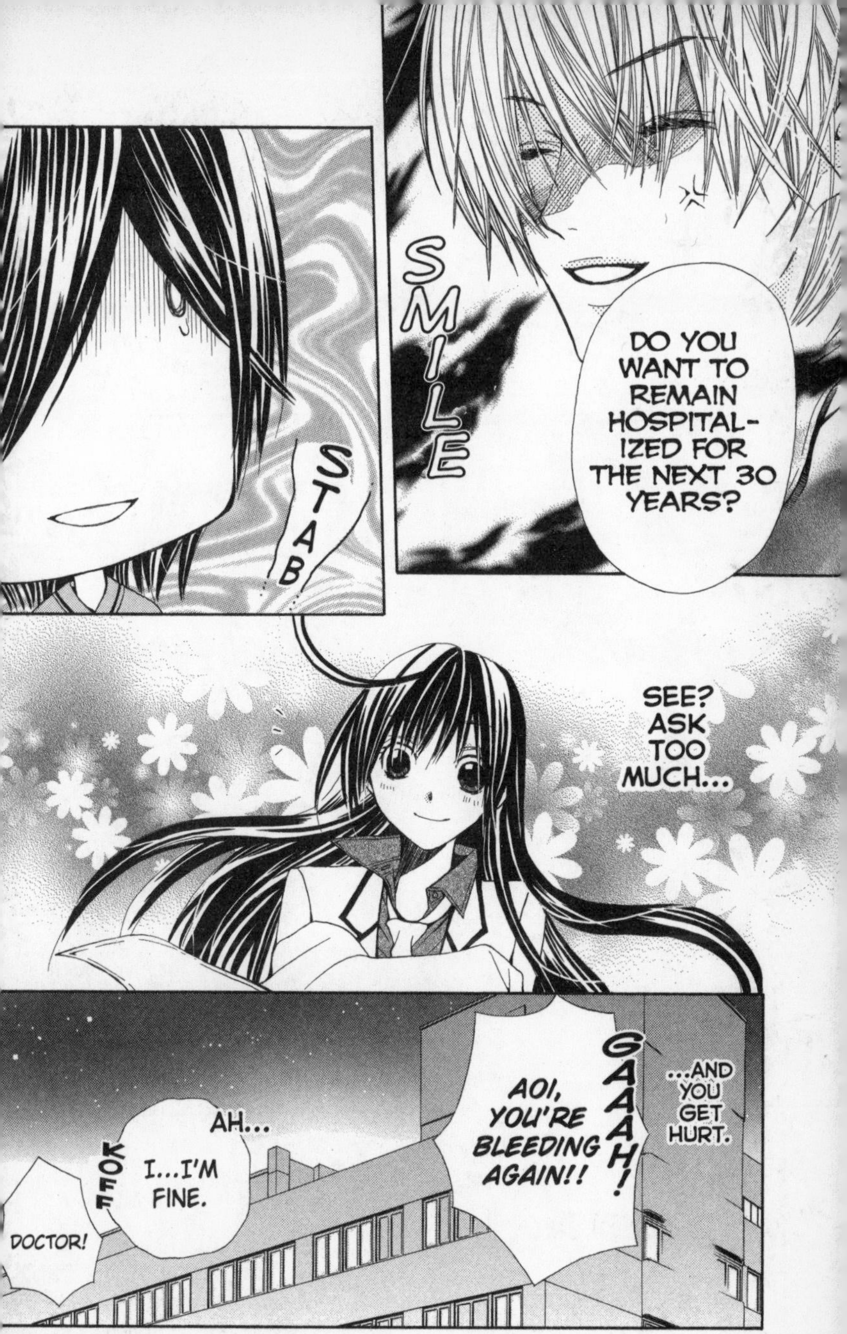
SMILE
DO YOU WANT TO REMAIN HOSPITAL-IZED FOR THE NEXT 30 YEARS?
STAB
SEE? ASK TOO MUCH...
...AND YOU GET HURT.
GAAAAH!
AOI, YOU'RE BLEEDING AGAIN!!
AH...
I...I'M FINE.
KOFF
DOCTOR!

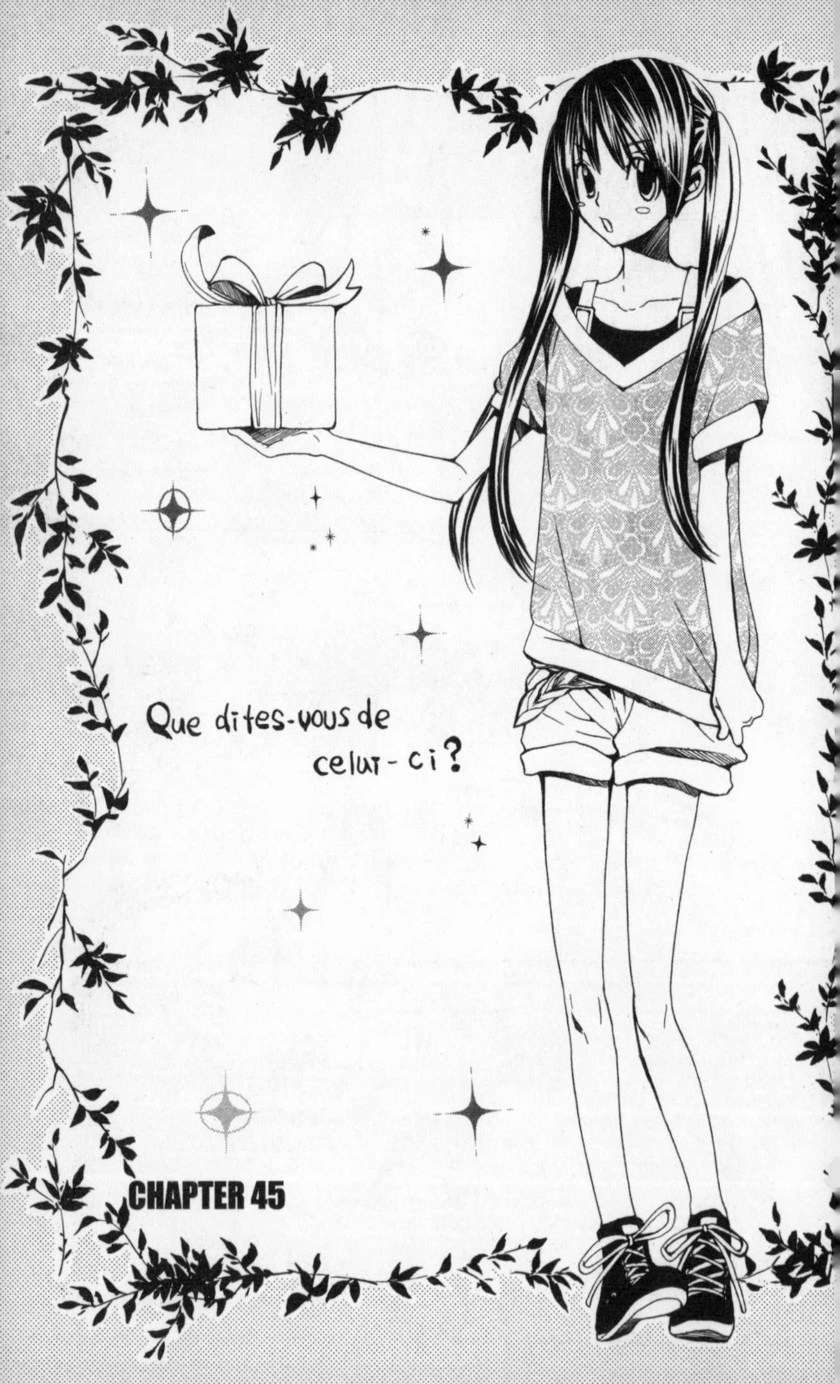
Que dites-vous de
celui-ci?
CHAPTER 45

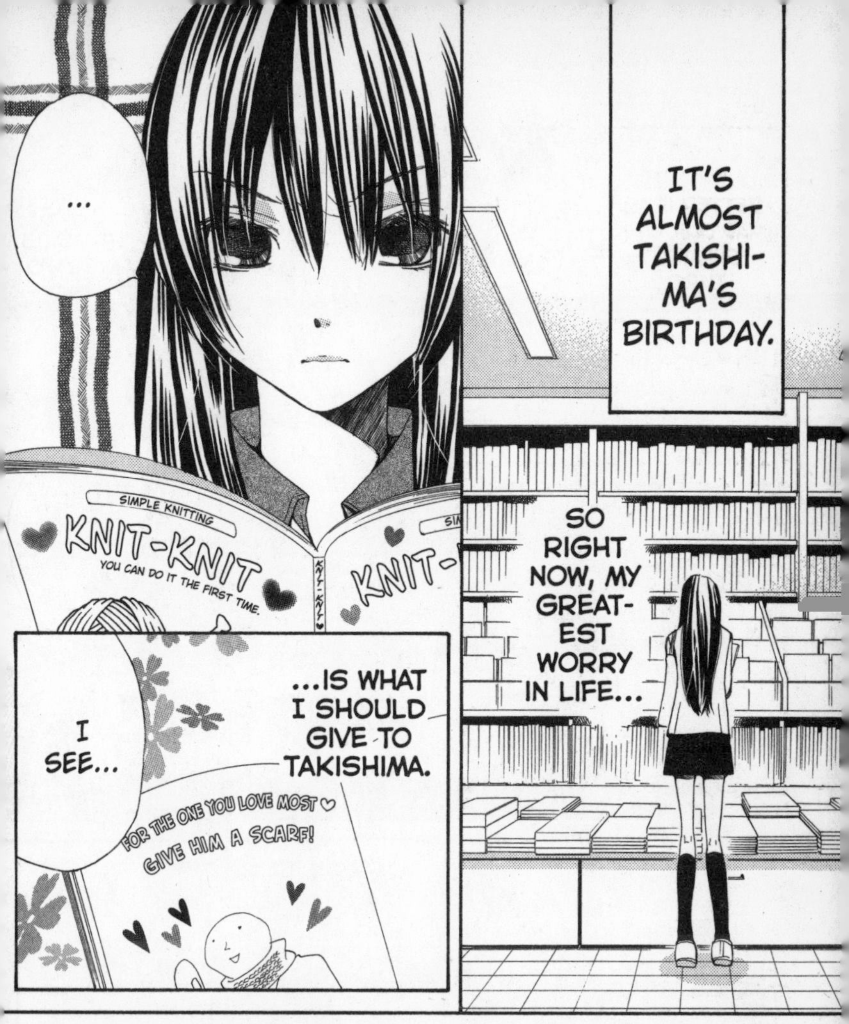
IT'S ALMOST TAKISHIMA'S BIRTHDAY.
SO RIGHT NOW, MY GREATEST WORRY IN LIFE...
...
SIMPLE KNITTING
KNIT-KNIT
YOU CAN DO IT THE FIRST TIME.
...IS WHAT I SHOULD GIVE TO TAKISHIMA.
I SEE...
FOR THE ONE YOU LOVE MOST ♡
GIVE HIM A SCARF!

• APPRECIATION FOR YOUR LETTERS •

THANK YOU FOR ALL YOUR LETTERS. I'M SORRY I CAN ONLY RESPOND ONCE A YEAR WITH A PRINTED FORM LETTER. I WILL USE THIS SPACE TO EXPRESS MY GRATITUDE. **LETTERS** THAT **WARM** THE HEART, ILLUSTRATIONS THAT **MOVE**, MUSIC DISCS WITH TUNES CHOSEN TO FIT THE CHARACTERS' PERSONALITIES, AND ALL THE PEOPLE WHO SENT S.A PLAYING CARDS, ACCESSORIES, FOOD, AND THE GIFT SUBSCRIPTION WHERE I COULD CHOOSE A FOOD BOOK (FROM WHICH I CHOSE RICE CAKES!). AND ALL THE OTHERS, WHO TRULY SENT A VARIETY OF LETTERS ABOUT YOUR INNERMOST FEELINGS, YOUR WORRIES AND YOUR MOST PERSONAL PHILOSOPHIES OF LOVE...ALL OF YOU ENCOURAGED ME. THANK YOU SO VERY MUCH! I'LL DO MY BEST TO CREATE COMICS THAT BRING AT LEAST A LITTLE BIT OF JOY TO ALL WHO READ THEM...MY SUPPORTERS.

THE SIZES OF THE WORDS ARE MESSED UP!

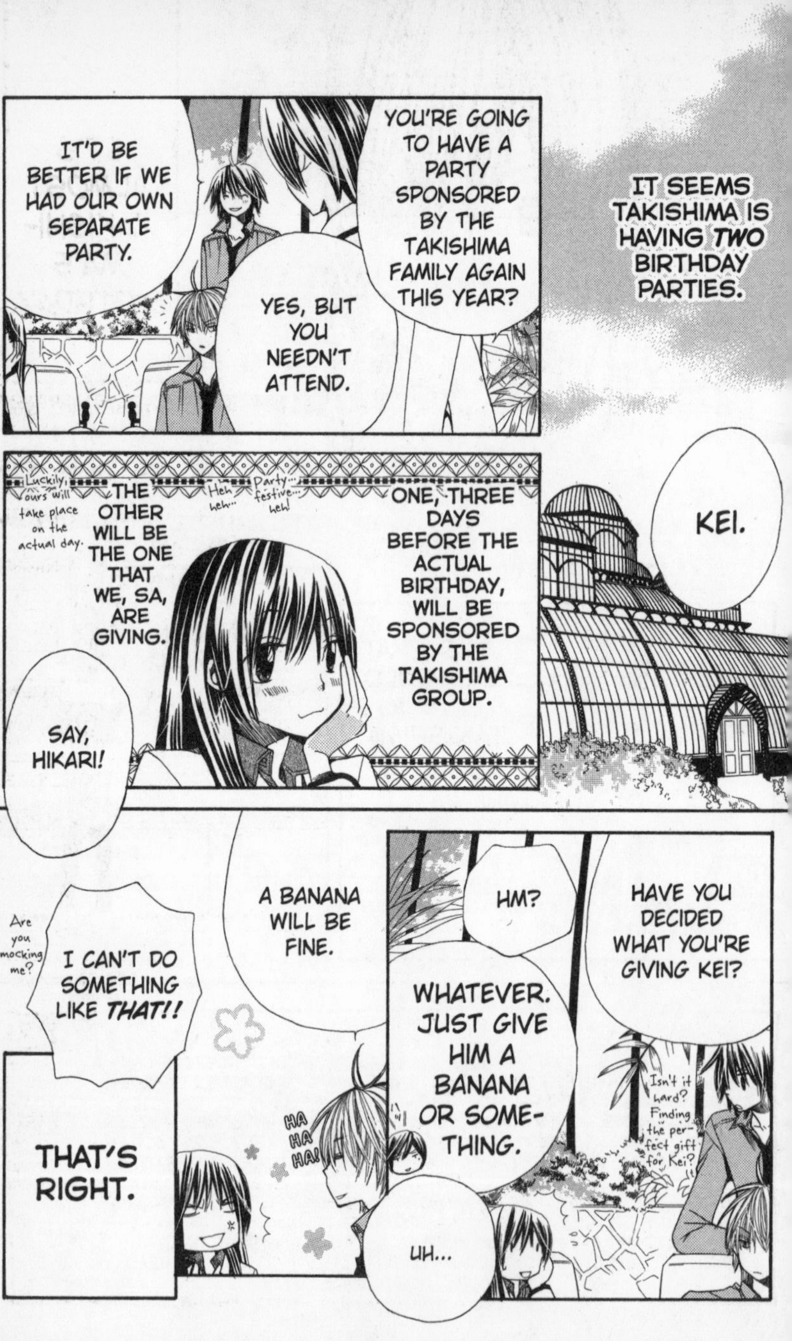
IT SEEMS TAKISHIMA IS HAVING *TWO* BIRTHDAY PARTIES.
KEI.
YOU'RE GOING TO HAVE A PARTY SPONSORED BY THE TAKISHIMA FAMILY AGAIN THIS YEAR?
YES, BUT YOU NEEDN'T ATTEND.
IT'D BE BETTER IF WE HAD OUR OWN SEPARATE PARTY.
ONE, THREE DAYS BEFORE THE ACTUAL BIRTHDAY, WILL BE SPONSORED BY THE TAKISHIMA GROUP.
Party... festive... heh!
Heh heh...
THE OTHER WILL BE THE ONE THAT WE, SA, ARE GIVING.
Luckily, ours will take place on the actual day.
SAY, HIKARI!
HAVE YOU DECIDED WHAT YOU'RE GIVING KEI?
HM?
Isn't it hard? Finding the perfect gift for Kei?
WHATEVER. JUST GIVE HIM A BANANA OR SOMETHING.
UH...
A BANANA WILL BE FINE.
HA HA HA!
I CAN'T DO SOMETHING LIKE *THAT!!*
Are you mocking me?
THAT'S RIGHT.

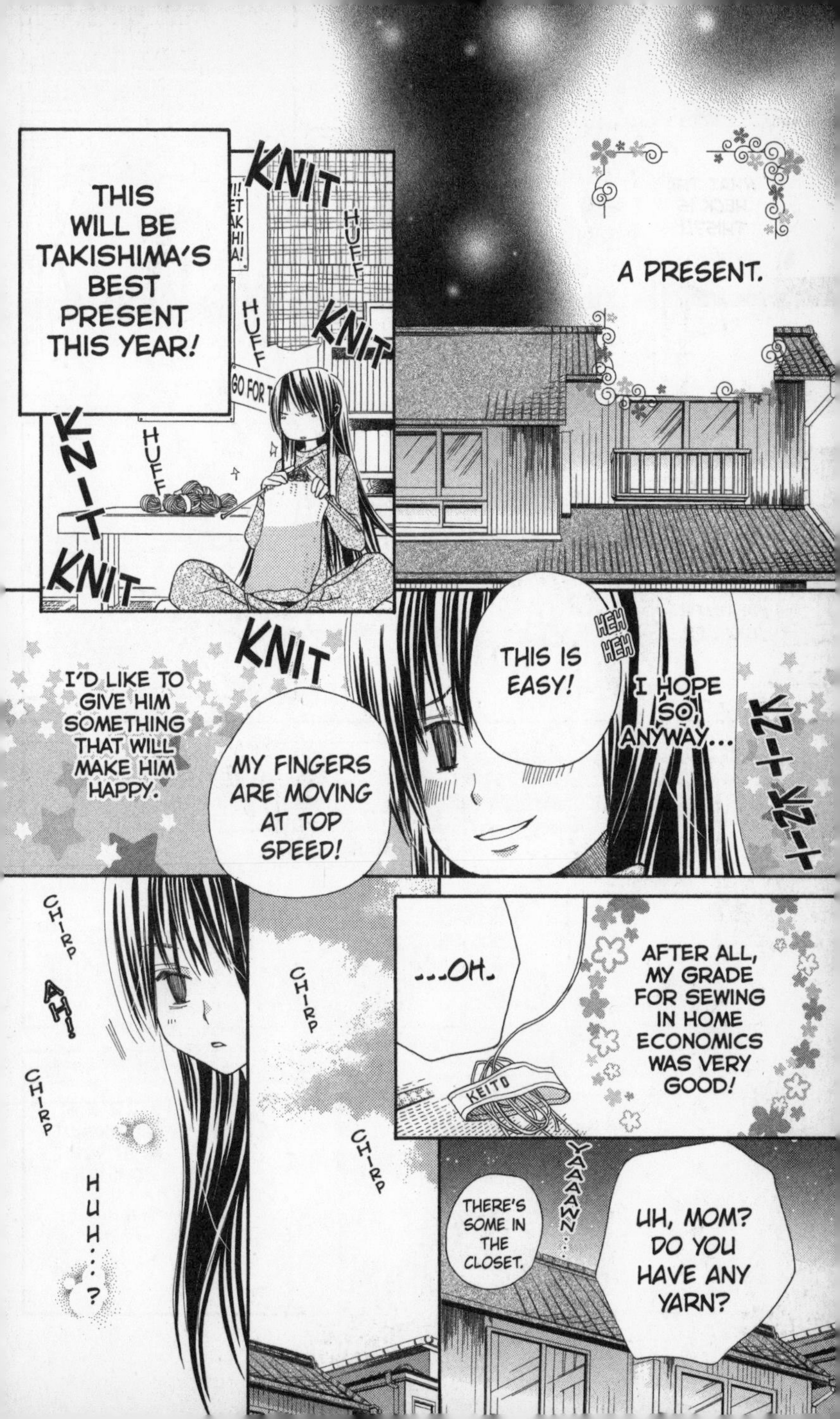
A PRESENT.
THIS WILL BE TAKISHIMA'S BEST PRESENT THIS YEAR!
KNIT
HUFF
KNIT
HUFF
KNIT
HUFF
KNIT
I HOPE SO, ANYWAY...
HEH HEH
THIS IS EASY!
KNIT KNIT
MY FINGERS ARE MOVING AT TOP SPEED!
KNIT
I'D LIKE TO GIVE HIM SOMETHING THAT WILL MAKE HIM HAPPY.
AFTER ALL, MY GRADE FOR SEWING IN HOME ECONOMICS WAS VERY GOOD!
...OH.
KEITO
UH, MOM? DO YOU HAVE ANY YARN?
YAAAAWN...
THERE'S SOME IN THE CLOSET.
CHIRP
CHIRP
CHIRP
AH!
CHIRP
HUH...?

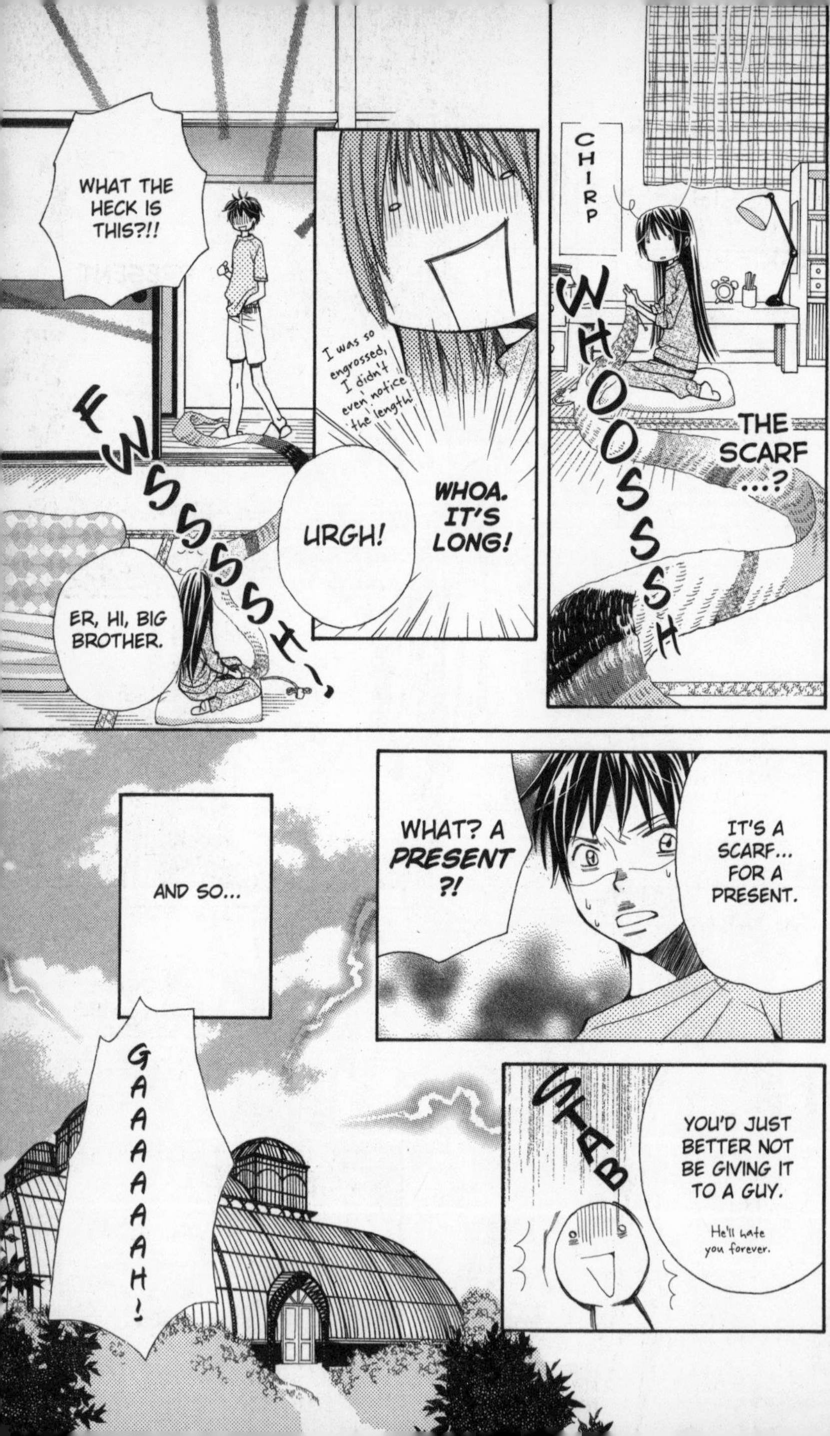
CHIRP
WHOOSSH
THE SCARF...?
I was so engrossed, I didn't even notice the length!
WHOA. IT'S LONG!
URGH!
WHAT THE HECK IS THIS?!!
FWSSSSSH!
ER, HI, BIG BROTHER.
IT'S A SCARF... FOR A PRESENT.
WHAT? A PRESENT?!
STAB
YOU'D JUST BETTER NOT BE GIVING IT TO A GUY.
He'll hate you forever.
AND SO...
GAAAAAAAAH!

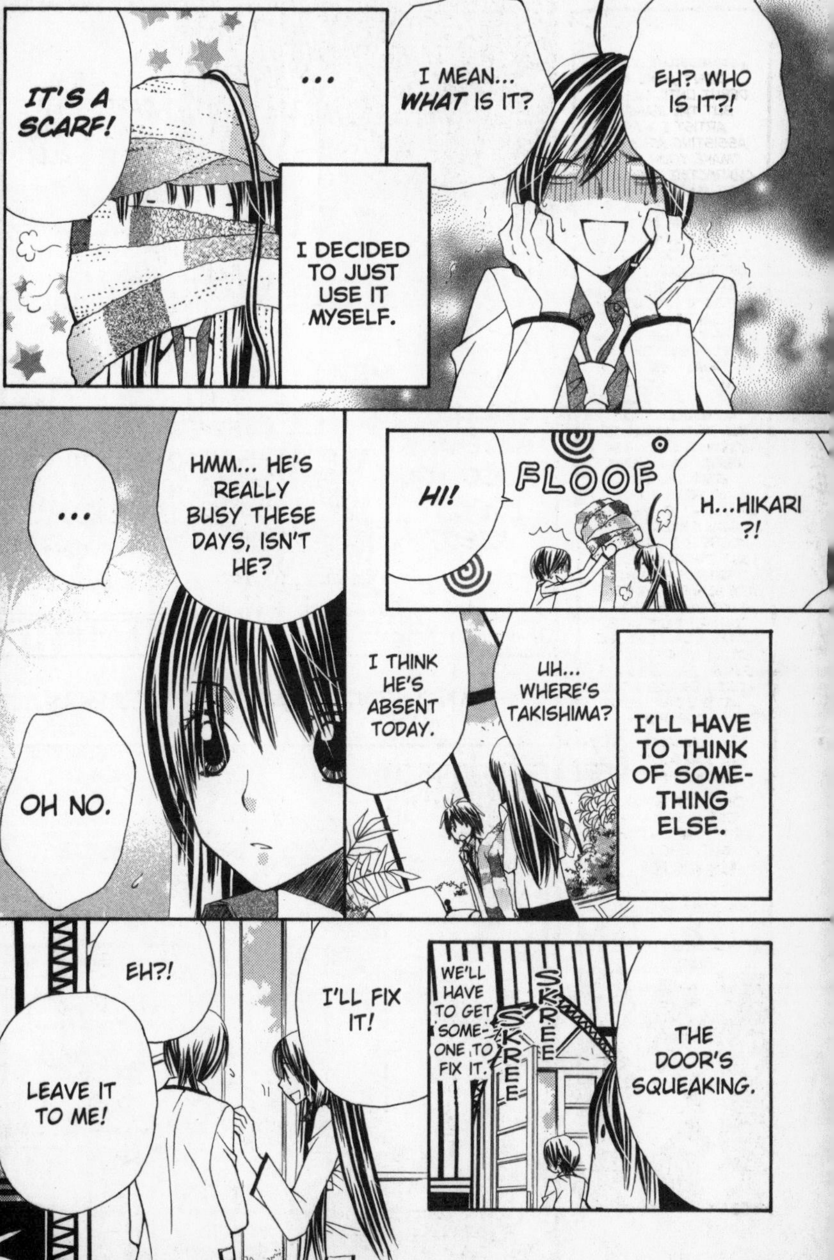
EH? WHO IS IT?!
I MEAN... *WHAT* IS IT?
...
I DECIDED TO JUST USE IT MYSELF.
IT'S A SCARF!
H...HIKARI ?!
FLOOF
HI!
I'LL HAVE TO THINK OF SOME-THING ELSE.
UH... WHERE'S TAKISHIMA?
I THINK HE'S ABSENT TODAY.
HMM... HE'S REALLY BUSY THESE DAYS, ISN'T HE?
...
OH NO.
THE DOOR'S SQUEAKING.
SKREE
SKREE
WE'LL HAVE TO GET SOME-ONE TO FIX IT.
I'LL FIX IT!
EH?!
LEAVE IT TO ME!

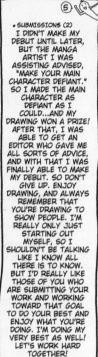

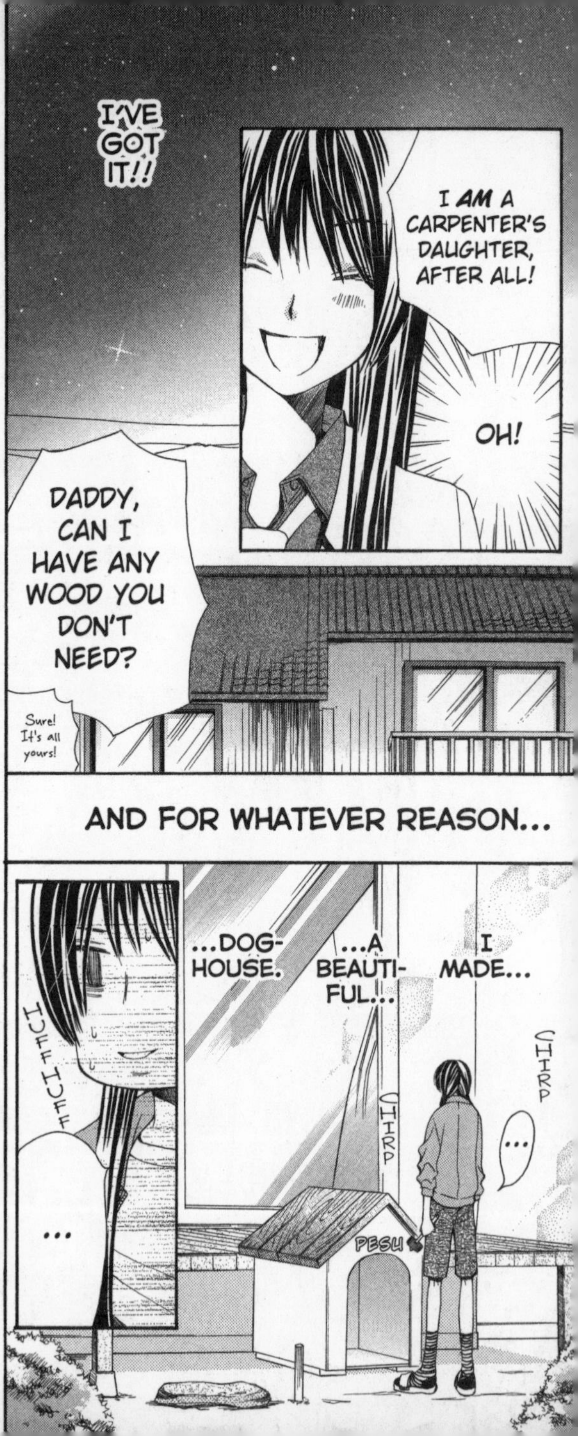
OH!
I'VE GOT IT!!
I AM A CARPENTER'S DAUGHTER, AFTER ALL!
DADDY, CAN I HAVE ANY WOOD YOU DON'T NEED?
Sure! It's all yours!
AND FOR WHATEVER REASON...
I MADE...
...A BEAUTIFUL...
...DOG-HOUSE.
CHIRP
...
CHIRP
PESU
HUFF HUFF
...

⑤

• SUBMISSIONS (2)
I DIDN'T MAKE MY DEBUT UNTIL LATER, BUT THE MANGA ARTIST I WAS ASSISTING ADVISED, "MAKE YOUR MAIN CHARACTER DEFIANT." SO I MADE THE MAIN CHARACTER AS DEFIANT AS I COULD...AND MY DRAWING WON A PRIZE! AFTER THAT, I WAS ABLE TO GET AN EDITOR WHO GAVE ME ALL SORTS OF ADVICE, AND WITH THAT I WAS FINALLY ABLE TO MAKE MY DEBUT. SO DON'T GIVE UP. ENJOY DRAWING, AND ALWAYS REMEMBER THAT YOU'RE DRAWING TO SHOW PEOPLE. I'M REALLY ONLY JUST STARTING OUT MYSELF, SO I SHOULDN'T BE TALKING LIKE I KNOW ALL THERE IS TO KNOW. BUT I'D REALLY LIKE THOSE OF YOU WHO ARE SUBMITTING YOUR WORK AND WORKING TOWARD THAT GOAL TO DO YOUR BEST AND ENJOY WHAT YOU'RE DOING. I'M DOING MY VERY BEST AS WELL! LET'S WORK HARD TOGETHER!

(WHAT? YOU DON'T WANT TO?) HFF HFF

OKAY, I'M RAMBLING NOW. I SHOULDN'T WRITE THESE LATE AT NIGHT, SHOULD I? HA HA HA...

WHAT? PUNCH LINE...? THERE ISN'T ONE!!

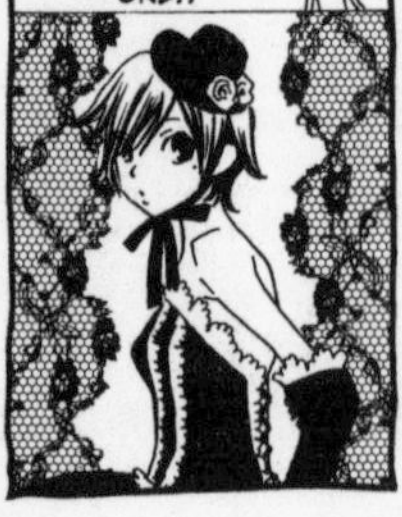

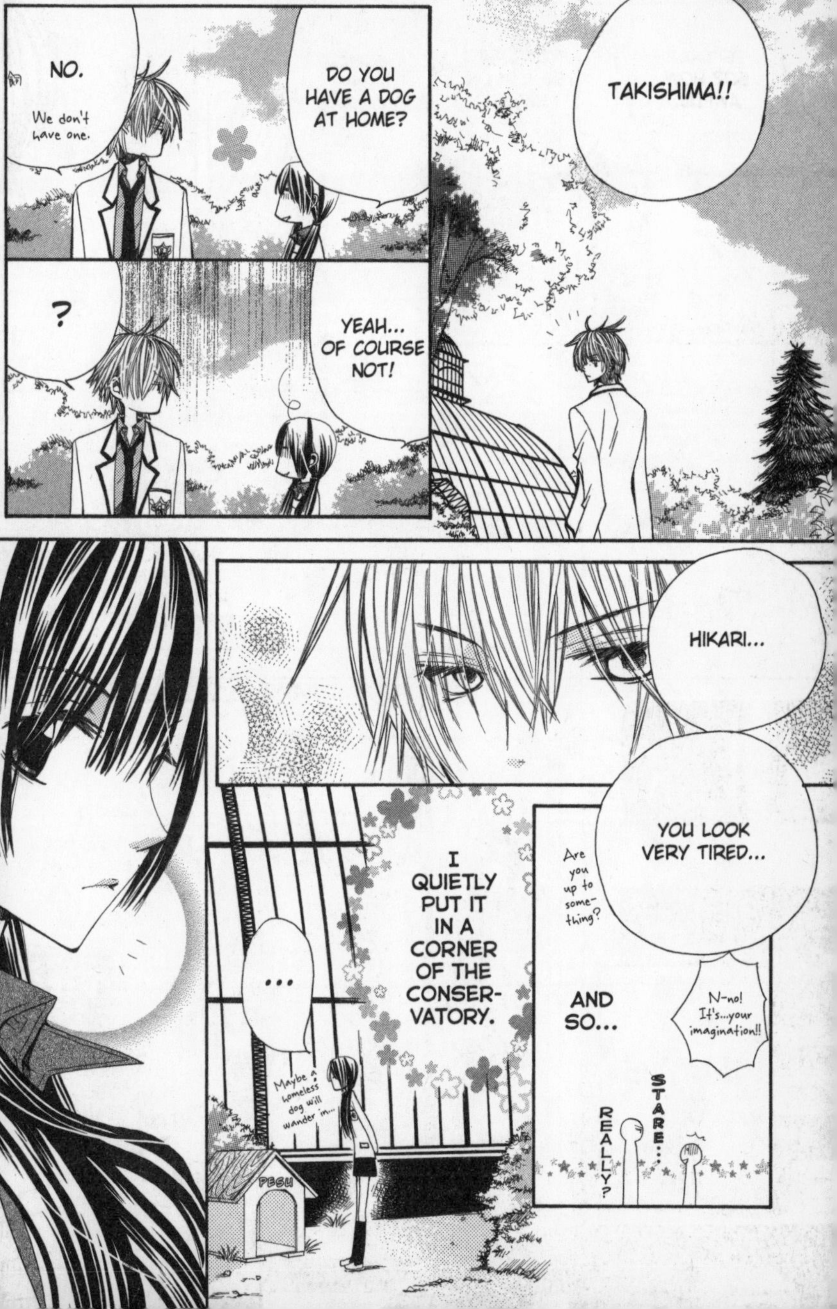
TAKISHIMA!!
DO YOU HAVE A DOG AT HOME?
NO.
We don't have one.
YEAH... OF COURSE NOT!
?
HIKARI...
YOU LOOK VERY TIRED...
Are you up to some-thing?
N-no! It's...your imagination!!
STARE...
REALLY?
AND SO...
I QUIETLY PUT IT IN A CORNER OF THE CONSER-VATORY.
...
Maybe a homeless dog will wander in...
PESU

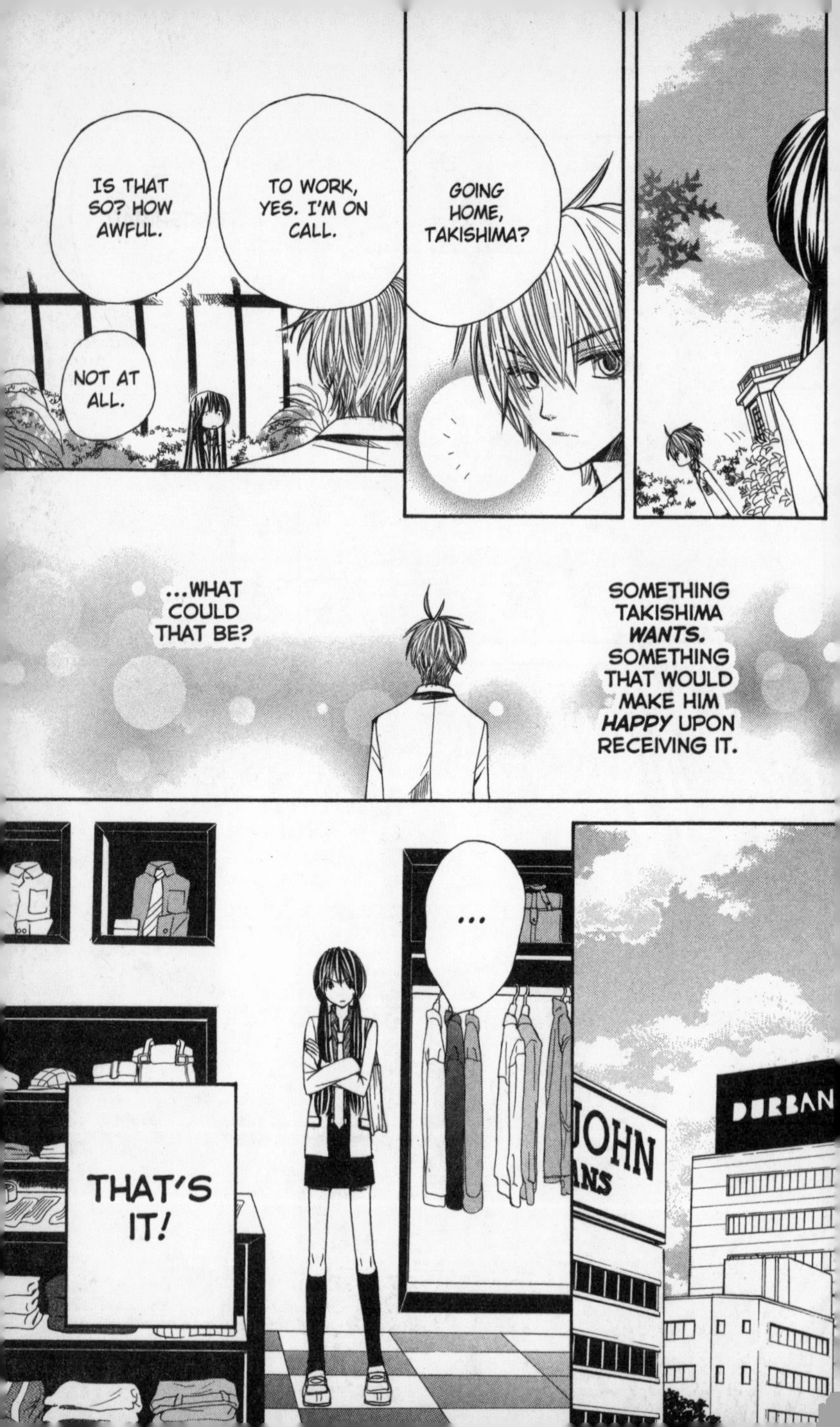
GOING HOME, TAKISHIMA?
TO WORK, YES. I'M ON CALL.
IS THAT SO? HOW AWFUL.
NOT AT ALL.
SOMETHING TAKISHIMA *WANTS.* SOMETHING THAT WOULD MAKE HIM *HAPPY* UPON RECEIVING IT.
...WHAT COULD THAT BE?
DURBAN
JOHN
...
THAT'S IT!

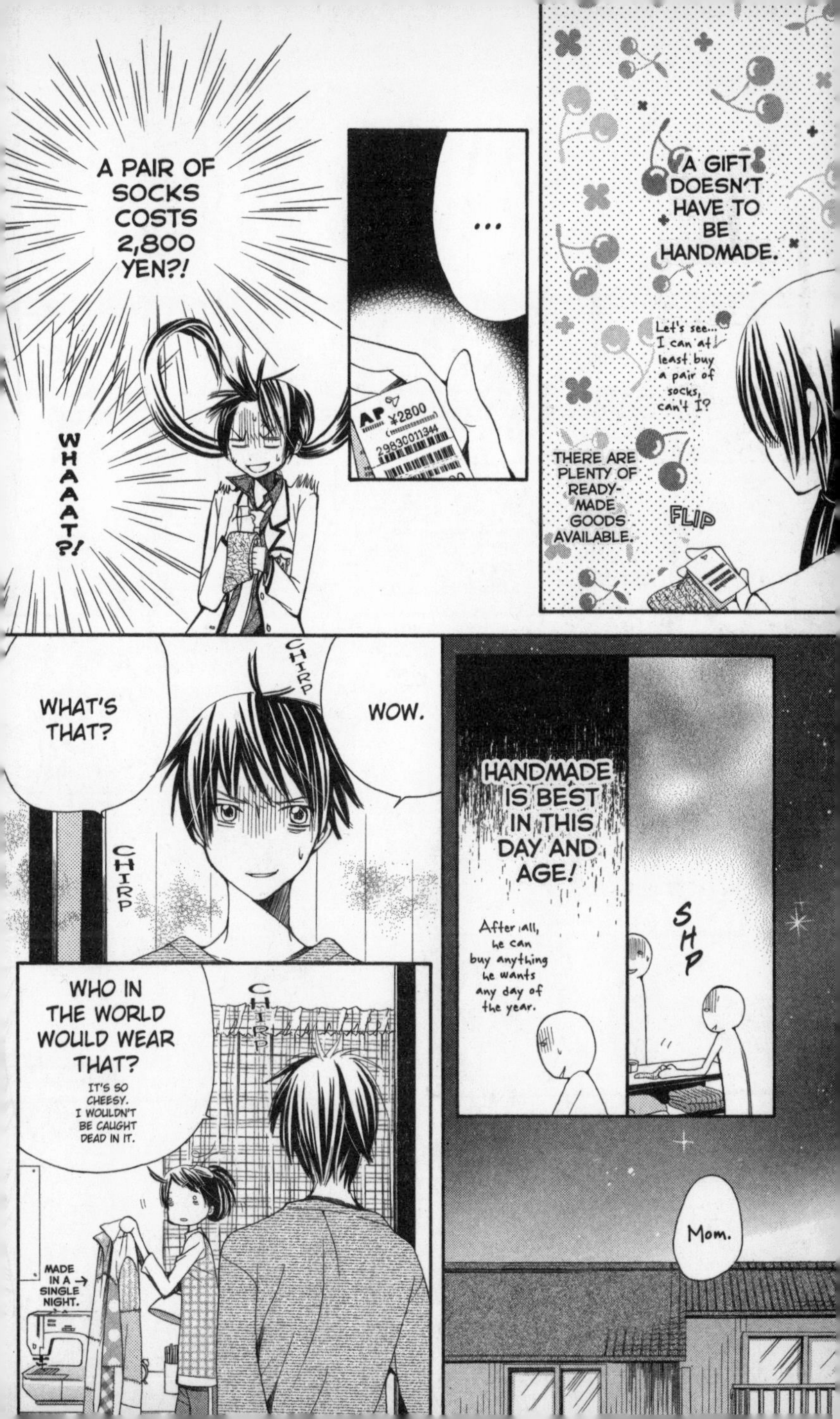
A GIFT DOESN'T HAVE TO BE HANDMADE.
Let's see... I can at least buy a pair of socks, can't I?
THERE ARE PLENTY OF READY-MADE GOODS AVAILABLE.
FLIP
...
AP ¥2800
A PAIR OF SOCKS COSTS 2,800 YEN?!
WHAAAAT?!
HANDMADE IS BEST IN THIS DAY AND AGE!
After all, he can buy anything he wants any day of the year.
SHP
Mom.
CHIRP
WOW.
WHAT'S THAT?
CHIRP
CHIRP
WHO IN THE WORLD WOULD WEAR THAT?
IT'S SO CHEESY. I WOULDN'T BE CAUGHT DEAD IN IT.
MADE IN A SINGLE NIGHT.

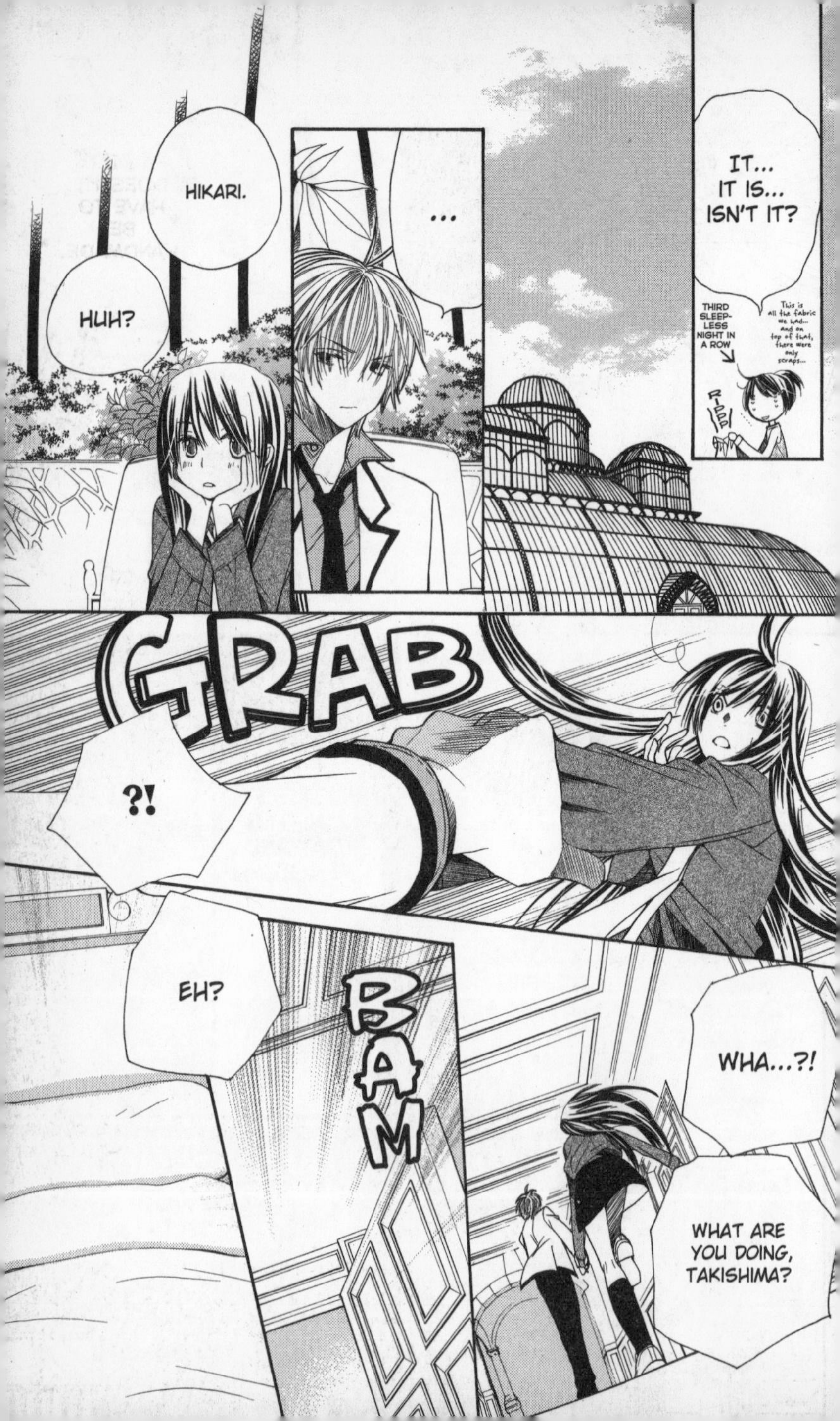
IT... IT IS... ISN'T IT?
This is all the fabric we had... and on top of that, there were only scraps...
THIRD SLEEP-LESS NIGHT IN A ROW
RIPP
...
HIKARI.
HUH?
GRAB
?!
WHA...?!
WHAT ARE YOU DOING, TAKISHIMA?
EH?
BAM

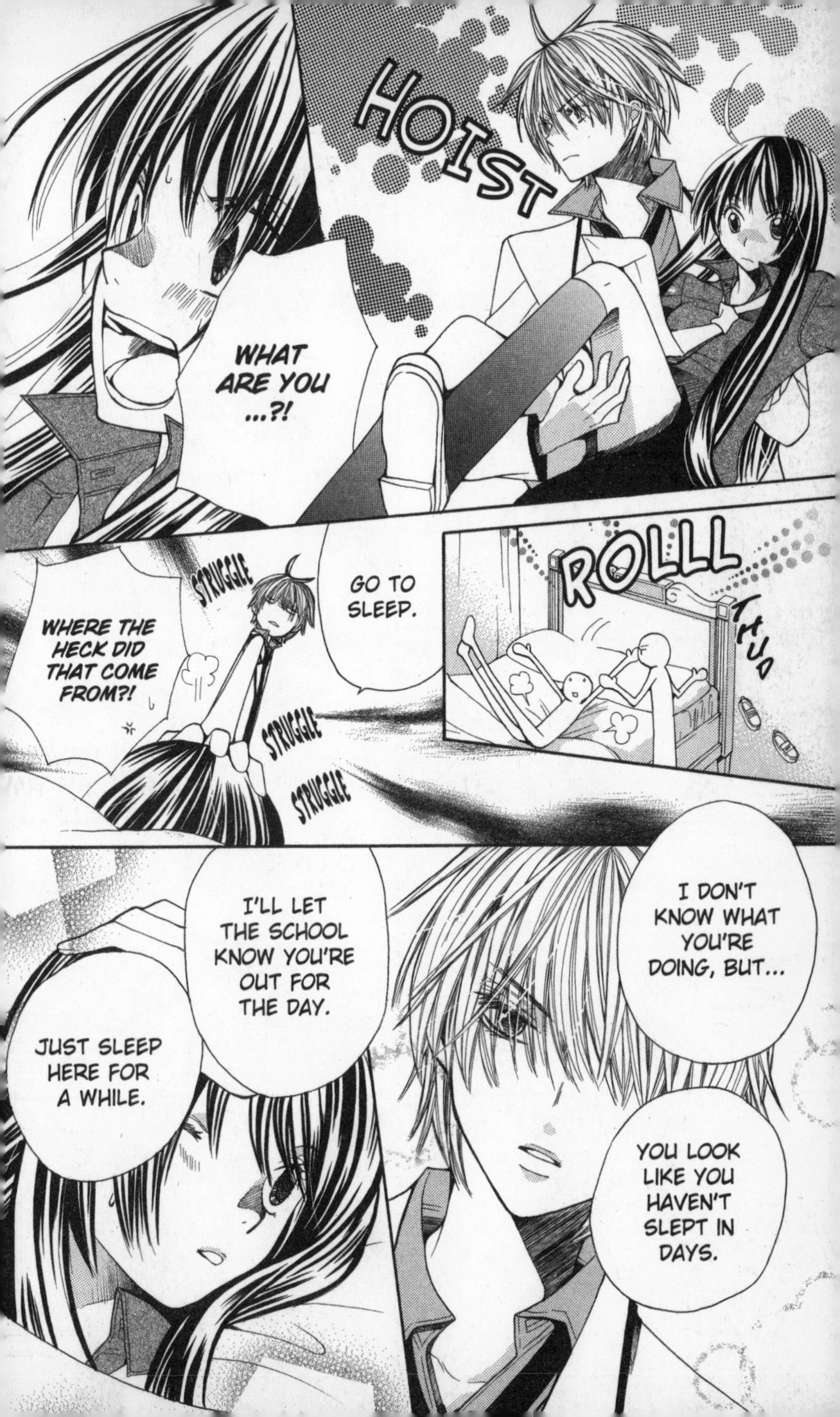
HOIST
WHAT ARE YOU ...?!
ROLLL
THUD
GO TO SLEEP.
STRUGGLE
WHERE THE HECK DID THAT COME FROM?!
STRUGGLE
STRUGGLE
I DON'T KNOW WHAT YOU'RE DOING, BUT...
YOU LOOK LIKE YOU HAVEN'T SLEPT IN DAYS.
I'LL LET THE SCHOOL KNOW YOU'RE OUT FOR THE DAY.
JUST SLEEP HERE FOR A WHILE.

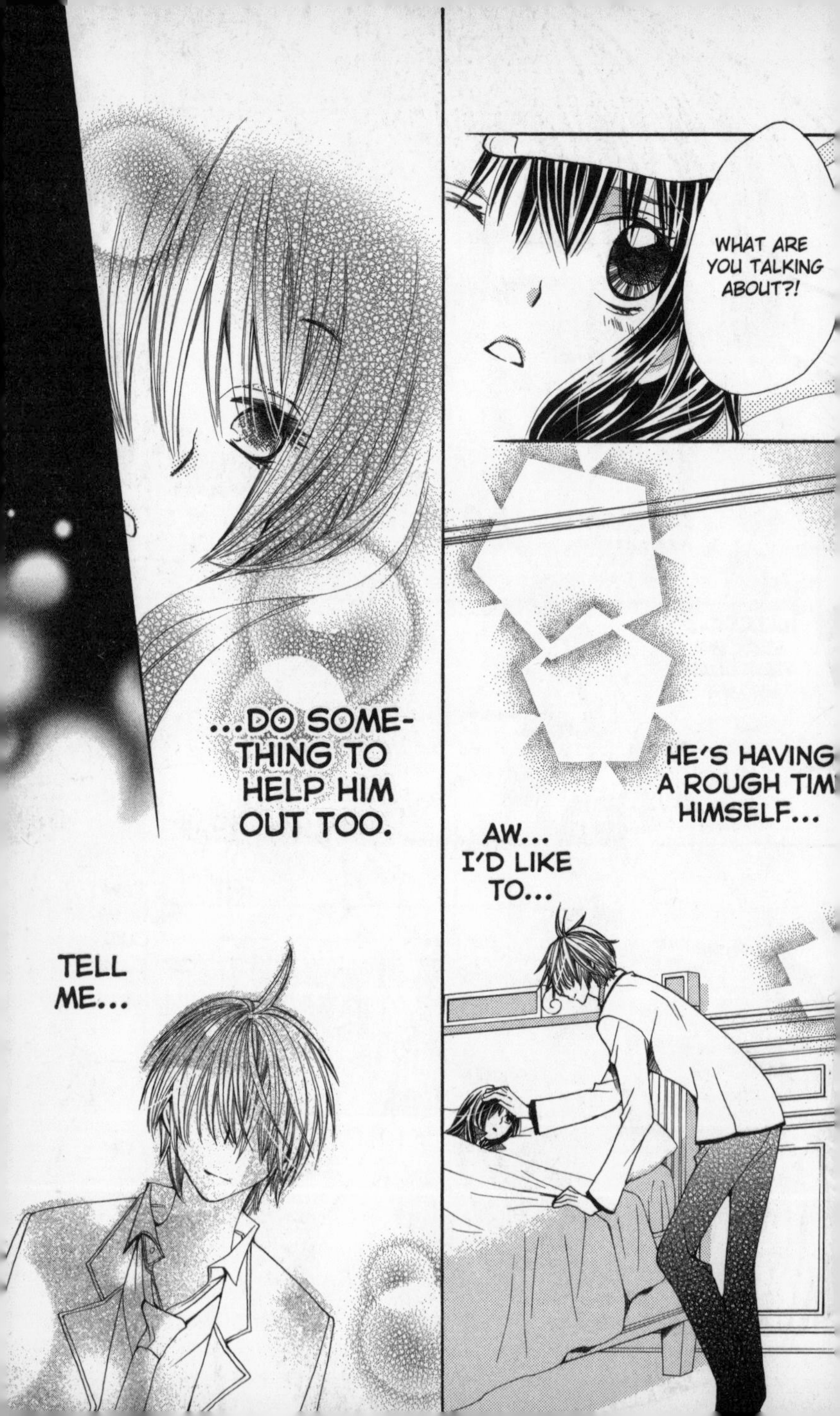
WHAT ARE YOU TALKING ABOUT?!
HE'S HAVING A ROUGH TIM HIMSELF...
AW... I'D LIKE TO...
...DO SOME-THING TO HELP HIM OUT TOO.
TELL ME...

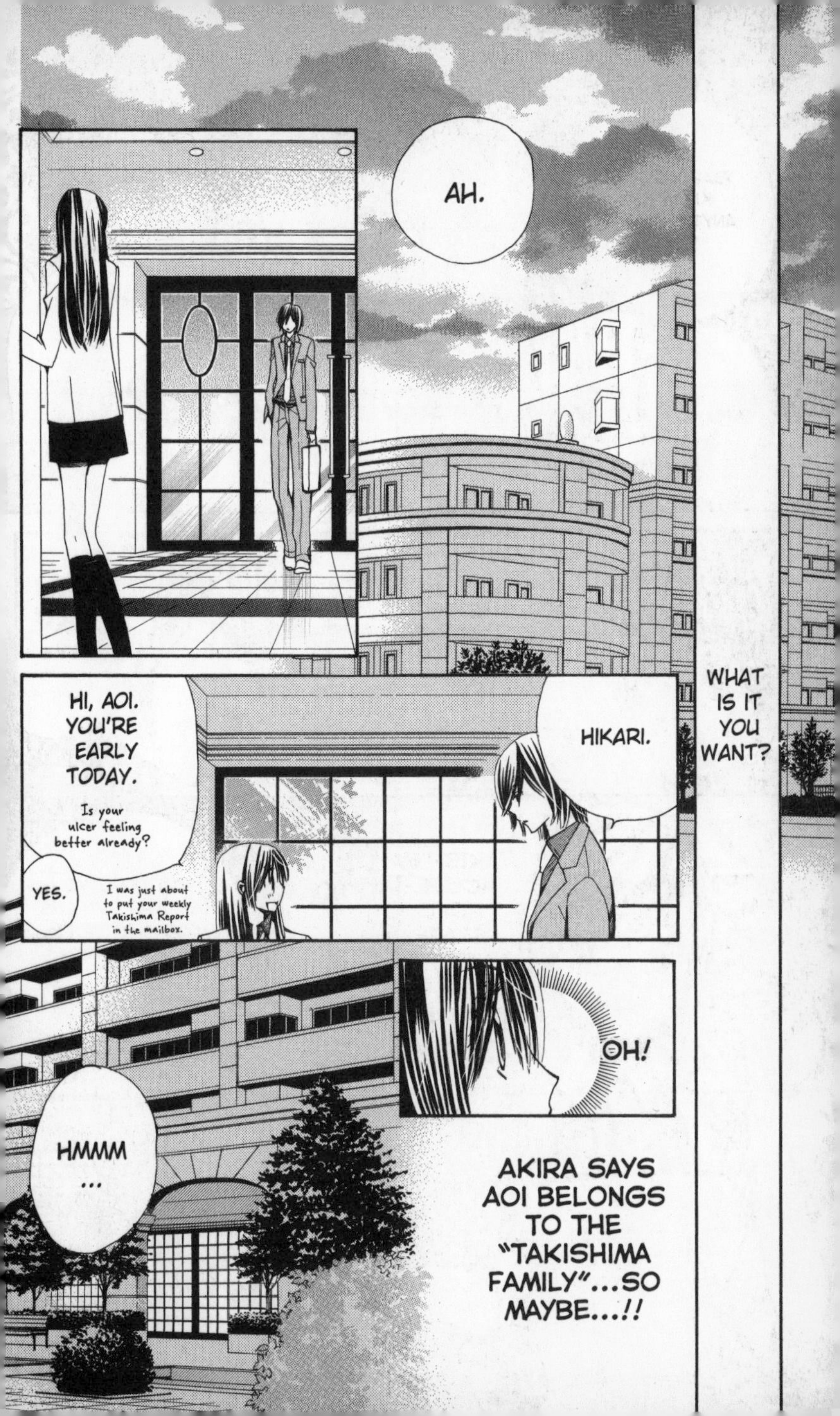
WHAT IS IT YOU WANT?
AH.
HIKARI.
HI, AOI. YOU'RE EARLY TODAY.
Is your ulcer feeling better already?
YES.
I was just about to put your weekly Takishima Report in the mailbox.
OH!
AKIRA SAYS AOI BELONGS TO THE "TAKISHIMA FAMILY"...SO MAYBE...!!
HMMM ...

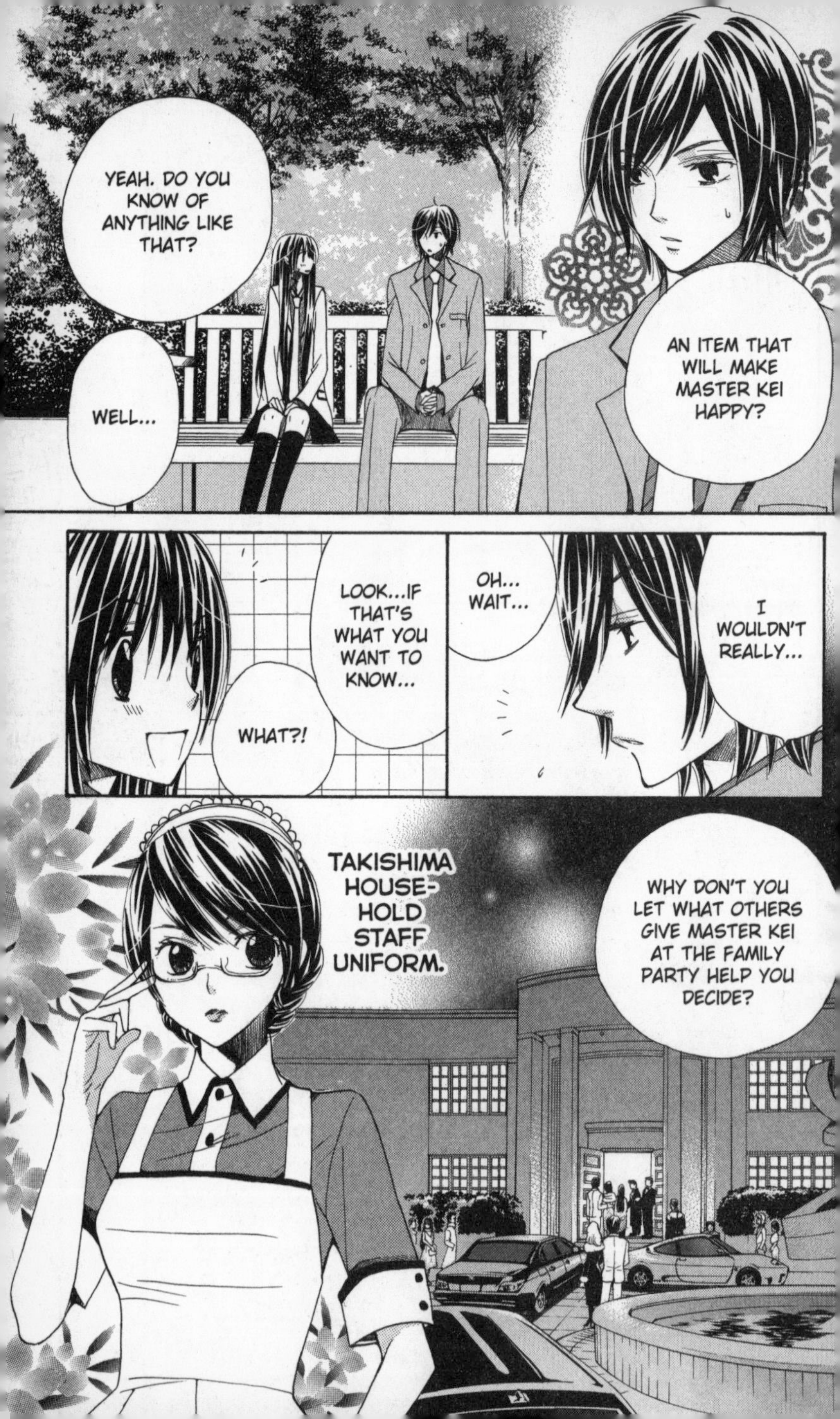
AN ITEM THAT WILL MAKE MASTER KEI HAPPY?
YEAH. DO YOU KNOW OF ANYTHING LIKE THAT?
WELL...
I WOULDN'T REALLY...
OH... WAIT...
LOOK...IF THAT'S WHAT YOU WANT TO KNOW...
WHAT?!
WHY DON'T YOU LET WHAT OTHERS GIVE MASTER KEI AT THE FAMILY PARTY HELP YOU DECIDE?
TAKISHIMA HOUSE-HOLD STAFF UNIFORM.

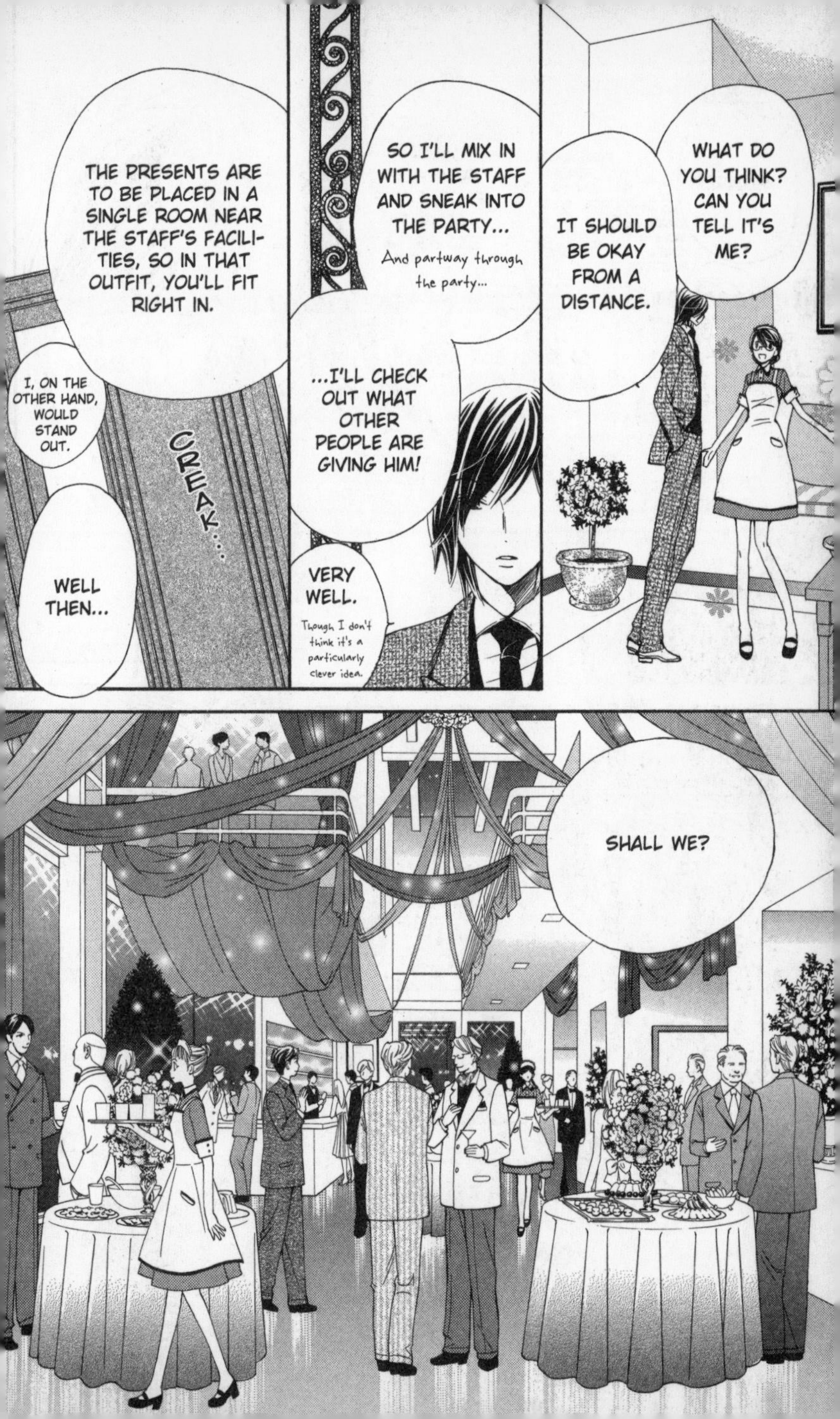
WHAT DO YOU THINK? CAN YOU TELL IT'S ME?
IT SHOULD BE OKAY FROM A DISTANCE.
SO I'LL MIX IN WITH THE STAFF AND SNEAK INTO THE PARTY...
And partway through the party...
...I'LL CHECK OUT WHAT OTHER PEOPLE ARE GIVING HIM!
VERY WELL.
Though I don't think it's a particularly clever idea.
THE PRESENTS ARE TO BE PLACED IN A SINGLE ROOM NEAR THE STAFF'S FACILI-TIES, SO IN THAT OUTFIT, YOU'LL FIT RIGHT IN.
I, ON THE OTHER HAND, WOULD STAND OUT.
CREAK...
WELL THEN...
SHALL WE?

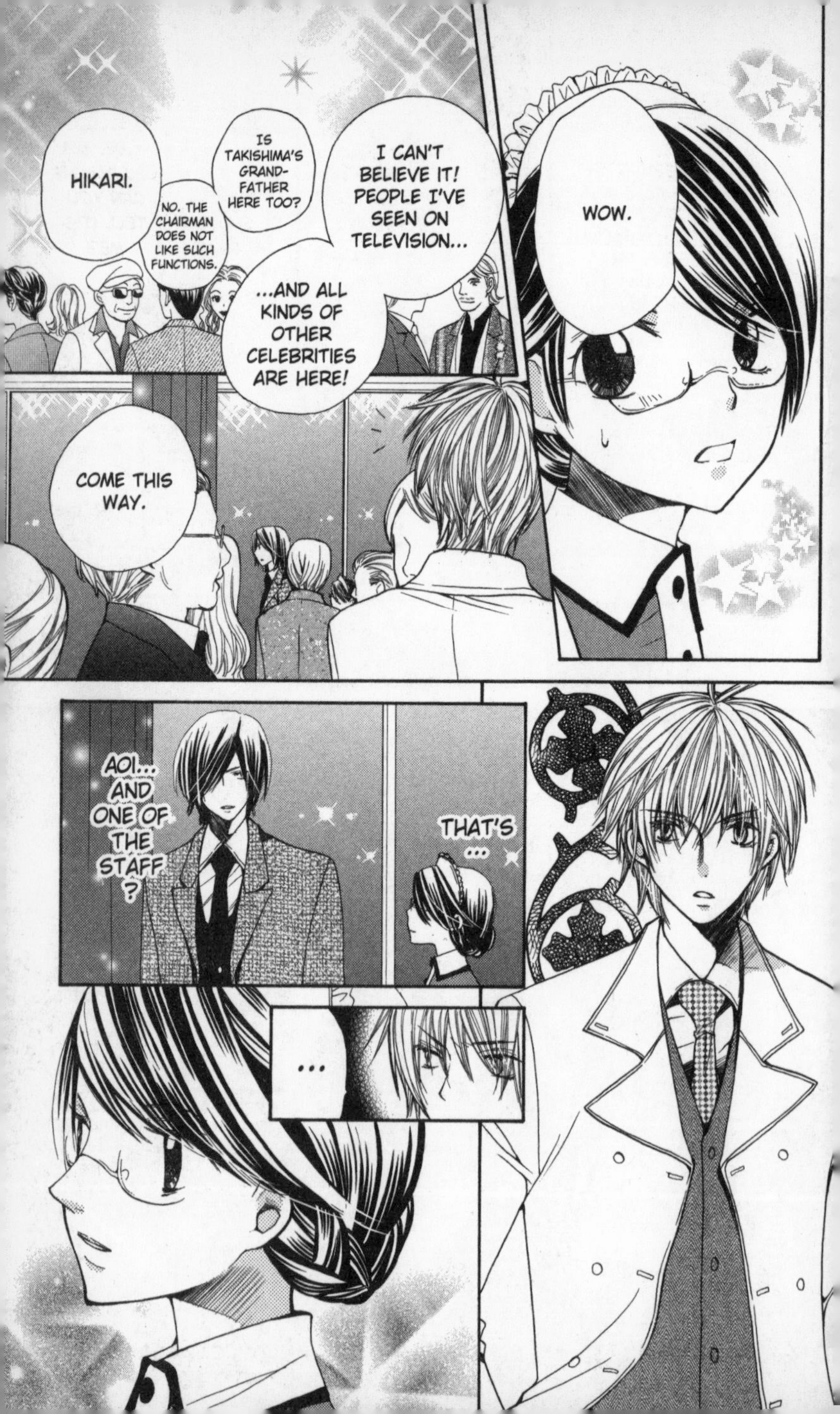
WOW.
I CAN'T BELIEVE IT! PEOPLE I'VE SEEN ON TELEVISION...
...AND ALL KINDS OF OTHER CELEBRITIES ARE HERE!
IS TAKISHIMA'S GRAND-FATHER HERE TOO?
NO. THE CHAIRMAN DOES NOT LIKE SUCH FUNCTIONS.
HIKARI.
COME THIS WAY.
THAT'S...
AOI... AND ONE OF THE STAFF?
...

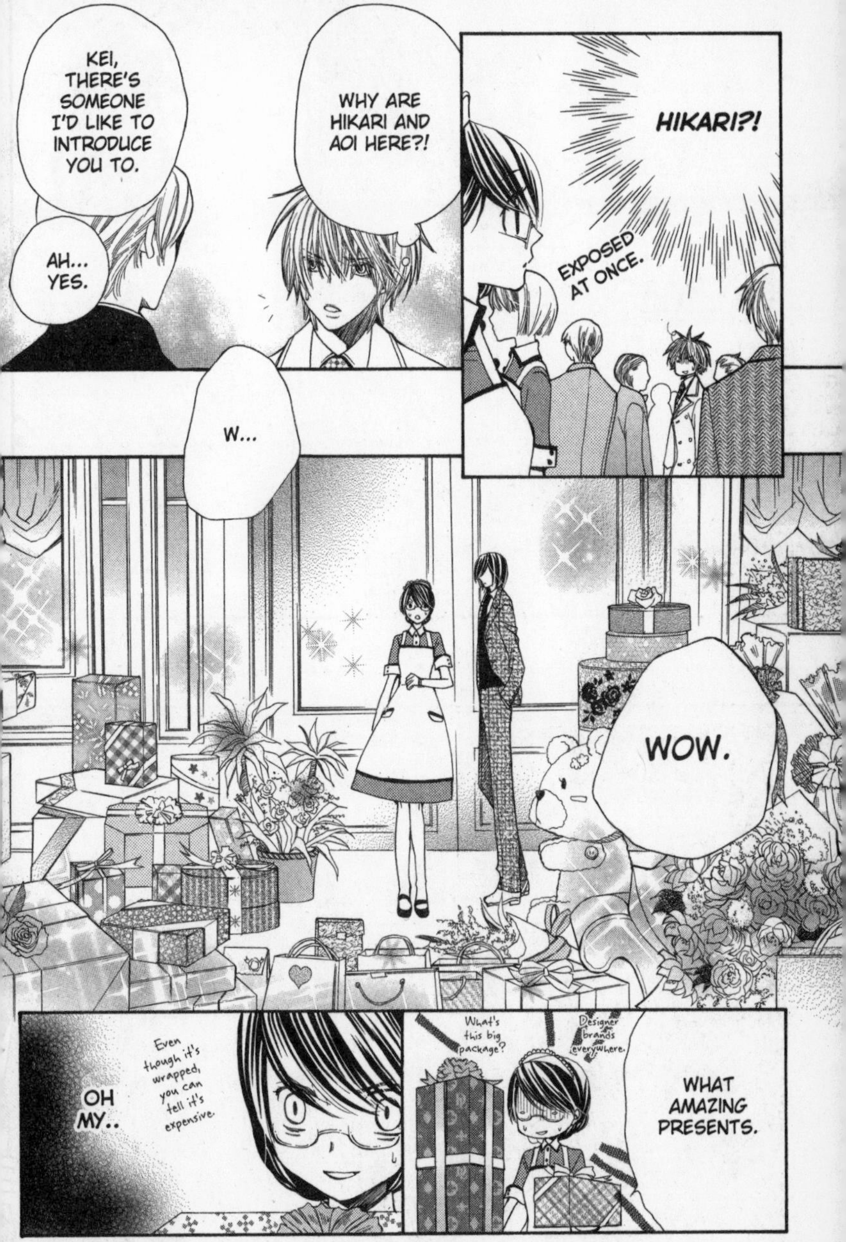
HIKARI?!
EXPOSED AT ONCE.
WHY ARE HIKARI AND AOI HERE?!
KEI, THERE'S SOMEONE I'D LIKE TO INTRODUCE YOU TO.
AH... YES.
W...
WOW.
WHAT AMAZING PRESENTS.
Designer brands everywhere.
What's this big package?
Even though it's wrapped, you can tell it's expensive.
OH MY..

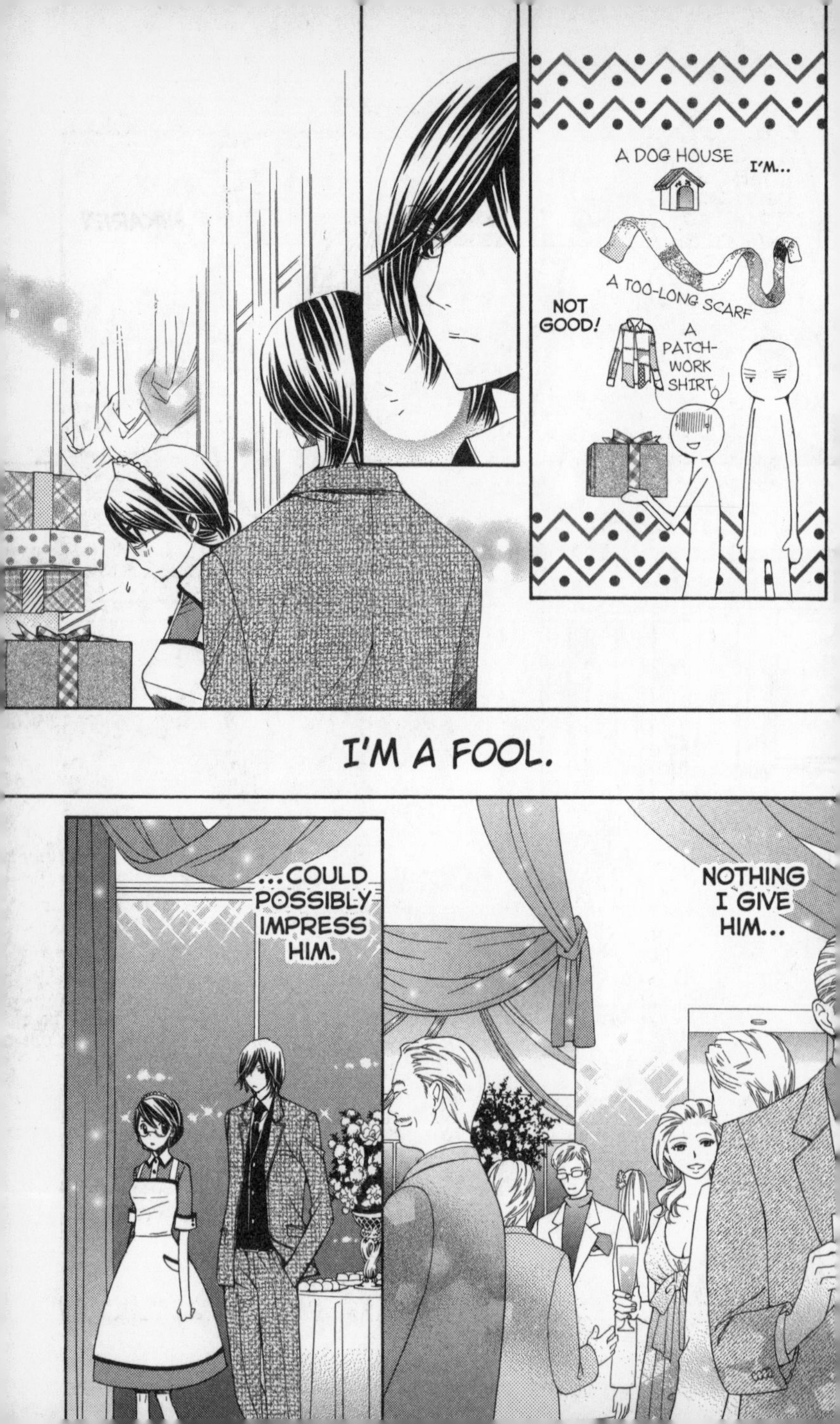
I'M...
A DOG HOUSE
A TOO-LONG SCARF
A PATCH-WORK SHIRT
NOT GOOD!
I'M A FOOL.
NOTHING I GIVE HIM...
...COULD POSSIBLY IMPRESS HIM.

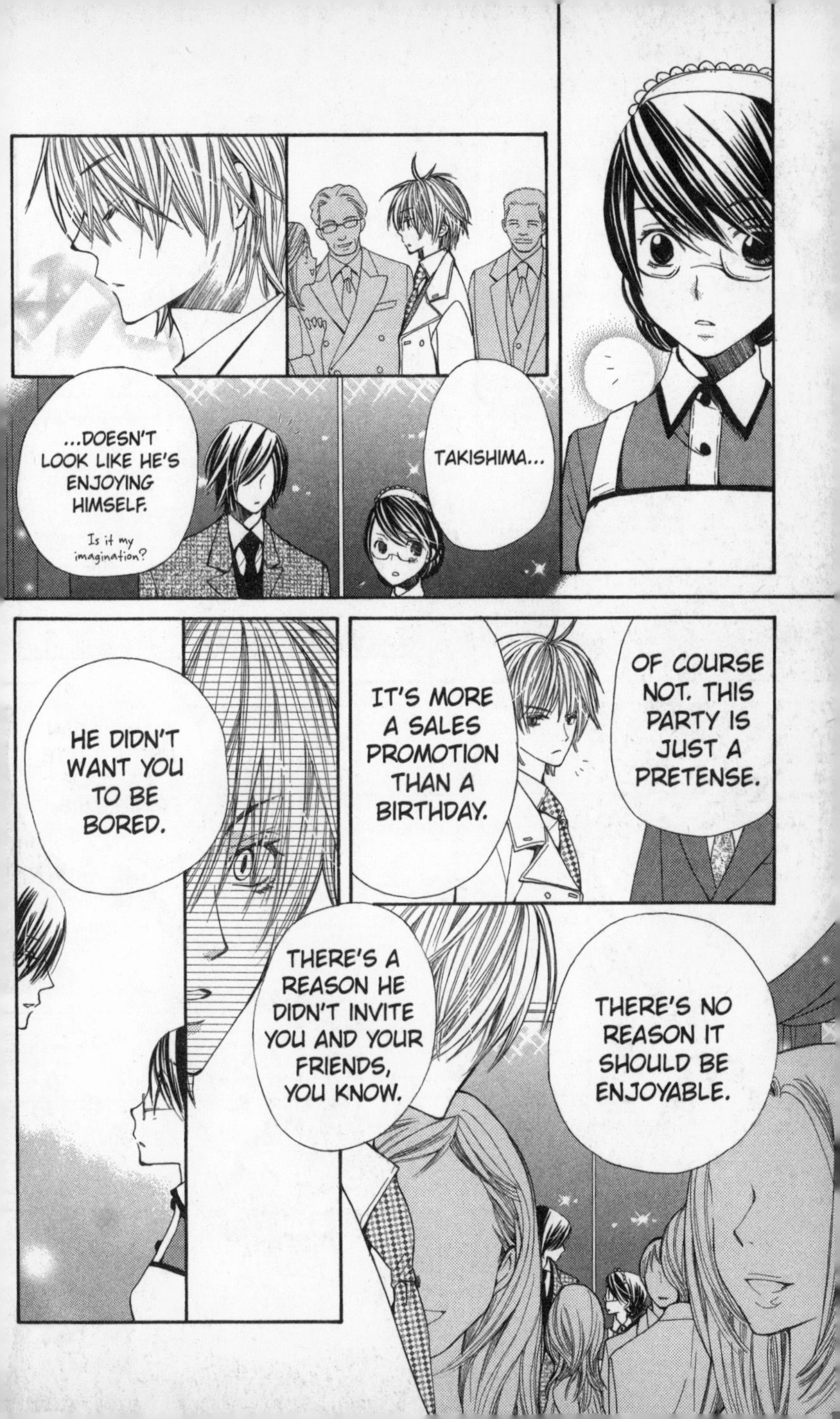
TAKISHIMA...
...DOESN'T LOOK LIKE HE'S ENJOYING HIMSELF.
Is it my imagination?
OF COURSE NOT. THIS PARTY IS JUST A PRETENSE.
IT'S MORE A SALES PROMOTION THAN A BIRTHDAY.
THERE'S NO REASON IT SHOULD BE ENJOYABLE.
THERE'S A REASON HE DIDN'T INVITE YOU AND YOUR FRIENDS, YOU KNOW.
HE DIDN'T WANT YOU TO BE BORED.

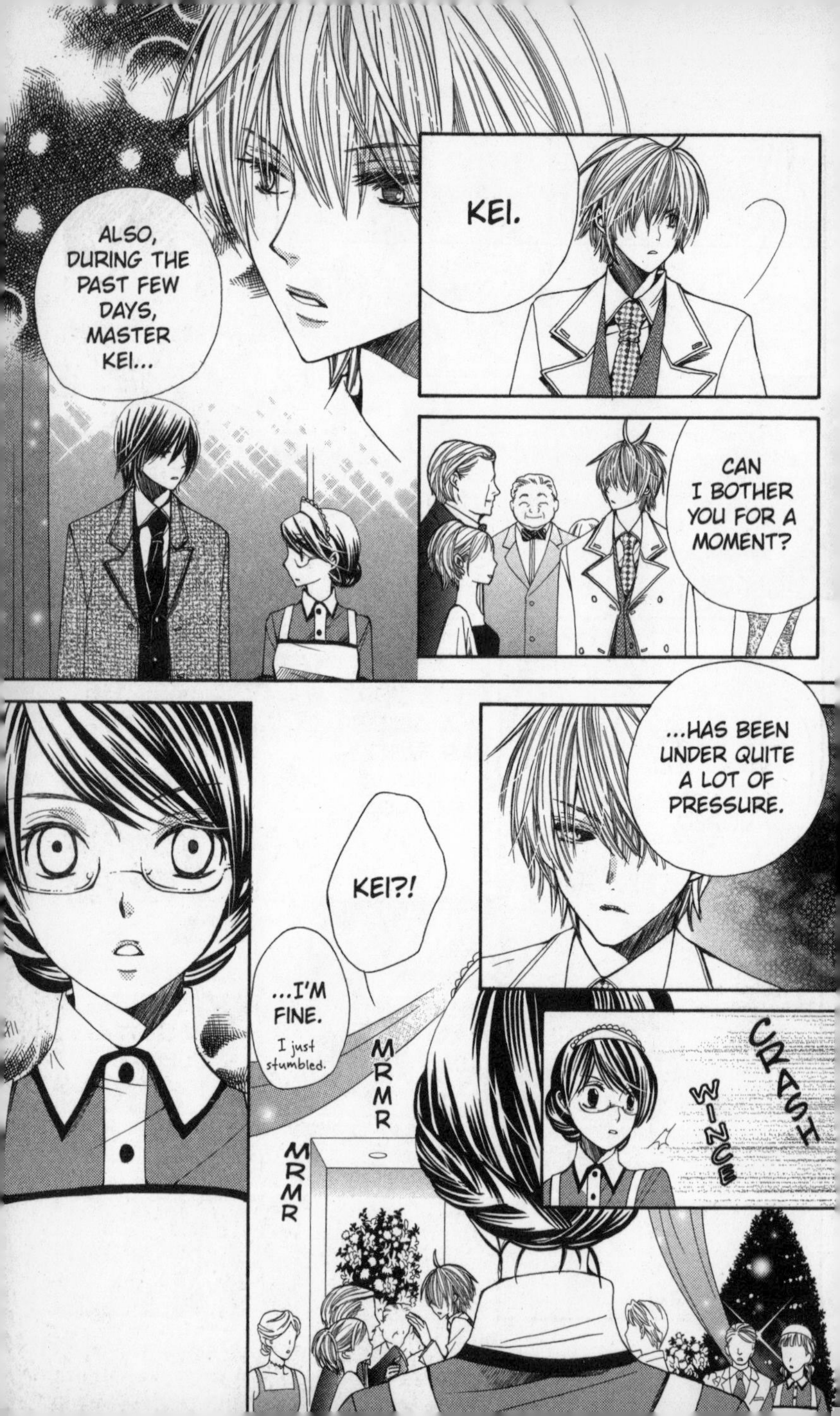
KEI.
CAN I BOTHER YOU FOR A MOMENT?
ALSO, DURING THE PAST FEW DAYS, MASTER KEI...
...HAS BEEN UNDER QUITE A LOT OF PRESSURE.
CRASH
WINCE
KEI?!
MRMR
MRMR
...I'M FINE.
I just stumbled.

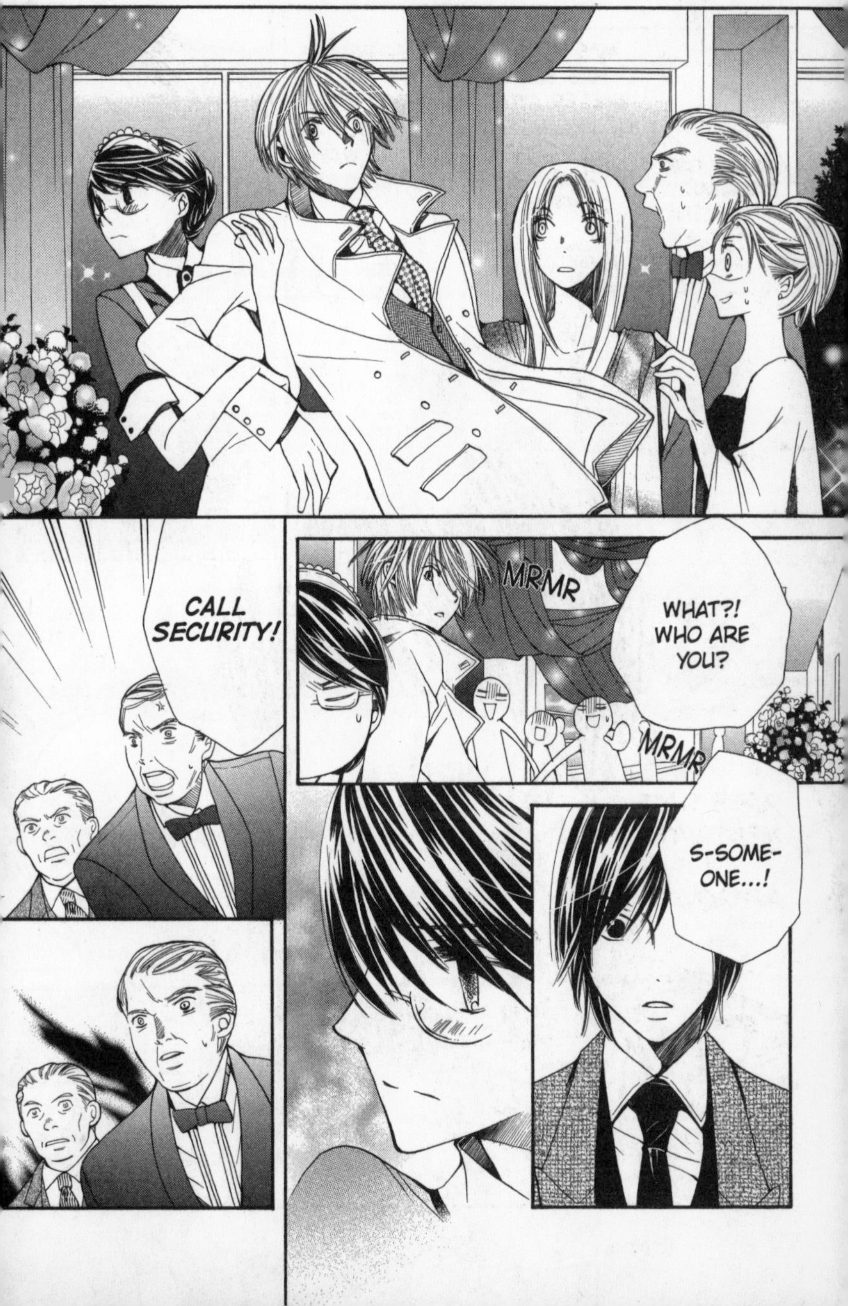
MRMR
WHAT?! WHO ARE YOU?
MRMR
S-SOME-ONE...!
CALL SECURITY!

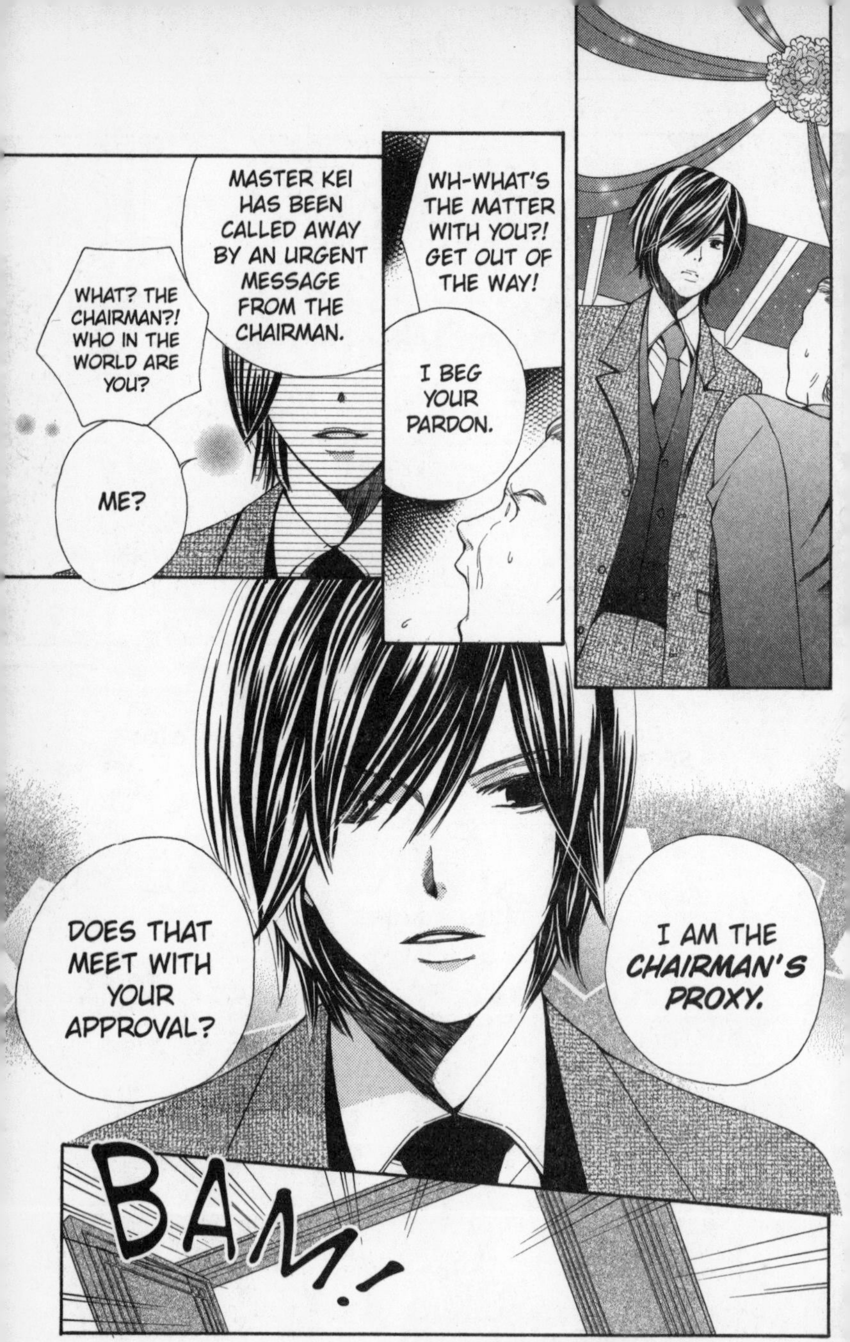
WH-WHAT'S THE MATTER WITH YOU?! GET OUT OF THE WAY!
I BEG YOUR PARDON.
MASTER KEI HAS BEEN CALLED AWAY BY AN URGENT MESSAGE FROM THE CHAIRMAN.
WHAT? THE CHAIRMAN?! WHO IN THE WORLD ARE YOU?
ME?
I AM THE *CHAIRMAN'S PROXY.*
DOES THAT MEET WITH YOUR APPROVAL?
BAM!

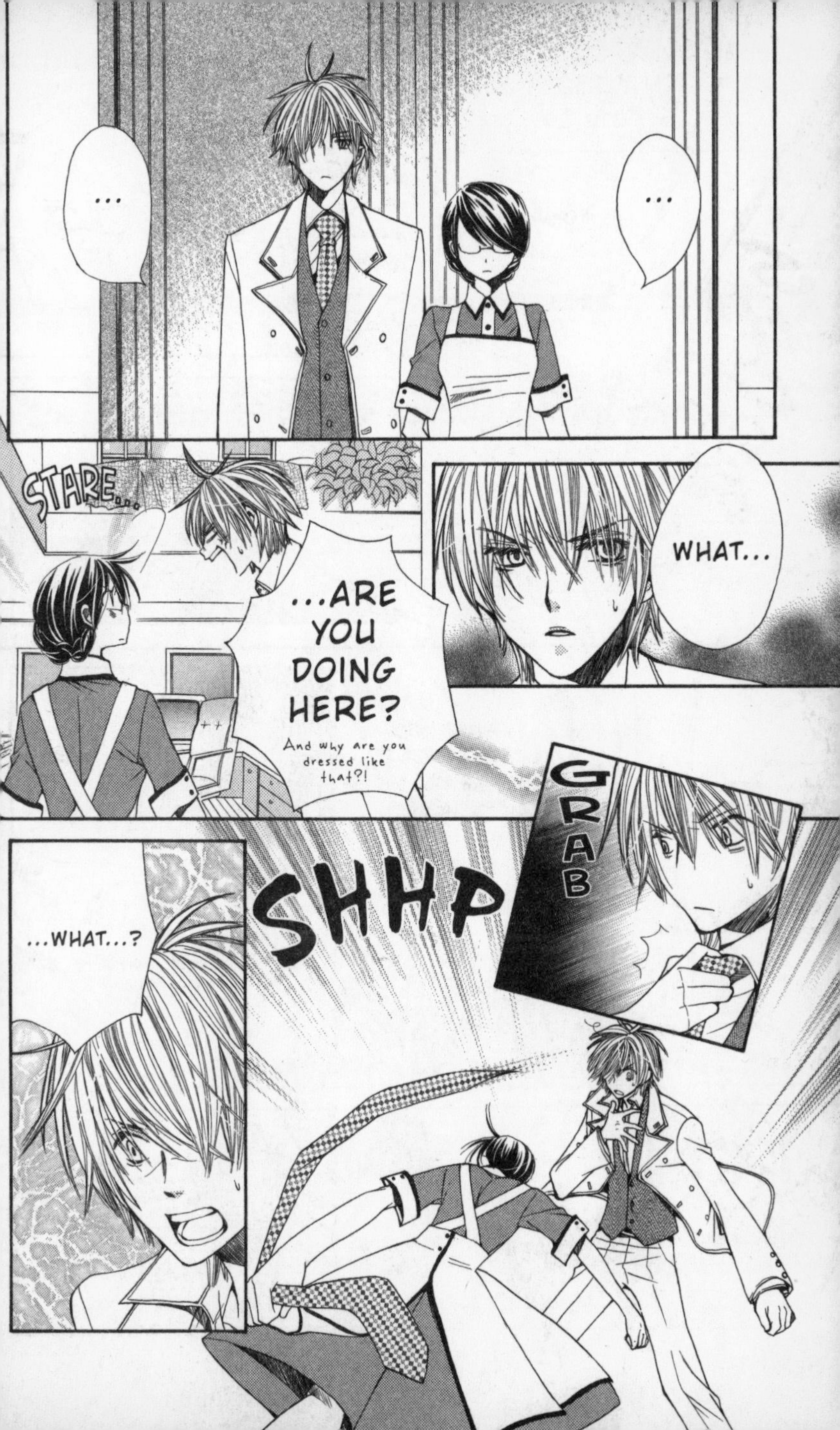
...
...
WHAT...
STARE...
...ARE YOU DOING HERE?
And why are you dressed like that?!
GRAB
SHHP
...WHAT...?

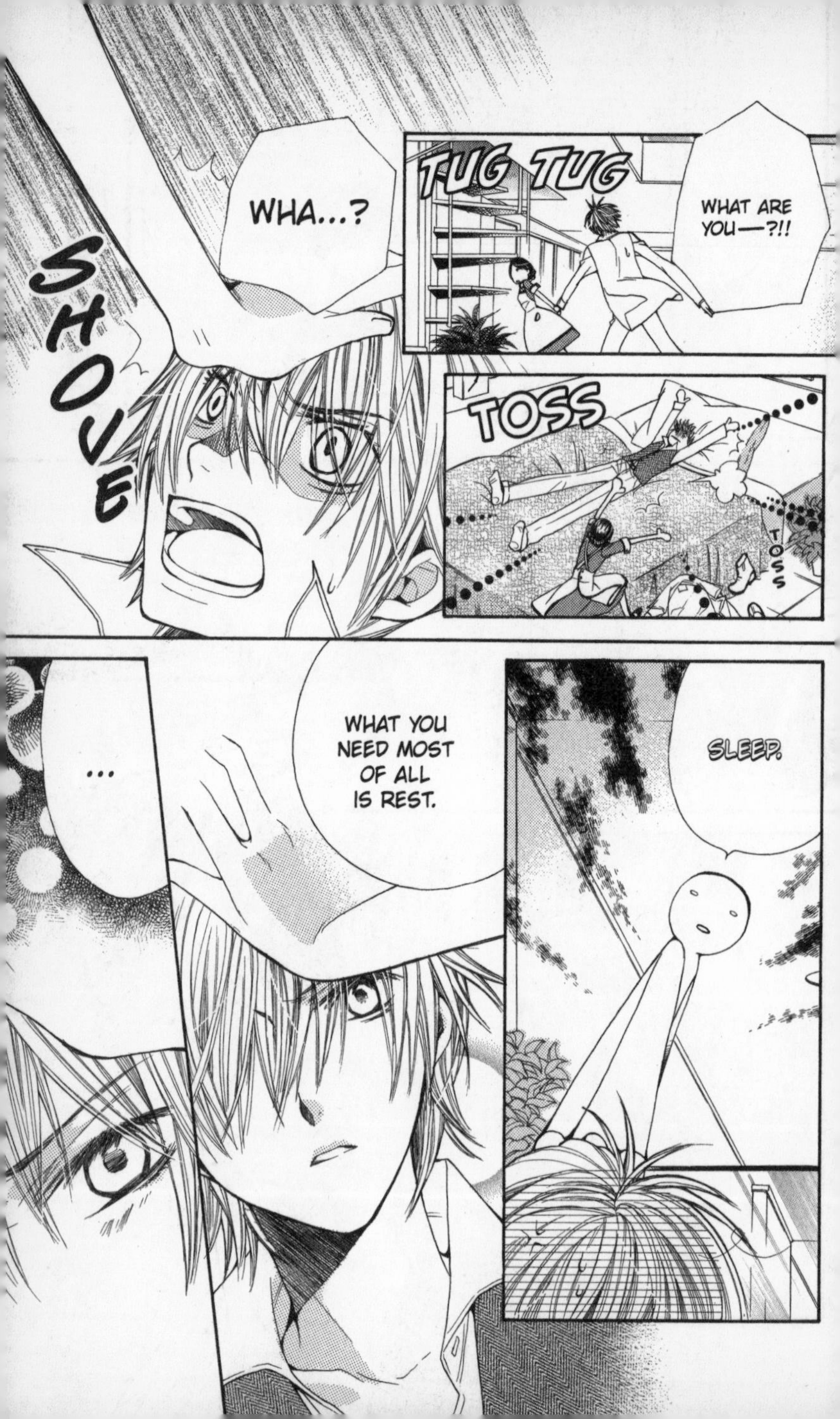
TUG TUG
WHAT ARE YOU—?!!
TOSS
TOSS
WHA...?
SHOVE
SLEEP.
WHAT YOU NEED MOST OF ALL IS REST.
...

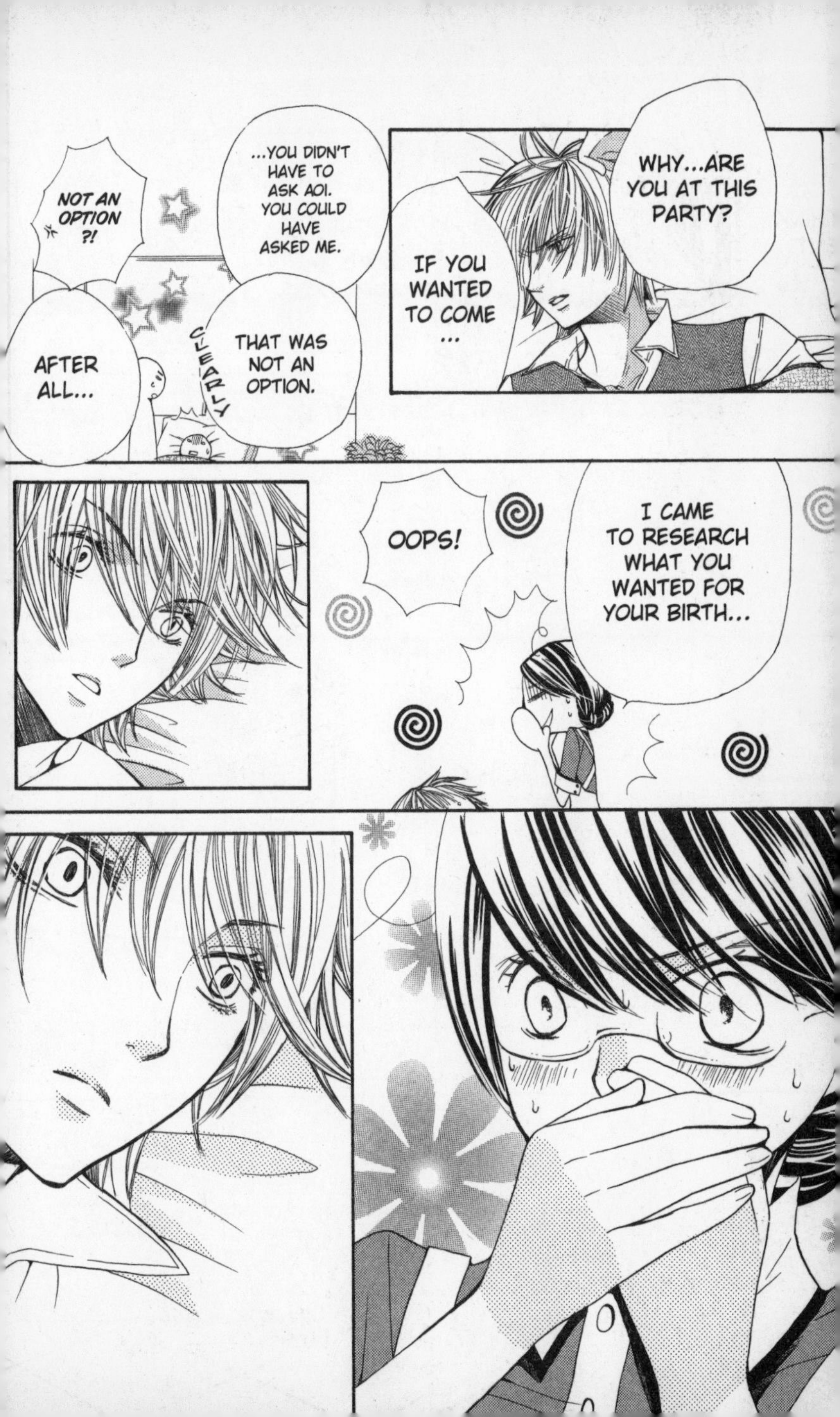
WHY...ARE YOU AT THIS PARTY?
IF YOU WANTED TO COME ...
...YOU DIDN'T HAVE TO ASK AOI. YOU COULD HAVE ASKED ME.
NOT AN OPTION ?!
CLEARLY
THAT WAS NOT AN OPTION.
AFTER ALL...
I CAME TO RESEARCH WHAT YOU WANTED FOR YOUR BIRTH...
OOPS!

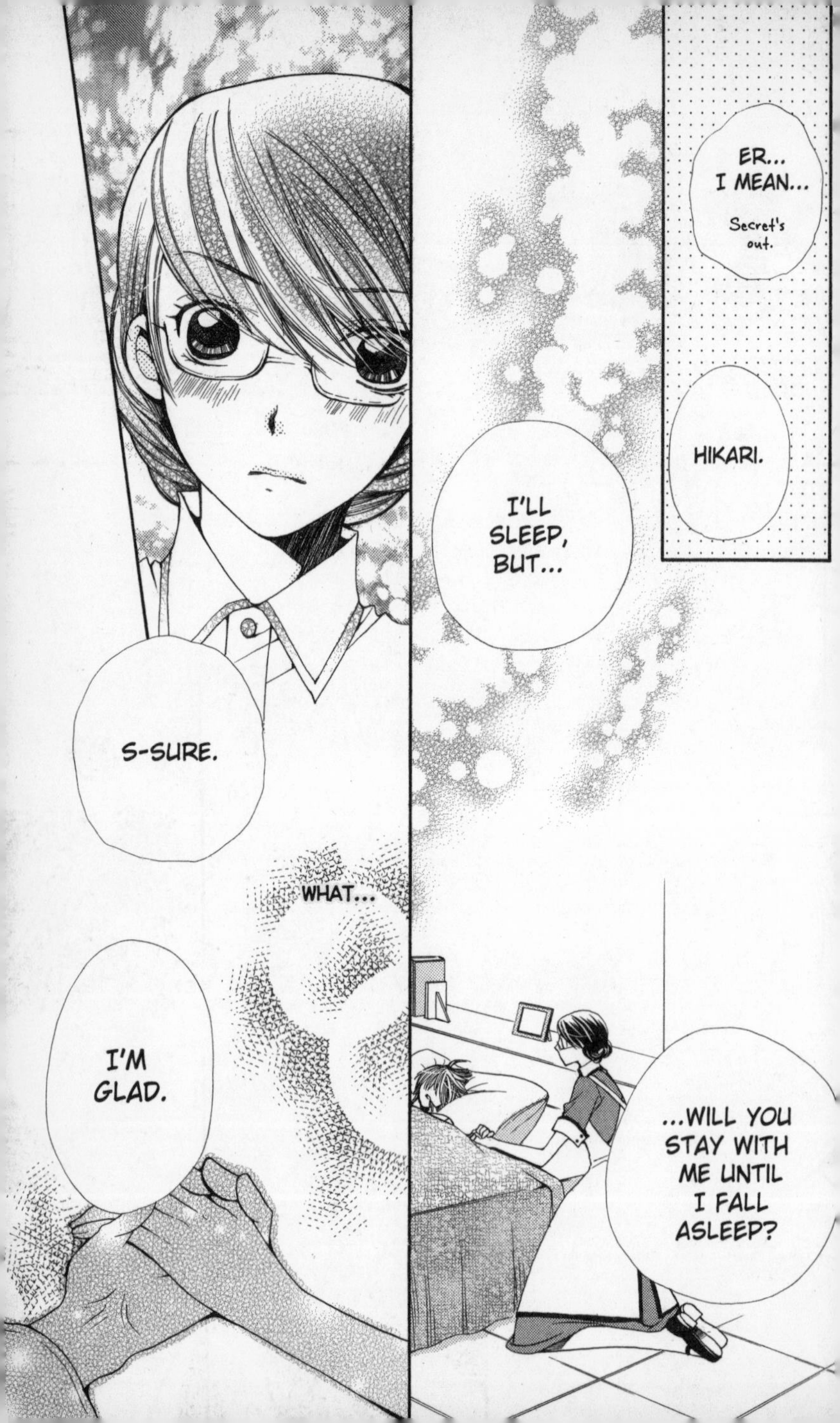
ER... I MEAN...
Secret's out.
HIKARI.
I'LL SLEEP, BUT...
...WILL YOU STAY WITH ME UNTIL I FALL ASLEEP?
S-SURE.
WHAT...
I'M GLAD.

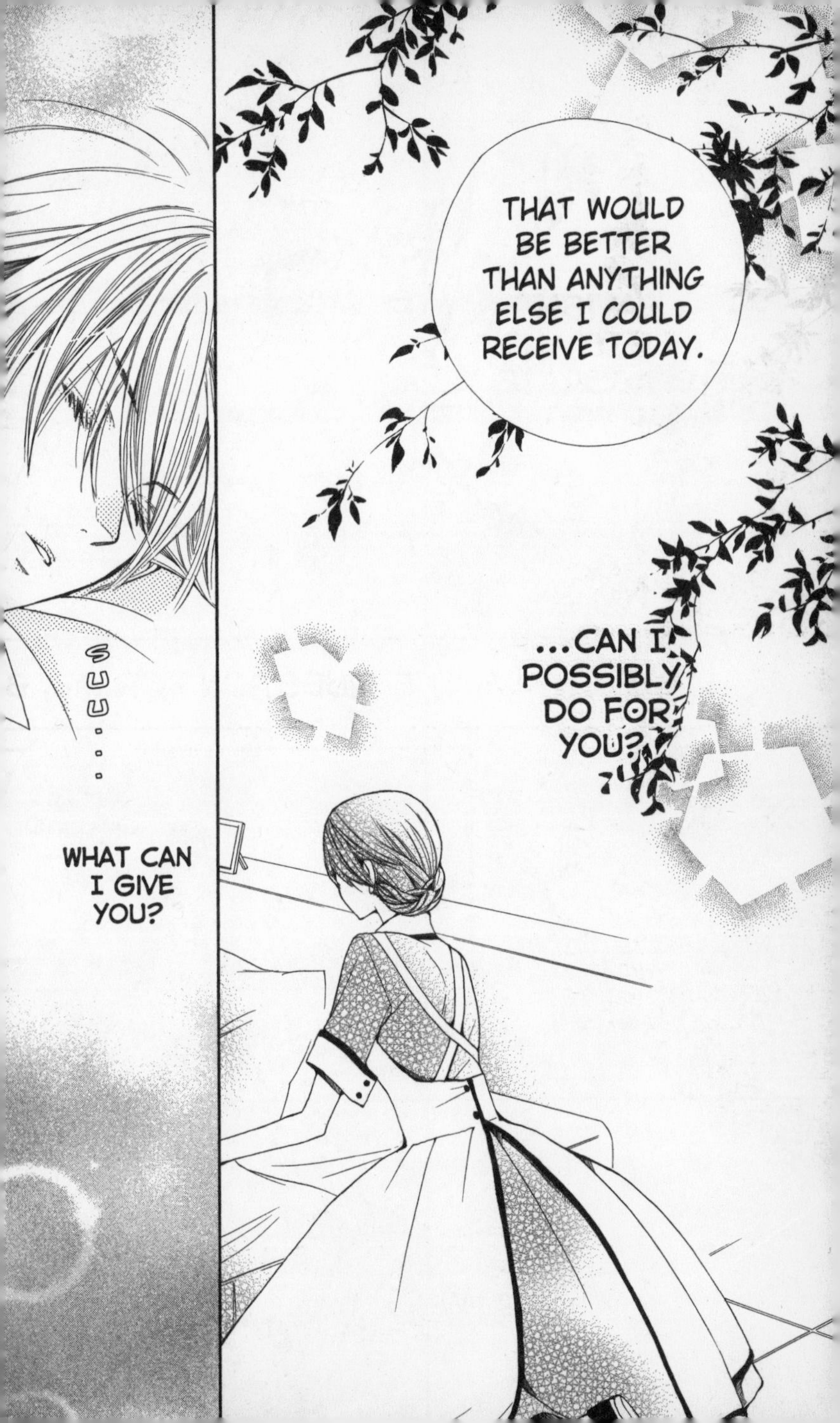
THAT WOULD BE BETTER THAN ANYTHING ELSE I COULD RECEIVE TODAY.
...CAN I POSSIBLY DO FOR YOU?
SUU...
WHAT CAN I GIVE YOU?

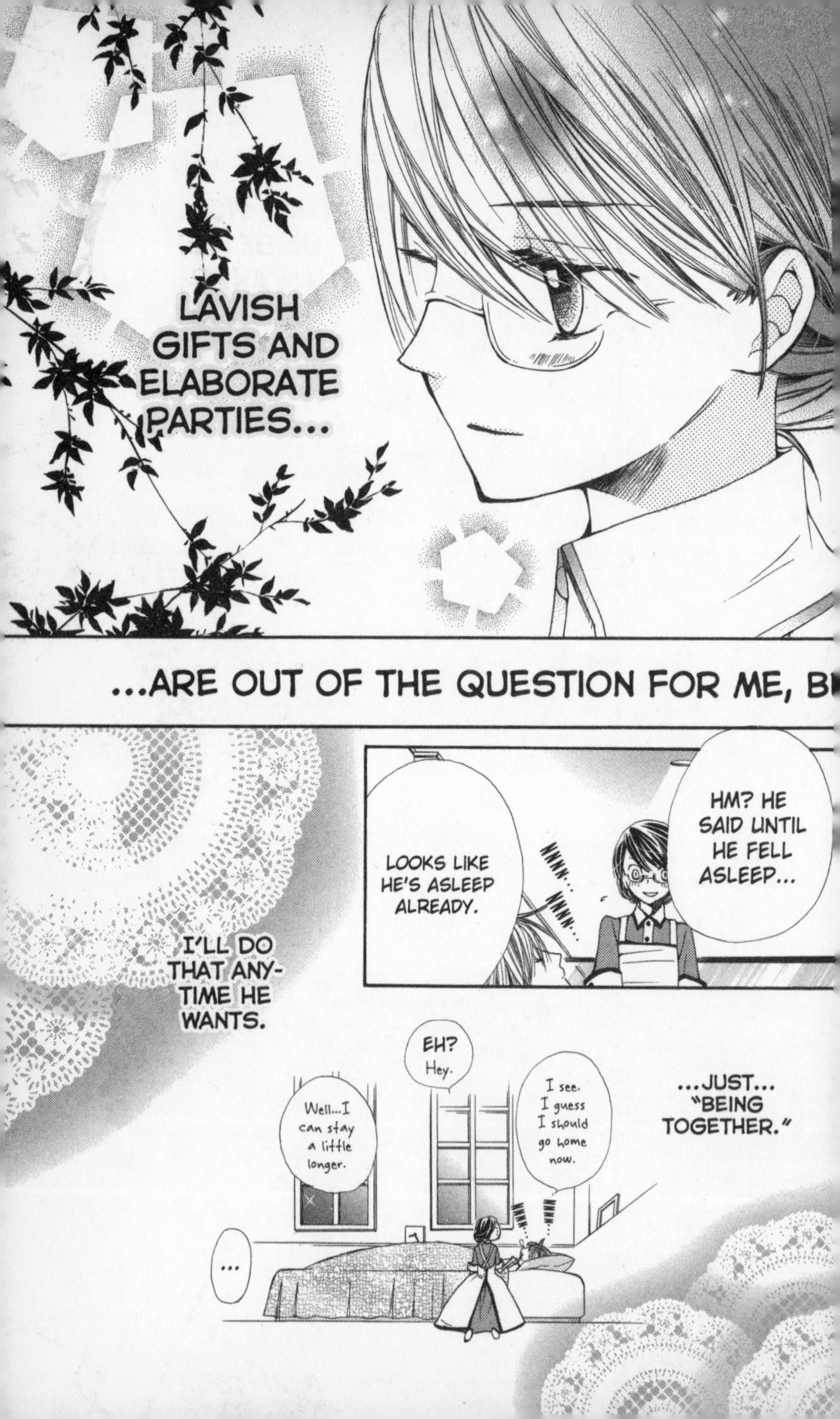
LAVISH GIFTS AND ELABORATE PARTIES...
...ARE OUT OF THE QUESTION FOR ME, B
HM? HE SAID UNTIL HE FELL ASLEEP...
NNNN...
LOOKS LIKE HE'S ASLEEP ALREADY.
I'LL DO THAT ANY-TIME HE WANTS.
...JUST... "BEING TOGETHER."
I see. I guess I should go home now.
NNNN...
EH? Hey.
Well...I can stay a little longer.
...

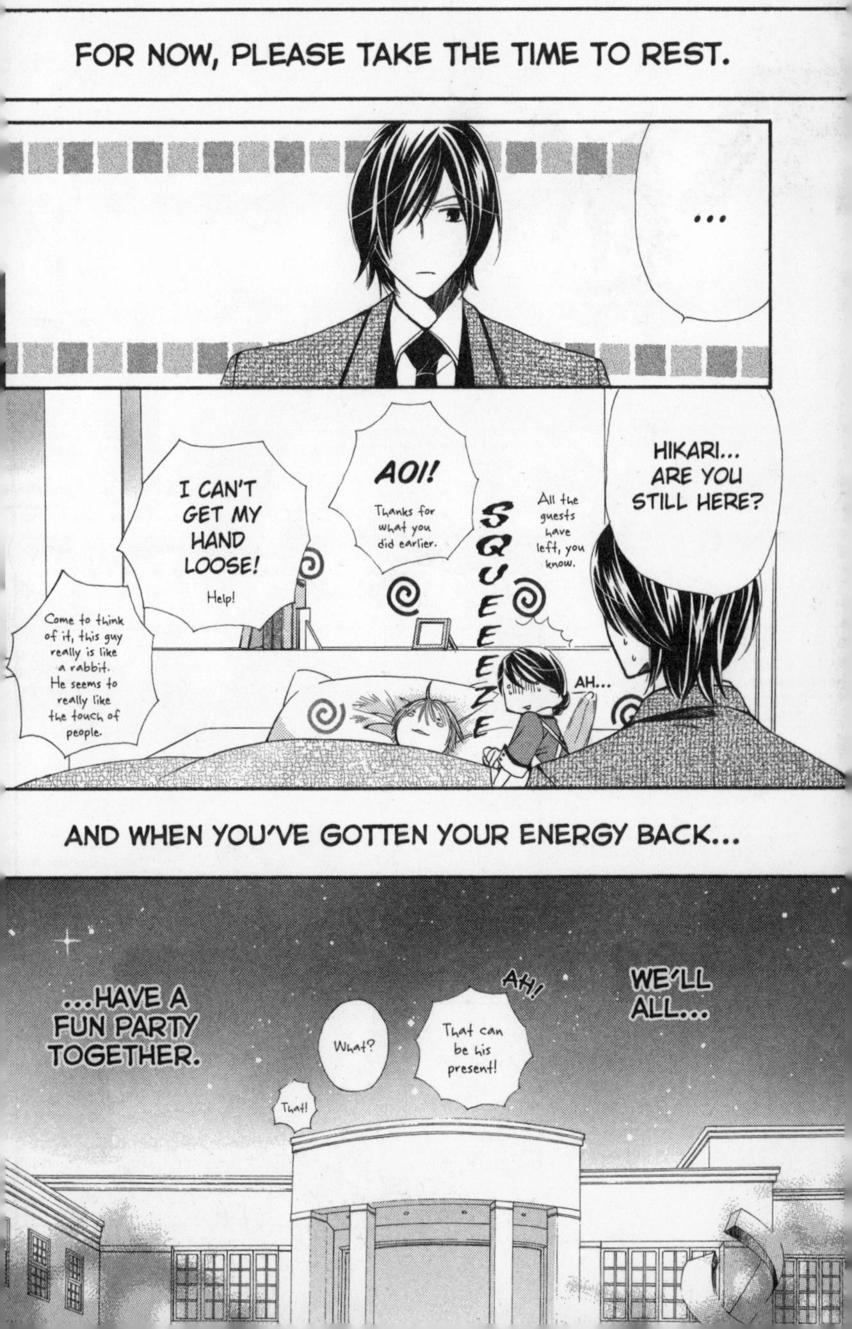
FOR NOW, PLEASE TAKE THE TIME TO REST.
...
HIKARI... ARE YOU STILL HERE?
All the guests have left, you know.
SQUEEEEZE
AH...
AOI!
Thanks for what you did earlier.
I CAN'T GET MY HAND LOOSE!
Help!
Come to think of it, this guy really is like a rabbit. He seems to really like the touch of people.
AND WHEN YOU'VE GOTTEN YOUR ENERGY BACK...
WE'LL ALL...
AH!
That can be his present!
What?
That!
...HAVE A FUN PARTY TOGETHER.

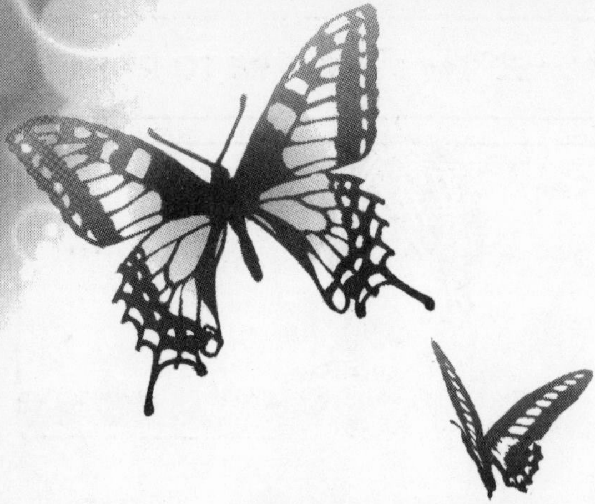

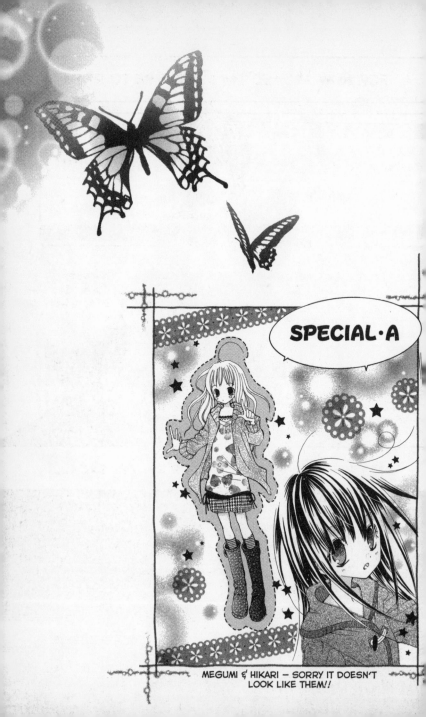

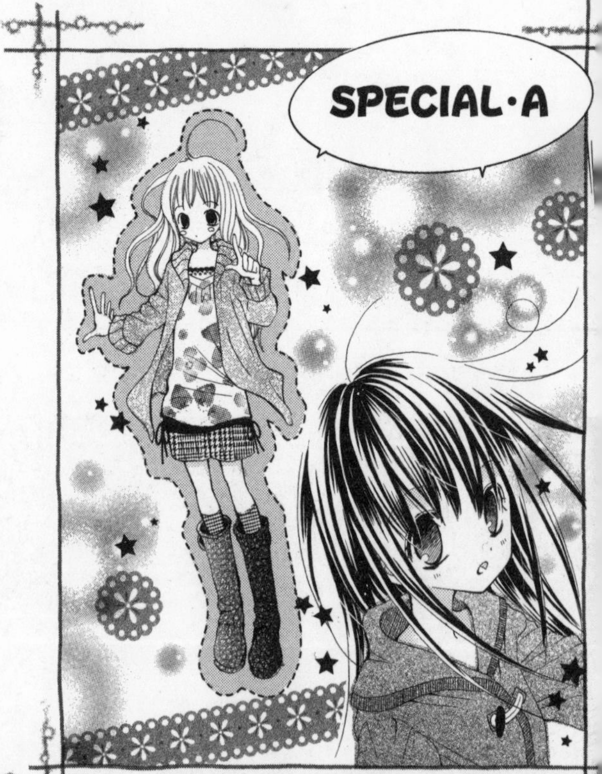
SPECIAL·A

MEGUMI & HIKARI – SORRY IT DOESN'T
LOOK LIKE THEM!!

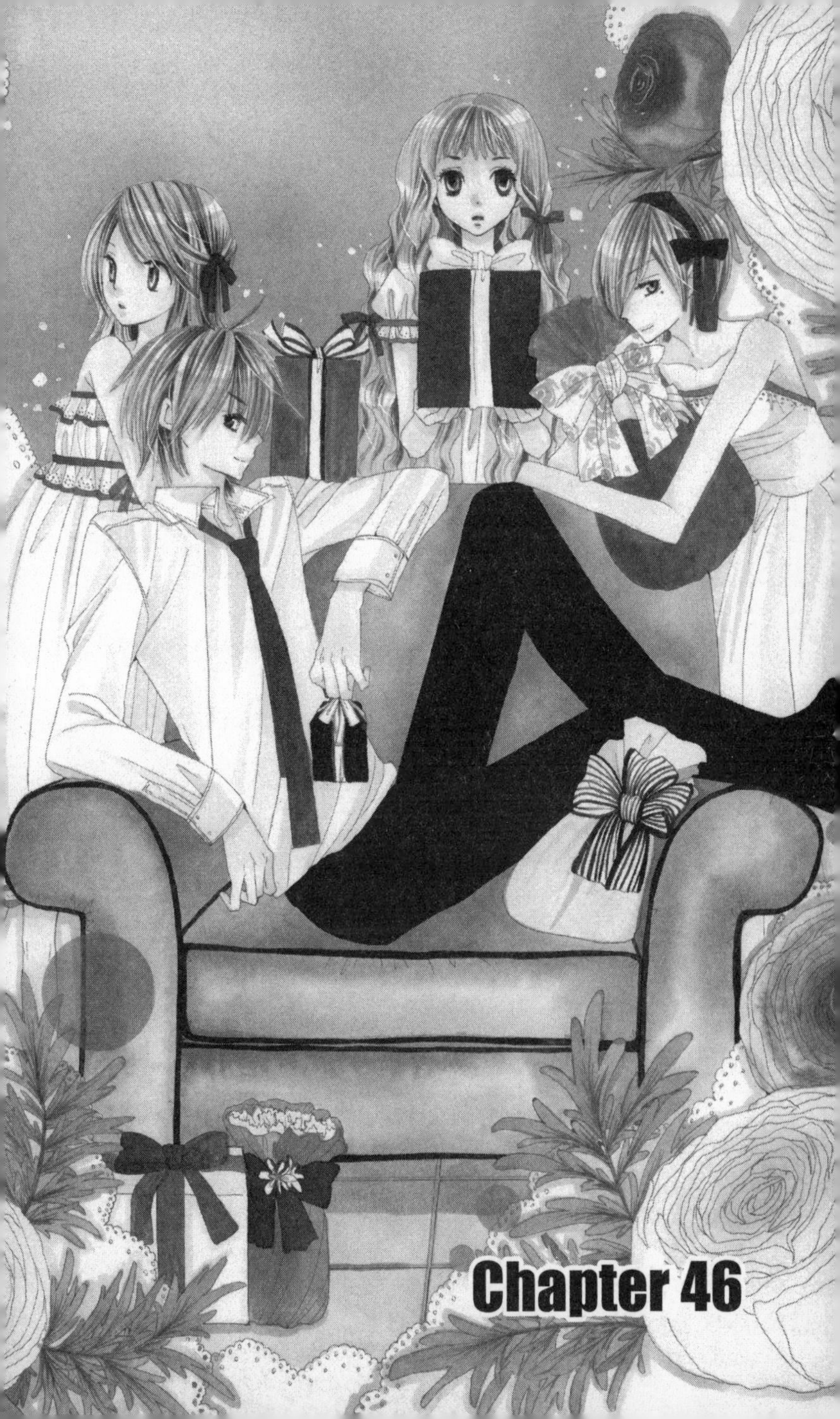

Chapter 46

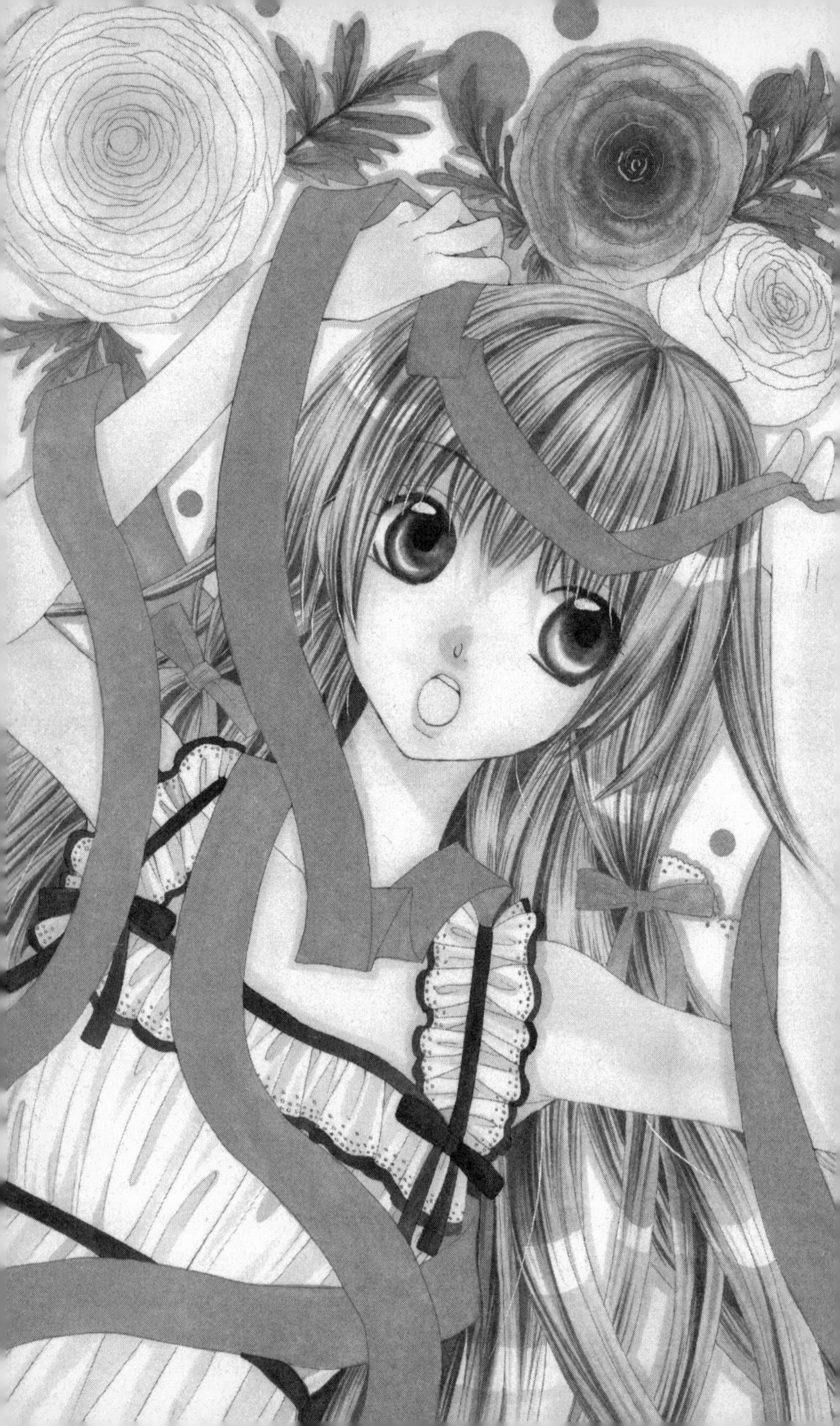

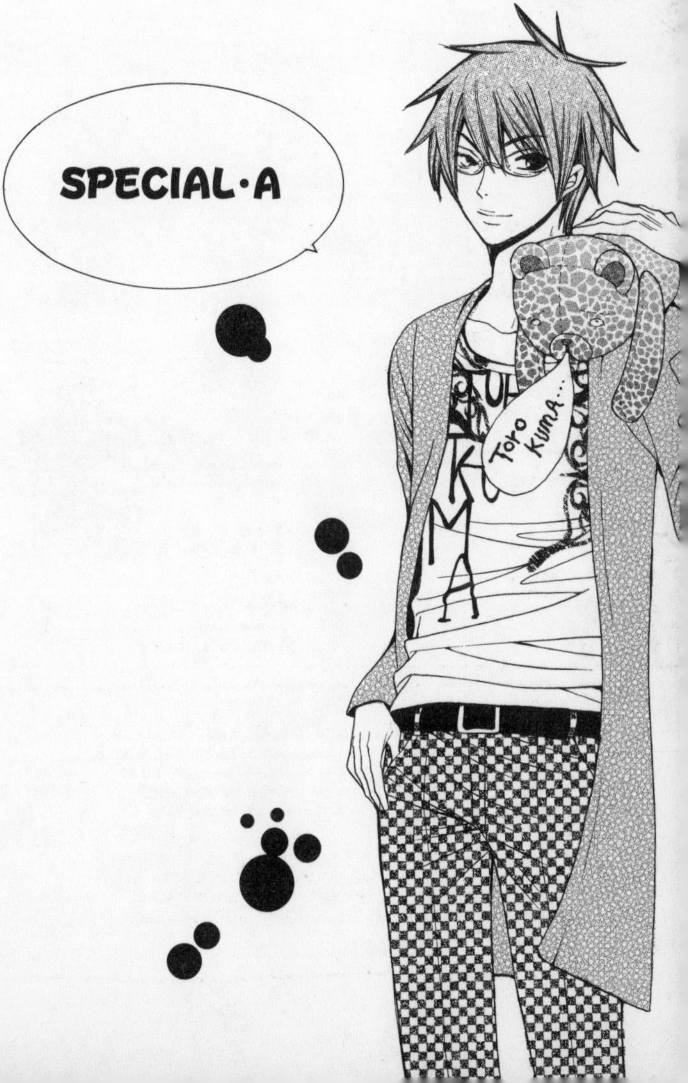
SPECIAL·A
Toro kuma...

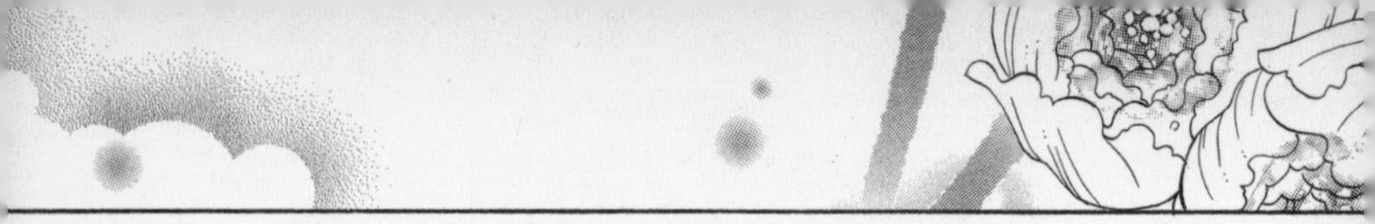

ONLY RECENTLY HAVE I FOUND BIRTHDAYS ENJOYABL

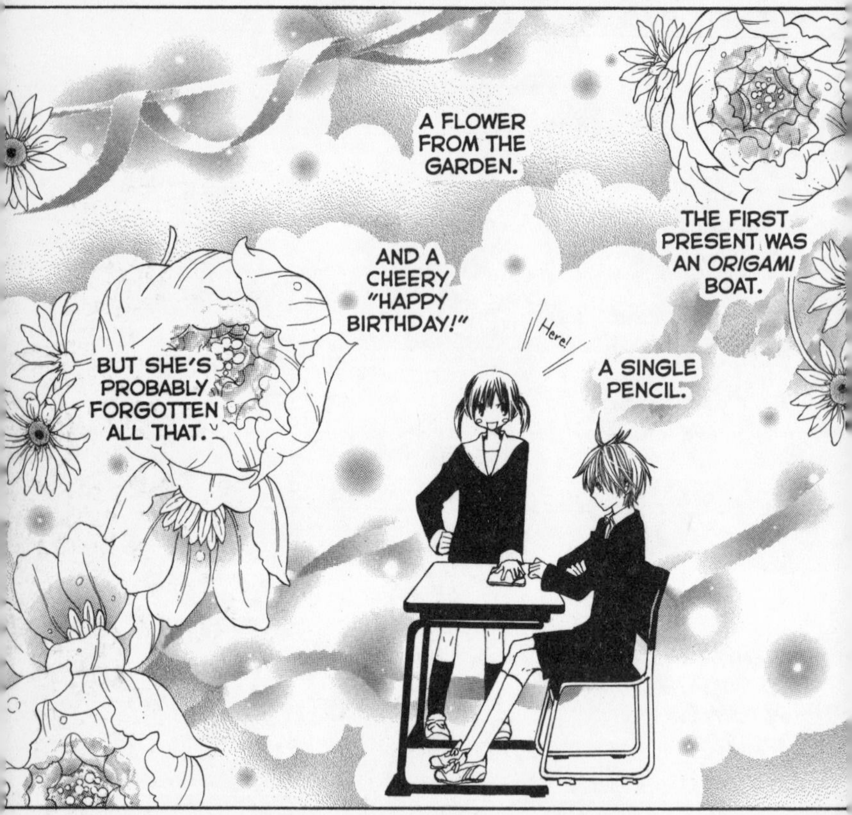
THE FIRST PRESENT WAS AN *ORIGAMI* BOAT.
A SINGLE PENCIL.
Here!
A FLOWER FROM THE GARDEN.
AND A CHEERY "HAPPY BIRTHDAY!"
BUT SHE'S PROBABLY FORGOTTEN ALL THAT.

•THIS AND THAT•

THIS IS THE LAST BOTTOM QUARTER PAGE. THANK YOU FOR STAYING WITH ME THROUGH IT ALL! THIS TIME I'M SPEAKING SERIOUSLY. HEE HEE! IT'S LIKE HOW A LETTER WRITTEN IN THE MIDDLE OF THE NIGHT CAN BE VERY EMBARRASSING WHEN READ IN THE MORNING. BUT IT'S ALREADY INKED! AH HA HA HA! I CAN'T ERASE IT!!

TO THOSE OF YOU WHO HAVE READ THIS FAR, TO MY ASSISTANTS WHO ALWAYS HELP ME, TO MY PREVIOUS EDITOR AND CURRENT EDITOR, AND TO MY FAMILY AND FRIENDS WHO SUPPORT ME: THANK YOU ALL SO MUCH! I HOPE WE CAN MEET AGAIN IN ANOTHER VOLUME!!

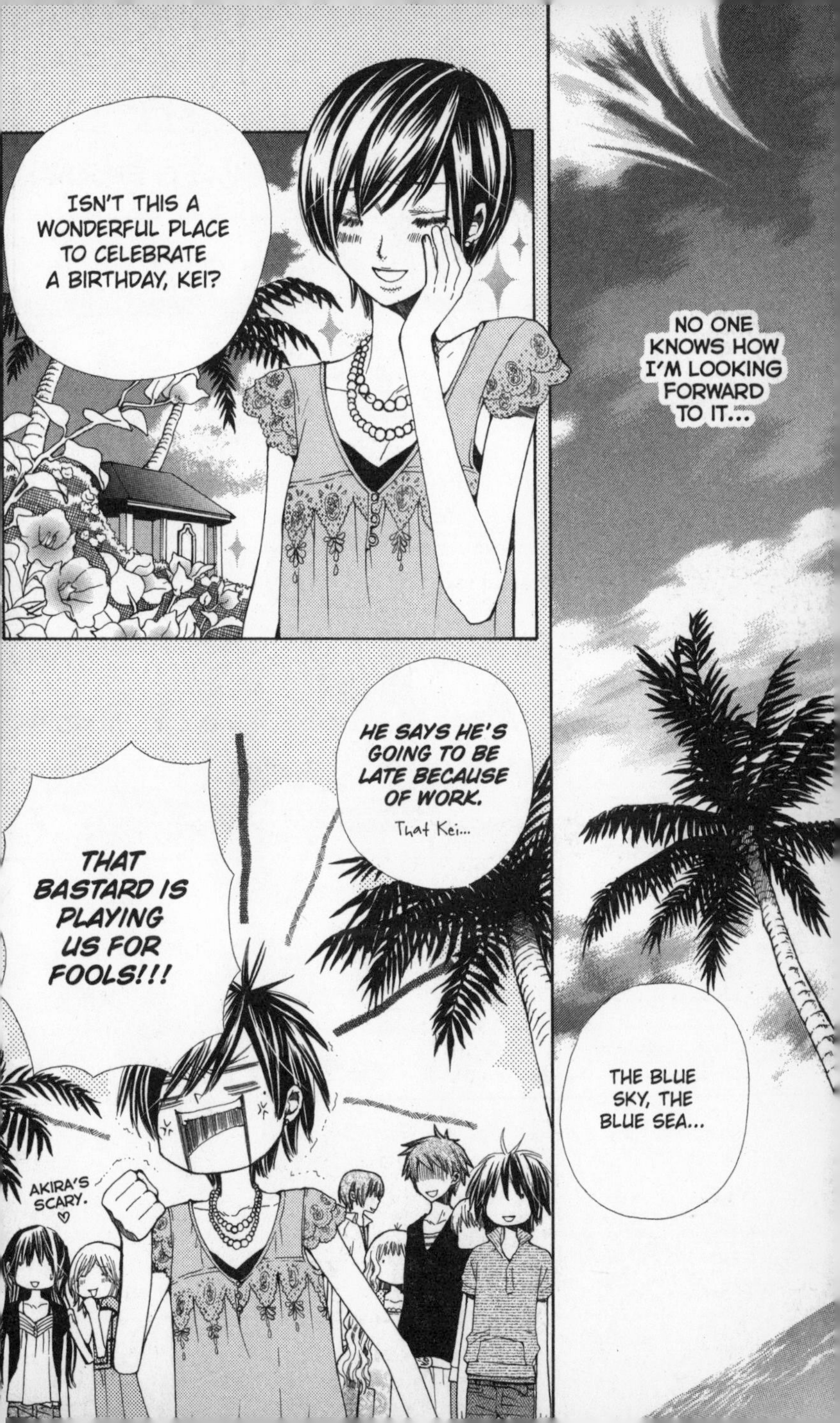
NO ONE KNOWS HOW I'M LOOKING FORWARD TO IT...
THE BLUE SKY, THE BLUE SEA...
ISN'T THIS A WONDERFUL PLACE TO CELEBRATE A BIRTHDAY, KEI?
HE SAYS HE'S GOING TO BE LATE BECAUSE OF WORK.
That Kei...
THAT BASTARD IS PLAYING US FOR FOOLS!!!
AKIRA'S SCARY. ♡

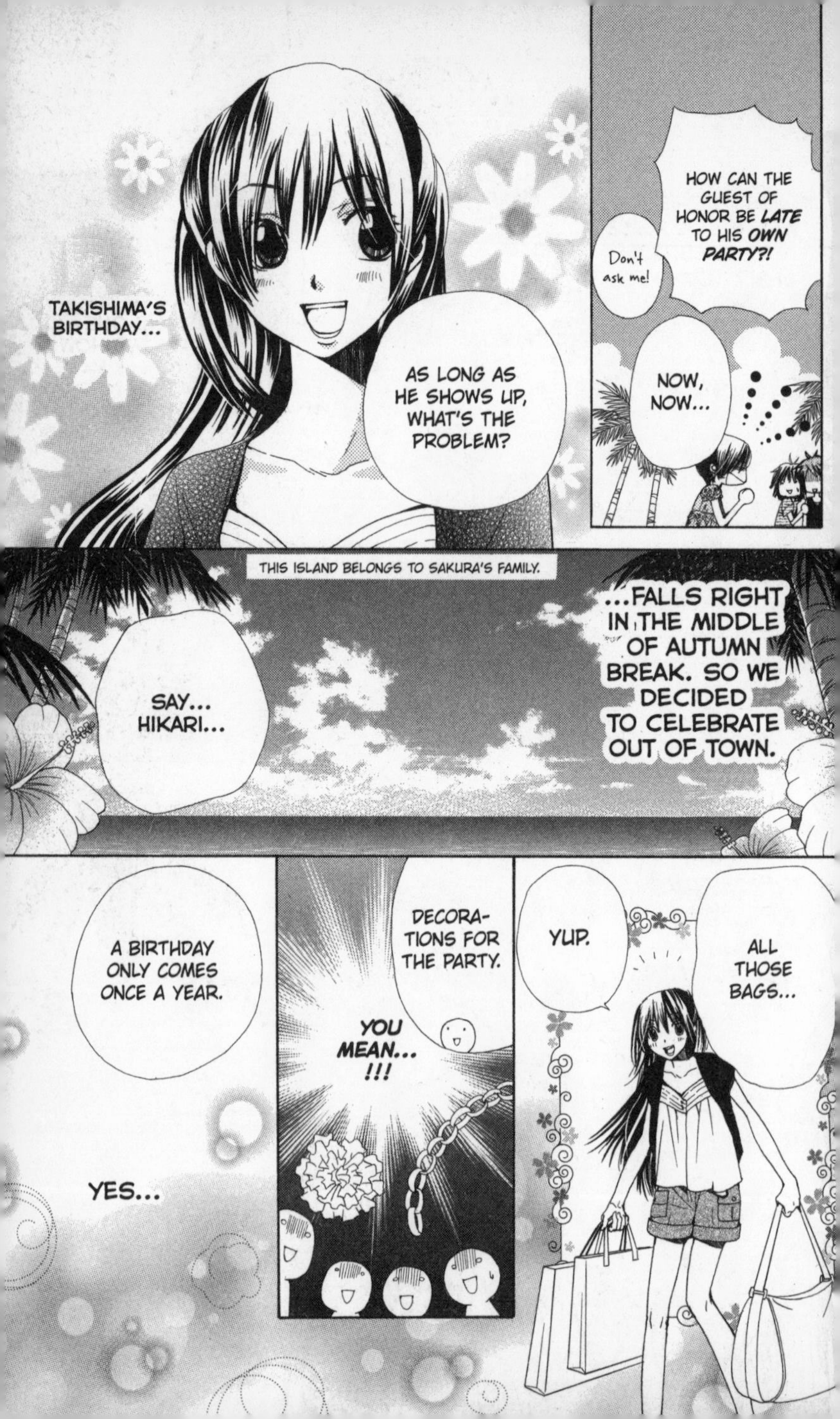
HOW CAN THE GUEST OF HONOR BE *LATE* TO HIS *OWN PARTY*?!
Don't ask me!
NOW, NOW...
AS LONG AS HE SHOWS UP, WHAT'S THE PROBLEM?
TAKISHIMA'S BIRTHDAY...
THIS ISLAND BELONGS TO SAKURA'S FAMILY.
...FALLS RIGHT IN THE MIDDLE OF AUTUMN BREAK. SO WE DECIDED TO CELEBRATE OUT OF TOWN.
SAY... HIKARI...
ALL THOSE BAGS...
YUP.
DECORATIONS FOR THE PARTY.
YOU MEAN... !!!
A BIRTHDAY ONLY COMES ONCE A YEAR.
YES...

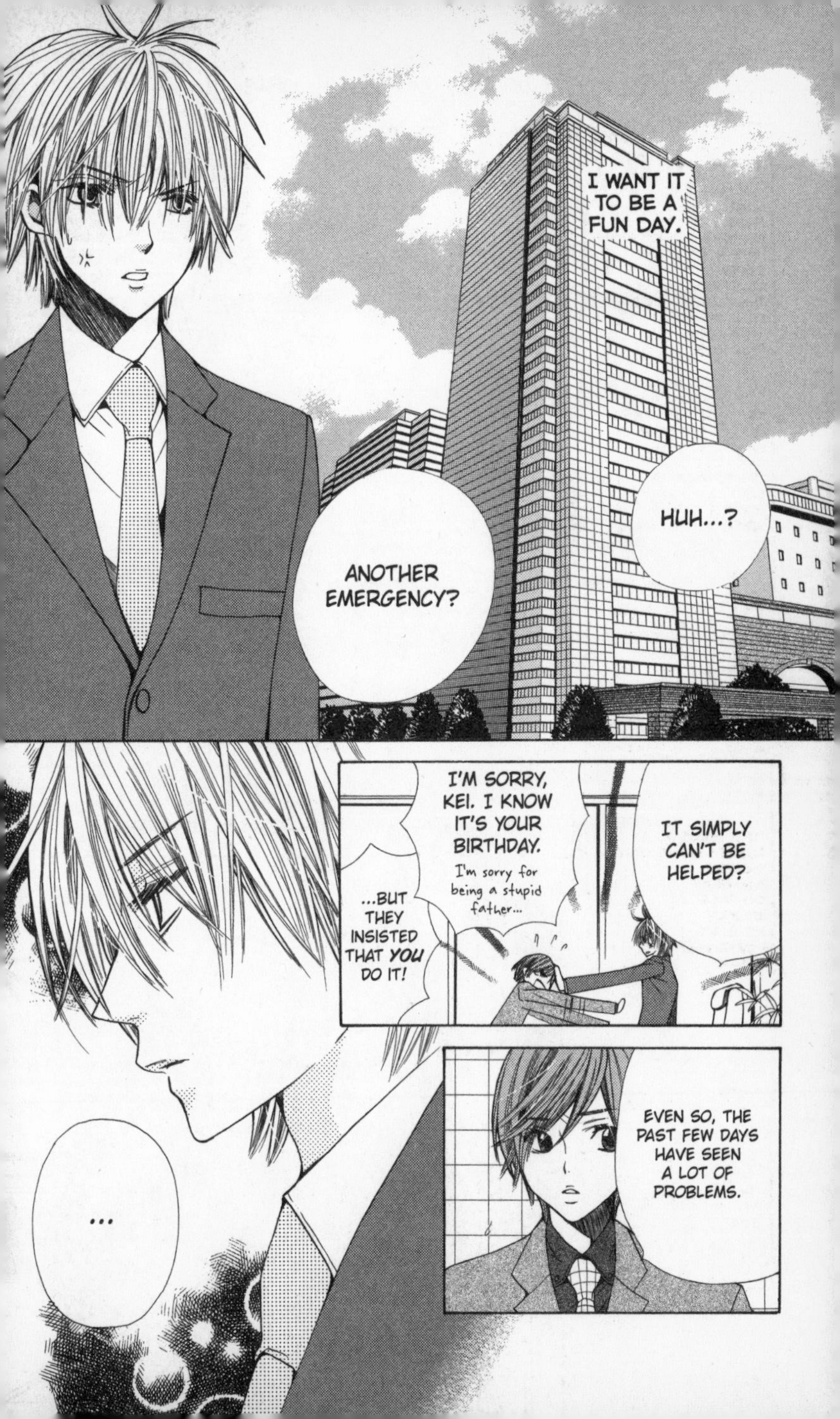
I WANT IT TO BE A FUN DAY.
HUH...?
ANOTHER EMERGENCY?
I'M SORRY, KEI. I KNOW IT'S YOUR BIRTHDAY.
I'm sorry for being a stupid father...
...BUT THEY INSISTED THAT *YOU* DO IT!
IT SIMPLY CAN'T BE HELPED?
EVEN SO, THE PAST FEW DAYS HAVE SEEN A LOT OF PROBLEMS.
...

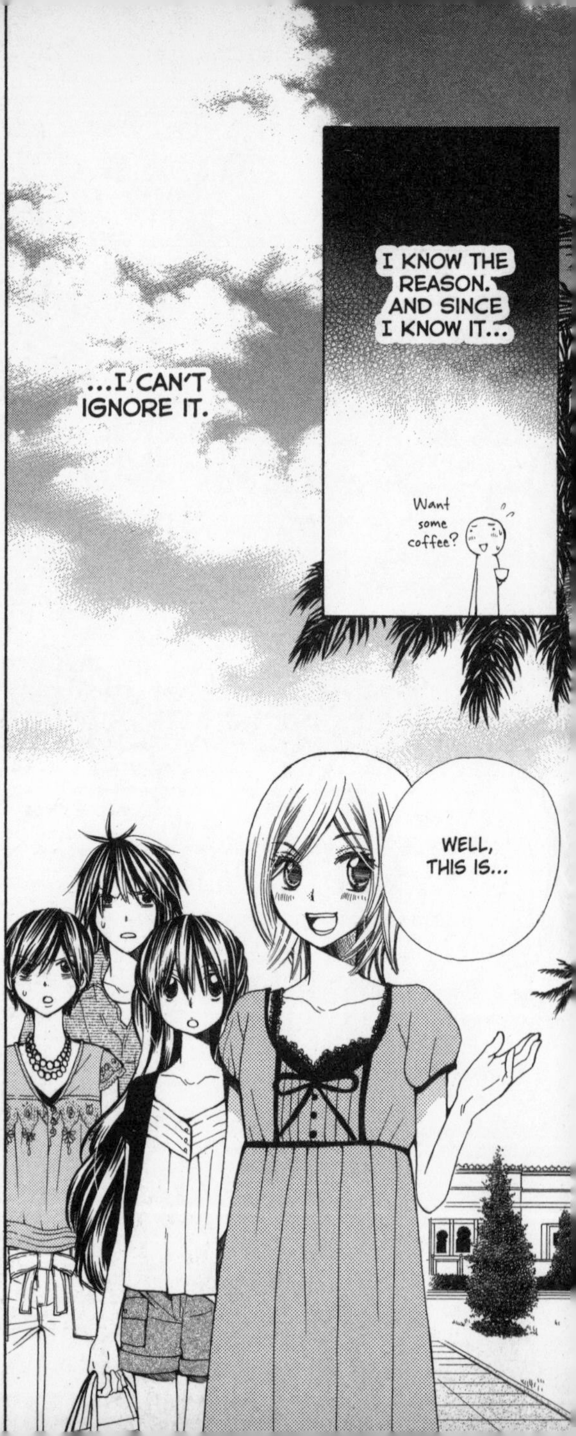
I KNOW THE REASON. AND SINCE I KNOW IT...
...I CAN'T IGNORE IT.
Want some coffee?
WELL, THIS IS...

6

·THIS AND THAT·

THIS IS MY FINAL QUARTER PAGE. THANK YOU FOR STAYING WITH ME UNTIL NOW! I DREW THE ILLUSTRATION ON THIS QUARTER PAGE FROM MY LIST OF READERS' REQUESTS.

HERE THEY ARE: GOTH-LOLI AND PUNK! WAIT A MINUTE...THAT'S NOT WHAT YOU MEANT? OH. I...I'M V-VERY S-SORRY... IT'S SO DIFFICULT. BUT I DID ENJOY DRAWING THEM! SO THANK YOU!

LOVE YOU. ♡ CREEPY!

THE FILLER ILLUSTRATION, "SPECIAL A" HIKARI AND MEGUMI, WAS DRAWN BY MY FRIEND MB. THEY WERE VERY CUTE. IT'S MOE. THANK YOU AGAIN!

LOVE YOU. ♡ STOP IT! ♡

IF IT PLEASES YOU, PLEASE SEND US YOUR THOUGHTS.
MAKI MINAMI
C/O SA EDITOR
VIZ MEDIA
P.O. BOX 77010
SAN FRANCISCO, CA 94107

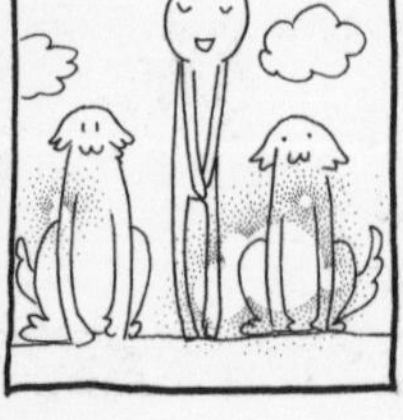
WITH ALL...
...MY HEART.

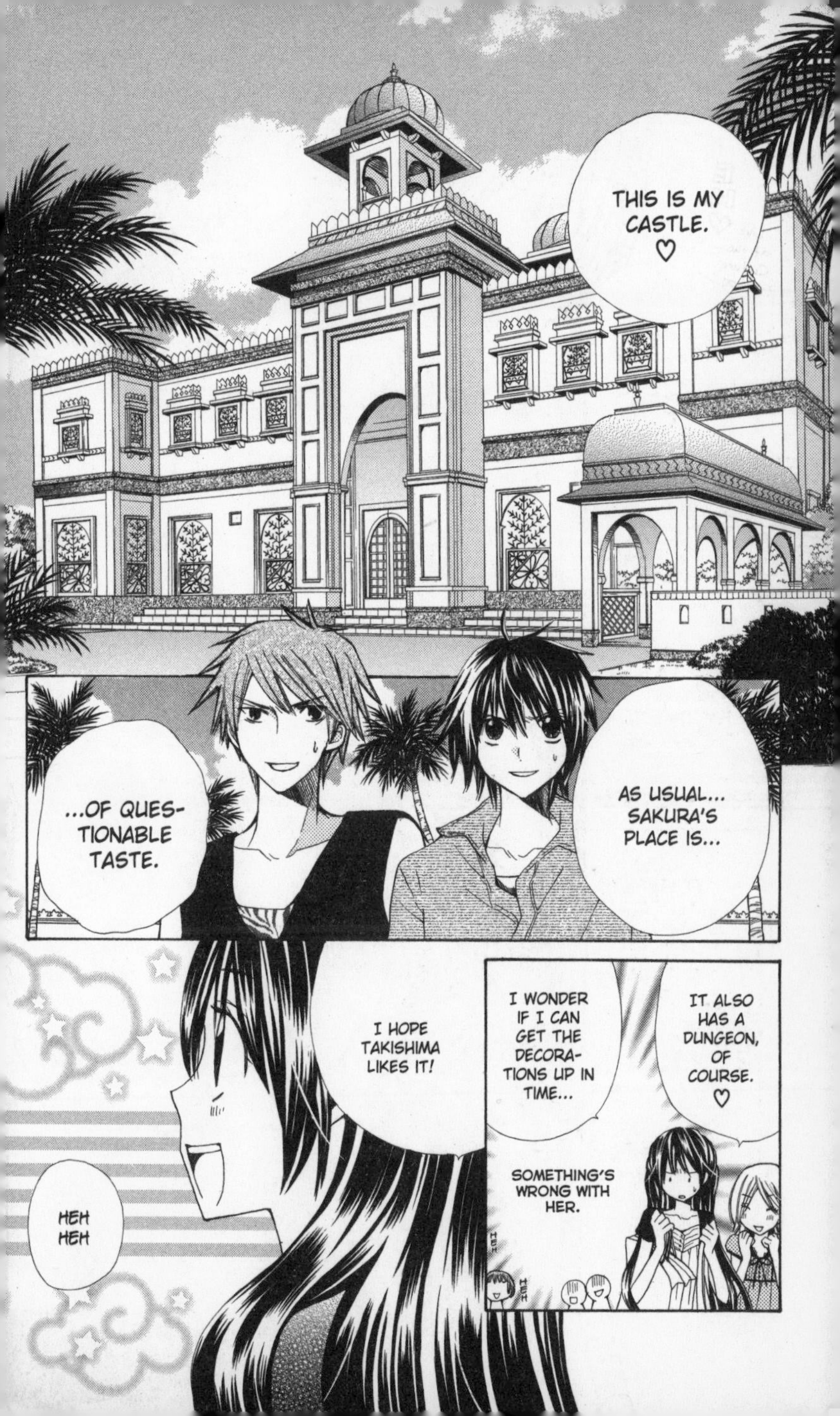
THIS IS MY CASTLE. ♡
AS USUAL... SAKURA'S PLACE IS...
...OF QUES-TIONABLE TASTE.
IT ALSO HAS A DUNGEON, OF COURSE. ♡
I WONDER IF I CAN GET THE DECORA-TIONS UP IN TIME...
SOMETHING'S WRONG WITH HER.
I HOPE TAKISHIMA LIKES IT!
HEH HEH

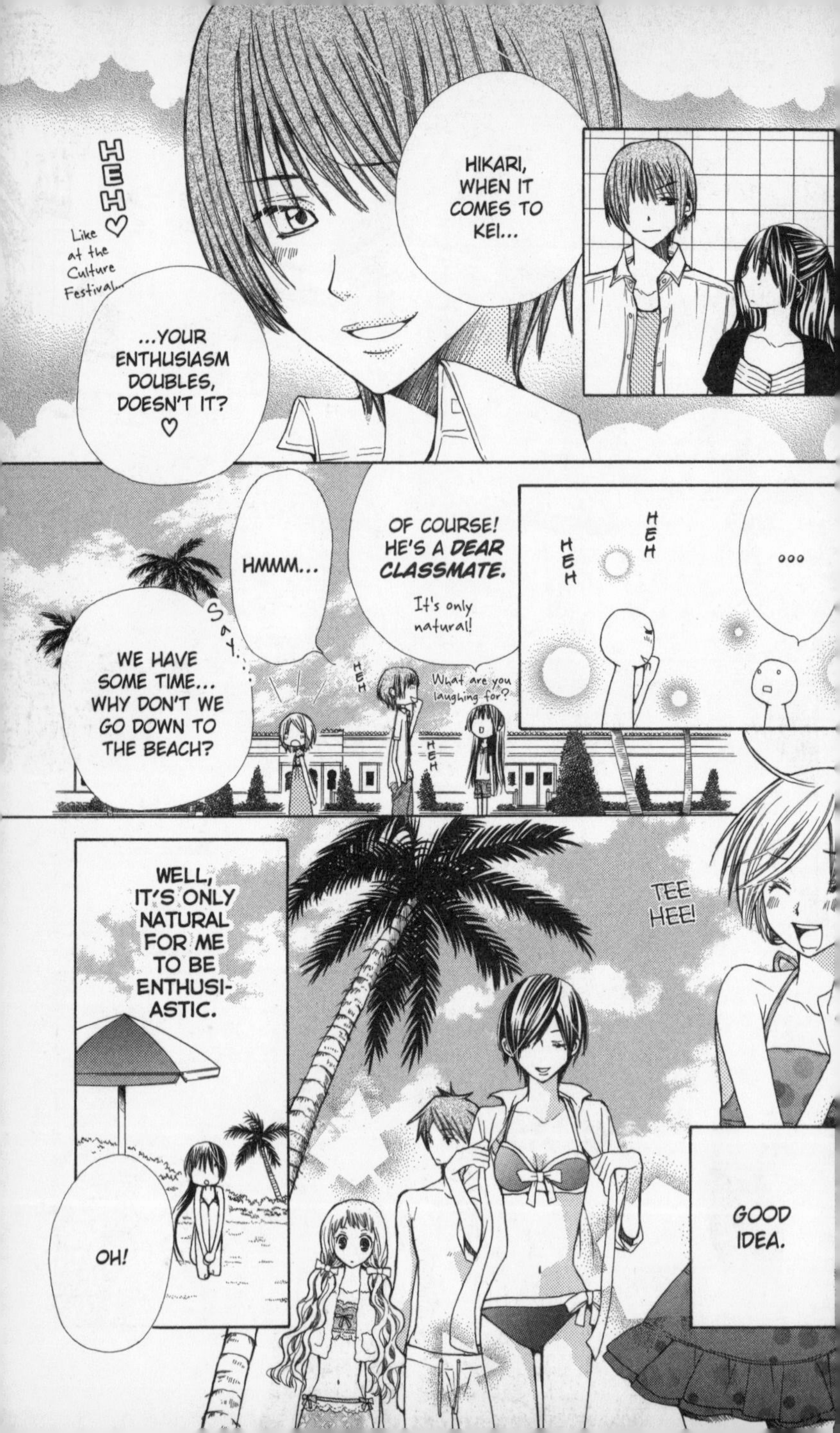
HIKARI, WHEN IT COMES TO KEI...
HEH HEH ♡
Like at the Culture Festival...
...YOUR ENTHUSIASM DOUBLES, DOESN'T IT? ♡
HEH
HEH
...
OF COURSE! HE'S A *DEAR CLASSMATE.*
It's only natural!
HMMM...
What are you laughing for?
HEH
HEH
Say...
WE HAVE SOME TIME... WHY DON'T WE GO DOWN TO THE BEACH?
GOOD IDEA.
TEE HEE!
WELL, IT'S ONLY NATURAL FOR ME TO BE ENTHUSI-ASTIC.
OH!

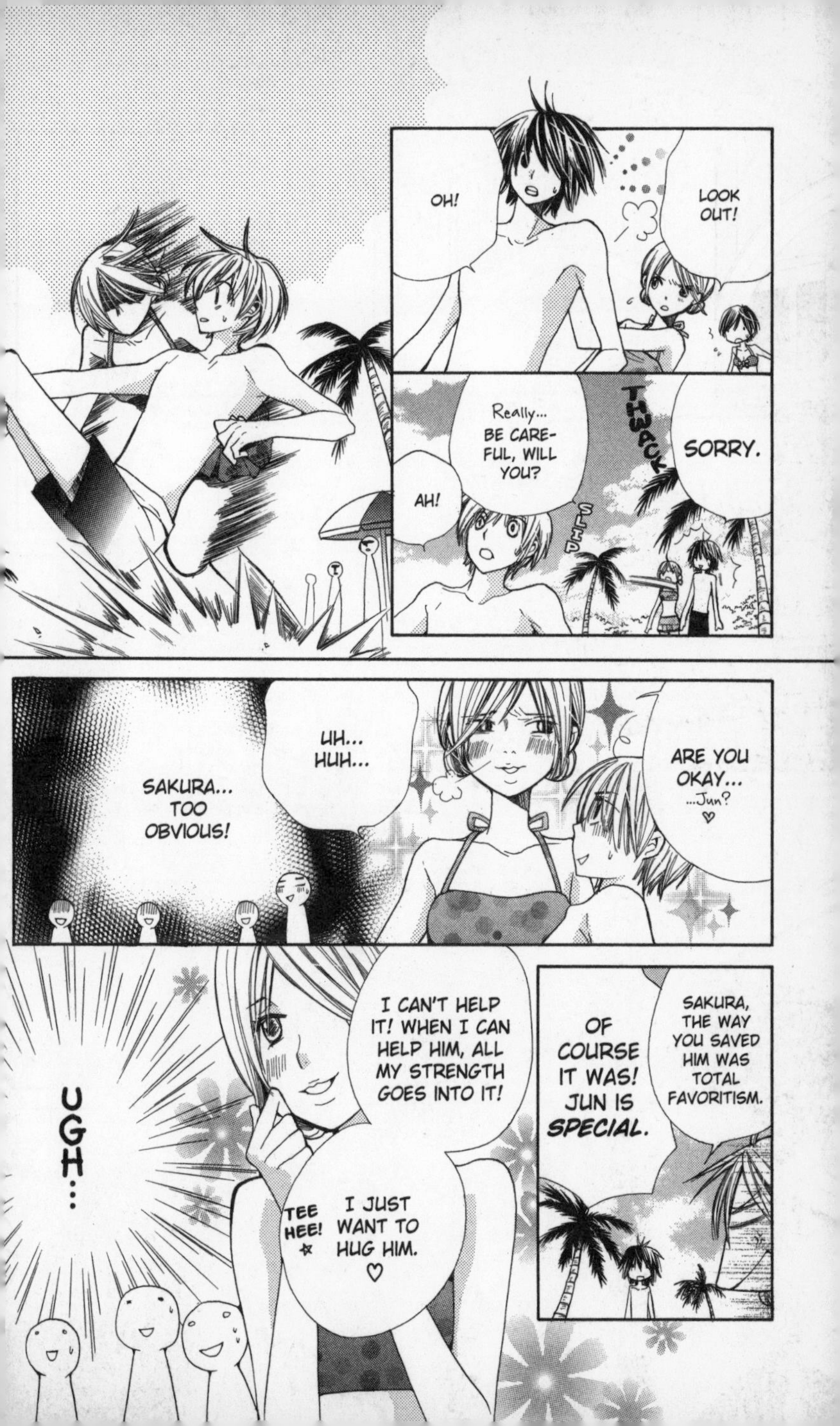
LOOK OUT!
OH!
SORRY.
THWACK
Really... BE CARE-FUL, WILL YOU?
SLIP
AH!
ARE YOU OKAY... ...Jun? ♡
UH... HUH...
SAKURA... TOO OBVIOUS!
SAKURA, THE WAY YOU SAVED HIM WAS TOTAL FAVORITISM.
OF COURSE IT WAS! JUN IS SPECIAL.
I CAN'T HELP IT! WHEN I CAN HELP HIM, ALL MY STRENGTH GOES INTO IT!
I JUST WANT TO HUG HIM. ♡
TEE HEE! ☆
UGH...

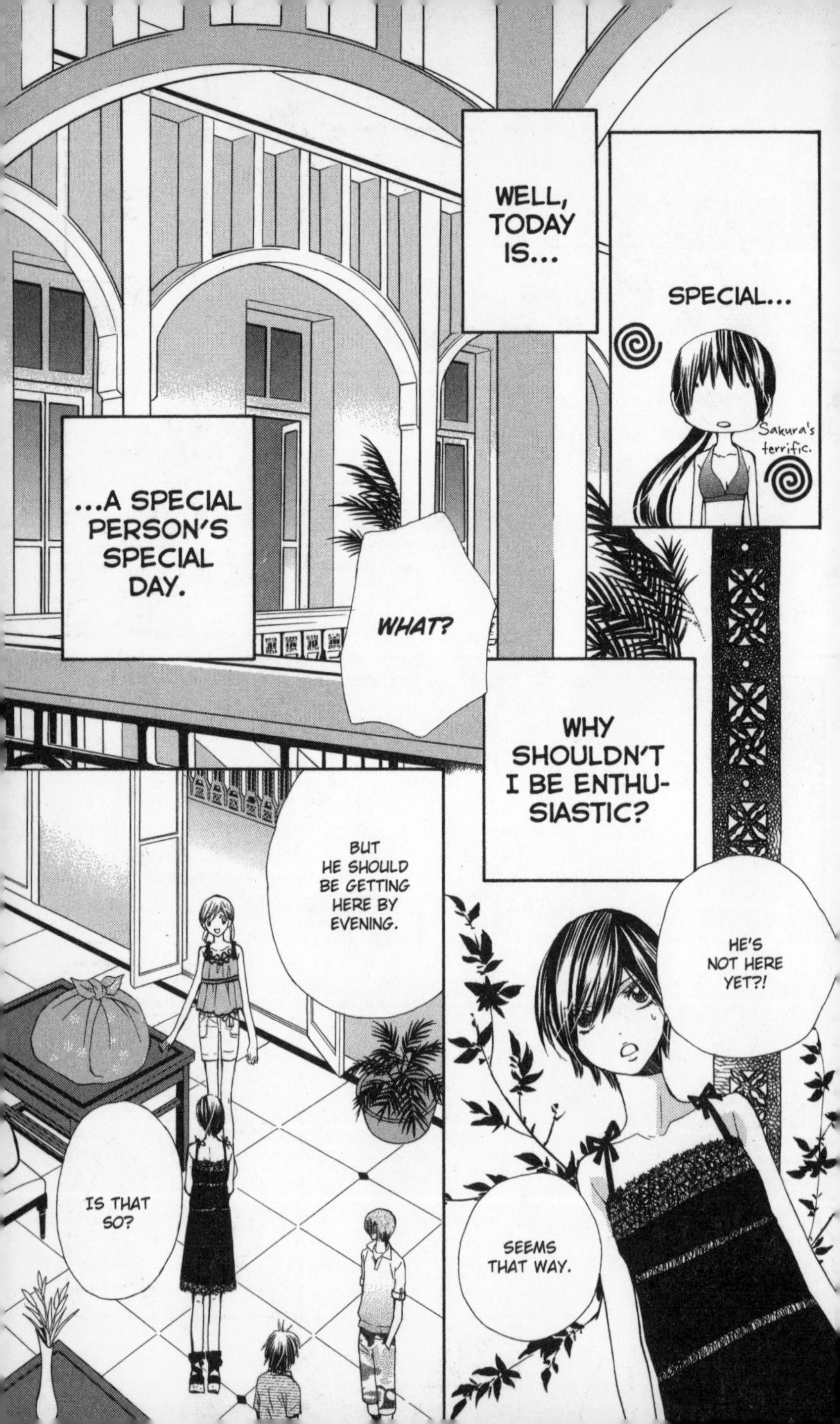
WELL, TODAY IS...
SPECIAL...
Sakura's terrific.
...A SPECIAL PERSON'S SPECIAL DAY.
WHAT?
WHY SHOULDN'T I BE ENTHU-SIASTIC?
HE'S NOT HERE YET?!
SEEMS THAT WAY.
BUT HE SHOULD BE GETTING HERE BY EVENING.
IS THAT SO?

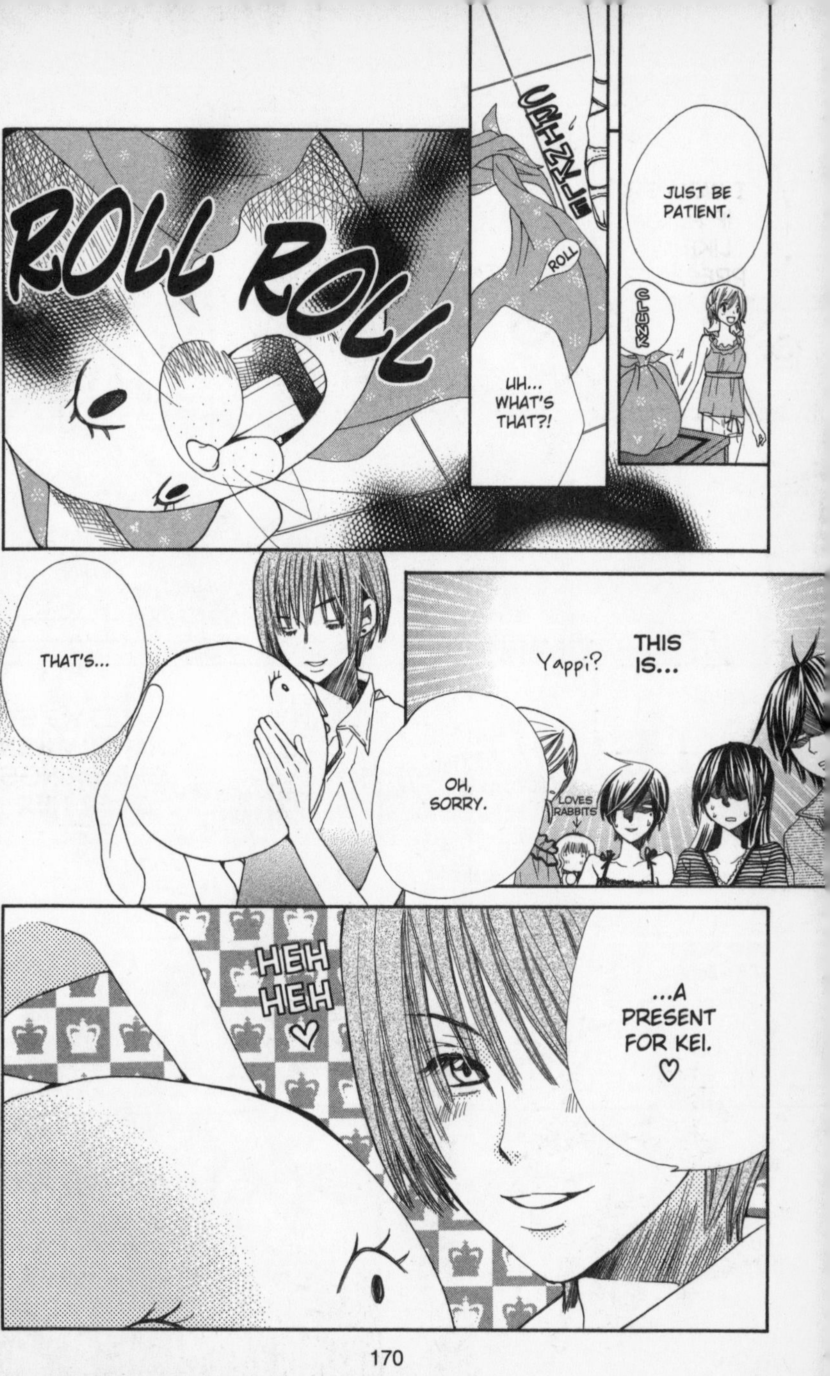
JUST BE PATIENT.
CLUNK
CRINKLE
ROLL
UH... WHAT'S THAT?!
ROLL ROLL
THIS IS...
Yappi?
LOVES RABBITS
OH, SORRY.
THAT'S...
...A PRESENT FOR KEI. ♡
HEH HEH ♡

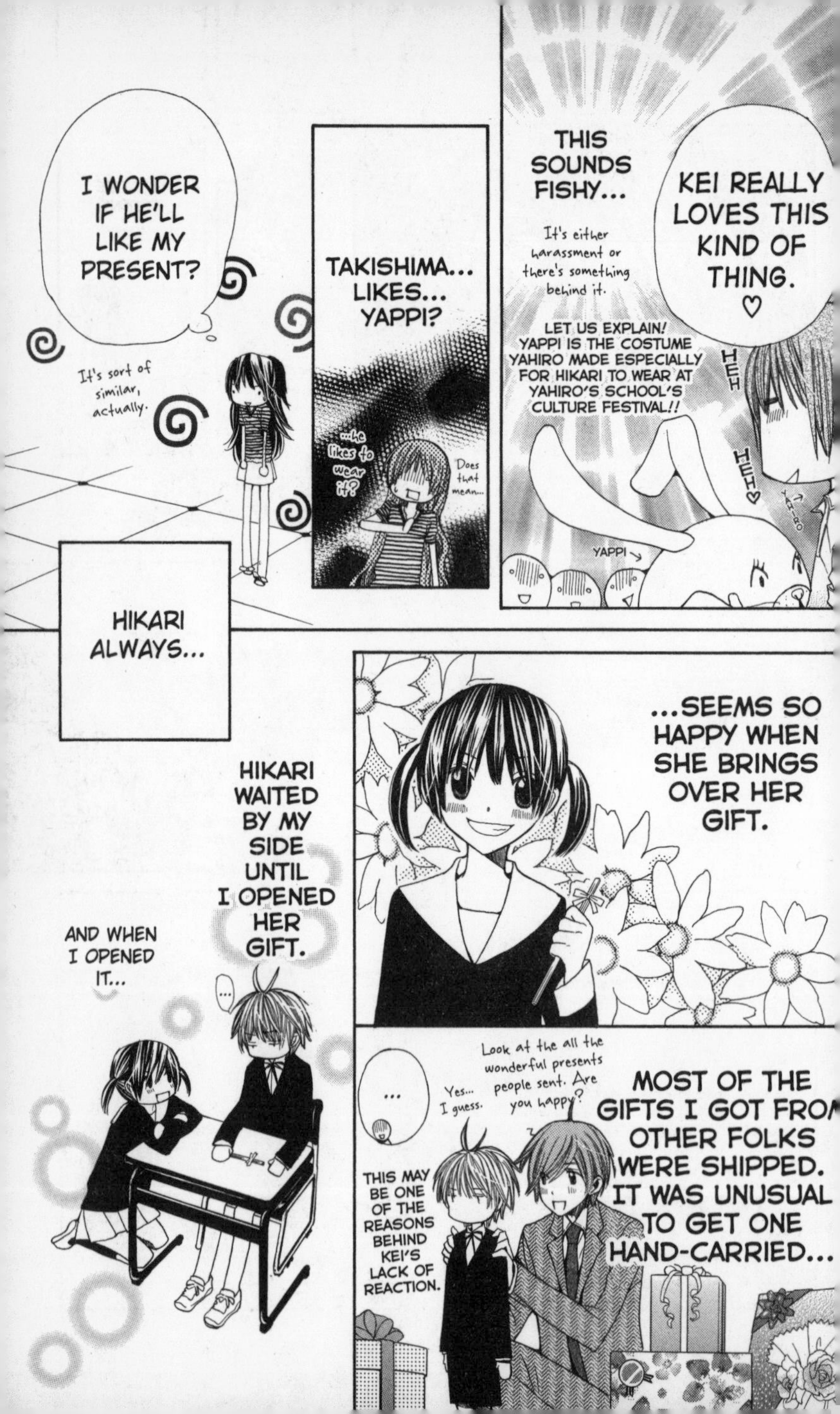
THIS SOUNDS FISHY...
It's either harassment or there's something behind it.
KEI REALLY LOVES THIS KIND OF THING. ♡
HEH
HEH♡
LET US EXPLAIN! YAPPI IS THE COSTUME YAHIRO MADE ESPECIALLY FOR HIKARI TO WEAR AT YAHIRO'S SCHOOL'S CULTURE FESTIVAL!!
YAHIRO
YAPPI
TAKISHIMA... LIKES... YAPPI?
Does that mean...
...he likes to wear it?
I WONDER IF HE'LL LIKE MY PRESENT?
It's sort of similar, actually.
HIKARI ALWAYS...
...SEEMS SO HAPPY WHEN SHE BRINGS OVER HER GIFT.
MOST OF THE GIFTS I GOT FROM OTHER FOLKS WERE SHIPPED. IT WAS UNUSUAL TO GET ONE HAND-CARRIED...
Look at the all the wonderful presents people sent. Are you happy?
Yes... I guess.
...
THIS MAY BE ONE OF THE REASONS BEHIND KEI'S LACK OF REACTION.
HIKARI WAITED BY MY SIDE UNTIL I OPENED HER GIFT.
AND WHEN I OPENED IT...
...

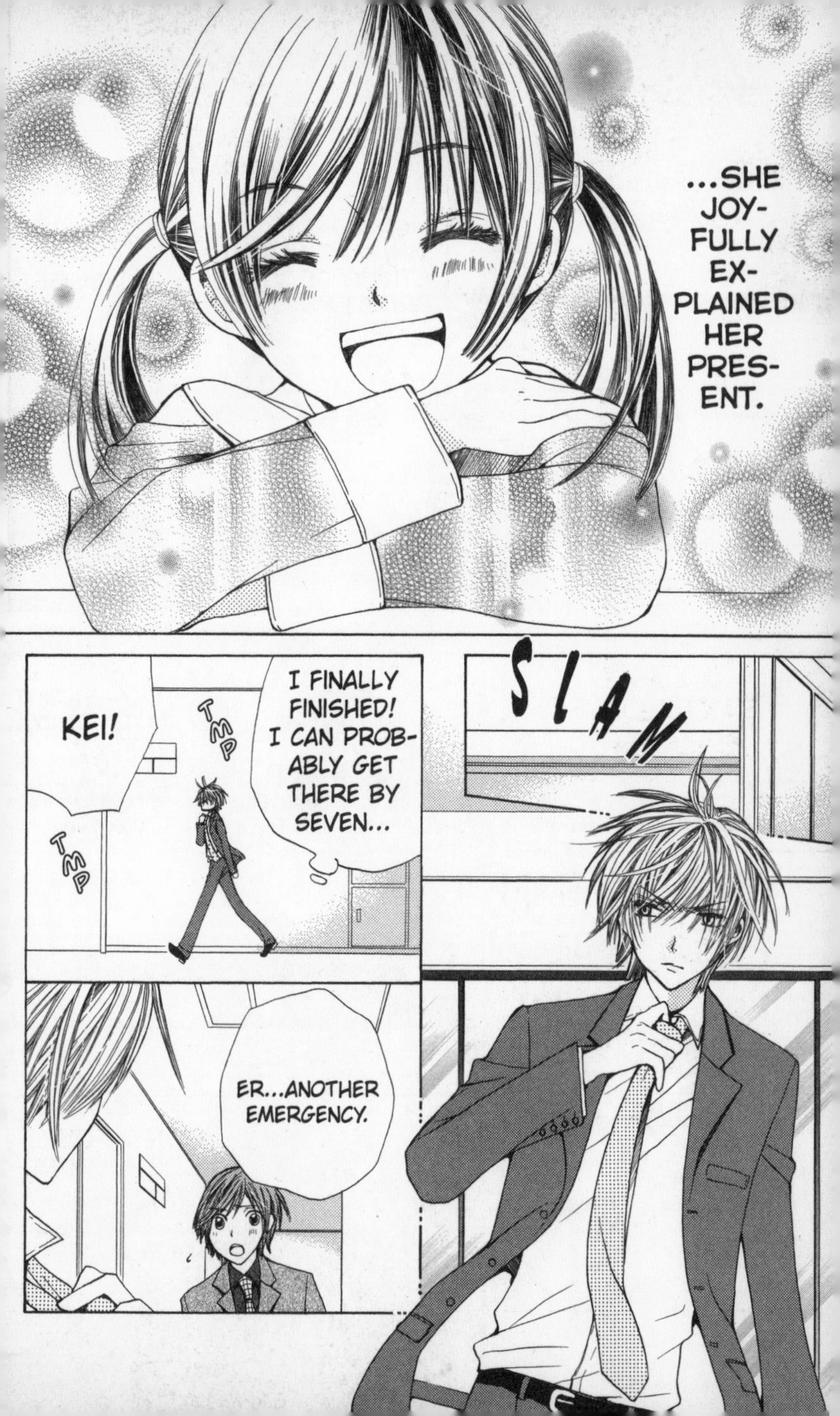
...SHE JOYFULLY EXPLAINED HER PRESENT.
SLAM
I FINALLY FINISHED! I CAN PROBABLY GET THERE BY SEVEN...
TMP
KEI!
TMP
ER...ANOTHER EMERGENCY.

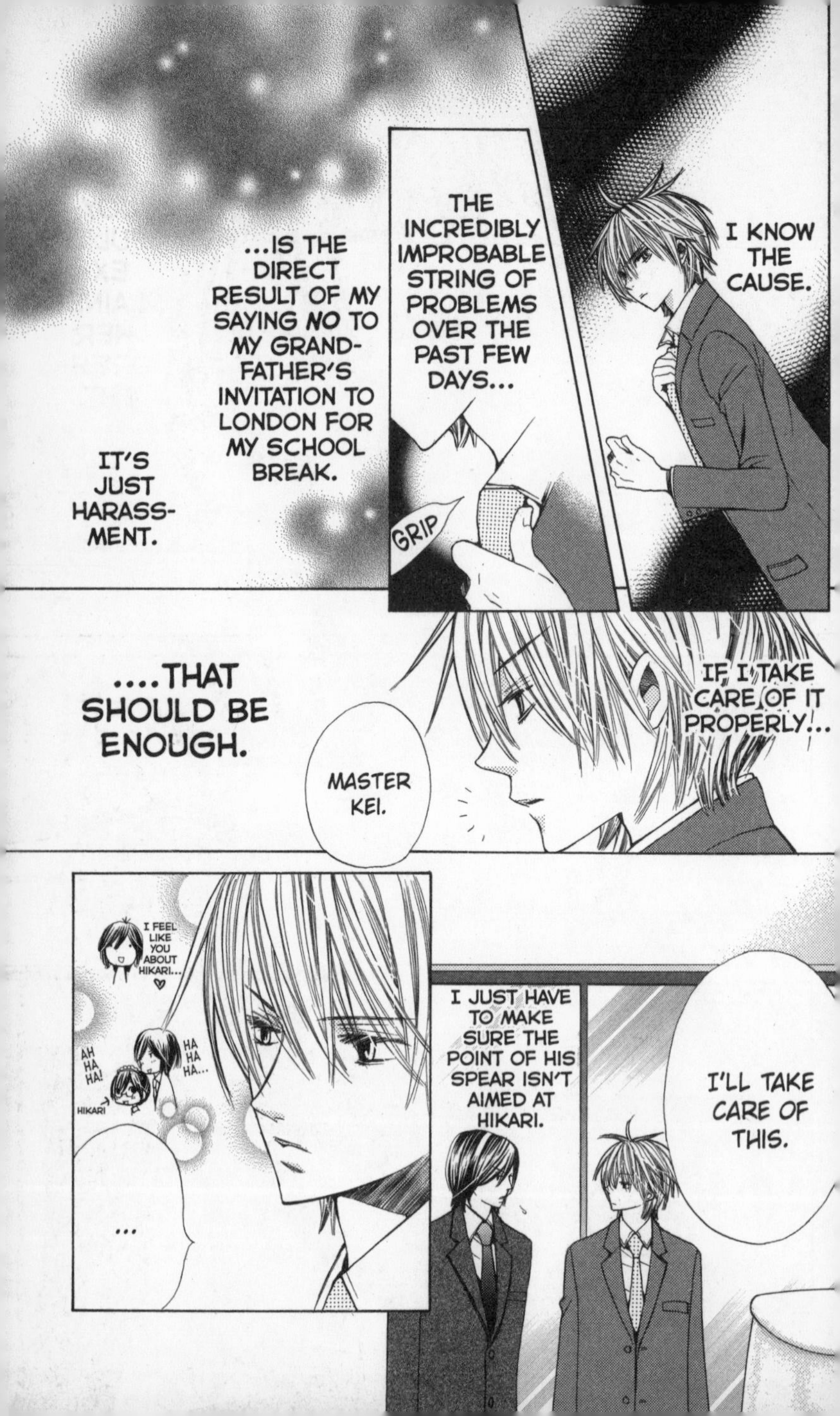
I KNOW THE CAUSE.
THE INCREDIBLY IMPROBABLE STRING OF PROBLEMS OVER THE PAST FEW DAYS...
GRIP
...IS THE DIRECT RESULT OF MY SAYING NO TO MY GRAND-FATHER'S INVITATION TO LONDON FOR MY SCHOOL BREAK.
IT'S JUST HARASS-MENT.
IF I TAKE CARE OF IT PROPERLY...
MASTER KEI.
....THAT SHOULD BE ENOUGH.
I'LL TAKE CARE OF THIS.
I JUST HAVE TO MAKE SURE THE POINT OF HIS SPEAR ISN'T AIMED AT HIKARI.
I FEEL LIKE YOU ABOUT HIKARI...
HA HA HA...
AH HA HA!
HIKARI
...

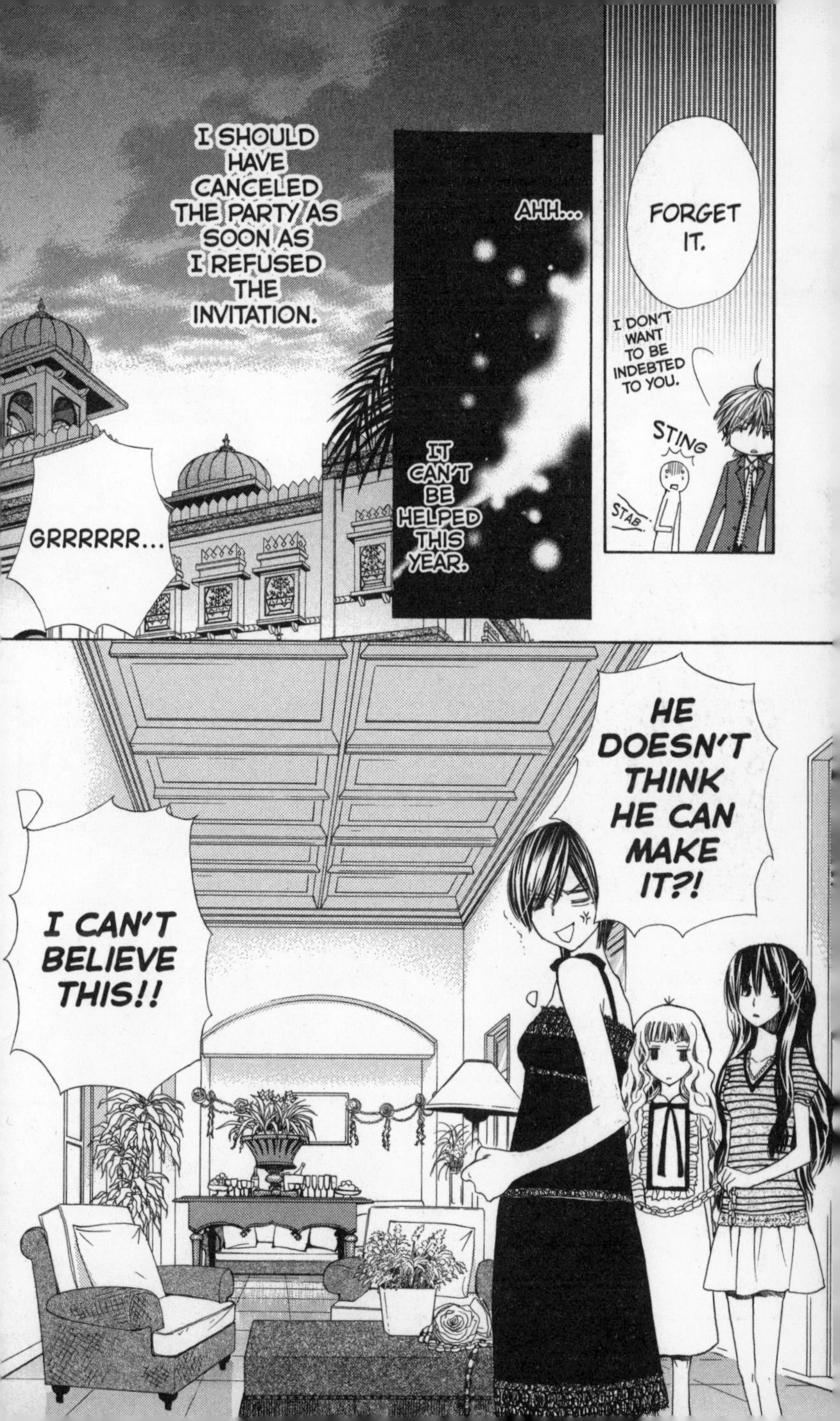
FORGET IT.
I DON'T WANT TO BE INDEBTED TO YOU.
STING
STAB
AHH...
IT CAN'T BE HELPED THIS YEAR.
I SHOULD HAVE CANCELED THE PARTY AS SOON AS I REFUSED THE INVITATION.
GRRRRRR...
HE DOESN'T THINK HE CAN MAKE IT?!
I CAN'T BELIEVE THIS!!

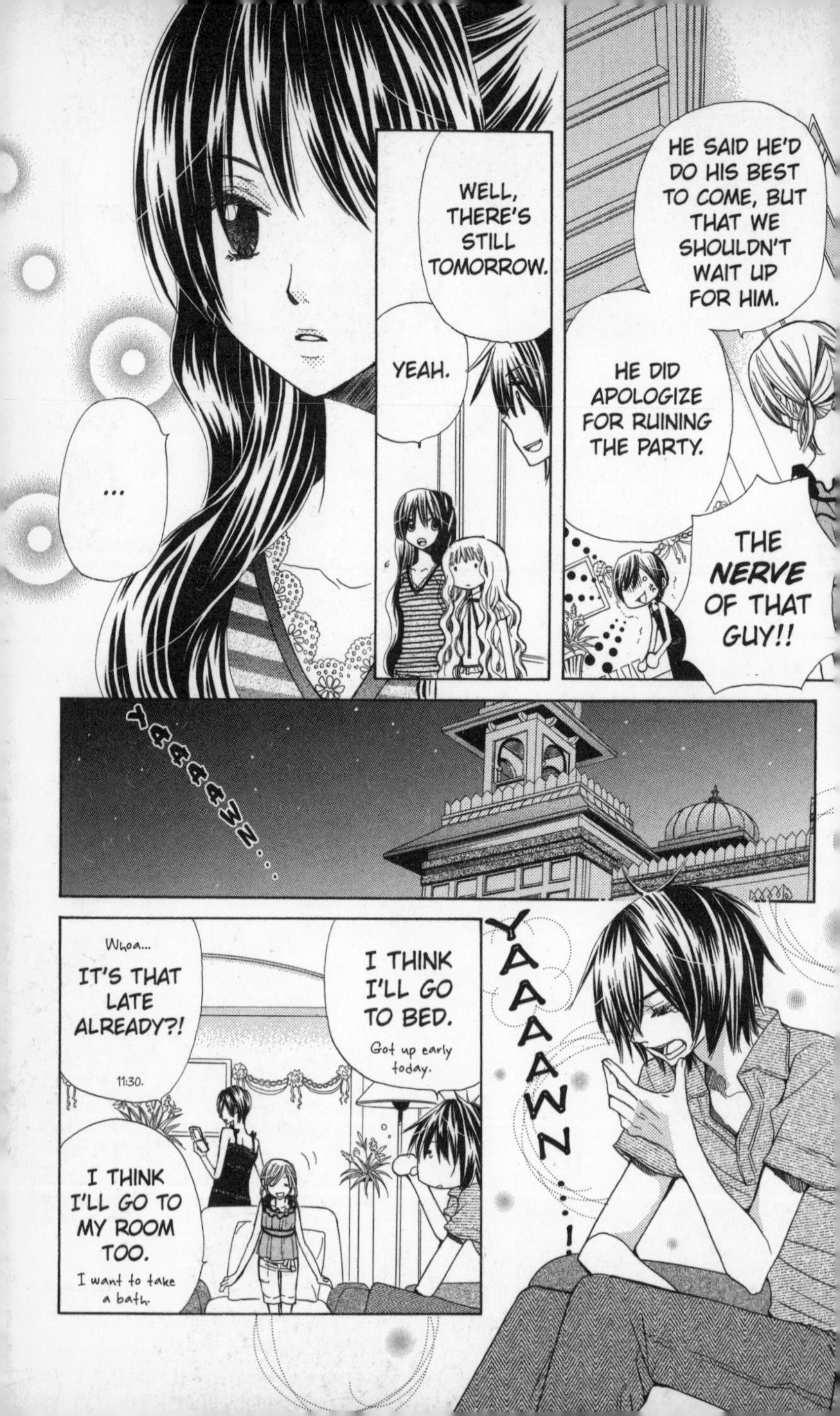
HE SAID HE'D DO HIS BEST TO COME, BUT THAT WE SHOULDN'T WAIT UP FOR HIM.
HE DID APOLOGIZE FOR RUINING THE PARTY.
THE *NERVE* OF THAT GUY!!
WELL, THERE'S STILL TOMORROW.
YEAH.
...
YAAAAWN...
YAAAAWN...!
I THINK I'LL GO TO BED.
Got up early today.
Whoa...
IT'S THAT LATE ALREADY?!
11:30.
I THINK I'LL GO TO MY ROOM TOO.
I want to take a bath.

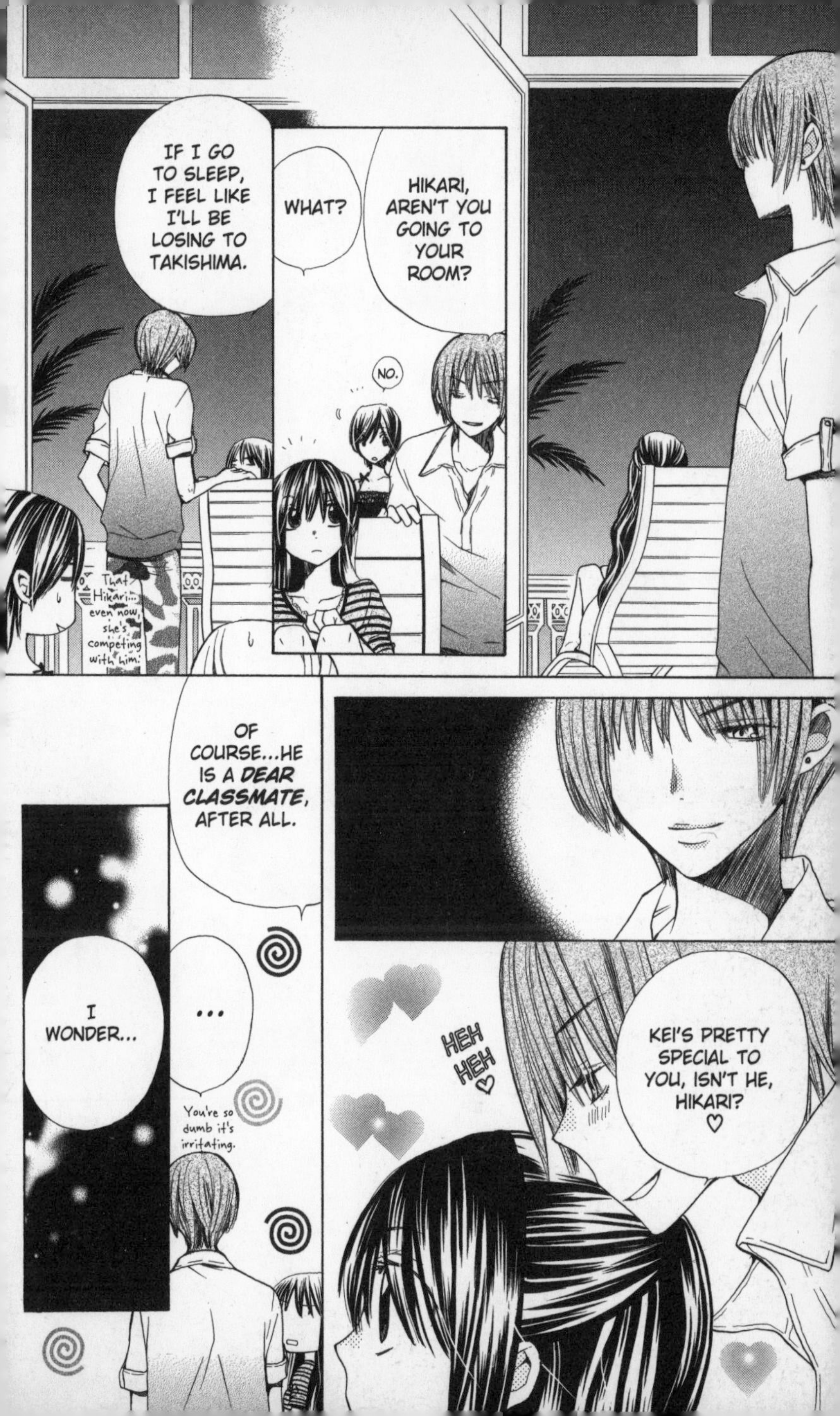
HIKARI, AREN'T YOU GOING TO YOUR ROOM?
WHAT?
NO.
IF I GO TO SLEEP, I FEEL LIKE I'LL BE LOSING TO TAKISHIMA.
That Hikari... even now, she's competing with him.
HEH HEH ♡
KEI'S PRETTY SPECIAL TO YOU, ISN'T HE, HIKARI? ♡
OF COURSE...HE IS A *DEAR CLASSMATE*, AFTER ALL.
...
You're so dumb it's irritating.
I WONDER...

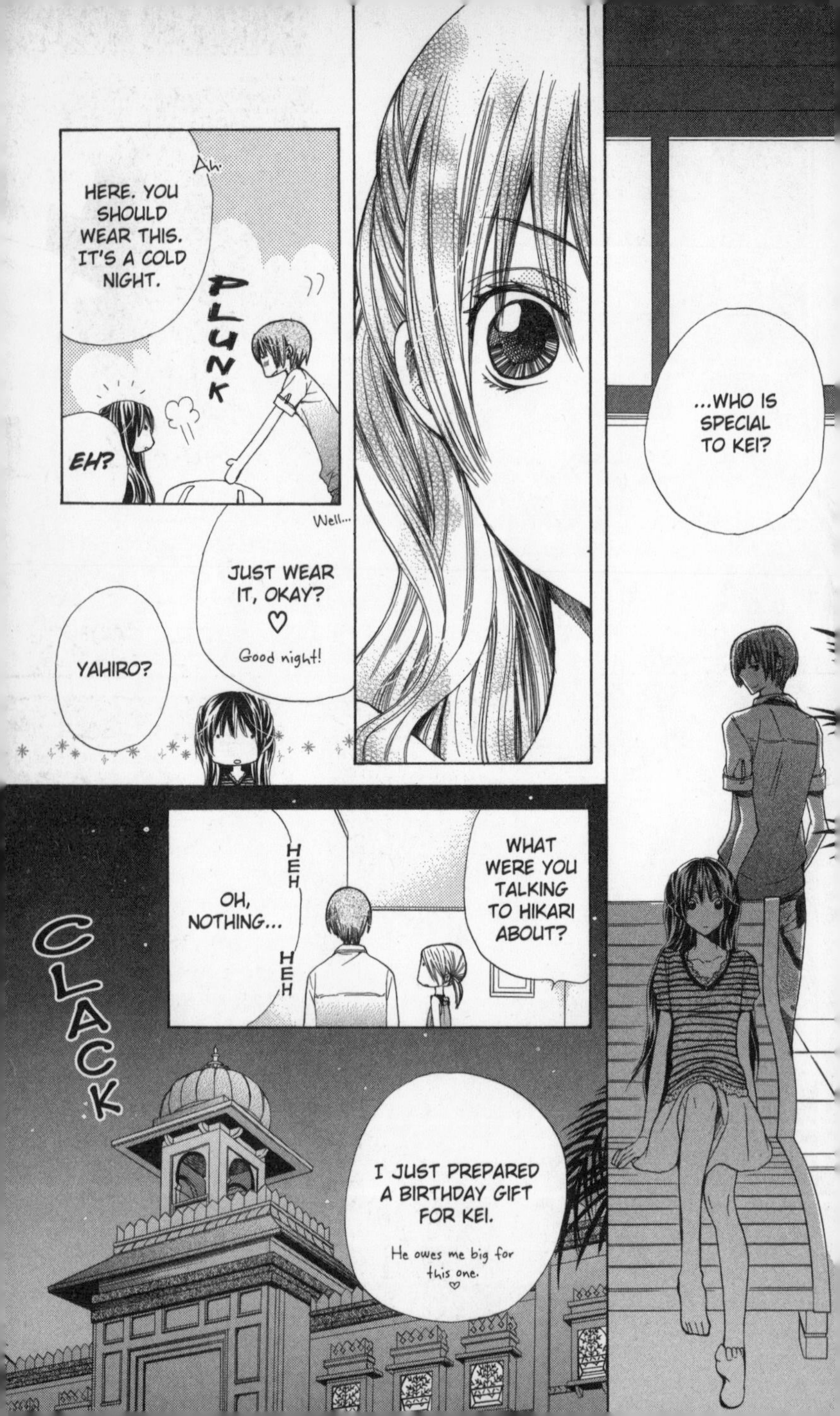
...WHO IS SPECIAL TO KEI?
Ah.
HERE. YOU SHOULD WEAR THIS. IT'S A COLD NIGHT.
PLUNK
EH?
Well...
JUST WEAR IT, OKAY? ♡
Good night!
YAHIRO?
WHAT WERE YOU TALKING TO HIKARI ABOUT?
OH, NOTHING...
HEH HEH
CLACK
I JUST PREPARED A BIRTHDAY GIFT FOR KEI.
He owes me big for this one. ♡

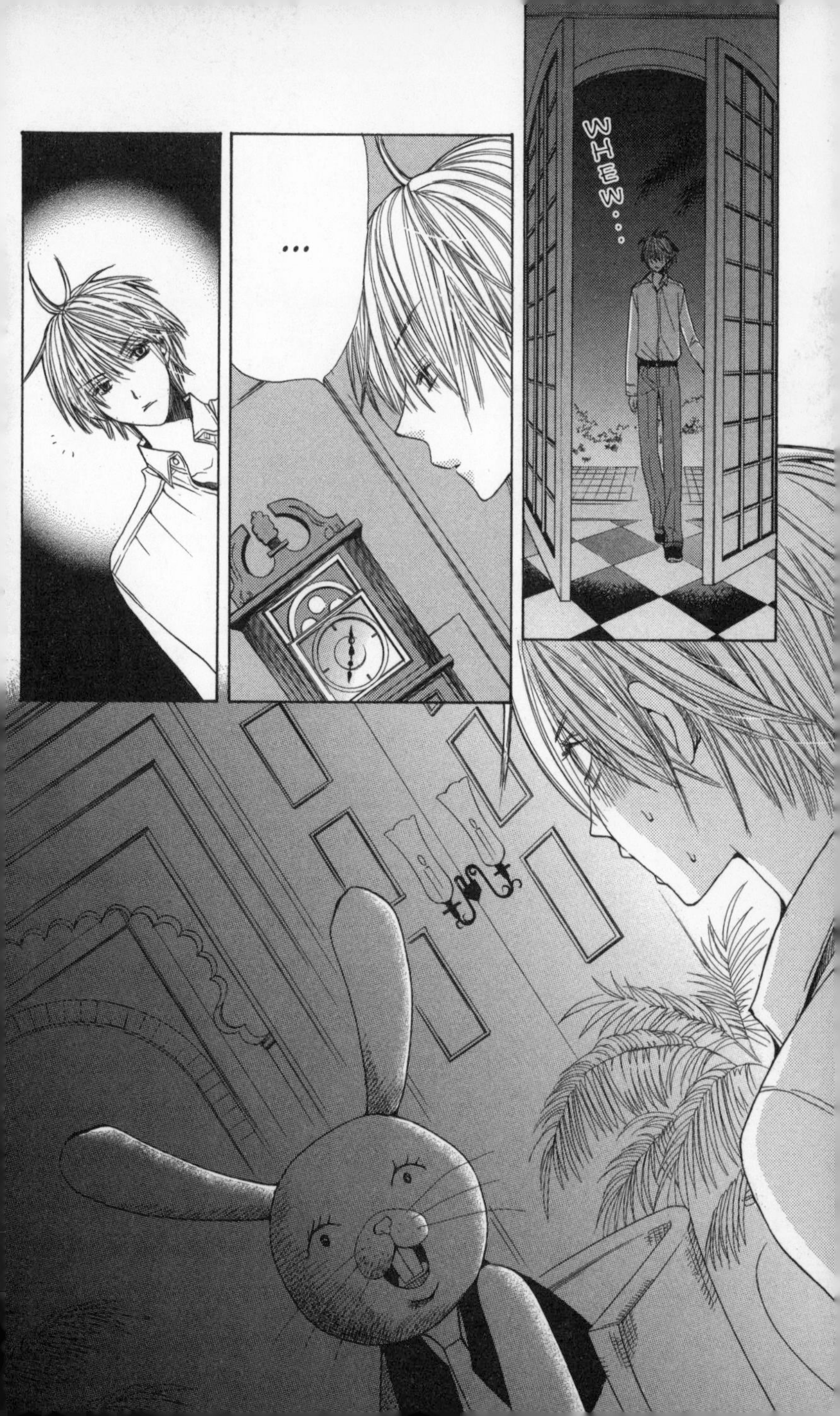
WHEW...
...

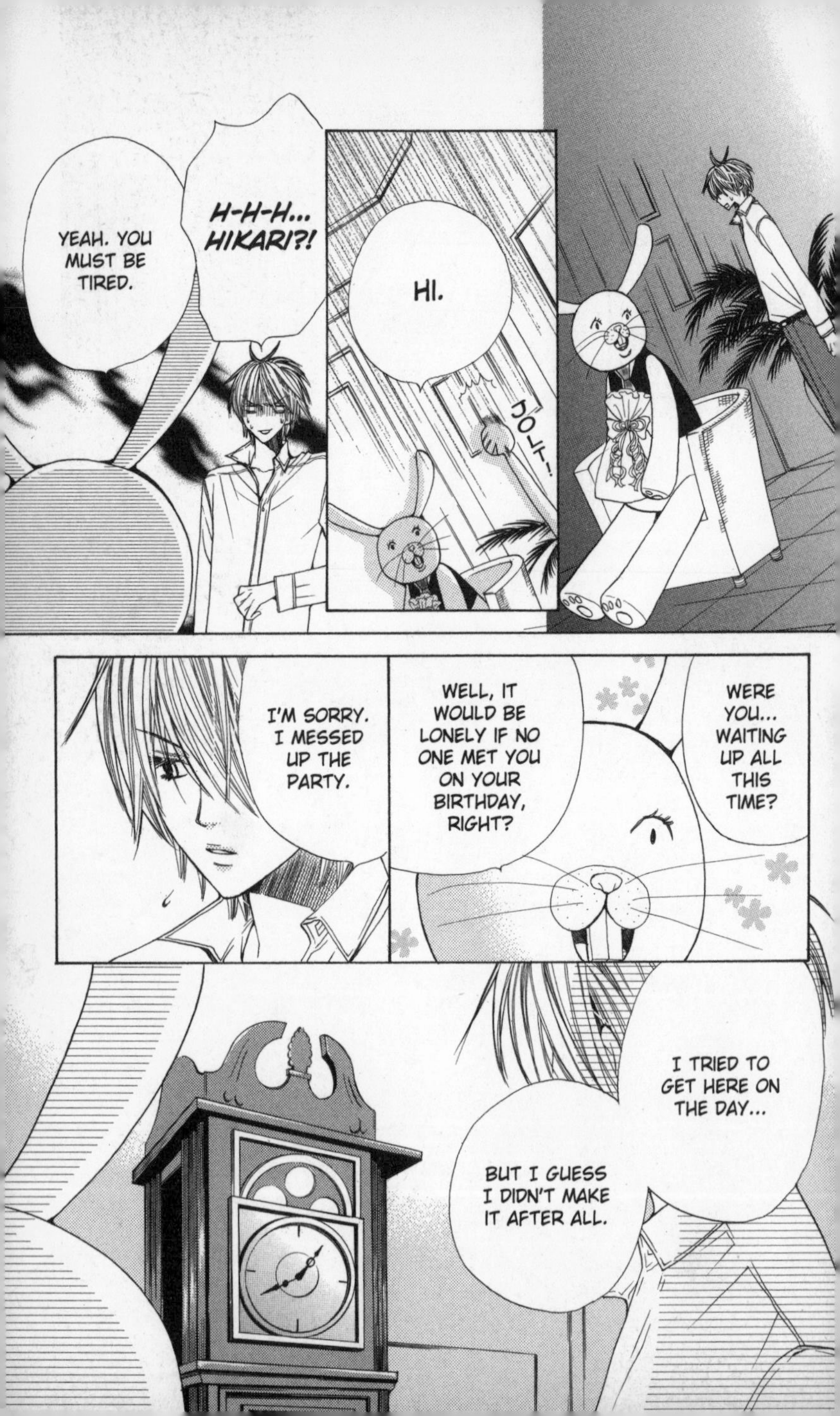
HI.
JOLT!
H-H-H... HIKARI?!
YEAH. YOU MUST BE TIRED.
WERE YOU... WAITING UP ALL THIS TIME?
WELL, IT WOULD BE LONELY IF NO ONE MET YOU ON YOUR BIRTHDAY, RIGHT?
I'M SORRY. I MESSED UP THE PARTY.
I TRIED TO GET HERE ON THE DAY...
BUT I GUESS I DIDN'T MAKE IT AFTER ALL.

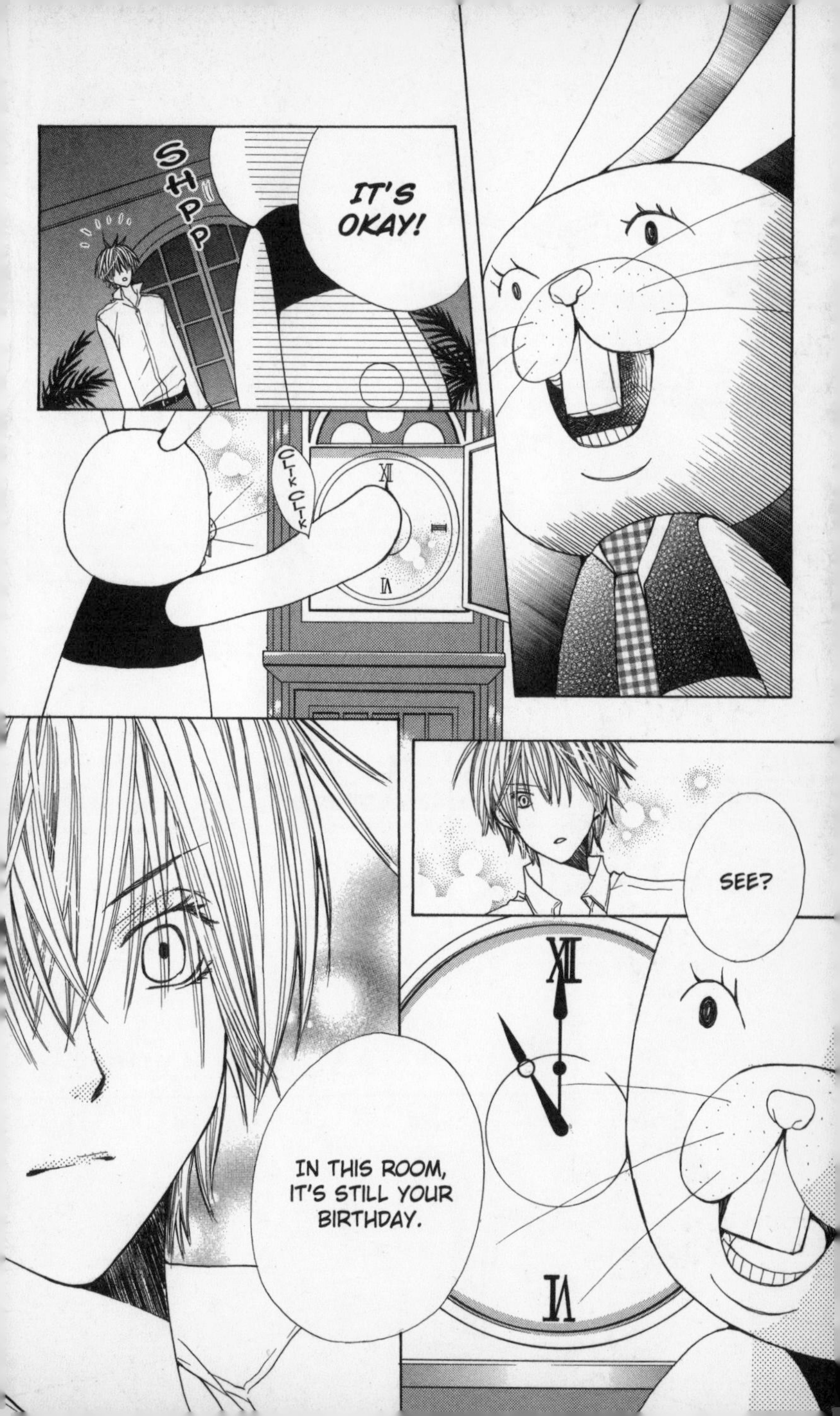

IT'S OKAY!
SHPP
CLIK CLIK
SEE?
IN THIS ROOM, IT'S STILL YOUR BIRTHDAY.

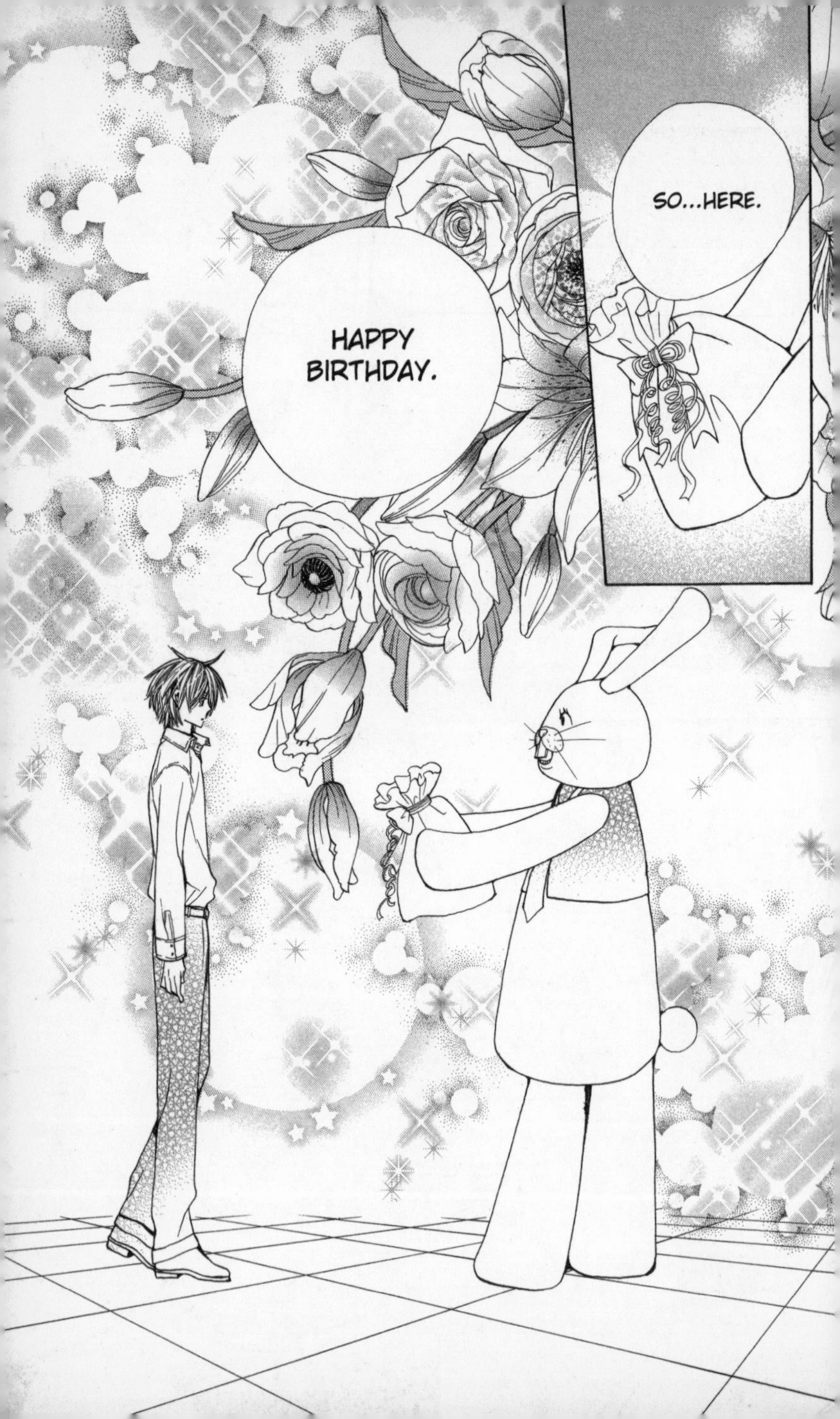
SO...HERE.
HAPPY BIRTHDAY.

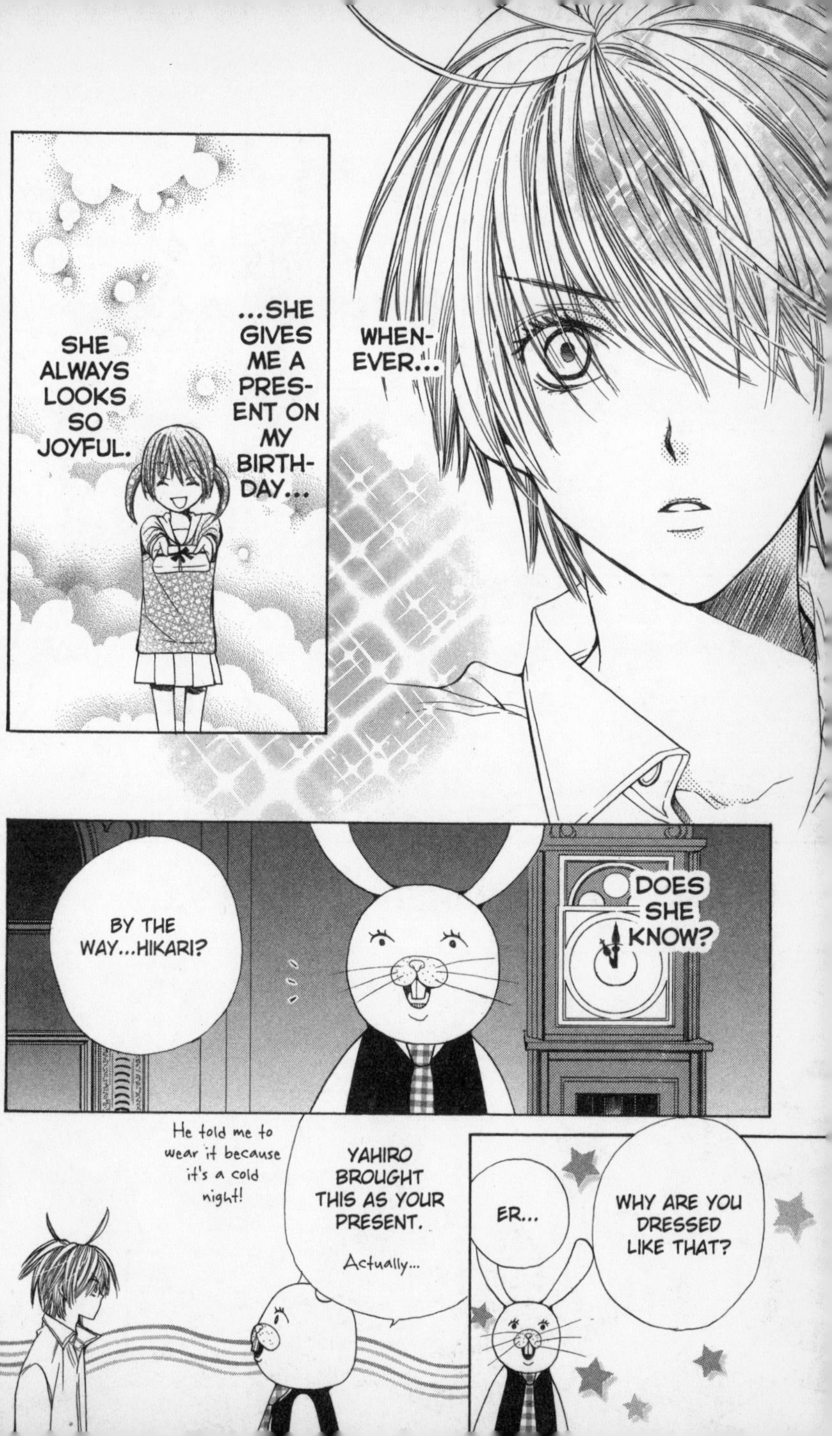
WHEN-EVER...
...SHE GIVES ME A PRESENT ON MY BIRTHDAY...
SHE ALWAYS LOOKS SO JOYFUL.
DOES SHE KNOW?
BY THE WAY...HIKARI?
WHY ARE YOU DRESSED LIKE THAT?
ER...
YAHIRO BROUGHT THIS AS YOUR PRESENT.
Actually...
He told me to wear it because it's a cold night!

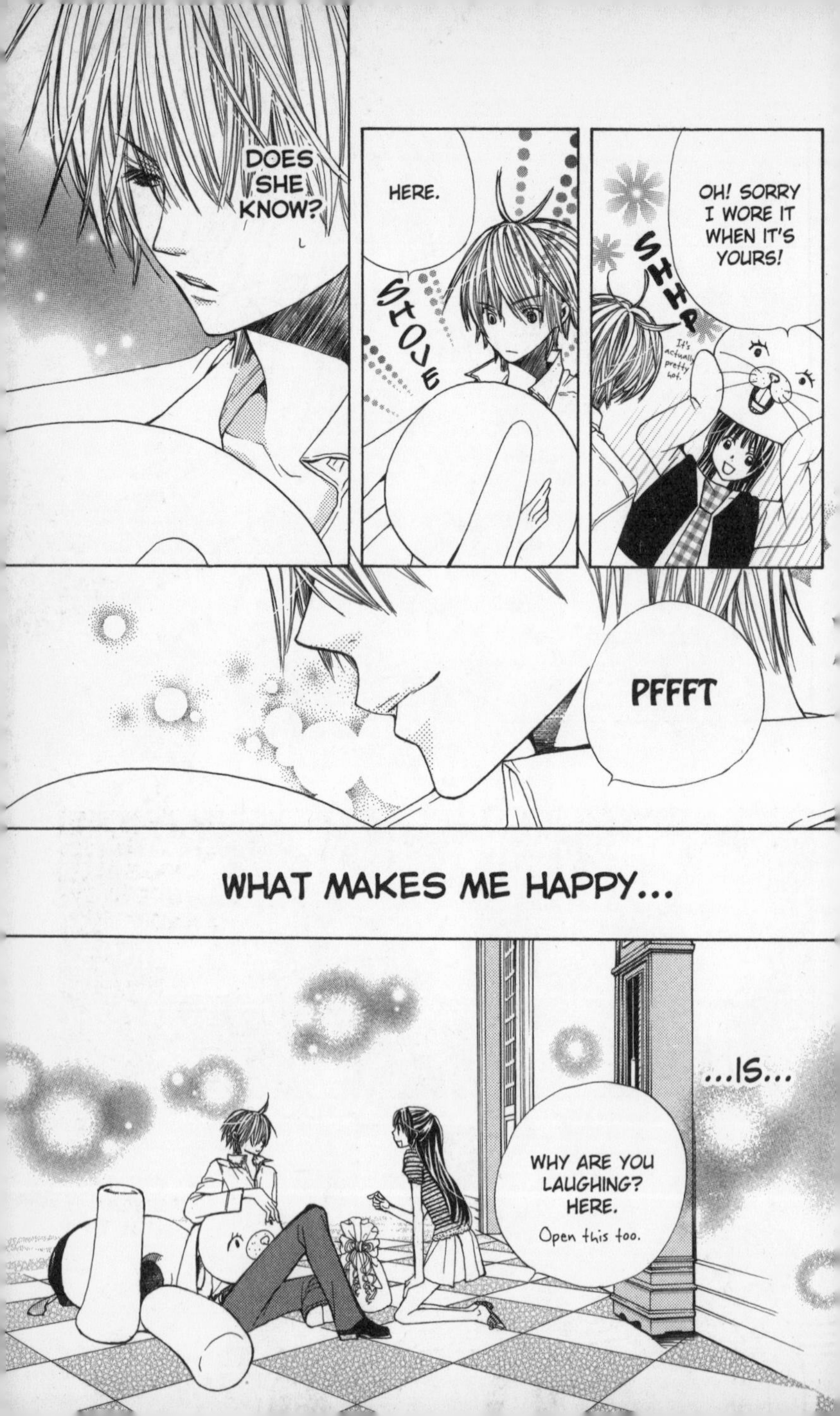
OH! SORRY I WORE IT WHEN IT'S YOURS!
SHHP
It's actually pretty hot.
HERE.
SHOVE
DOES SHE KNOW?
PFFFT
WHAT MAKES ME HAPPY...
...IS...
WHY ARE YOU LAUGHING? HERE.
Open this too.

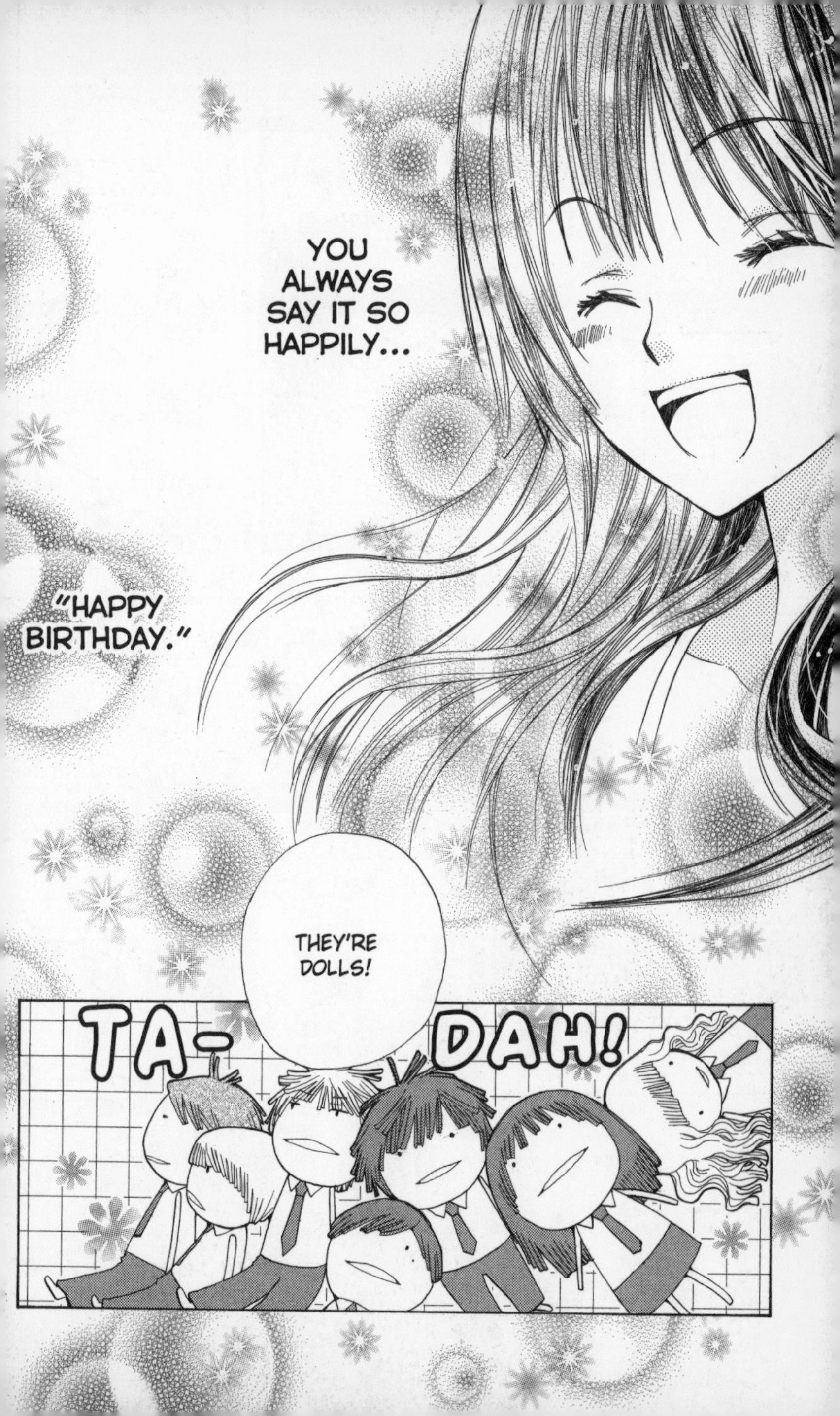
YOU ALWAYS SAY IT SO HAPPILY...
"HAPPY BIRTHDAY."
THEY'RE DOLLS!
TA-DAH!

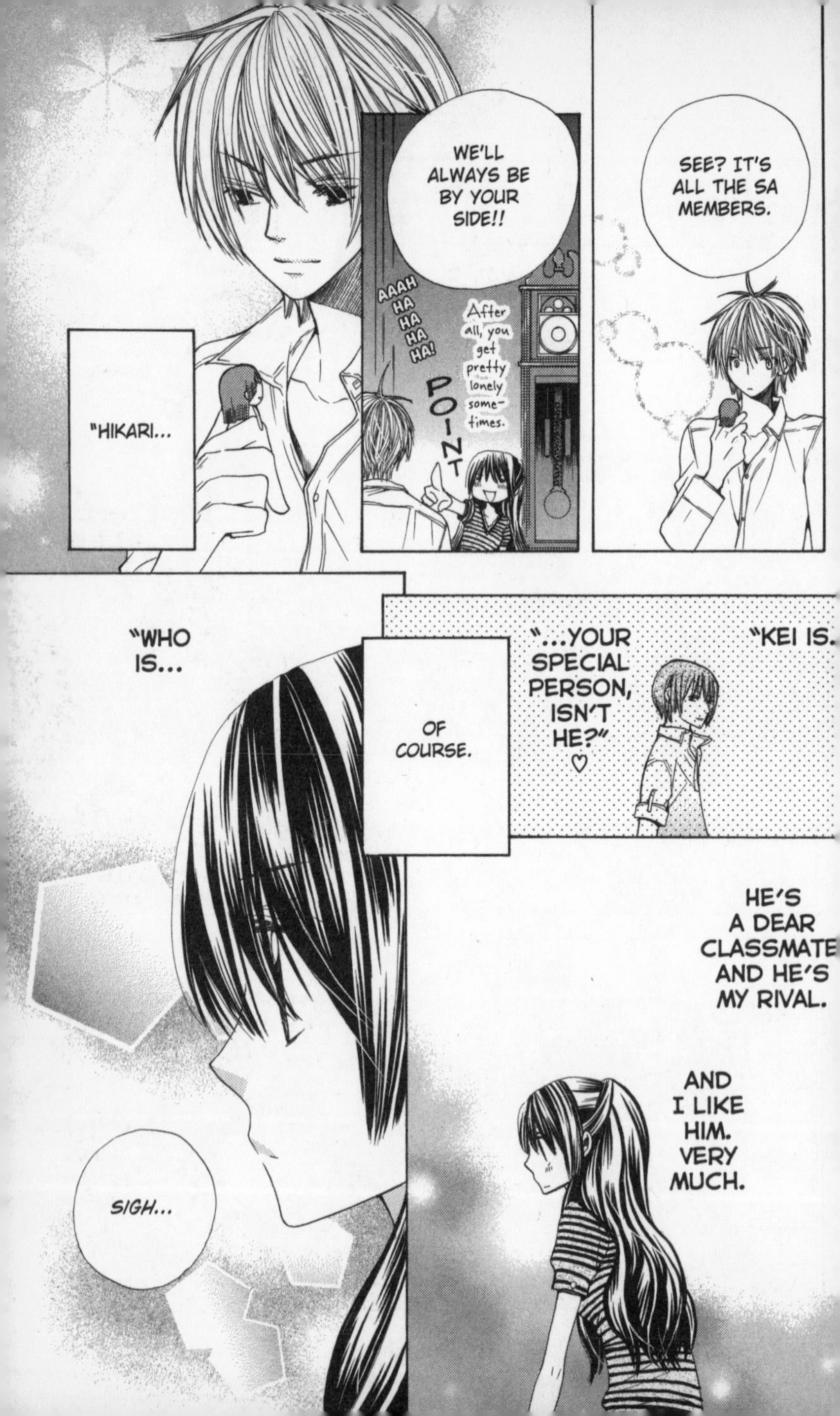
SEE? IT'S ALL THE SA MEMBERS.
WE'LL ALWAYS BE BY YOUR SIDE!!
AAAH HA HA HA HA!
After all, you get pretty lonely some-times.
POINT
"HIKARI...
"KEI IS.
"...YOUR SPECIAL PERSON, ISN'T HE?" ♡
OF COURSE.
HE'S A DEAR CLASSMATE AND HE'S MY RIVAL.
AND I LIKE HIM. VERY MUCH.
"WHO IS...
SIGH...

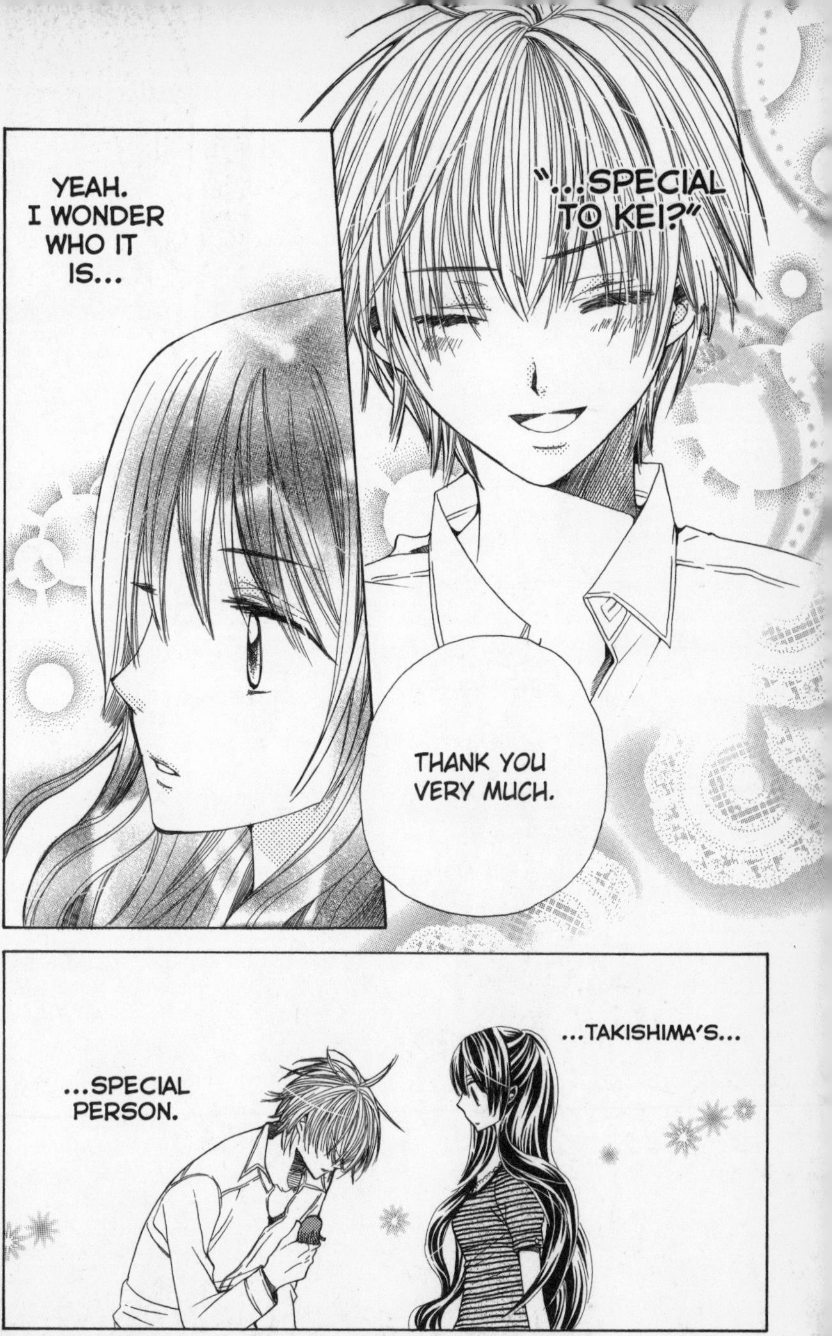
"...SPECIAL TO KEI?"
THANK YOU VERY MUCH.
YEAH. I WONDER WHO IT IS...
...TAKISHIMA'S...
...SPECIAL PERSON.

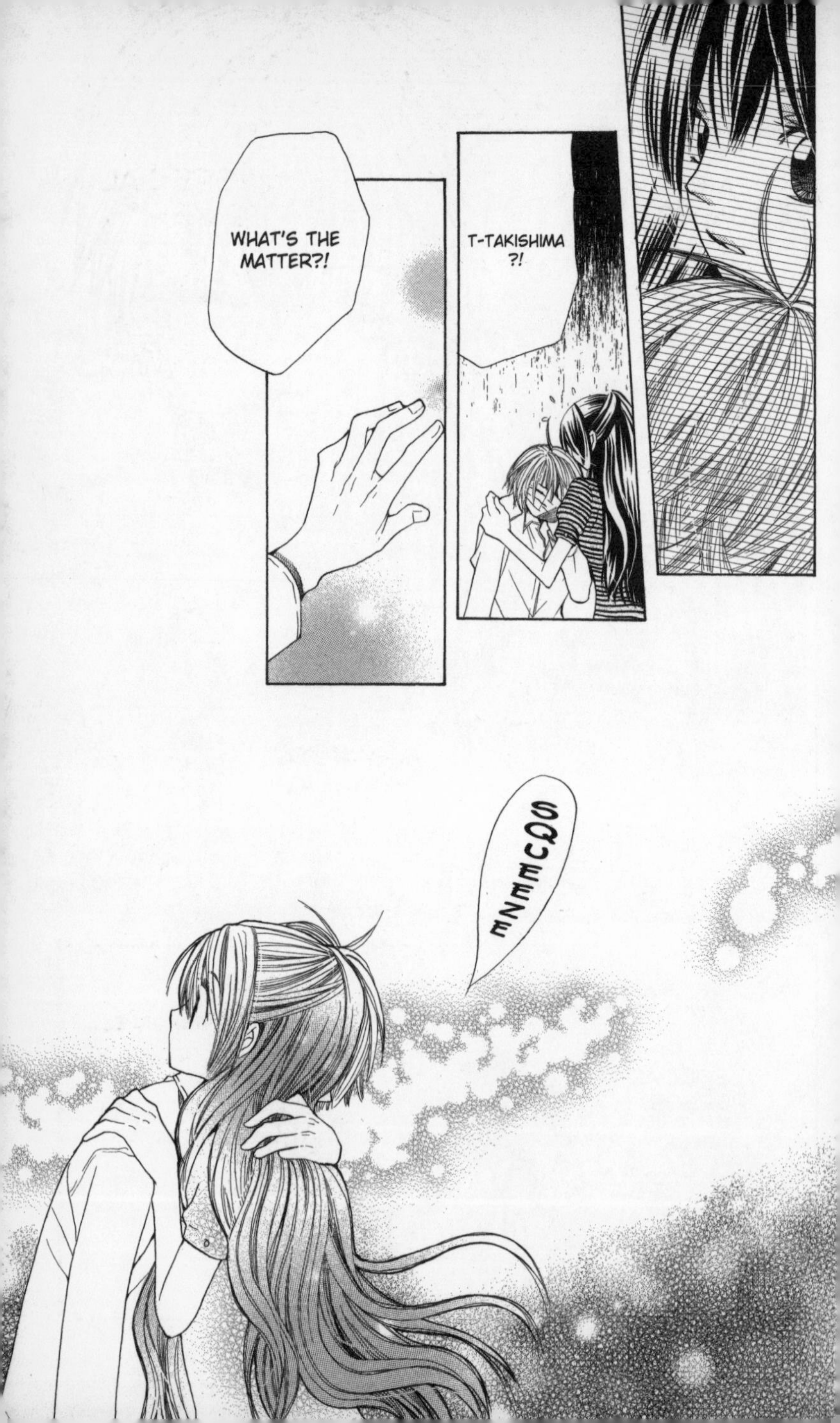
T-TAKISHIMA ?!
WHAT'S THE MATTER?!
SQUEEZE

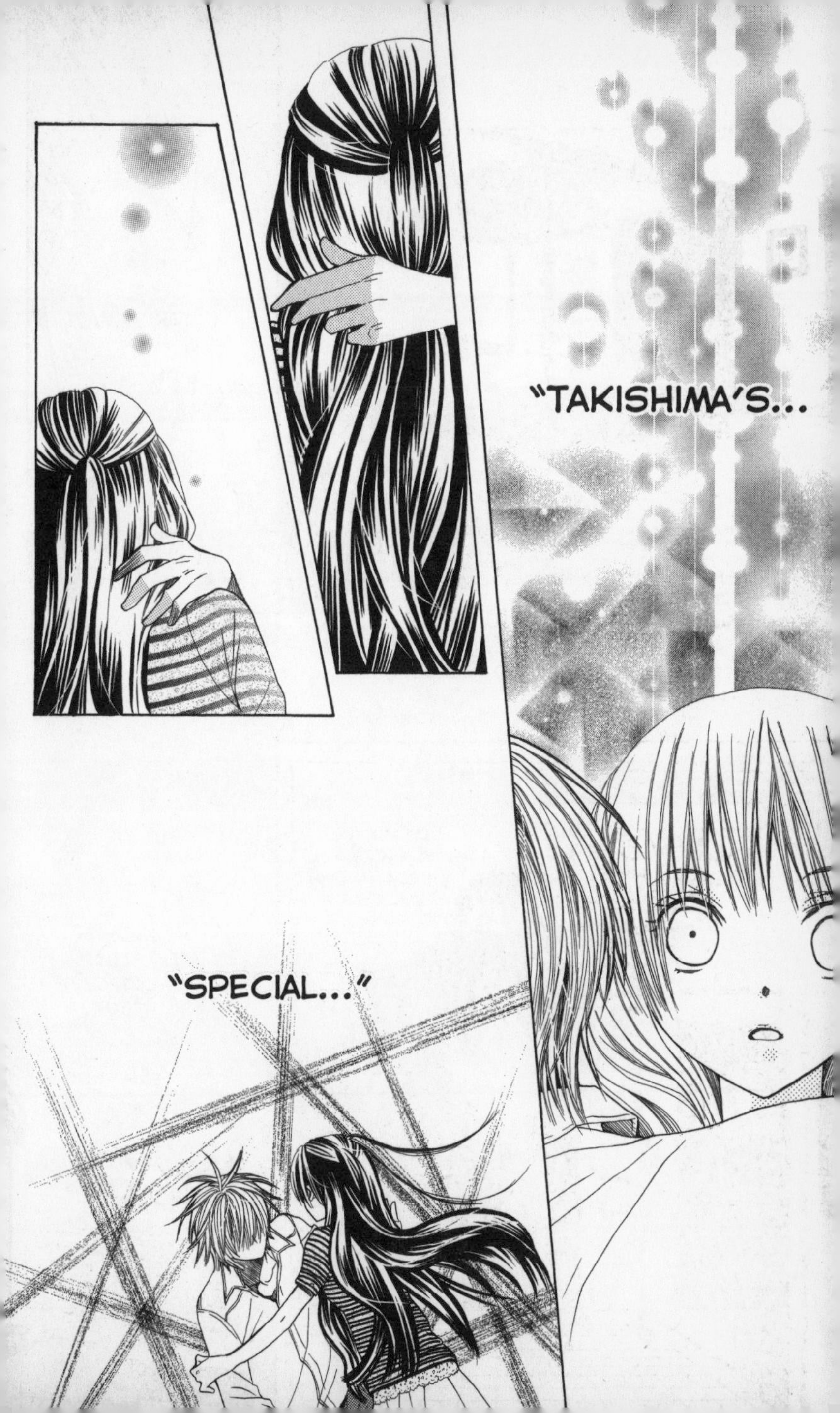
"TAKISHIMA'S...
"SPECIAL..."

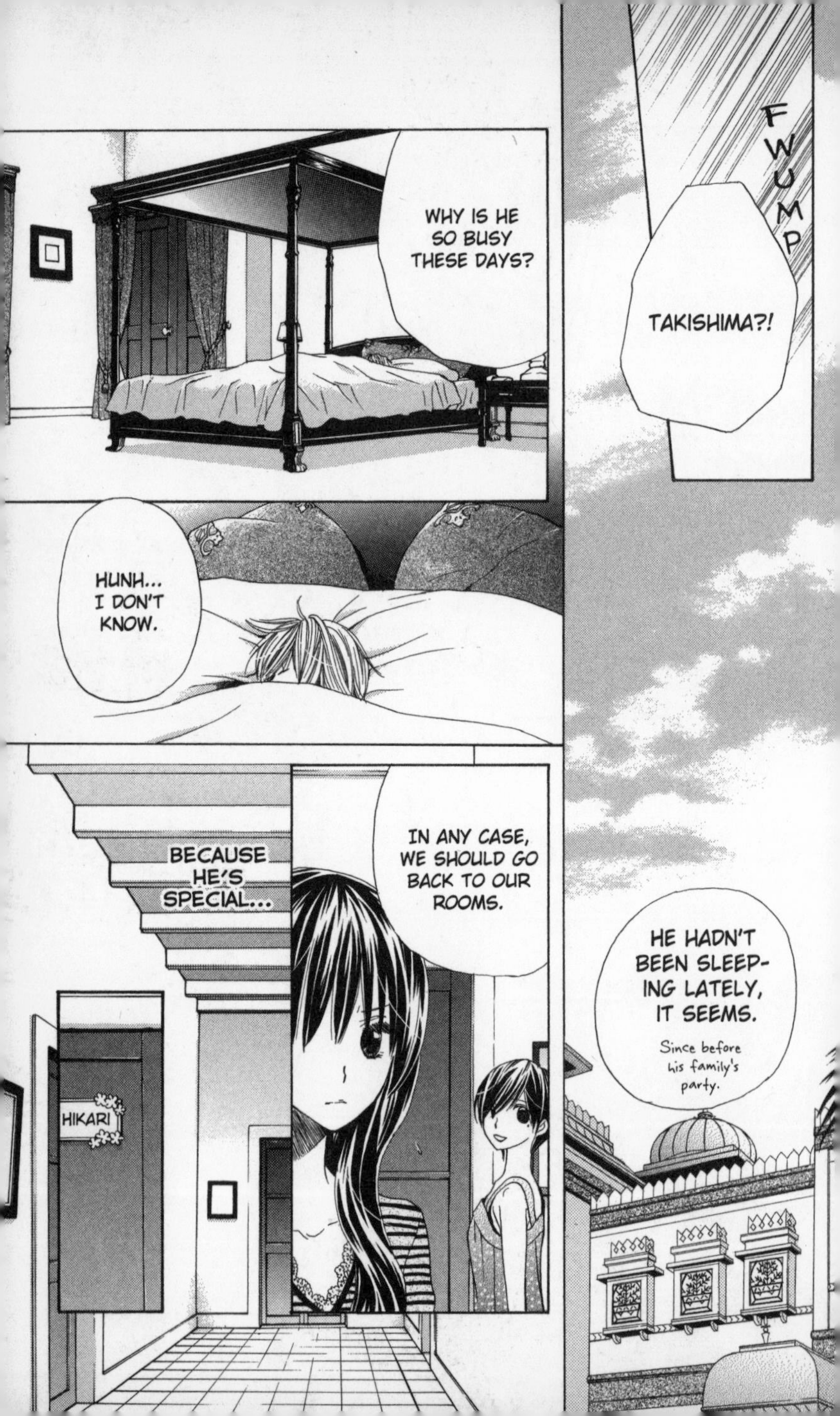
FWUMP
TAKISHIMA?!
HE HADN'T BEEN SLEEPING LATELY, IT SEEMS.
Since before his family's party.
WHY IS HE SO BUSY THESE DAYS?
HUNH... I DON'T KNOW.
IN ANY CASE, WE SHOULD GO BACK TO OUR ROOMS.
BECAUSE HE'S SPECIAL...
HIKARI

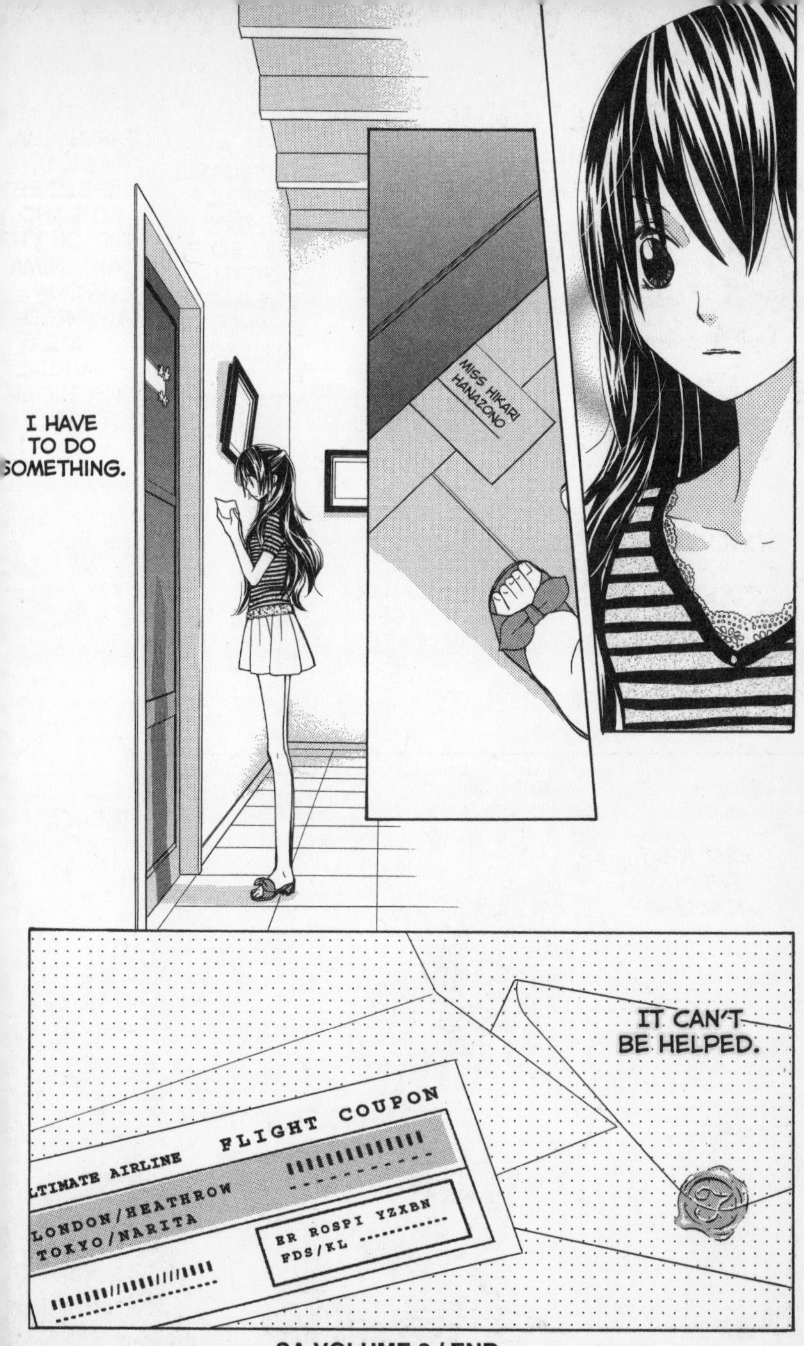
MISS HIKARI HANAZONO
I HAVE TO DO SOMETHING.
IT CAN'T BE HELPED.
FLIGHT COUPON
LTIMATE AIRLINE
LONDON/HEATHROW
TOKYO/NARITA
BR ROSPI YZXBN
FDS/KL

SA VOLUME 8 / END

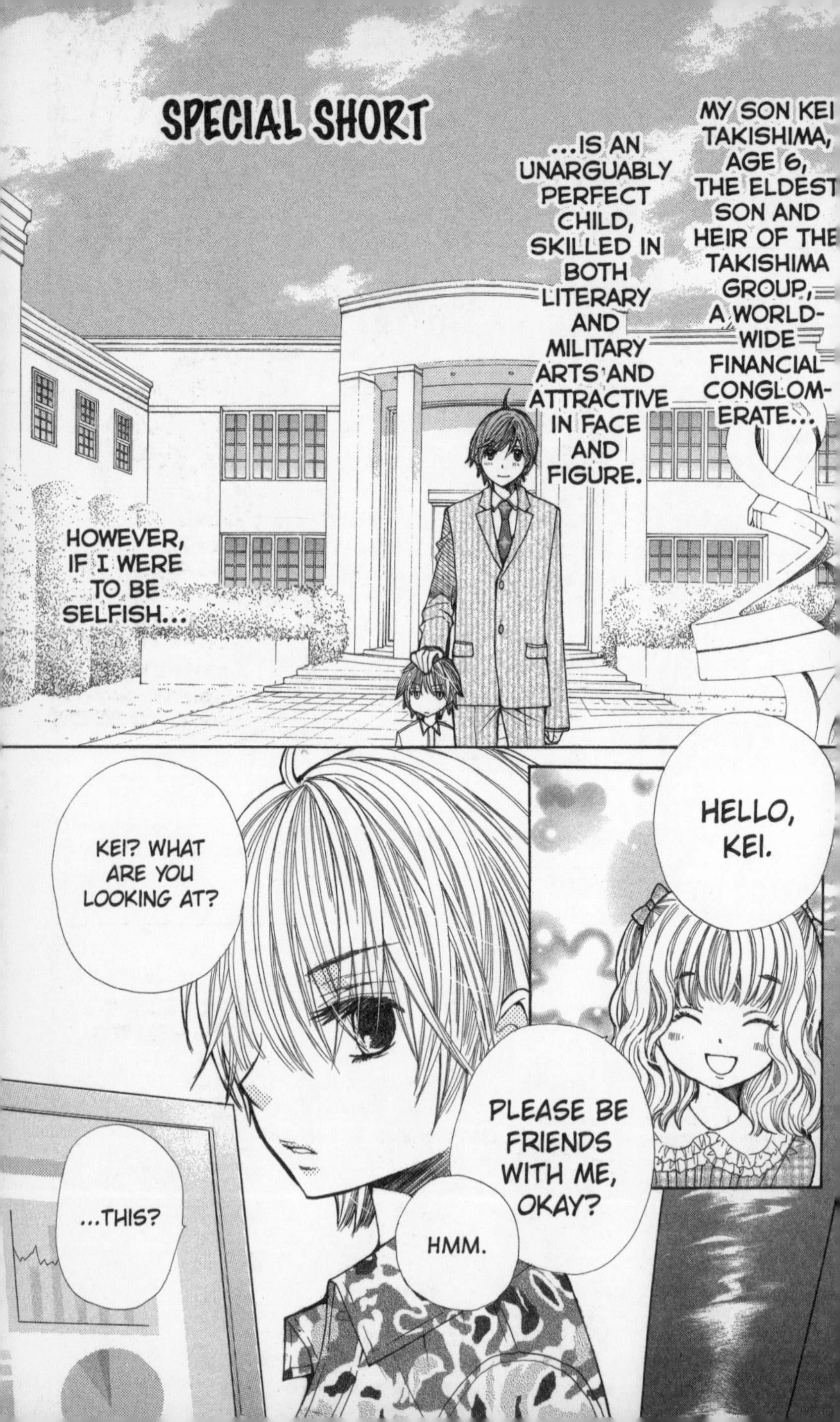
SPECIAL SHORT
MY SON KEI TAKISHIMA, AGE 6, THE ELDEST SON AND HEIR OF THE TAKISHIMA GROUP, A WORLD-WIDE FINANCIAL CONGLOM-ERATE...
...IS AN UNARGUABLY PERFECT CHILD, SKILLED IN BOTH LITERARY AND MILITARY ARTS AND ATTRACTIVE IN FACE AND FIGURE.
HOWEVER, IF I WERE TO BE SELFISH...
HELLO, KEI.
PLEASE BE FRIENDS WITH ME, OKAY?
HMM.
KEI? WHAT ARE YOU LOOKING AT?
...THIS?

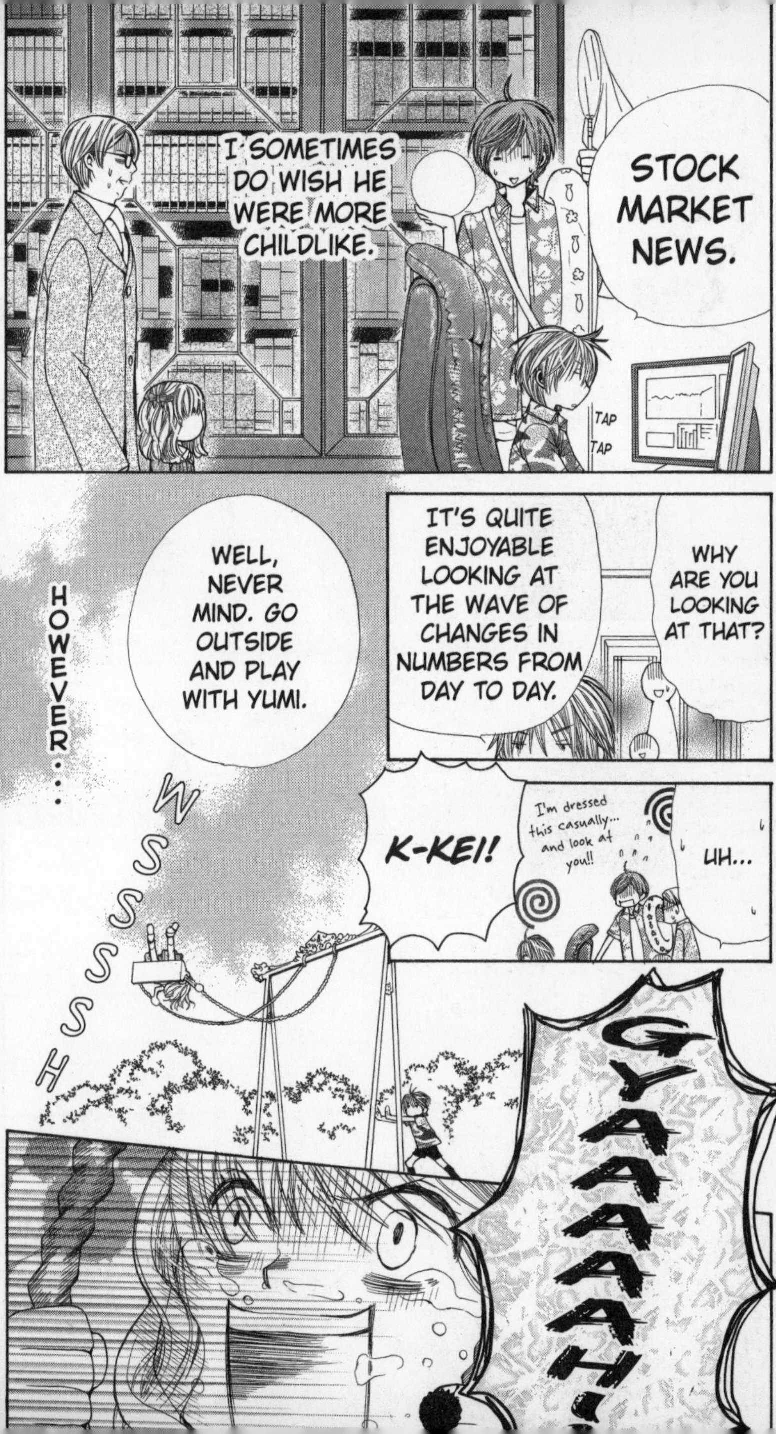
STOCK MARKET NEWS.
TAP TAP
I SOMETIMES DO WISH HE WERE MORE CHILDLIKE.
WHY ARE YOU LOOKING AT THAT?
IT'S QUITE ENJOYABLE LOOKING AT THE WAVE OF CHANGES IN NUMBERS FROM DAY TO DAY.
UH...
I'm dressed this casually... and look at you!!
K-KEI!
WELL, NEVER MIND. GO OUTSIDE AND PLAY WITH YUMI.
HOWEVER...
WSSSSSH
GYAAAAAH!

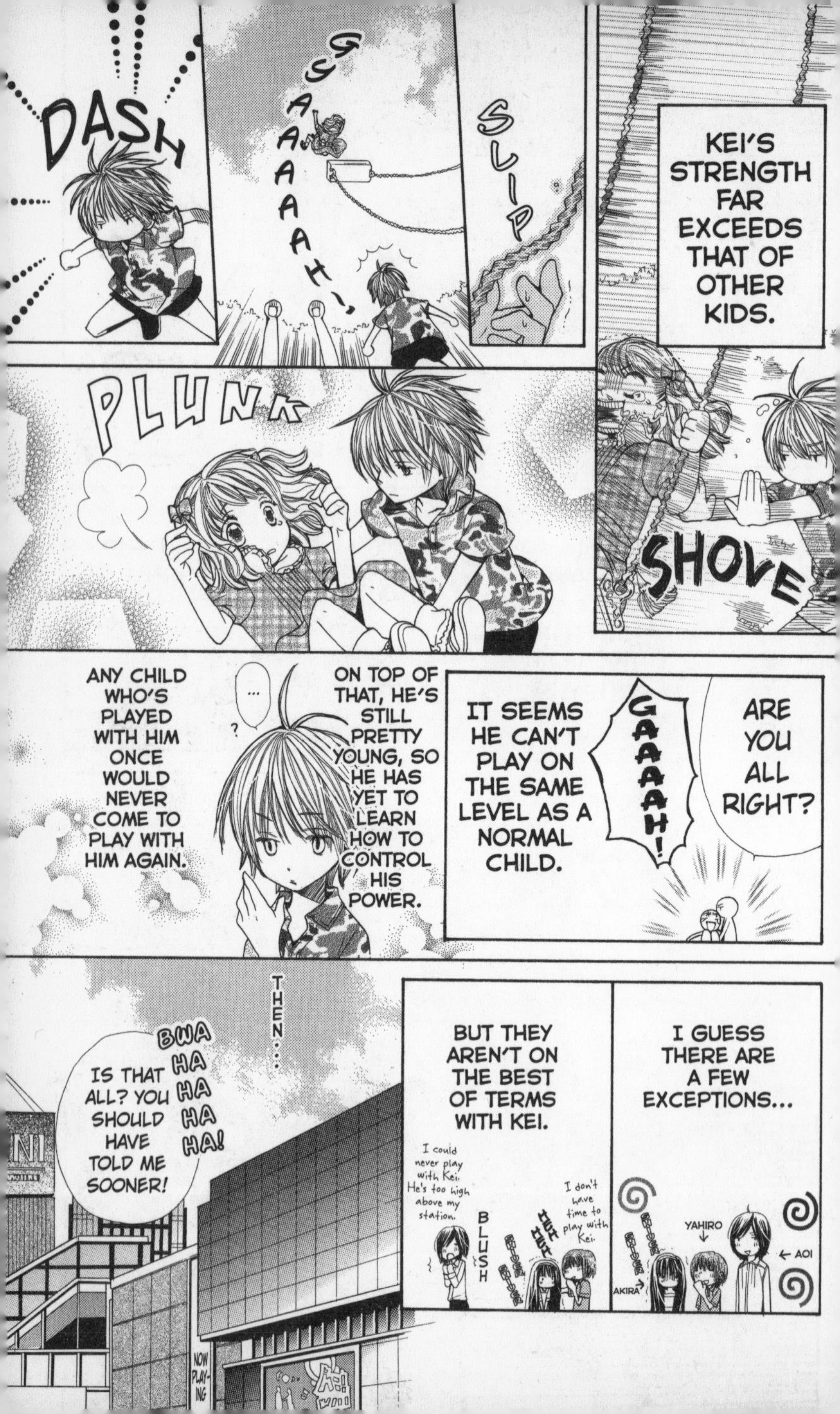
KEI'S STRENGTH FAR EXCEEDS THAT OF OTHER KIDS.
SLIP
GYAAAAAAH~!
DASH
SHOVE
PLUNK
ARE YOU ALL RIGHT?
GAAAAAH!
IT SEEMS HE CAN'T PLAY ON THE SAME LEVEL AS A NORMAL CHILD.
ON TOP OF THAT, HE'S STILL PRETTY YOUNG, SO HE HAS YET TO LEARN HOW TO CONTROL HIS POWER.
...
?
ANY CHILD WHO'S PLAYED WITH HIM ONCE WOULD NEVER COME TO PLAY WITH HIM AGAIN.
I GUESS THERE ARE A FEW EXCEPTIONS...
AOI
YAHIRO
SHIVER SHIVER
AKIRA
BUT THEY AREN'T ON THE BEST OF TERMS WITH KEI.
I don't have time to play with Kei.
HEH HEH
SHIVER SHIVER
BLUSH
I could never play with Kei. He's too high above my station.
THEN...
BWA HA HA HA HA!
IS THAT ALL? YOU SHOULD HAVE TOLD ME SOONER!
NOW PLAYING

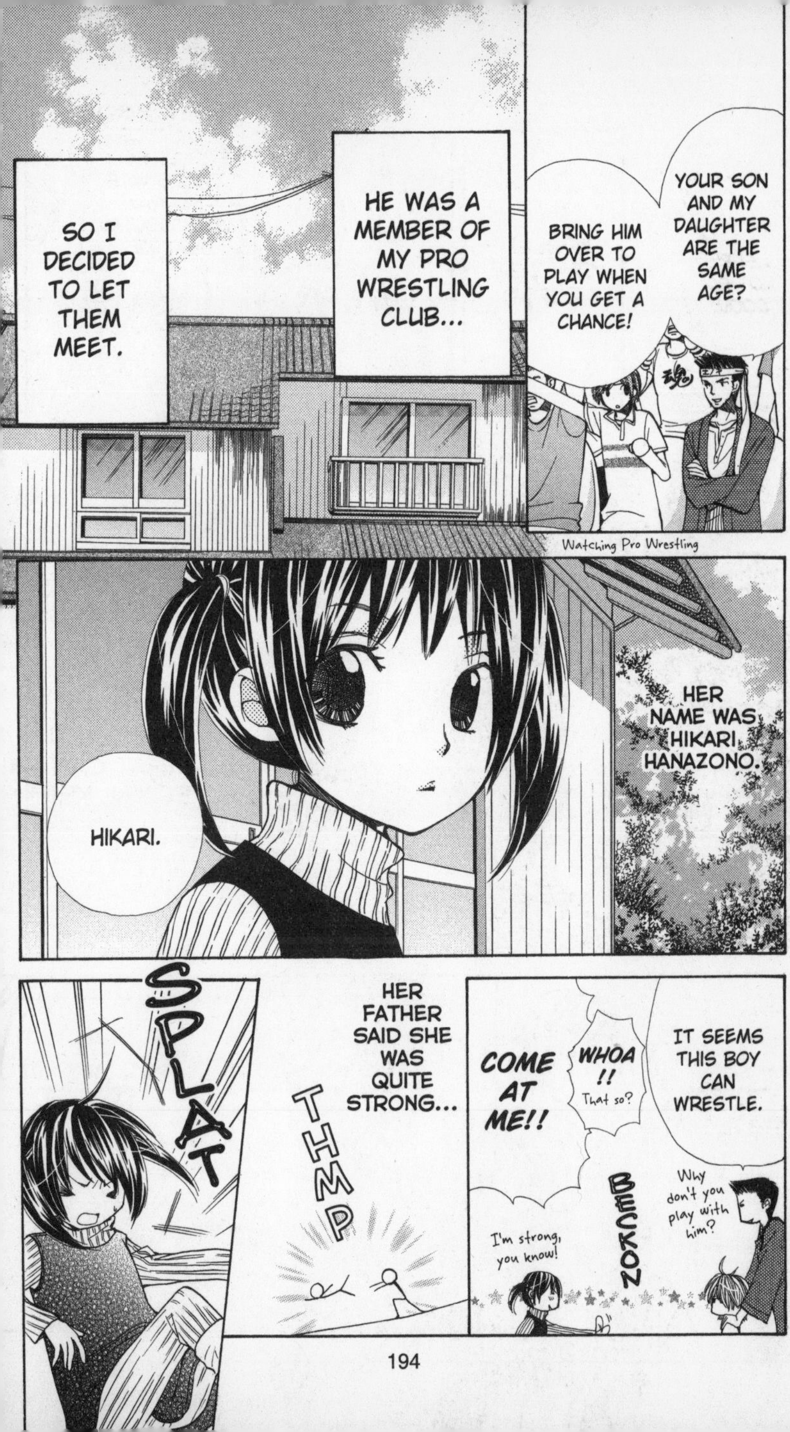
YOUR SON AND MY DAUGHTER ARE THE SAME AGE?
BRING HIM OVER TO PLAY WHEN YOU GET A CHANCE!
Watching Pro Wrestling
HE WAS A MEMBER OF MY PRO WRESTLING CLUB...
SO I DECIDED TO LET THEM MEET.
HER NAME WAS HIKARI HANAZONO.
HIKARI.
IT SEEMS THIS BOY CAN WRESTLE.
Why don't you play with him?
WHOA!! That so?
BECKON
COME AT ME!!
I'm strong, you know!
HER FATHER SAID SHE WAS QUITE STRONG...
THMP
SPLAT

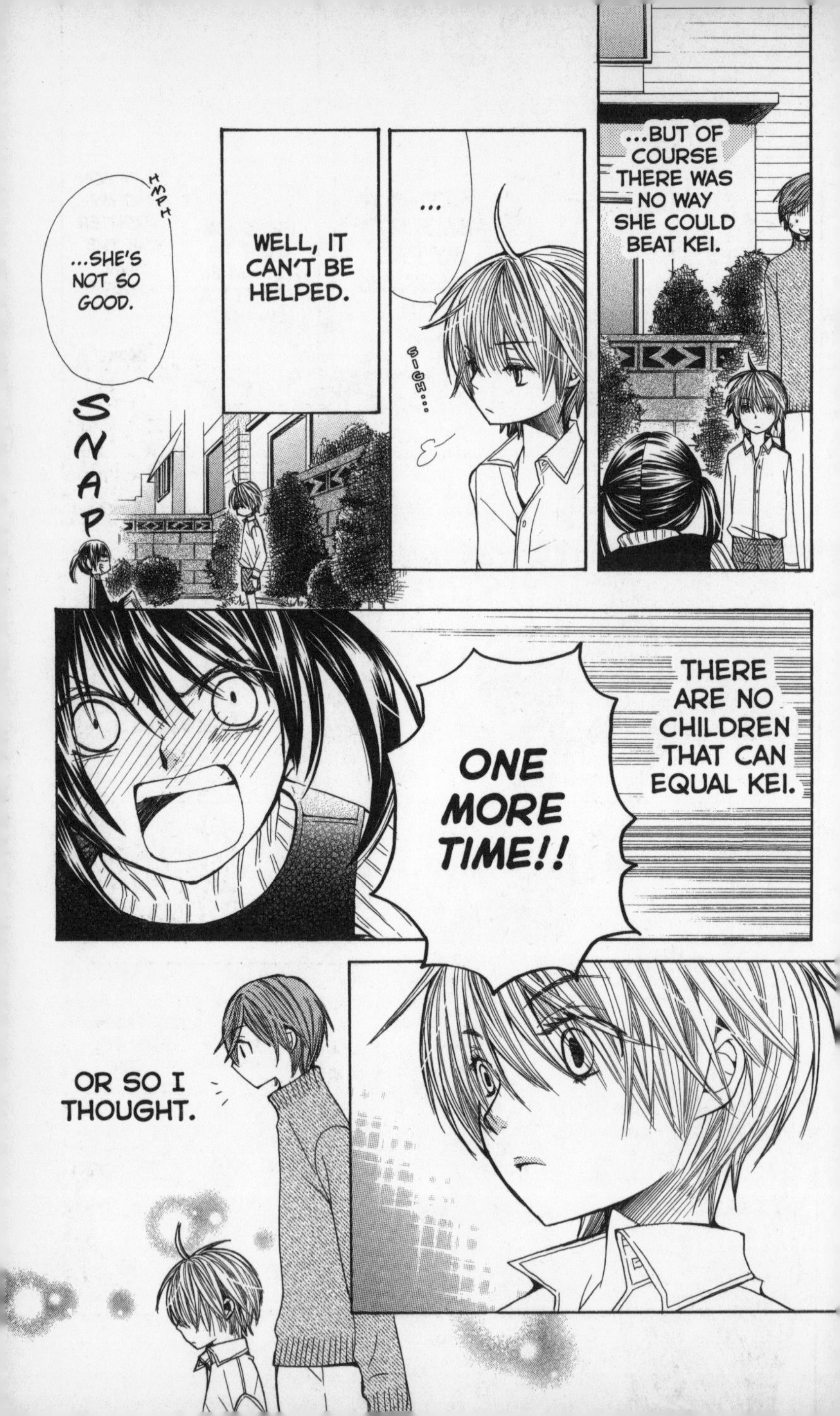
...BUT OF COURSE THERE WAS NO WAY SHE COULD BEAT KEI.
...
SIGH...
WELL, IT CAN'T BE HELPED.
HMPH
...SHE'S NOT SO GOOD.
SNAP
THERE ARE NO CHILDREN THAT CAN EQUAL KEI.
ONE MORE TIME!!
OR SO I THOUGHT.

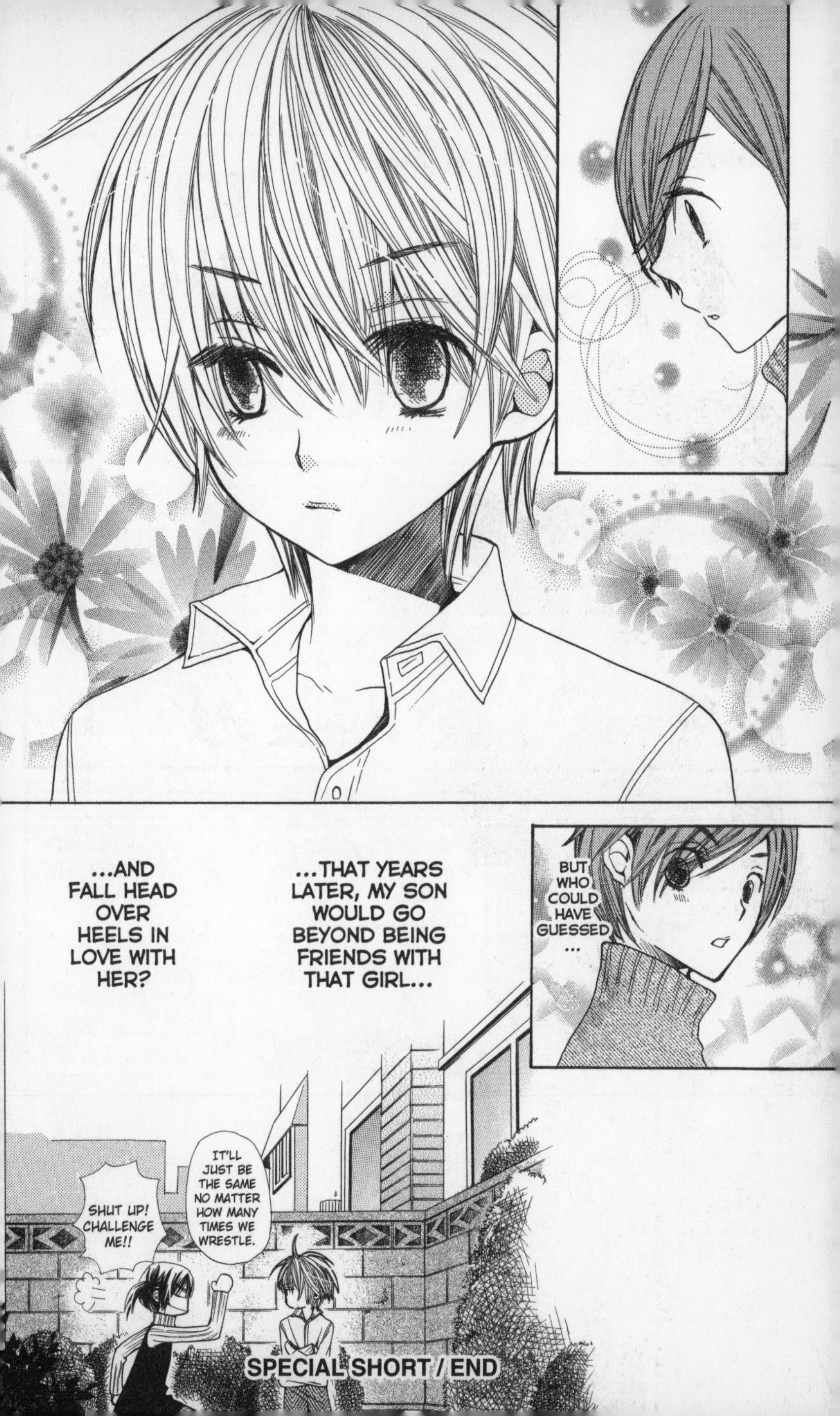
BUT WHO COULD HAVE GUESSED...
...THAT YEARS LATER, MY SON WOULD GO BEYOND BEING FRIENDS WITH THAT GIRL...
...AND FALL HEAD OVER HEELS IN LOVE WITH HER?
IT'LL JUST BE THE SAME NO MATTER HOW MANY TIMES WE WRESTLE.
SHUT UP! CHALLENGE ME!!
SPECIAL SHORT / END

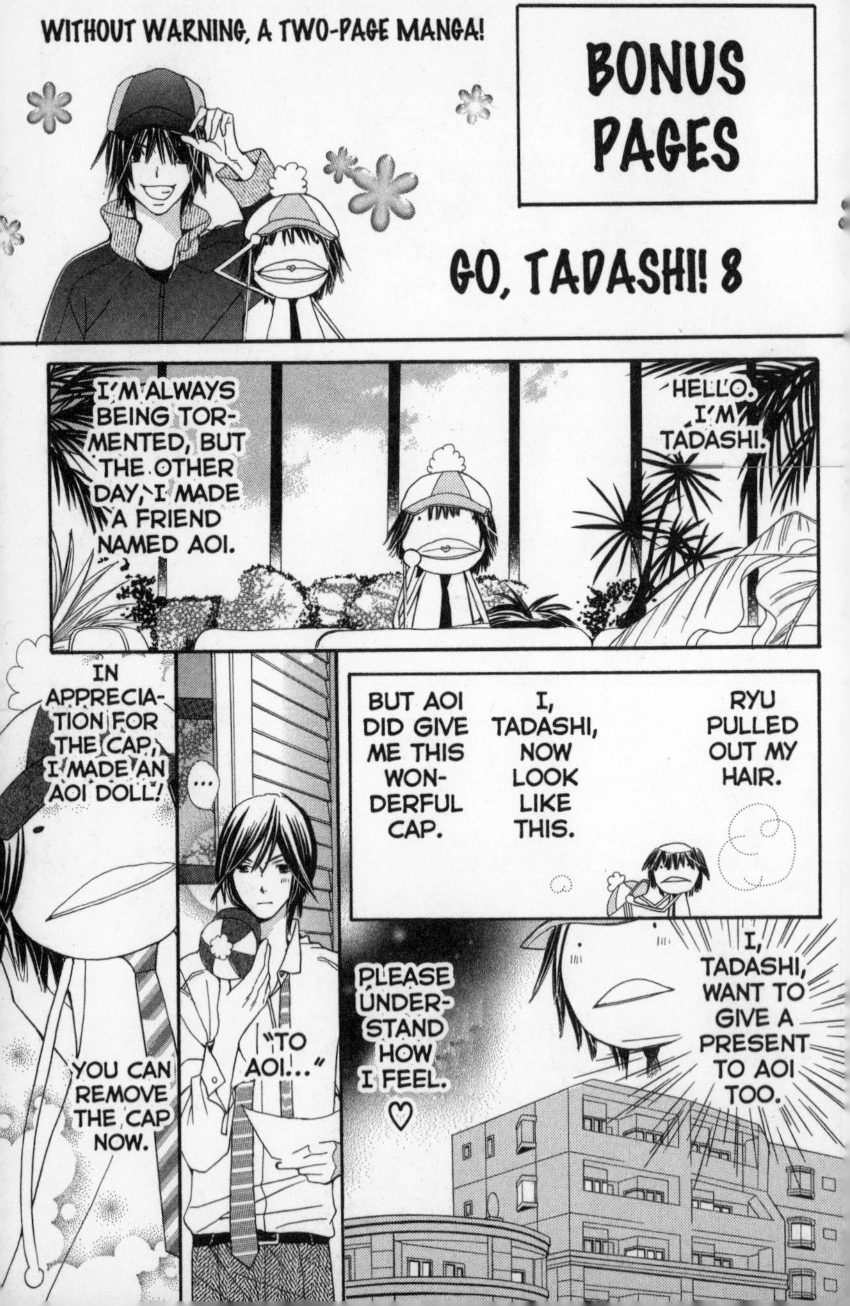
BONUS PAGES
GO, TADASHI! 8
WITHOUT WARNING, A TWO-PAGE MANGA!
HELLO. I'M TADASHI.
I'M ALWAYS BEING TORMENTED, BUT THE OTHER DAY, I MADE A FRIEND NAMED AOI.
RYU PULLED OUT MY HAIR.
I, TADASHI, NOW LOOK LIKE THIS.
BUT AOI DID GIVE ME THIS WONDERFUL CAP.
I, TADASHI, WANT TO GIVE A PRESENT TO AOI TOO.
PLEASE UNDERSTAND HOW I FEEL. ♡
...
"TO AOI..."
IN APPRECIATION FOR THE CAP, I MADE AN AOI DOLL!
YOU CAN REMOVE THE CAP NOW.

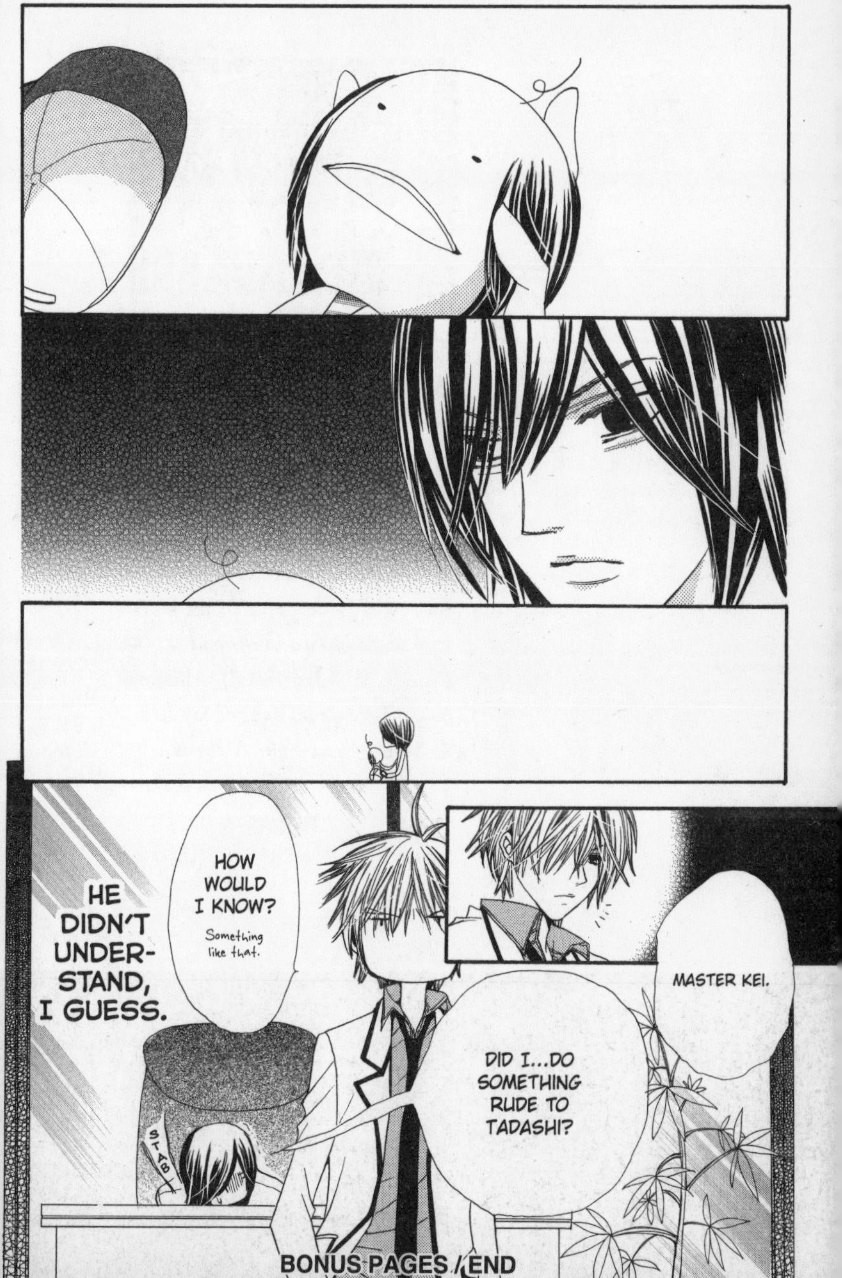
MASTER KEI.
DID I...DO SOMETHING RUDE TO TADASHI?
HOW WOULD I KNOW?
Something like that.
HE DIDN'T UNDERSTAND, I GUESS.
STAB

BONUS PAGES / END

Maki Minami is from Saitama
prefecture in Japan. She debuted
in 2001 with *Kanata no Ao*
(Faraway Blue). Her other works
include *Kimi wa Girlfriend*
(You're My Girlfriend), *Mainichi
ga Takaramono* (Every Day Is a
Treasure) and *Yuki Atataka*
(Warm Winter). *S•A* was serialized in
Japan's *Hana to Yume* magazine and
made into an anime in 2008.

S•A

Vol. 8

The Shojo Beat Manga Edition

STORY & ART BY

MAKI MINAMI

English Adaptation/Amanda Hubbard
Translation/JN Productions
Touch-up Art & Lettering/HudsonYards
Design/Izumi Hirayama
Interior Design/Deirdre Shiozawa
Editor/Jonathan Tarbox

Editor in Chief, Books/Alvin Lu
Editor in Chief, Magazines/Marc Weidenbaum
VP, Publishing Licensing/Rika Inouye
VP, Sales & Product Marketing/Gonzalo Ferreyra
VP, Creative/Linda Espinosa
Publisher/Hyoe Narita

Printed in Canada

Published by VIZ Media, LLC
P.O. Box 77010
San Francisco, CA 94107

Shojo Beat Manga Edition
10 9 8 7 6 5 4 3 2 1
First printing, January 2009

www.viz.com

store.viz.com

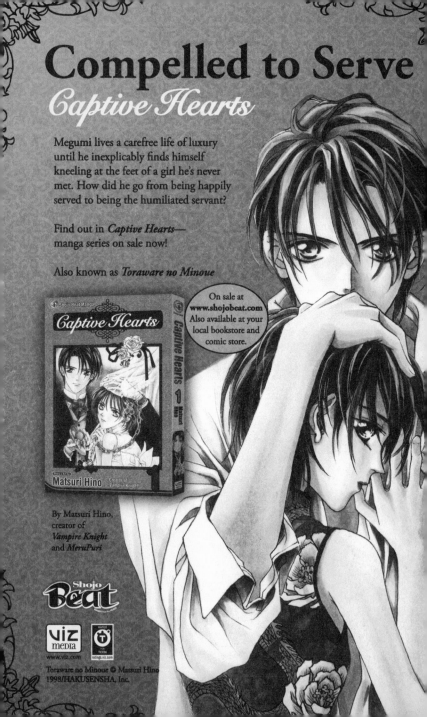

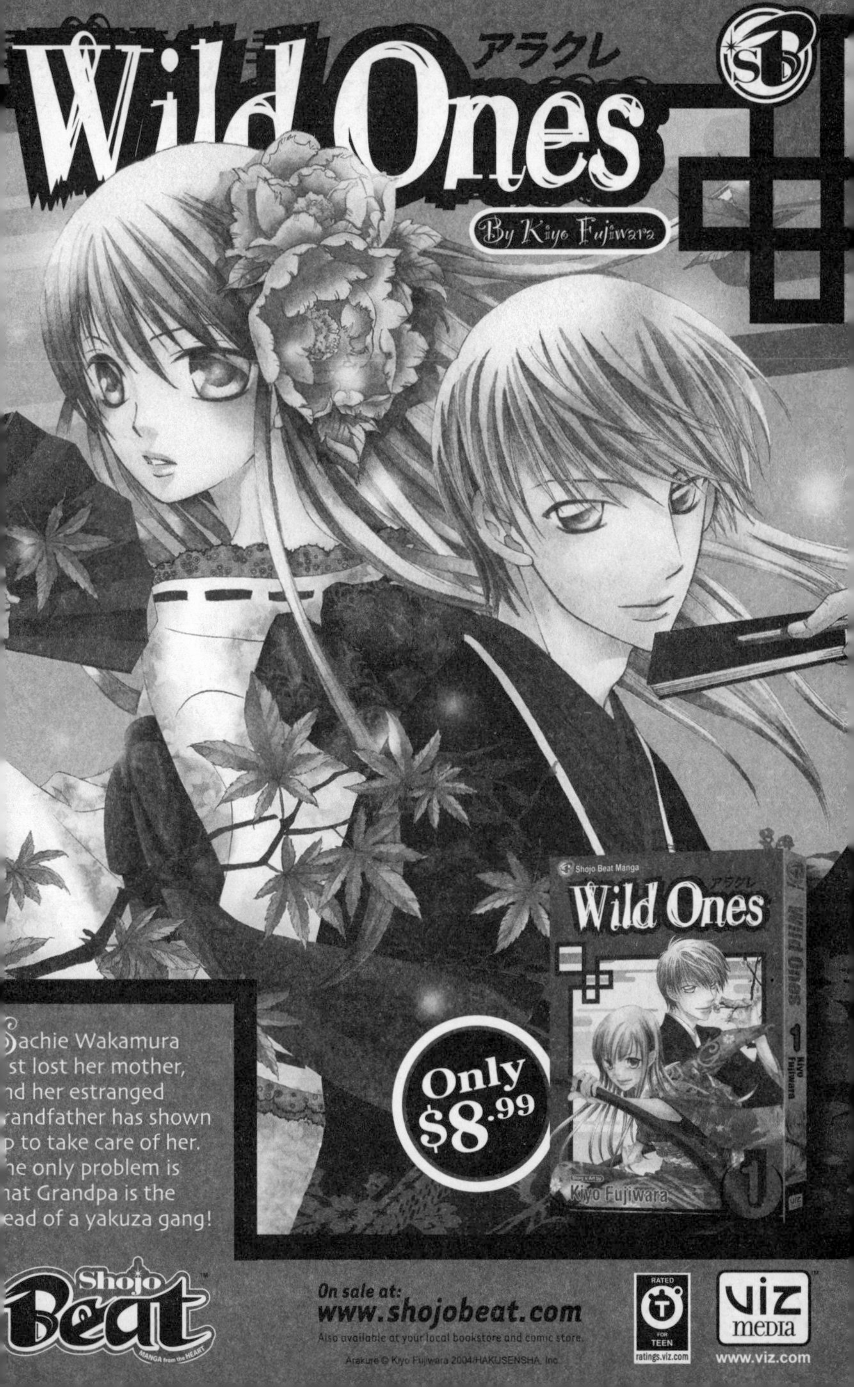

Wild Ones
アラクレ
SB
By Kiyo Fujiwara
Shojo Beat Manga
Wild Ones
アラクレ
Story & Art by
Kiyo Fujiwara
1
Only $8.99
Sachie Wakamura
st lost her mother,
nd her estranged
randfather has shown
p to take care of her.
he only problem is
hat Grandpa is the
ead of a yakuza gang!
Shojo Beat
MANGA from the HEART
On sale at:
www.shojobeat.com
Also available at your local bookstore and comic store.
Arakure © Kiyo Fujiwara 2004/HAKUSENSHA, Inc.
RATED T FOR TEEN
ratings.viz.com
VIZ MEDIA
www.viz.com

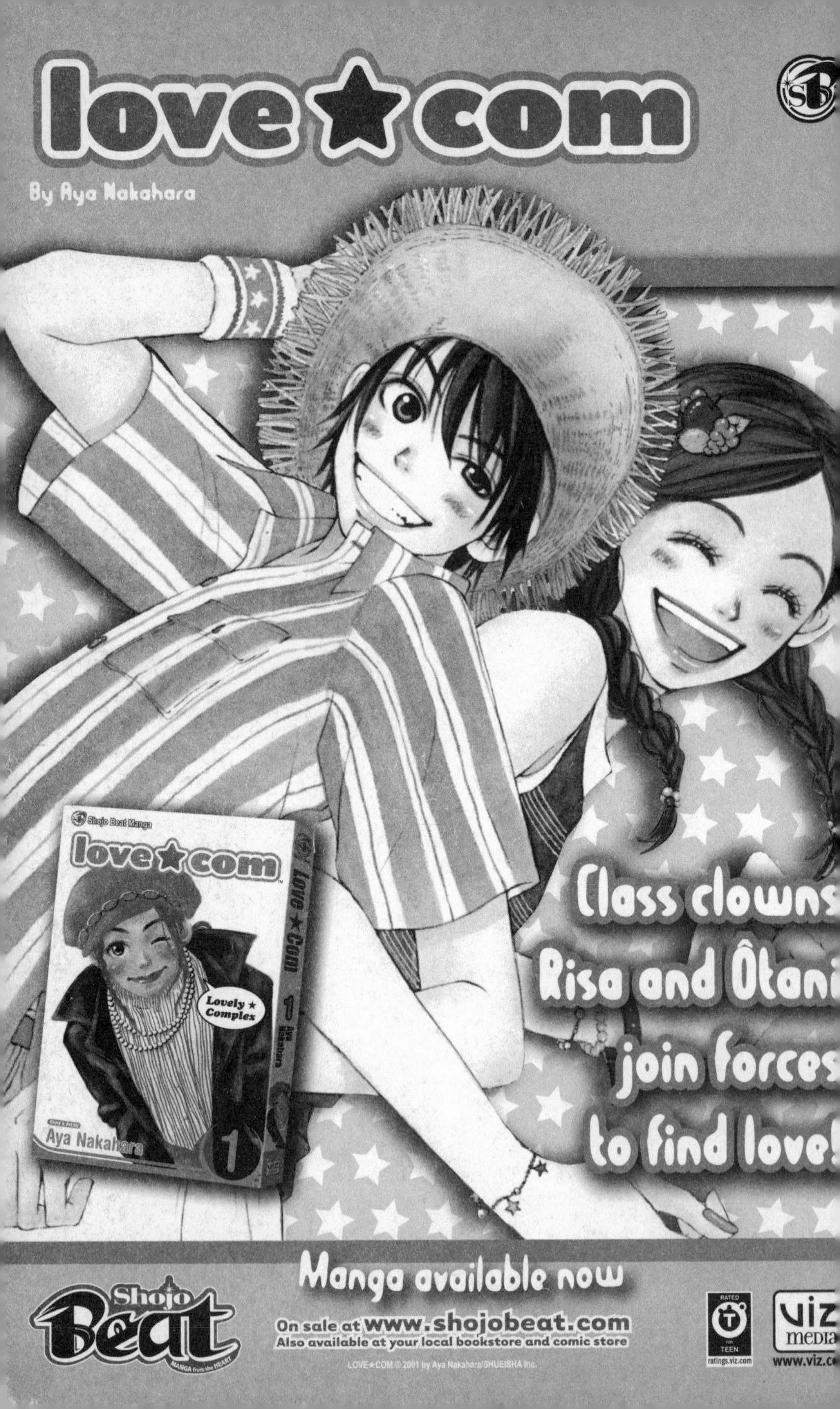
love★com
By Aya Nakahara
Shojo Beat Manga
love★com
Love★Com
1
Aya Nakahara
Lovely★Complex
Story & Art by
Aya Nakahara
1
Class clowns
Risa and Ôtani
join forces
to find love!
Manga available now
Shojo Beat
MANGA from the HEART
On sale at www.shojobeat.com
Also available at your local bookstore and comic store
LOVE★COM © 2001 by Aya Nakahara/SHUEISHA Inc.
RATED T FOR TEEN
ratings.viz.com
viz media
www.viz.c

High School DEBUT

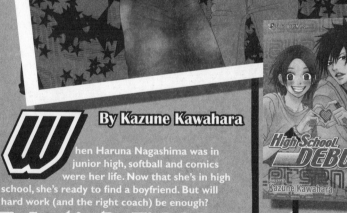

By Kazune Kawahara

When Haruna Nagashima was in junior high, softball and comics were her life. Now that she's in high school, she's ready to find a boyfriend. But will hard work (and the right coach) be enough?

Find out in the *High School Debut* manga series—available now!